EMILY DICKINSON

AN ANNOTATED BIBLIOGRAPHY

Writings, Scholarship, Criticism, and Ana
1850-1968

EDITED BY
WILLIS J. BUCKINGHAM

INDIANA UNIVERSITY PRESS
BLOOMINGTON & LONDON

Published in Canada by Fitzhenry & Whiteside Limited,
Don Mills, Ontario

Library of Congress catalog card number: 75-108205
ISBN: 253-31947-1
Manufactured in the United States of America

for my
mother and father

EMILY DICKINSON

An Annotated Bibliography

If fame belonged to me,
I could not escape her.

—ED to TWH

Contents

MISCELLANEA

UNPUBLISHED MATERIALS

Preface

This volume seeks to provide a comprehensive listing of published materials relating to Emily Dickinson, incorporating previous Dickinson bibliographies in a single work. It does not include detailed bibliographical description of editions of the poems and letters; its emphasis is rather on scholarship, criticism, and the history of Emily Dickinson's reputation. It therefore takes within its scope foreign-language editions and criticism, fiction and drama based on the poet's life, tributes by creative artists, and other miscellaneous items.

The impulse behind this bibliography has been inclusive rather than selective. Only short introductions to Emily Dickinson in anthologies and encyclopedias have been categorically excluded, and in other cases it is seldom that an item has been rejected on the grounds of its slight importance to Dickinson studies.

The bibliography is divided into twenty-four separately numbered sections (see the table of contents). Some of the sections are arranged chronologically, as Sections 3 and 4 (editions of the poems and letters). In other sections, an alphabetical arrangement seemed more appropriate, as in Section 6 (signed articles). The reader is advised to consult the index of persons, periodicals, and subjects whenever he does not find an item in the section or place that he expects it.

To aid in their location, anonymous items are listed by subject wherever convenient. For example, unsigned reviews are always listed with the book reviewed. Similarly, when an anonymous article has to do with an Emily Dickinson celebration or exhibition, it is listed with the commemoration materials in Section 22. If the writer of an anonymous book or article is known, the entry is placed under his name. The remaining anonymous materials are collected in Section 7 and arranged chronologically.

Listed as "reviews" are articles or notices dealing in any way with a particular work. For example, press releases announcing the discovery of the manuscripts which led to the publication of *Further Poems*, 1929 (3.138) are included among the reviews of that volume.

The explication index includes textual as well as critical discussions of individual poems. Each explication entry cites the author's last name,

bibliography entry number, and relevant page numbers of the book or article in which the explication is found. When an explication has been reprinted, a short title of the printing to which the page numbers refer will
follow the author's name, e.g., Frye, *Fables of Identity*, 6.375, 215. Explications of each poem are arranged chronologically so that a reader may
follow, if he wishes, successive interpretations as they build upon one
another. Most book-length studies of Emily Dickinson contain their own
index to poems and the reader is directed to these listings for further help
in locating discussions of particular poems. Explications appearing in unpublished theses are not indexed.

    The final index lists names of all persons and periodicals, and includes
a number of subject headings. These subject listings are far from exhaustive, and they are offered as an aid rather than as a substitute for research.
Relevant page numbers are given in the case of books and some long articles, but these references, too, are intended only as a point of departure;
the whole work should be searched and its indexes, when they are provided,
should be consulted. Bibliography entry numbers always contain a decimal
and may thus easily be distinguished from page numbers.

    Additions to this bibliography made after its numbering was completed
have been given a decimal number with a letter suffix, e.g., 6.34a. I have
not added items published after 1968. Cross-reference numbers in brackets
refer to the location of main entries.

    This work builds gratefully upon the labors of others. Among those
whose efforts have preceded mine, I wish to mention in particular Mr.
Charles Green, who, until his retirement, had been at work on a revision
of the 1930 Jones Library bibliography (1.8). I am immensely indebted to
that Library and especially to its present Curator of Special Collections,
Winnifred D. Sayer, for aid in making use of the materials gathered by Mr.
Green and his staff. I have also drawn heavily upon the excellent Dickinson
bibliography prepared in 1948 by Russell St. Clair Smith (1.15). For many
additions and corrections I have relied upon recent bibliographies by Susan
Freis (1.20), Sheila Clendenning (1.23), and Klaus Lubbers (5.114). My listing of scholarship in Italian and German owes much to the work of Paola
Guidetti (8.61) and Hans Galinsky (10.51).

    It is a pleasure to express my appreciation to the Department of En-
glish, Indiana University, and to Professor Donald Gray and the late Professor William Riley Parker, for travel grants which made it possible to
examine items in distant libraries. For the advice and encouragement of
other members of the Department, among them Professors J. Albert Robbins
and Edwin H. Cady, I have been especially fortunate. Some of those who
have helped with foreign-language materials are Professor Keiichi Harada
of Chiba University, Japan; Mr. Guenter Baumann of the University of Kiel;
Mr. H. Jay Harris, Miss Elena Fraboschi, Miss Barbara Garland, and Miss
Eloah Giacomelli, all of Indiana University. I am grateful for help, of various kinds, from Mrs. Marguerite Harris, Mr. Frederick L. Morey, Professor John J. McAleer of Boston College, and from Mr. J. Richard Phillips
of the Robert Frost Library, Amherst College. The staff of the Indiana University Library, and of other libraries, have been courteous and helpful. To
Mr. Charles Campbell I am especially thankful for assistance in preparing
the manuscript. Mrs. Donald F. Gaines of the Indiana University Press has
done much to make the work more accurate and consistent in form.

Bloomington, Indiana   W.J.B.
August, 1969

EMILY DICKINSON

An Annotated Bibliography

BIBLIOGRAPHIES
AND CONCORDANCES

1.

Bibliographies
and Related Materials

The arrangement of this section is chronological within its subdivisions: "Descriptive Bibliographies" (1.1-4), "Guides to Secondary Materials" (1.5-23), and "Guides to ED's Manuscripts and Reading" (1.24-34). Items of bibliographical interest listed in other sections may be located in the index, s.v. "bibliographies."

DESCRIPTIVE BIBLIOGRAPHIES

1.1   *Yale University Library. Emily Dickinson.* Compiled by William H. McCarthy, Jr. New Haven, Conn.: Bibliographical Press, Yale Univ. Library, 1930. 16 pp.
     75 copies published on Dec. 10, 1930.
     Catalog of an exhibition commemorating the ED Centenary. Although its descriptions are limited to editions of the poems and letters on display, it is the only published work to attempt title-page transcription with line endings marked or to offer a full list of contents with page numbers. See also 22.20.
     Reviewed:
     Rollins (6.854)

1.2   Jones Library, Inc., Amherst. "Books by Emily Dickinson." Unpublished typescript. Dated by hand, April 4, 1939. 7 pp.
     A handlist compiling in chart form 94 different printings or bindings for 13 separate Dickinson volumes published before 1935. Each entry notes the number of the edition or impression, the publisher, the date of publication, and furnishes a brief description of the binding. One of the sheets supplies more detail about variant bindings of the three volumes of poetry published in the 1890's.

1.3   Millicent Todd Bingham. "Appendix III: Books by Emily Dickinson" in *Ancestors' Brocades,* 1945 (5.5), pp. 412-15; see also pp. 69, 80, 89, 181, 225, 308, 345. Describes bindings and other features of Dickinson volumes published in the 1890's.

3

[1.15]   Russell St. Clair Smith. "A Dickinson Bibliography." 1948.

1.4   Jacob Blanck. "Emily Dickinson" in *Bibliography of American Literature*. 8 or 9 vols. planned. New Haven, Conn.: Yale Univ. Press, 1955——, II (1957), 446-54.

> A descriptive listing of first editions and other separates. It is the only bibliography of ED which indicates gatherings or describes typographic variations between printings. Some musical settings and ED poems reprinted in early anthologies are also noted.

GUIDES TO SECONDARY MATERIALS

1.5   Margaret Frances Parmalee. "Emily Dickinson: A Reading List of Books and Periodicals on Her Life and Poetry." Unpublished M.A. thesis, Univ. of Michigan, 1928.

> This compilation was fully superseded by the 1930 Jones Library bibliography (1.8).

1.6   *Emily Dickinson: A Bibliography*. Compiled by Alfred Leete Hampson. Northampton, Mass.: Hampshire Bookshop, 1930. 36 pp.

> Softcover. 500 copies published May 1930 at $2.50.
>
> A chronologically arranged, unnumbered listing of editions of the poems and letters and 126 secondary items in books and periodicals. There is no annotation or description. Reprints an essay by Elizabeth McCausland in celebration of the ED Centenary (6.681).

Reviewed:
> Grattan (6.415)
> McCausland (6.681)
> Wells (6.1086)

Unsigned reviews:

1.7   *Publishers' Weekly*, CXVII (May 25, 1930), 2622.

1.8   *Emily Dickinson, December 10, 1830 — May 15, 1886. A Bibliography*. With a Foreword by George F. Whicher. Amherst, Mass.: Jones Library, Inc., 1930. 63 pp.

> Softcover. 500 copies published Nov. 1930 at $.75. Reprinted in 1931.
>
> Compiled by the Jones Library staff, this unannotated, unnumbered bibliography lists editions (without description) and more than 300 secondary items in the following categories: books, periodicals, newspapers, theses, musical settings, poems in tribute, local history material. The arrangement within sections is chronological. With the exception of a few musical settings and some of the sources for local history, this volume is fully incorporated in the present work. A prefatory note to the bibliography, pp. 5-7, describes the publication history of editions of the poems, and George F. Whicher contributes a Centennial appraisal of ED's achievement, pp. 9-15 (see 6.1118).

Reviewed:
> Taggard (6.968)

Troxell (6.1008)
Unsigned Reviews:

1.9   *American Literature*, III (Nov. 1931), 363.
1.10   *New York Herald Tribune Books*, VII (April 12, 1931), 31.
1.11   *Publishers' Weekly*, CXVIII (Dec. 20, 1930), 2740-41.
1.12   *Saturday Review*, VII (June 6, 1931), 888.
1.13   *Springfield Daily News*, Dec. 6, 1930.
[22.15]   *Springfield Sunday Union and Republican*, Dec. 7, 1930, p. 4-A.

1.14   Millicent Todd Bingham. "Appendix II: Early Reviews of Books by Emily Dickinson, 1830-1896" in *Ancestors' Brocades*, 1945 (5.5), pp. 406-11.
       Supplements the Jones Library bibliography (1.8) with a list of early reviews drawn from Mrs. Todd's scrapbook clippings of newspaper comment on the Dickinson volumes she edited in the 1890's. This listing is incorporated in the present volume.

1.15   Russell St. Clair Smith. "A Dickinson Bibliography." Unpublished M.A. thesis, Brown Univ., 1948. 179 pp.
       The first part of this work describes editions of the poems and letters to 1945. It is the most complete single source for title-page transcription, collation of gatherings and signatures, and summary of contents (with page numbers). Selected later impressions of the volumes of poetry published in the 1890's are analyzed for discrepancies and checkpoints. The second part lists more than 800 secondary materials of all types, of which half are reviews of books by and about the poet. Poems reprinted in anthologies and a handful of items of little importance are not incorporated in the present work. The author supplies a prefatory critical estimate of Dickinson biography and editing, pp. vii-xxii.

1.16   Jones Library, Inc., Amherst. "Selected List of Essays and Reviews in Newspapers and Periodicals." Unpublished typescript, n.d. 56 pp.
       601 entries (some duplicates) from 1862-1950 are chronologically arranged. An earlier handlist of 12 pages for the years 1930-34 is also available at the Library. Both listings are fully included in the present work.

1.17   William White. "Homage to Emily Dickinson: Tributes by Creative Artists." *Bulletin of Bibliography*, XX (May-Aug. 1951), 112-15.
       A bibliography of tributes to ED by poets, novelists, playwrights, and other artists. Additional poems in tribute are listed by Charles R. Green, pp. 114-15. Except for musical settings, the present volume incorporates both lists.

1.18   Martha S. Bell. "Special Women's Collections in U.S. Libraries." *College and Research Libraries*, XX (May 1959), 235-42.
       Describes the ED collection in the Jones Library, Amherst, p. 237.

1.19   Joseph M. Kuntz. *Poetry Explication, A Checklist of Interpretation Since 1925 of British and American Poems Past and Present*. Rev. ed. Denver: Alan Swallow, 1962.
       Lists explications of Dickinson poems, pp. 73-9. All are incorporated in the explication index of the present work.

[6.851] J. Albert Robbins. "Nineteenth-Century Poetry" in *American Literary Scholarship,* 1963—.

1.20 Susan Freis. "Emily Dickinson: A Check List of Criticism, 1930-1966." *Papers of the Bibliographical Society of America,* **LXI** (Fourth Quarter, 1967), 359-85.
465 items are gathered in a continuously numbered, four-part listing (the sections alphabetically arranged) of books, periodical articles, parts of books, and Ph.D. dissertations about ED. Annotation is limited to noting reprints and review articles. The compilation is especially useful for locating explications of Dickinson poems in general works on poetry. About a dozen items were judged too insignificant for inclusion in the present work.

1.21 Frederick L. Morey, ed. *Emily Dickinson Bulletin.* No. 1 (Jan. 1968). "Published periodically during the academic year" (there were 6 numbers in 1968) by the editor, 4508 38th St., Brentwood, Md. 20722.
Issues in 1968 featured checklists of secondary materials, description of Dickinson holdings in various libraries (see 1.29), notes and queries, and brief articles. Back issues are available from the editor.

1.22 Hensley C. Woodbridge. "ED and the Hispanic-Speaking World." *Emily Dickinson Bulletin* (1.21), No. 5 (Oct. 1968), pp. 1-5.
A 28-item list of scholarship and criticism on ED in Spanish. It is fully incorporated in the present work.

1.23 Sheila T. Clendenning. *Emily Dickinson: A Bibliography.* N.p. [Kent, Ohio]: Kent State Univ. Press, 1968. 145 pp.
An enumerative, annotated listing of ED editions (without description) and such secondary materials as books and articles about the poet, Ph.D. dissertations, and some translations. It includes explication and author indexes and an introductory essay (pp. xi-xxii) on the history of ED scholarship. Omits short reviews and ana. Some early reprintings noted on pp. 18-20 and a few other items, along with about 30 explication entries, those of marginal usefulness, are not included in the present work.

[5.114] Klaus Lubbers. "Sources" in *Emily Dickinson: The Critical Revolution* (1968), pp. 265-323.

GUIDES TO EMILY DICKINSON'S MANUSCRIPTS
AND READING

Manuscripts

1.24 *Manuscripts Presented by Millicent Todd Bingham to Amherst College, 1956-1957.* Microfilm reproduction of ED's manuscripts by the Folger Shakespeare Library, Washington, D.C., April 1957. 3 reels.
Contents:
Reel 1: Poems selected by the author and preserved for her own records.

Reel 2: Letters including poems.
Reel 3: Letters and drafts.
This microfilm reproduces the most significant portion of the
Bingham collection. For a guide to its use, see 1.25.

1.25   Millicent Todd Bingham. *Guide to the Use of the Microfilm of the
        Emily Dickinson Manuscripts Presented by Millicent Todd
        Bingham to Amherst College, 1956-1957.* Amherst: mimeo-
        graphed, Oct. 1957. 12 pp.
        A catalog of manuscripts in the Millicent Todd Bingham Col-
        lection at the Robert Frost Library, Amherst College. See 1.24
        for a microfilm of this collection.

1.26   Jay Leyda. "Locations of Manuscripts, Illustrations, Memorabi-
        lia" in *Years and Hours,* 1960 (5.49), II, 489-503.
        A guide to the location of sources gathered in Jay Leyda's two-
        volume anthology of biographical materials.

1.27   Joseph Jones, *et. al. American Literary Manuscripts.* Austin:
        Univ. of Texas Press, 1960, p. 103.
        Lists Dickinson holdings in twenty American libraries.

1.28   Philip M. Hamer. *A Guide to Archives and Manuscripts in the
        United States.* New Haven, Conn.: Yale Univ. Press, 1961,
        pp. 229-30, 236, 256.
        Notes Dickinson holdings in the Amherst College Library, the
        Jones Library, Amherst, the Boston Public Library, and the
        Harvard Univ. Library.

1.29   Frederick L. Morey. "Major ED Collections," *Emily Dickinson
        Bulletin* (1.21), No. 2 (Mar. 1968), pp. 1-2; "Minor Collections,"
        No. 4 (June 1968), pp. 2-9.
        Briefly describes the holdings of ED manuscripts and secondary
        materials at 14 libraries.

1.30   Ruth Miller. "Appendix I: The Fascicle Numbering" in *The Po-
        etry of Emily Dickinson,* 1968 (5.54), pp. 289-332.
        A list of the poems "according to fascicles or packets into
        which they were gathered, presumably by Emily Dickinson"
        (p. 289). Where authorities disagree on the numbering of the
        manuscript sheets, the variant arrangements are listed.

1.31   Houghton Library, Harvard University. "Dickinson Papers: Lists
        and Notes." Typescript, n.d. 93 pp.
        Contents: "Inventory of poems" made by William McCarthy as
        received from Alfred Leete Hampson, pp. 3-57; "Guide to re-
        arrangement of packets" as determined by Thomas H. Johnson,
        Theodora Ward, and Michael Wineberg, pp. 58-61; "Inventory
        of letters" prepared by William McCarthy, pp. 62-83; "Summary
        of family papers" compiled by Jay Leyda who also arranged the
        papers in the boxes and made some annotations on the folders,
        pp. 84-87; and "Genealogies," pp. 88-93.

1.32   Robert Frost Library, Amherst College. Card index to the Todd-
        Bingham collection of Dickinson manuscripts and related ma-
        terials. In addition to manuscripts of the poems and letters
        (see 1.24-25), the extensive Amherst College holdings include
        all of Mrs. Todd's papers and correspondence relating to her
        work as editor of the Dickinson volumes published in the 1890's.

Diaries and other family materials in the possession of Millicent Todd Bingham have been deposited at the Yale Univ.
Library.

Emily Dickinson's Reading

1.33   Harvard University. *Handlist of Books Found in the Home of
            Emily Dickinson at Amherst, Mass., Spring, 1950.* Cambridge,
            Mass.: 1951. Negative microfilm reproduction. 97 pp.
            This microfilm is available at a number of libraries. The
            Houghton Library, Harvard, which owns the original typescript
            of this handlist, also has a 58-page typewritten list of books
            found in ED's home which remain in the Harvard Library.
[5.14]   Jack L. Capps. "An Annotated Bibliography of Emily Dickinson's
            Reading" in *Emily Dickinson's Reading* (1966), pp. 147-88.
1.34   Ruth Miller. "Appendix III: Emily Dickinson's Reading" in *The
            Poetry of Emily Dickinson,* 1968 (5.54), pp. 385-430.
            Lists some of the books found in the Dickinson home which re-
            main in the Harvard Library, and reprints selections from
            other volumes which Harvard returned to Amherst to suggest
            that they, too, may have been of interest to ED.

2.

Concordances

2.1 Frank Hardy Lane. "A Concordance to the Poems of Emily Dickinson." Bound typescript. n.d. 919 pp. Unpublished.
Contains a concordance, pp. 1-883; a list of proper names, quotations, and allusions, pp. 884-96; and a bibliography, pp. 897-919. Probably done between 1930 and 1945. Placed on sale in 1968 by International Bookfinders, Box 3003, Beverly Hills, Calif.

2.2 Louise Kline Kelly. "A Concordance of Emily Dickinson's Poems." Unpublished Ph.D. thesis, Pennsylvania State College, 1951.
Indexes nouns, verbs, adjectives, and adverbs; gives the line-context of words occurring less than ten times, the page and line number for words occurring more frequently.

2.3 S. P. Rosenbaum. *A Concordance to the Poems of Emily Dickinson.* Ithaca, N.Y.: Cornell Univ. Press, 1964. 899 pp.
A computer concordance indexing poems and variants based on *Poems,* 1955 (3.197). Provides for each word its line-context, line number, first line of the poem, and poem number. Includes an index of words in order of frequency, pp. 865-99.
Reviewed:

Franklin (5.28)	Rosenbaum (6.861)
Griffith (6.428)	Todd (6.997)
Robbins (6.851; *ALS,*	Tugwell (6.1011a)
1964, p. 131)	White (6.1158)

Unsigned reviews:

2.4 *American Literature,* XXXVII (May 1965), 230.

2.5 *Publishers' Weekly,* CLXXXVII (Jan. 4, 1965), 100-01.

2.6 *Springfield Sunday Republican,* Nov. 29, 1964.

PUBLICATION OF
EMILY DICKINSON'S
POEMS AND LETTERS

3.

Publication of Poems, Including First Printings

3.1   "A Valentine." *Springfield Republican,* Feb. 20, 1852, p. [2].
      "Sic transit gloria mundi," ED's first published poem. Origi-
      nally written as a valentine to William Howland. Unsigned.

3.2   "The May-Wine." *Springfield Republican,* May 4, 1861, p. 8.
      "I taste a liquor never brewed." Unsigned.

3.3   "The Sleeping." *Springfield Republican,* Mar. 1, 1862, p. 2.
      "Safe in their Alabaster Chambers." Unsigned.

3.4   "My Sabbath." *Round Table,* I (Mar. 12, 1864), 195.
      "Some keep the Sabbath going to Church." Unsigned.

3.5   "Sunset." *Springfield Republican,* Mar. 30, 1864, p. 6.
      "Blazing in Gold and quenching in Purple." Unsigned.

3.6   "The Snake." *Springfield Republican,* Feb. 14, 1866, p. 1.
      "A narrow Fellow in the Grass." Unsigned. For an account of
      ED's alleged reaction to the publication of this poem, see Whi-
      cher, *This Was a Poet* (5.104), p. 325. R. W. Franklin discusses
      the text and first publication of this poem, see *Editing* (5.28), p.
      167 note 31.

3.7   "Success" in *A Masque of Poets, Including Guy Vernon, a Novel-*
      ette in Verse [ed. George Parsons Lathrop]. *No Name Series.*
      Boston: Roberts Brothers, 1878, p. 174. Unsigned.
        2000 copies published Nov. 15, 1878, at $1.00. 301 pp. Re-
        issued as a Roberts Brothers' "red line" edition, Dec. 10,
        1878, 500 copies, at $1.50.
      "Success is counted sweetest." The fourth and last lines were
      altered, perhaps by Helen Hunt Jackson, who solicited the manu-
      script. This volume is discussed, and its contributors identi-
      fied, by Aubrey H. Starke (6.950). See also Winterich (6.1197).

3.8   "Renunciation." *Scribner's Magazine,* VIII (Aug. 1890), 240.
      First printing of "There came a Day at Summer's full." See
      also 6.159b.

[6.476]   Thomas Wentworth Higginson. "An Open Portfolio" (Sept. 25, 1890).

3.9   *Poems by Emily Dickinson.* Edited by Two of Her Friends, Mabel
      Loomis Todd and T. W. Higginson. Boston: Roberts Brothers,
      1890. 152 pp.

500 copies published Nov. 12, 1890, at $1.50. For description of this edition and its reprintings, see 1.1-4 and Smith, 1.15. The 4th impression (1891) corrected several errata which had persisted through previous reprintings. The first English edition, London: Osgood, McIlvaine, [Aug.] 1891, 158 pp., followed the 4th American impression. Reissued: London, 1904 (3.112). Reissued with the 2nd Series, Cleveland, 1948 (3.189) and with the 2nd and 3rd Series, Gainesville, Fla., 1967 (3.212).

Contains 116 poems. Preface by T. W. Higginson (6.477), pp. [iii]-vi. On the editing and reception of this volume, see especially Bingham, *Ancestors' Brocades* (5.5), Franklin, *Editing* (5.28), and Lubbers, *Critical Revolution* (5.114). Higginson's personal copy is owned by the Boston Public Library.

Reviewed:

Aïdé (6.17)	Lang (6.592, 6.594; see also 3.29-30)
Bates (6.76-78)	M., W. (6.636)
Bridges (6.146)	Moulton (6.734)
Brooks (6.152)	Nichols (6.747)
Chadwick (6.193)	Payne (6.782)
Cutting (6.250)	Pellew (6.787)
Dole (6.290)	T., A. (6.965)
Higginson (6.477c)	Thompson (6.993)
Howells (6.516)	Whiting (6.1169)
Hughes (6.519)	Wortman (6.1206)
Kirkland (6.576)	Young (6.1208-1209)

Unsigned reviews:

3.10   *Amherst Record*, Dec. 3, 1890, p. 4.
        10 sentence-length excerpts from reviews of *Poems*, 1890.

3.11   *Atlantic Monthly*, LXVII (Jan. 1891), 128-29.
        Horace Scudder may have written this review; see Lubbers, *Critical Revolution* (5.114), p. 259 note 11.

3.12   *Bookseller* [London], No. 402 (May 6, 1891), p. 447.
        Excerpt reprinted: Bingham, *Ancestors' Brocades* (5.5), p. 182.

3.13   *Boston Beacon*, Dec. 13, 1890.

3.14   *Boston Saturday Evening Gazette*, Nov. 23, 1890.

3.15   *Boston Sunday Globe*, Dec. 14, 1890, p. 25.

3.16   *Boston Herald*, Dec. 29, 1890, p. 6.

3.17   *Boston Evening Transcript*, Dec. 15, 1890, p. 6.
        This review may have been written by Charles Edwin Hurd, see Lubbers, *Critical Revolution* (5.114), p. 259 note 10.

3.18   *Brooklyn Standard Union*, Jan. 31, 1891.

3.19   *Catholic World*, LII (Jan. 1891), 600-04.

3.20   *Christian Intelligencer*, LXII (May 27, 1891), 12.

3.21   *Concord* [N.H.] *People and Patriot*, Jan. 2, 1891.

3.22   *Congregationalist*, LXXV (Dec. 5, 1890), 426.

3.23   *Critic*, n.s. XIV (Dec. 13, 1890), 305-06.

3.24   *Critic*, n.s. XIV (Dec. 27, 1890), 339.

3.25   *Current Literature*, VI (April 1891), 498-99.

3.26   *Graphic* [London], XLIV (Sept. 12, 1891), 305.
        Excerpt reprinted: Bingham, *Ancestors' Brocades* (5.5), p. 182.

3.27   *Independent*, XLII (Dec. 11, 1890), 1759.
          Attributed to Kinsley Twining; see Lubbers, *Critical Revolution*
          (5.114), p. 236 note 28. Bingham, in *Ancestors' Brocades* (5.5),
          p. 77, notes that the author was thought to be Maurice Thomp-
          son.
3.28   *Literary World* [Boston], XXI (Dec. 6, 1890), 466.
3.29   *London Daily News*, Jan. 2, 1891.
          Reprinted: Blake and Wells, *Recognition* (5.13), pp. 24-7.
          Excerpt reprinted: Bingham, *Ancestors' Brocades* (5.5), pp.
          100-01.
          May have been written by Andrew Lang; see next entry.
3.30   *London Daily News*, Oct. 3, 1891.
          Excerpt reprinted: Bingham, *Ancestors' Brocades* (5.5), pp.
          182-83.
          This review — and the preceding one — may have been written by
          Andrew Lang, a literary editor of the *Daily News*. For a reply
          to his criticism of ED, see Sanborn, 6.875.
3.31   *New York Commercial Advertiser*, Jan. 6, 1891, p. 4.
3.32   *New York Evening Sun*, Jan. 12, 1891.
          My search did not locate this item cited by Bingham, *Ancestors'
          Brocades* (5.5), p. 407.
3.33   *New York Daily Tribune*, Nov. 15, 1890, p. 8.
3.34   *New York Daily Tribune*, Jan. 4, 1891, Part II, p. 14.
3.35   *New York Daily Tribune*, Mar. 15, 1891.
3.36   *Overland Monthly*, XVII, Series 2 (May 1891), pp. 549-50.
3.37   *Packer Alumna* [Packer Collegiate Institute, Brooklyn, N.Y.], VII
          (June 1891), 139.
3.38   *Providence Sunday Journal*, Dec. 7, 1890, p. 13.
3.39   *Providence Sunday Journal*, June 14, 1891, p. 13.
3.40   *Review of Reviews* [London], IV (Sept. 1891), 308.
3.41   *San José* [Calif.] *Mercury*, April 19, 1891.
3.42   *Saturday Review* [London], LXXII (July 18, 1891), 94.
          Excerpt reprinted: Bingham, *Ancestors' Brocades* (5.5), p. 182.
3.43   *Saturday Review* [London], LXXII (Sept. 5, 1891), 279.
          Reprinted: Blake and Wells, *Recognition* (5.13), pp. 38-41.
3.44   *Scribner's Magazine*, IX (Mar. 1891), 395-96.
          Reprinted: Blake and Wells, *Recognition* (5.13), pp. 34-36.
3.44a   *Spectator* [London), LXVIII (April 2, 1892), 472.
3.45   *Springfield Republican*, Nov. 16, 1890, p. 4.
          Excerpt reprinted: Whicher, *This Was a Poet* (5.104), p. 320.

3.46   "Poems by the Late Emily Dickinson." *Independent*, XLIII (Feb.
          5, 1891), 181.
          First printing of "God made a little Gentian," "I held a Jewel
          in my fingers," and "Went up a year this evening!"
3.47   "Nobody." *Life* [N.Y.], XVII (Mar. 5, 1891), 146.
          First printing of "I'm Nobody! Who are you?"
3.48   "Two Lyrics." *Independent*, XLIII (Mar. 12, 1891), 369.
          First printing of "Just lost, when I was saved!" and "Through
          the strait pass of suffering."
3.49   *Christian Register*, LXX (April 2, 1891), 212.
          First printing of "God is a distant — stately Lover."

3.50   "Morning." *St. Nicholas,* XVIII (May 1891), 491.
          First printing of "Will there really be a 'Morning'?"
3.51   "The Sleeping Flowers." *St. Nicholas,* XVIII (June 1891), 616.
          First printing of "Whose are the little beds, I asked."
[6.473]   Thomas Wentworth Higginson. "Emily Dickinson's Letters"
          (Oct. 1891).
3.52   *Poems by Emily Dickinson.* Edited by Two of Her Friends, T. W.
          Higginson and Mabel Loomis Todd. *Second Series.* Boston:
          Roberts Brothers, 1891. 230 pp.
               960 copies published Nov. 9, 1891 in plain ($1.25) and deluxe
          ($1.50) bindings. For description of this edition and its re-
          printings, see 1.1-4 and Smith, 1.15. The 1st and 2nd Series
          were combined in one volume published May 1893, at $2.00.
          Reissued with the 1st Series, Cleveland, 1948 (3.112) and
          with the 1st and 3rd Series, Gainesville, Fla., 1967 (3.212).
          Contains 167 poems. Preface by Mabel Loomis Todd (6.1003),
          pp. [3]-8. On the editing and reception of this volume, see es-
          pecially Bingham, *Ancestors' Brocades* (5.5), Franklin, *Editing*
          (5.28), and Lubbers, *Critical Revolution* (5.114).
          Reviewed:

Bridges (6.145)	Moulton (6.733)
Chamberlain (6.194)	Schauffler (6.891)
Higginson (6.477d)	Stoddard (6.956)
Hughes (6.519)	Wingate (6.1195)
M., W. (6.636)	

          Unsigned reviews:
3.53   *Amherst Record,* Dec. 2, 1891, p. 4.
3.53a   *Atlantic Monthly,* LXIX (Feb. 1892), 277.
3.54   *Book Buyer,* VIII (Jan. 1892), 650-51.
3.55   *Boston Beacon,* Nov. 14, 1891.
3.56   *Boston Budget,* Nov. 15, 1891.
               Excerpt reprinted: Bingham, *Ancestors' Brocades* (5.5), p. 176.
          This review may have been written by Lilian Whiting; see Lub-
          bers, *Critical Revolution* (5.114), p. 260 note 17.
3.57   *Boston Courier,* Nov. 22, 1891.
               Excerpt reprinted: Bingham, *Ancestors' Brocades* (5.5), p. 174.
3.58   *Boston Evening Transcript,* Dec. 9, 1891, p. 6.
               Excerpt reprinted: Bingham, *Ancestors' Brocades* (5.5), p. 175.
          This and the following item may have been written by Charles
          Edwin Hurd; see Lubbers, *Critical Revolution* (5.114), p. 259
          note 10.
3.59   *Boston Evening Transcript,* Dec. 15, 1891, p. 6.
3.60   *Boston Traveller,* Nov. 28, 1891.
3.61   *Catholic World,* LIV (Dec. 1891), 448.
3.62   *Chautauquan,* XIV (Jan. 1892), 509-10.
3.63   *Chicago Tribune,* Dec. 12, 1891, p. 12.
               Reprinted: Blake and Wells, *Recognition* (5.13), pp. 45-9.
               Excerpt reprinted: Bingham, *Ancestors' Brocades* (5.5), p. 176.
3.64   *Christian Intelligencer,* LXIII (Jan. 13, 1892), 12.
3.65   *Christian Register,* LXX (Dec. 31, 1891), 868-69.
3.66   *Christian Union,* XLV (June 18, 1892), 1212.
               Excerpt reprinted: Bingham, *Ancestors' Brocades* (5.5), pp.
          176-77.

3.67   *Cleveland Plain Dealer,* Dec. 6, 1891.
3.68   *Concord* [N.H.] *People and Patriot,* Feb. 1892.
3.69   *Congregationalist,* **LXXV** (Dec. 31, 1891), 459.
        Excerpt reprinted: Bingham, *Ancestors' Brocades* (5.5), pp.
        174-75.
3.70   *Critic,* n.s. **XVI** (Dec. 19, 1891), 346.
        Reprinted: Blake and Wells, *Recognition* (5.13), pp. 50-1.
        For a reply, see 6.956.
3.71   *Independent,* **XLIII** (Sept. 3, 1891), 1321.
3.72   *Light* [Worcester, Mass.], **IV** (Dec. 5, 1891), 322.
3.73   *Literary World,* **XXII** (Dec. 19, 1891), 486.
        Excerpt reprinted: Bingham, *Ancestors' Brocades* (5.5), p. 175.
3.74   *New York World,* Dec. 6, 1891, p. 26.
        Excerpt reprinted: Bingham, *Ancestors' Brocades* (5.5), p. 175.
3.75   *Overland Monthly,* **XIX** (Feb. 1892), 218-19.
3.76   *Springfield Republican,* Nov. 8, 1891, p. 6.
        Excerpt reprinted: Bingham, *Ancestors' Brocades* (5.5), p. 174.
3.77   *Springfield Republican,* Dec. 10, 1891, p. 5.
        Excerpt reprinted: Bingham, *Ancestors' Brocades* (5.5), p. 174.

3.78   "A Nameless Rose." *Youth's Companion,* **LXIV** (Dec. 24, 1891), 672.
        First printing of "Nobody knows this little Rose."
3.79   *The Handbook of Amherst, Massachusetts.* Prepared and Published
        by Frederick H. Hitchcock. Amherst, Mass.: 1891.
        Partial first printing of "The murmuring of Bees, has ceased."
        Two other **ED** poems appearing here were reprinted from
        Poems, 1891 (3.52).
3.80   "Autumn." *Youth's Companion,* **LXV** (Sept. 8, 1892), 448.
        First printing of "The name — of it — is 'Autumn.'"
3.81   "Saturday." *Youth's Companion,* **LXV** (Sept. 22, 1892), 468.
        First printing of "From all the Jails the Boys and Girls."
3.82   "In September." *Youth's Companion,* **LXV** (Sept. 29, 1892), 484.
        First printing of "September's Baccalaureate."
3.83   *Youth's Companion,* **LXVI** (May 18, 1893), 256.
        First printing of "I met a King this afternoon!" and "I'm the
        little 'Heart's Ease'!"
3.84   *Book Buyer,* n.s. **XI** (Oct. 1894), 425.
        First printing of "They might not need me — yet they might."
[4.3]   *Letters of Emily Dickinson,* ed. Mabel Loomis Todd. 2 vols.
        (1894).
        Many poems make their first appearance within the text of this,
        the earliest edition of **ED**'s letters.
3.85   *Outlook,* **LIII** (Jan. 25, 1896), 140.
        First printing of "'Tis little I — could care for Pearls" and "We
        learn in the Retreating" and partial first printing of "This World
        is not Conclusion."
3.86   "Time's Healing." *Independent,* **XLVIII** (May 21, 1896), 677.
        First printing of "They say that 'Time assuages.'"
3.87   "Parting." *Scribner's Magazine,* **XIX** (June 1896), 780.
        First printing of "My life closed twice before its close."
3.88   "Verses." *Independent,* **XLVIII** (July 2, 1896), 885.
        First printing of "Hope is a subtle Glutton," "It dropped so

low — in my Regard," "The Past is such a curious Creature,"
and partial first printing of "Proud of my broken heart, since
thou dids't break it."

3.89   *Poems by Emily Dickinson.* Edited by Mabel Loomis Todd.
Third Series. Boston: Roberts Brothers, 1896. 200 pp.
1000 copies published on Sept. 1, 1896 in plain ($1.25) and
deluxe ($1.50) bindings. For description of this edition and
its reprintings, see 1.1-4 and Smith, 1.15. Reprinted with
the 1st and 2nd Series, Gainesville, Fla., 1967 (3.212).
Contains 166 poems. Preface by Mabel Loomis Todd (6.1004),
pp. [vii]-viii. On the editing and reception of this volume see
especially Bingham, *Ancestors' Brocades* (5.5), Franklin, *Editing* (5.28), and Lubbers, *Critical Revolution* (5.114).

Reviewed:

Abbott (6.5)	Hughes (6.519)
C., E.R. (6.163)	Musser (6.741)
Carmen (6.181)	Payne (6.783)
Child (6.202)	Whiting (6.1168)
Higginson (6.477g)	Williams (6.1181)

Unsigned reviews:

3.90   *Book News* [Philadelphia], XV (Oct. 1896), 56.
Reprinted from an undated *Hartford Post.*

3.91   *Boston Beacon,* Oct. 1896. [The date is uncertain; see Bingham,
Ancestors' Brocades (5.5), p. 410).

3.92   *Boston Courier,* Sept. 6, 1896.

3.93   *Boston Evening Transcript,* Aug. 8, 1896, p. 12.
This review may have been written by Charles Edwin Hurd; see
Lubbers, *Critical Revolution* (5.114), p. 259 note 10.

3.94   *Bradley: His Book* [Springfield, Mass.], II (Dec. 1896), 66.
Attributed to Van der Dater by Lubbers, *Critical Revolution*
(5.114), p. 305.

3.94a   *Chautauguan,* XXIV (Mar. 1897), 750.

3.95   *Chicago Journal,* Sept. 26, 1896, p. 9.
Excerpt reprinted: Bingham, *Ancestors' Brocades* (5.5), p. 346.

3.96   *Chicago Tribune,* Oct. 3, 1896, p. 10.

3.97   *Church* [Boston], II (Nov. 1896), 44.

3.98   *Independent,* XLVIII (Oct. 29, 1896), 1463.

3.99   *Literary World,* XXVII (Oct. 31, 1896), 361.

3.100   *New York Commercial Advertiser,* Oct. 10, 1896, p. 14.

3.101   *New York Daily Tatler,* I (Nov. 11, 1896), 5.

3.102   *New York Times,* Sept. 25, 1896, p. 10.

3.103   *New York Daily Tribune,* Aug. 23, 1896, Part III, p. 22.
Excerpt reprinted: Bingham, *Ancestors' Brocades* (5.5), p. 345.

3.104   *Newport News,* May 16, 1899.

3.105   *Overland Monthly,* XXX (Aug. 1897), 190.

3.106   *Philadelphia Telegraph,* Sept. 19, 1896.

3.107   *Public Opinion* [Washington, D.C.], XXI (Oct. 22, 1896), 537.

3.108   *Springfield Sunday Republican,* Sept. 13, 1896, p. 13.

3.109   "Nature's Way." *Youth's Companion,* LXXII (Jan. 20, 1898), 36.
First printing of "Were nature mortal lady."

3.110   "Fame." *Independent,* L (Feb. 3, 1898), 137.
First printing of "Fame is a bee."

3.111   "Spring's Orchestra." *Independent*, L (June 2, 1898), 705.
          First printing of "The saddest noise, the sweetest noise."
3.112   *Poems by Emily Dickinson.* London: Methuen, 1904. 152 pp.
          Contains only the poems of the 1890 edition (3.9). The sheets
          were imported from America and a new title page inserted.
          Reviewed:
3.113   *Athenaeum* [London], No./4036 (Mar. 4, 1905), pp. 269-70.
3.114   *The Single Hound, Poems of a Lifetime by Emily Dickinson.* With
          an Introduction by Her Niece, Martha Dickinson Bianchi.
          Boston: Little, Brown, 1914. 151 pp.
               595 copies published on Sept. 19, 1914, at $1.25.
          Contains 143 poems. Preface by Martha Dickinson Bianchi,
          pp. [v]-xix.
          Reviewed:
               Braithwaite (6.137)   D., J.J. (6.253)
               Burrows (6.161)   Monroe (6.718)
               Colson (6.223)   Sergeant (6.904)
          Unsigned reviews:
3.115   *Boston Herald*, Oct. 24, 1914, p. 8.
3.116   *Chicago Evening Post*, Dec. 4, 1914, Holiday Literary Supplement,
          p. 4.
3.117   *Chicago Daily Tribune*, Oct. 10, 1914, p. 10.
          This review was written by Elia W. Peattie.
3.118   *New York Times Book Review*, Sept. 19, 1915, p. 333.
3.119   *Review of Reviews* [N.Y.], LI (Feb. 1915), 248.
3.120   *Springfield Republican*, Sept. 22, 1914, p. 15.
3.121   *Springfield Sunday Republican*, Oct. 18, 1914, p. 17.
3.122   *Springfield Republican*, Oct. 22, 1914, p. 5.

3.123   *The Complete Poems of Emily Dickinson.* With an Introduction by
          Her Niece, Martha Dickinson Bianchi. Boston: Little, Brown;
          Toronto: McClelland, 1924. 330 pp.
               2000 copies published on July 2, 1924, at $3.50. First En-
          glish edition: London: Martin Secker, 1924. Pocket Edition:
          Boston: Little, Brown, 1926; London: Martin Secker, 1928.
          Contains 597 poems, four of which make their first appearance.
          Introduction, pp. v-ix. An additional introductory note by Mme.
          Bianchi appears in the Pocket Edition, pp. xi-xii.
          Reviewed:
               A., M. (6.2)   Hill (6.478)   Walsh (6.1064)
               Bates (6.80)   Jones (6.551)   Wasson (6.1074)
               Blunden (6.117)   M., F. (6.633)   Whicher (6.1117)
               Brégy (6.140)   Pearson (6.785)   Wicks (6.1173)
               Chew (6.200)   Sapir (6.878)   Williams (6.1178)
               Fletcher (6.354)   Taggard (6.969)   Yust (6.1211)
          Unsigned reviews:
3.124   *Boston Globe*, April 12, 1925, p. 73.
3.125   *Literary Digest*, LXXXII (Aug. 2, 1924), 34, 38.
3.126   *Springfield Republican*, Oct. 26, 1924, p. 7-A.
3.127   *Selected Poems of Emily Dickinson.* Edited by Conrad Aiken.
          London: Cape, 1924. 272 pp.
               Published in Sept. 1924.
          Contains 220 poems. Preface by Conrad Aiken (6.20), pp. 5-22.

Reviewed:
   Lubbock (6.628)   Porter (6.814)

   Monro (6.717)   T., J. M. (6.965a)

Unsigned reviews:

3.128   *English Review*, XXXVIII (Nov. 1924), 728.

3.129   *Saturday Review* [London], CXXXVIII (Nov. 1, 1924), 447.

3.130   *Springfield Sunday Republican*, Feb. 1, 1925, p. 7-A.

3.131   *Times* [London] *Literary Supplement*, No. 1189 (Oct. 30, 1924), pp. 673-74.

3.132   *Emily Dickinson*. (The Pamphlet Poets). N.Y.: Simon and Schuster, [*ca.* 1927]. 31 pp. $.75.

      Contains 24 poems selected by Louis Untermeyer, with an introduction by him, pp. 5-6.

3.133   "Twenty New Poems by Emily Dickinson." *London Mercury*, XIX (Feb. 1929), [350]-359.

      In the same number there is a brief editorial note on the poems by J. C. Squire, p. 337. All are included in *Further Poems* (3.138).

3.134   "Unpublished Poems by Emily Dickinson." *Atlantic Monthly*, CXLIII (Feb. 1929), [180-86], and (Mar. 1929), [326-32].

      Each number contains ten poems, one of which is duplicated in the *London Mercury* listed above (3.133). All are included in *Further Poems* (3.138).

3.135   "New Poems by Emily Dickinson." *Saturday Review*, V (Mar. 9, 1929), 751.

      First printing of eight poems, all of which were published in *Further Poems* (3.138).

3.136   *New York Herald Tribune Books* V (Mar. 10, 1929), 1, 4.

      First printing of seven poems. Two others appearing here were first published the preceding month in the *London Mercury* (3.133). All were collected in *Further Poems* (3.138).

3.137   "Four Poems by Emily Dickinson." *Nation*, CXXVIII (Mar. 13, 1929), 315.

      All were published simultaneously in *Further Poems* (see next entry).

3.138   *Further Poems of Emily Dickinson*. Withheld From Publication by Her Sister Lavinia. Edited by Her Niece Martha Dickinson Bianchi and Alfred Leete Hampson. Boston: Little, Brown, 1929. 208 pp.

      2000 copies published on Mar. 16, 1929, at $2.50. 465 numbered copies of a deluxe, large paper edition were published on the same date. The first English edition (London: Secker) was published on Oct. 12, 1929.

      Contains 191 poems and an appendix including poems which had previously appeared in fragmentary form.

Reviewed:

Aiken (6.21, 6.23)	D., M. E., (6.254)	Green (6.419-420)
Arvin (6.54)	Deutsch (6.279)	H., A.R. (6.432)
Blunden (6.117)	Elliott (6.312)	Hampson (6.438)
Braithwaite (6.136)	Friedlaender	Harris (6.450)
Brickell (6.144)	(6.370)	Hicks (6.465)

Hillyer (6.479-   Mumford (6.736)   Tasker (6.979)
  480, 6.485)   North (6.756)   Twitchett (6.1015)
Humphries (6.523)   O'Halloran (6.765)   Untermeyer (6.1021)
Hutchison (6.526)   Prescott (6.823)   Van Doren, M.
K., B.M. (6.560)   Sackville-West   (6.1041)
Kreymborg (6.583)   (6.870)   Welby (6.1083)
Luskin (6.629)   Spencer (6.940)   Wells (6.1091)
McCausland   Squire (6.947)   Whitman (6.1172)
  (6.678-680)
  Unsigned reviews:

3.139   *Book Chat From Beacon Hill* [Boston], V, No. 1, n.d., p. 1.
3.140   *Boston Herald*, Mar. 17, 1929, Magazine Section, p. 5.
3.141   *Catholic World*, CXXX (Oct. 1929), 115.
3.142   *Christian Science Monitor*, Jan. 25, 1929, p. 1.
3.143   *Christian Science Monitor*, April 3, 1929, p. 14.
3.144   *Hampshire Daily Gazette* [Northampton, Mass.], Jan. 25, 1929.
3.145   *Hampshire Daily Gazette* [Northampton, Mass.], Mar. 18, 1929.
3.145a *New York Times*, Jan. 25, 1929, p. 3.
3.145b *Springfield Republican*, Jan. 25, 1929, p. 1.
3.146   *Springfield Republican*, Mar. 24, 1929, p. 7-E.
3.147   *Springfield Republican*, April 12, 1929, p. 12.
3.148   *Springfield Union*, Jan. 26, 1929.
           Two articles: a news release and an editorial.
3.149   *Time*, XIII (April 8, 1929), 46.
3.150   *Times* [London] *Literary Supplement*, No. 1448 (Oct. 31, 1929),
           p. 869.

3.151   *The Poems of Emily Dickinson.* Edited by Martha Dickinson
        Bianchi and Alfred Leete Hampson. *Centenary Edition.* Bos-
        ton: Little Brown, 1930. 401 pp.
           Published on Nov. 21, 1930, at $4.00. For the first English
           edition, see 3.158. Reissued in 1937 with additional poems
           (3.173).
           Contains 787 poems, of which one ("Fitter to see Him, I may
           be") makes its first appearance here. Includes an introduction
           . by Mme. Bianchi, pp. [v]-xii.
        Reviewed:
           Britt (6.148)   Maynard (6.674)
           Hansen (6.439)   Vernon (6.1048)
           Marcellino (6.647)
        Unsigned reviews:
3.152   *Boston Sunday Post*, Dec. 7, 1930.
           My search did not locate this item cited in the Jones Library
           handlist (1.16), p. 29.
3.153   *Boston Transcript*, Dec. 27, 1930, p. 2.
3.154   *Saturday Review*, VII (Dec. 6, 1930), 443.
3.155   *Springfield Sunday Union and Republican*, May 18, 1930, p. 7-E.
3.156   *Springfield Sunday Union and Republican*, Nov. 30, 1930, p. 7-E.

3.157   Barney, Margaret Higginson, and Frederic Ives Carpenter. "Un-
        published Poems of Emily Dickinson." *New England Quar-
        terly*, V (April 1932), 217-20.
           Includes six poems later collected in *Bolts of Melody*, 1945

(3.177). Two of the six were reprinted in the *New York Herald Tribune*, April 17, 1932, Section 2, p. 6.

3.158   *The Poems of Emily Dickinson.* Edited by Martha Dickinson
        Bianchi and Alfred Leete Hampson. Definitive Complete Edi-
        tion. London: Secker, 1933.
        A reprint of the 1930 *Centenary Edition* (3.151).
        Reviewed:

Armstrong (6.48)	Read (6.838)
French (6.368)	Thompson (6.992)

3.159   *Poems For Youth.* Edited by Alfred Leete Hampson; Foreword
        by May Lamberton Becker; Illustrations by George and Doris
        Hauman. Boston: Little, Brown, 1934. 119 pp. $2.00. With
        two exceptions, all of the poems in this book appear in *Poems,
        1930* (3.151). Editorial note, pp. [7]-[8]; Foreword, pp. [9]-
        [12].
        Reviewed:

B., F. (6.59)	S., P.P. (6.869)
Becker (6.86)	Skinner (6.928)
Eaton (6.307)	

Unsigned reviews:

3.160   *Boston Herald,* Dec. 8, 1934.
        My search did not locate this item cited in the Jones Library
        handlist (1.16), p. 42.
3.161   *Springfield Sunday Union and Republican*, Dec. 9, 1934, p. 7-E.
3.162   "Glory." *Atlantic Monthly,* CLV (June 1935), 703.
        First printing of "My Triumph lasted till the Drums."
3.163   "Two Unpublished Poems." *Yale Review,* XXV (Autumn 1935), 76.
        First printing of "Somehow myself survived the Night" and
        partial first printing of "More Life — went out — when He
        went."
3.164   "If I Should Be A Queen." *Atlantic Monthly,* CLVI (Nov. 1935),
        560.
        First printing of "I'm saying every day."
3.165   "Two Poems." *Saturday Review,* XIII (Nov. 9, 1935), 12.
        First printing of "A Tooth upon Our Peace" and "She staked
        her Feathers — Gained an Arc."
3.166   *Commonweal,* XXIII (Nov. 29, 1935), 124.
        First printing of "We grow accustomed to the Dark."
3.167   *Unpublished Poems of Emily Dickinson.* Edited by Her Niece
        Martha Dickinson Bianchi and Alfred Leete Hampson. Boston:
        Little Brown, 1935. 157 pp.
        The deluxe edition, limited to 525 numbered copies, was
        published on Nov. 23, 1935, at $7.50. The trade edition was
        published in Feb. 1936 at $2.50.
        Reviewed:

Becker (6.87)	Hutchison (6.529)	S., P.P. (6.868)
Bogan (6.120)	Leisy (6.605)	Salls (6.873)
Eshleman (6.321)	Mary Irmina (6.665)	Sedgwick (6.902)
Flaccus (6.352a)	Matthiessen (6.669)	Sprague (6.946)
Gannett (6.388)	McCarthy (6.667)	Taggard (6.970)
Holmes (6.504)	McLean (6.686)	Van Doren, M. (6.1043)

Unsigned reviews:

3.168   *American Mercury*, **XXXVII** (Feb. 1936), 253.
3.169   *Amherst Record*, Nov. 27, 1935, p. 8.
3.170   *Publishers' Weekly*, **CXXVIII** (Oct. 5, 1935), 1269.
3.171   *Springfield Republican*, Oct. 1, 1935, p. 8.
3.172   *Springfield Republican*, Nov. 24, 1935, p. 7-E.

3.173   *The Poems of Emily Dickinson*. Edited by Martha Dickinson
        Bianchi and Alfred Leete Hampson. Introduction by Alfred
        Leete Hampson. Boston: Little Brown; London: Cape, 1937.
        484 pp.
            Published Feb. 1937, at $3.50. The English edition was re-
        issued in 1947 (3.183). The title of the American edition
        was changed in Dec. 1946 to *Poems by Emily Dickinson*.
        Combines *Poems*, 1930 (3.151) and *Unpublished Poems*, 1935
        (3.167). Introduction, pp. [vi]-ix.
        Reviewed:

    Holmes (6.505)   Stonier (6.959)
    Murdock (6.738)   Underhill (6.1017)
    de Selincourt (6.903)   Whiting (6.1166)

        Unsigned reviews:

3.174   *New York Herald Tribune Books*, May 2, 1937, p. 12.
3.175   *Springfield Republican*, Feb. 26, 1937, p. 10.
3.176   *Times* [London] *Literary Supplement*, No. 1860 (Sept. 25, 1937),
        p. 690.

[5.104] George F. Whicher. *This Was a Poet* (1938), p. 144.
         First printing of "Blossoms will run away."

[10.79] *Emily Dickinson, Selected Poems*. Selected by S. Vestdijk (1940).

3.177   *Bolts of Melody. New Poems of Emily Dickinson*. Edited by
        Mabel Loomis Todd and Millicent Todd Bingham. New York
        and London: Harper, 1945. 352 pp.
            Published April 4, 1945, at $3.00. This edition was reissued
        by an English publisher (London: Cape) in 1947 (3.182).
        Includes a foreword by Mark Van Doren, pp. v-vi, and an in-
        troduction by Millicent Todd Bingham, pp. vii-xxviii.
        Reviewed:

    Aiken (6.19)   Jakeman (6.535)   Rosenberger (6.862)
    Beal (6.81)   Kennedy (6.566)   Scott (6.900)
    Bogan (6.122-123)   Laycock (6.602)   Sewall (6.912)
    C., S.C. (6.168)   Linscott (6.621)   Stunz (6.960)
    Deutsch (6.276)   M., M. (6.634)   Swallow (6.963)
    Fletcher (6.353)   Matthiessen (6.670)   Taggard (6.971)
    Gannett (6.393)   Maynard (6.673)   Wells (6.1097)
    Goldsmith (6.408)   McLean (6.685)   Whicher (6.1126,
    H., C. (6.432a)   Middleton (6.701)   6.1128)
    Hackett (6.434)   Raymund (6.837)   Wilson (6.1188)
    Hillyer (6.483)   Winterich (6.1199)

        Unsigned reviews:

3.178   *Boston Daily Globe*, April 5, 1945, p. 10.
3.179   *Time*, **XLV** (April 16, 1945), 100, 102, 104.
3.180   *United States Quarterly Booklist*, I (Sept. 1945), 12.

3.181   "Poems of Emily Dickinson: Hitherto Published Only in Part," ed. Millicent Todd Bingham. *New England Quarterly*, XX (Mar. 1947), 3-50.

Prints and discusses 56 poems, of which 45 were previously published in part. Includes comment on problems in editing.

3.182   *Bolts of Melody. New Poems of Emily Dickinson.* Edited by Mabel Loomis Todd and Millicent Todd Bingham. London: Cape, 1947.

A reissue of *Bolts of Melody*, 1945 (3.177).

Published jointly with *Poems*, 1947. See next entry for reviews.

3.183   *Poems of Emily Dickinson.* Edited by Martha Dickinson Bianchi and Alfred Leete Hampson. London: Cape, 1947.

A reissue of *Poems*, 1937 (3.173).

Reviewed jointly with *Bolts of Melody*, 1947 (3.182):

Arlott (6.47)	McCarthy (6.675)
G., H (6.381)	Trewin (6.1006)
Hansen (6.442)	West (6.1106)

Unsigned reviews:

3.184   *Durham University Journal*, n.s. IX (Dec. 1947), 29-31.

3.185   *Times* [London] *Literary Supplement*, No. 2379 (Sept. 6, 1947), p. 452.

3.186   *Times* [London] *Literary Supplement*, No. 2392 (Dec. 6, 1947), p. 628.

3.187   *Emily Dickinson. Love Poems and Others.* Mount Vernon, N.Y.: Peter Pauper Press, n.d. [1948]. 93 pp.

Published early in 1948 at $2.00. First English edition: London: Mayflower; Vision, 1956. Also published in a volume containing fewer poems as *Emily Dickinson. Love Poems.* Mount Vernon, N.Y.: Peter Pauper Press, n.d. [1961?]. 61 pp. $1.00.

Both volumes contain unnumbered poems selected from *Poems*, 1890 (3.9) and *Poems*, 1891 (3.52). There are 141 poems in the first collection, 75 in the second. The latter volume includes an unsigned preface, "A Note on Emily Dickinson," pp. [3-4].

3.188   *An Emily Dickinson Year Book.* Edited by Helen H. Arnold. Drawings by Louise B. Graves. Northampton, Mass.: The Hampshire Bookshop, 1948. 132 pp.

Published in May 1948 in a limited, autographed edition at $5.00 and in the trade edition at $3.50.

Contains extracts from the poems and letters. Foreword by Helen Arnold, pp. vii-xii.

3.189   *Emily Dickinson: Poems, First and Second Series.* Edited by Two of Her Friends, Mabel Loomis Todd and T.W. Higginson. Illustrations by Leon Jacobson; Introduction by Carl Van Doren. Cleveland: World (Living Library); Toronto: McClelland, 1948. 256 pp.

A reissue of *Poems*, 1890 (3.9) and *Poems*, 1891 (3.52).

Reviewed:

Whicher (6.1136)

Unsigned reviews:

3.190   *New York Herald Tribune Weekly Book Review*, Aug. 15, 1948,
            p. 13.
3.191   *New York Times Book Review*, Aug. 22, 1948, p. 12.
3.192   *Springfield Daily News*, June 24, 1948.
3.193   *Selected Poems of Emily Dickinson.* Introduction by Conrad
            Aiken. N.Y.: Random House (Modern Library), n.d. [1948].
            231 pp.
            Contains 430 poems selected from *Poems*, 1890 (3.9), *Poems*,
            1891 (3.52), and *Poems*, 1896 (3.89). Introduction, pp. vii-xvi,
            reprinted from *Selected Poems*, 1924 (3.127).
3.194   George F. Whicher. "Some Uncollected Poems by Emily Dickin-
            son." *American Literature*, XX (Jan. 1949), 436-40.
            Notes several poems first published in periodicals that were
            not included in subsequent collections.
[4.76]   Theodora Ward, ed., *Letters to Holland* (1951). Includes the first
            appearance of six poems.
3.195   *Poems of Emily Dickinson.* Selected and Edited With a Commen-
            tary by Louis Untermeyer, and Illustrated With Drawings by
            Helen Sewall. N.Y.: Limited Editions Club, 1952. 286 pp.
               Published in 1500 copies only, bound in leather. Reissued
               by the Heritage Press, N.Y., 1952, as a volume in their
               American Poets Series, at $5.00.
3.196   *Hampshire Daily Gazette* [Northampton, Mass.], Dec. 18, 1952.
            First printing of "Her sovereign people."
3.197   *The Poems of Emily Dickinson, Including Variant Readings Crit-*
            ically Compared With All Known Manuscripts. Edited by
            Thomas H. Johnson. 3 vols. Cambridge, Mass.: Belknap
            Press of Harvard Univ. Press, 1955. Paged continuously,
            1266 pp.
               London: Oxford Univ. Press; Toronto: Saunders, 1955.
               See also *Complete Poems*, 1960 (3.207) and *Final Harvest*,
               1962 (3.208).
            Usually recognized as definitive, this edition contains 1,775
            numbered poems, arranged chronologically. The editor pro-
            vides three introductory essays: "Creating the Poems," pp.
            xvii-xxxviii; "Editing the Poems 1890-1945," pp. xxxix-xlviii;
            and "Characteristics of the Handwriting," [by Theodora Van
            Wagenen Ward] pp. xlix-lix. Manuscript and publication in-
            formation accompany the text of each poem. Back matter in-
            cludes biographical sketches of recipients of poems, tabulation
            of poems by year, titles of poems supplied by ED, and other
            appendices, as well as a subject index.
            Reviewed:

Anderson (6.37)	Franklin (5.28, esp. pp. 95-113)
Arvin (6.52)	Harding (6.446)
Blackmur (6.108)	Hillyer (6.489)
Bogan (6.121)	Iwayama (12.13)
Cambon (8.45)	Knox (6.580)
Ciardi (6.212)	Leary (6.603)
Ferguson (6.340)	Leyda (6.614)

Ransom (6.835)   Warren (6.1072)
Spicer (6.942)   White (6.1161a)
Turner (6.1013)   Wilson (6.1187)
Untermeyer (6.1022)
Unsigned reviews:

3.198   *Publishers' Weekly*, CLXIX (Jan. 14, 1956), 106-09.
3.199   *Times* [London] *Literary Supplement*, No. 2811 (Jan. 13, 1956),
         pp. 13-15.

3.200   *Eighteen Poems. Emily Dickinson.* Northampton, [Mass.]: Api-
         ary Press, 1957. 28 pp.
              100 copies printed on the Washington hand press at Smith
              College, Northampton, Mass.

3.201   *Riddle Poems.* [Northampton, Mass.]: Gehenna Press, 1957.
         Unpaged.
              "Two hundred copies of this book have been printed by
              Esther & Leonard Baskin & Richard Warren." $5.00.
              Contains 15 poems selected by Jay Leyda.
         Reviewed:
              White (6.1161)

3.202   *Selected Poems of Emily Dickinson.* Edited with an Introduction
         and Notes by James Reeves. Poetry Bookshelf Series. N.Y.:
         Macmillan; London: Heinemann, 1959. 113 pp.
              First issued at $2.00. Reprinted, 1960, 1963. Published in
              1966 by Barnes & Noble (New York).
              Contains 181 poems, following the text and chronology of
              Poems, 1955 (3.197). Introduction, pp. ix-lii (see 6.841), and
              notes to 38 poems, pp. 103-13.
         Reviewed:
              Adams (6.9)   Fitts (6.352)
              Corke (6.233)   Franklin (5.28, pp. 126-27)
              Everett (6.323)   Templeman (6.984)
         Unsigned reviews:

3.203   *College English* XXI (Mar. 1960), 357.
3.204   *Times* [London] *Literary Supplement*, No. 2977 (Mar. 20, 1959),
         p. 162.

3.205   *Selected Pòems and Letters of Emily Dickinson.* Together with
         Thomas Wentworth Higginson's Account of His Correspondence
         with the Poet and His Visit to Her in Amherst. Edited with an
         Introduction by Robert N. Linscott. Garden City, N.Y.: Dou-
         bleday Anchor Books, 1959. 343 pp. Softcover.
         Reprints about 400 poems and more than 100 letters. The
         poems follow the text of the volumes published in 1890, 1891,
         and 1896.

3.206   *Emily Dickinson.* Selected, with an Introduction and Notes, by
         John Malcolm Brinnin. *The Laurel Poetry Series.* N.Y.:
         Dell, 1960. 160 pp. Softcover.
              Contains 173 poems, following the text of *Poems*, 1937 (3.173),
              Bolts of Melody, 1945 (3.177), and, in eight instances, *Poems*,
              1955 (3.197). In his introduction, "ED, the Legend and the
              Poet," pp. 7-20, Mr. Brinnin finds that ED posed in her life
              and work as a blunt, half-crazed Medea, a recluse and mystic,

a dutiful daughter and village eccentric, and a girlishly saucy Victorian maiden. He praises her prosodic innovation and argues that much of her popularity rests on the textual altera- tions of her early editors.

3.207   *The Complete Poems of Emily Dickinson.* Edited by Thomas H. Johnson. Boston: Little, Brown, 1960. 770 pp.
Reprints in one volume the text of *Poems,* 1955 (3.197), delet- ing the variants and the publication and manuscript informa- tion of the three-volume edition. "Introduction," pp. v-xi.
Reviewed:

duPont (6.303)	Hicks (6.466)	Matchett (6.667)
Ferguson (6.338)	Hollis (6.502)	McLaughlin (6.683a)
Franklin (5.28,	Kazin (6.562)	Miller (6.709)
pp. 127, 133-37)	Lane (6.591)	Nordell (6.753)
G., C. (6.379-380)	Lauter (6.598)	Perrine (6.788)
Harding (6.447)		Shepard (6.918)

3.208   *Final Harvest: Emily Dickinson's Poems.* Selection and Intro- duction by Thomas H. Johnson. Boston: Little, Brown, 1962. 331 pp.
Issued in softcover, 1964.
A selection of 575 poems based on the editor's three-volume 1955 edition (3.197). Introduction to this edition, "The Vision and Veto of Emily Dickinson" (6.550), pp. vii-xiv.
Reviewed:

Hogan (6.497)	Holmes (6.503)	White (6.1156)

3.209   "Emily Dickinson: Three Newly-Found Poems," ed. Oscar Wil- liams. *Mutiny,* No. 12 (1963), pp. [58-59].
Prints as poems three verses "hidden in prose" among the letters of ED.

3.210   *Poems of Emily Dickinson.* Selected by Helen Plotz. Drawings by Robert Kipniss. N.Y.: Crowell; Toronto: Ambassador, 1964. 157 pp.
A selection of poems intended mainly for young people.
Reviewed:

Dalgliesh (6.259)	Engle (6.318)	White (6.1159)

[5.23]   *14 by Emily Dickinson, with Selected Criticism,* ed. Thomas M. Davis (1964).

3.211   Higgins, David J. M. "Twenty-five Poems by Emily Dickinson: Unpublished Variant Versions." *American Literature,* XXXVIII (Mar. 1966), 1-21.
Prints and discusses hitherto unpublished textual variants of twenty-five poems. Noted by Robbins, *ALS, 1966* (6.851), pp. 142-43.

3.212   *Poems (1890-1896),* by Emily Dickinson. A Facsimile Reproduc- tion of the Original Volumes Issued in 1890, 1891, and 1896. Introd. George Monteiro. Three Volumes in One. Gainesville, Florida: Scholars' Facsimiles & Reprints, 1967. 596 pp. $15.00.
A facsimile edition of the three Todd-Higginson volumes: *Poems,* 1890 (3.9), 1891 (3.52), and 1896 (3.89). The introduc- tion (pp. vii-xxii) discusses ED's early editing and critical reception.

3.213   *A Choice of Emily Dickinson's Verse.* Selected with an Introduc-
        tion by Ted Hughes. London: Faber and Faber, 1968. 68 pp.
        16s.
        Contains 104 poems, following the text of *Poems*, 1955 (3.197).
        Introduction, pp. 9-15.
        Reviewed:
        White (6.1160)

3.214   *Judge Tenderly of Me. The Poems of Emily Dickinson.* Selected
        with an Afterword by Winfield Townley Scott. Illus. by Bill
        Greer. Kansas City, Mo.: Hallmark Editions, 1968. 62 pp.
        $2.50.
        Contains 41 poems following, with a few exceptions, the text
        and chronology of *Poems*, 1955 (3.197). "Afterword," pp. 57-
        62.

3.215   *Two Poems by Emily Dickinson.* Illus. and calligraphy by Marie
        Angel. Foreword by Philip Hofer and Eleanor M. Garvey.
        N.Y.: Walker and Co., 1968. [16] pp. $3.00.
        A small booklet enclosed in a cardboard "frame" cover fea-
        turing illuminated drawings of butterflies to illustrate the
        poems "My Cocoon tightens — Colors tease" and "The butter-
        fly upon the Sky." The lettering is "arranged as a harmonious
        composition emphasizing the significant words."

3.216   *Emily Dickinson: A Letter to the World.* Poems for young
        readers chosen and introduced by Rumer Godden. Decorated
        by Prudence Seward. London: The Bodley Head, 1968. 70 pp.
        16*s.*
        Contains 44 poems following the text exactly as printed in
        Poems, 1955 (3.197). Introduction, pp. 7-14.

4.

Publication of Letters and
Prose Fragments, Including
First Printings

4.1   *Indicator, A Literary Periodical* [Amherst College], II, No. 7
(Feb. 1850), pp. 223-24.
     Prints the text of a Valentine letter attributed to ED and per-
haps written originally for *Forest Leaves,* a small paper of
the Amherst Academy (see Tuckerman, 6.1010, p. 113). Reprinted in *Letters,* 1958 (4.90), I, 91-93. First reprinted in
Taggard, *Life and Mind* (5.81), p. 67. For a press release on
Miss Taggard's discovery of this item, see 7.29.

[6.473]   Thomas Wentworth Higginson. "Emily Dickinson's Letters"
(Oct. 1891).

4.2   *Kappa Alpha Theta,* VI, No. 3 (April 1892), 117-18.
     First printing of a Dec. 1881 letter to Mrs. Holland.

4.3   *Letters of Emily Dickinson.* Edited by Mabel Loomis Todd. 2
vols. Boston: Roberts Brothers, 1894. Paged continuously,
454 pp.
        1000 copies were published on Nov. 21, 1894, at $2.00. For
description of this edition and its reprintings, see 1.1-4 and
Smith, 1.15. The two volumes were bound as one in some
reprintings, one of which (Boston: Little, Brown, 1906), was
erroneously advertised as a "new edition." The *de facto*
second edition appeared in 1931 (4.52).
     "Introductory" by Mabel Loomis Todd (6.1001), pp. [v]-xii.
Many poems make their first appearance within the text of the
letters.
     Reviewed:

Abbott (6.4)	Howe (6.515)	Stoddard (6.957)
Block (6.115)	Hughes (6.519)	Todd (6.999)
Crowell (6.240)	Jordan (6.554)	Wetcho (6.1110)
Cutting (6.249)	North (6.755)	Whiting (6.1167)
Dall (6.260)	Schappes (6.884)	Wortman (6.1205)

     Unsigned reviews:

4.4   *Amherst Record,* Dec. 19, 1894, p. 4.

4.5   *Book Buyer*, n.s. XI (Nov. 1894), 485-86.
4.6   *Book Buyer*, n.s. XI (Jan. 1895), 758.
4.7   *Boston Beacon*, Jan. 19, 1895.
4.8   *Boston Herald*, Nov. 27, 1894, p. 7.
4.9   *Boston Home Journal*, n.s. VIII (Nov. 24, 1894), 5.
4.10   *Chicago Journal*, Dec. 22, 1894, p. 9.
4.11   *Chicago Tribune*, Dec. 1, 1894, p. 10.
4.12   *Christian Register*, LXXIV (April 11, 1895), 234.
4.13   *Concord* [N.H.] *People and Patriot*, Jan. 21, 1895.
4.14   *Congregationalist* [Boston], LXXIX (Dec. 27, 1894), 973-74.
4.15   *Critic*, n.s. XXIII (Feb. 16, 1895), 119.
4.16   *Denver Times*, Dec. 7, 1894.
4.17   *Evangelist* [N.Y.], LXV (Nov. 29, 1894), 16.
4.18   *Hartford Courant*, Dec. 21, 1894, p. 6.
4.19   *Hartford Courant*, Dec. 28, 1894.
        My search did not locate this item cited in Bingham, *Ancestors'*
        Brocades (5.5), p. 410.
4.20   *Independent*, XLVII (Feb. 21, 1895), 245.
4.21   *Literary World* [Boston], XXV (Dec. 15, 1894), 445-46.
4.22   *New Orleans Times-Democrat*, Dec. 2, 1894.
        Attributed to Lilian Whiting by Lubbers, *Critical Revolution*
        (5.114), p. 313.
4.23   *New York Evening Post*, Dec. 18, 1894, p. 12.
4.24   *New York Times*, Nov. 25, 1894, Part III, p. 23. Condensed and
        reprinted in *Book News*, XIII (Feb. 1895), 267-68.
4.25   *New York Daily Tribune*, Jan. 20, 1895, Part III, p. 20.
4.26   *Outlook*, LI (Mar. 23, 1895), 481.
4.27   *Philadelphia Evening Bulletin*, Dec. 15, 1894.
4.28   *Philadelphia Public Ledger*, Dec. 7, 1894.
4.29   *Philadelphia Telegraph*, Dec. 8, 1894.
4.30   *Review of Reviews* [N.Y.], XI (Jan. 1895), 110-11.
4.31   *San Francisco Chronicle*, Dec. 30, 1894.
4.32   *Springfield Sunday Republican*, Dec. 2, 1894, p. 11.
4.33   *Spy* [Worcester, Mass.], Dec. 2, 1894.

[6.999] Mabel Loomis Todd. "Emily Dickinson's Letters" (May 1895).
4.34   Helen Knight Bullard Wyman. "Emily Dickinson as Cook and
         Poetess." *Boston Cooking School Magazine,* XI, No. 1 (June-
         July 1906).
         First printing of one letter and part of another to Lucretia
         Bullard, dated by Johnson about 1864; see *Letters*, 1958 (4.90),
         III, 907-08. (The second letter first appeared in full in the
         Mount Holyoke News and the *Boston Transcript* [Part 4, p. 8]
         for Nov. 9, 1929.) The *Boston Cooking School* article also in-
         cludes reminiscences of ED by Mrs. Wyman, the poet's niece.
         A brief excerpt of Mrs. Wyman's article is reprinted in Leyda,
         Years and Hours (5.49), II, 479.
4.35   Martha Dickinson Bianchi. "Selections from the Unpublished
         Letters of Emily Dickinson to Her Brother's Family." *Atlantic*
         Monthly, CXV (Jan. 1915), 35-42.
         The letters first printed here are incorporated, with minor

textual changes, in Mme. Bianchi's *Life and Letters* (4.36) and
ED: Face to Face (4.59).

4.36　　Martha Dickinson Bianchi. *The Life and Letters of Emily Dickinson.* Boston and N.Y.: Houghton Mifflin; London: Cape,
1924. 386 pp. $4.00. Reissued in 1930.

Excerpt reprinted:
"School Days" in *Modern Biography,* ed. Marietta Hyde
(6.532), pp. 92-102.

Part I, pp. 3-105, consists of a biographical sketch of ED and
includes hitherto unpublished letters. Part II, pp. 109-381,
reprints, with textual changes and omissions, letters first
published in the 1894 Todd edition (4.3). G.F. Whicher in *This
Was a Poet* (5.104), p. 312, notes that important corrections
were made in the fifth printing (1929) of this work.

Reviewed:

Arvin (6.53)	Fletcher (6.354)	Parton (6.771)
B., H. (6.60)	Gorman (6.410)	Porter (6.814)
Bates (6.80)	Grattan (6.415)	Rede (6.839)
Benét (6.89)	Green (6.421)	Root (6.856)
Bianchi (6.95)	Harris (6.451)	Sapir (6.878)
Boynton (6.129)	Hicks (6.462)	Schappes
Bradford (6.134)	Humphries (6.522)	(6.884-885)
Brégy (6.140)	Hutchison (6.527)	Smith (6.930)
Busse (10.44)	Keys (6.570)	Taggard (6.969)
Chew (6.200)	Kurth (6.586)	Vinci-Roman
Colton (6.225)	Libaire (6.615)	(6.1050)
Crowell (6.240)	Lubbock (6.628)	Whicher (6.1117)
Douglas (6.298)	Murphy (6.739)	Williams (6.1178)
F., J.F. (6.325)	Orr (6.766)	Woolsey (6.1204)

Unsigned reviews:

4.37　　*Amherst Writing,* XXXVIII (May 1924), 28-30.
[5.83]　　*Chicago Evening Post,* June 27, 1930, p. 8.
4.38　　*Current Opinion,* LXXVI (June 1924), 780.
4.39　　*Literary Digest,* LXXXII (Aug. 2, 1924), 34, 38.
4.40　　*Piper* [Boston: Houghton Mifflin], Mar. 1924, pp. 1-3.
4.41　　*Pittsburgh Monthly Bulletin,* XXIX (July 1924), 377.
4.42　　*Review of Reviews* [N.Y.], LXIX (May 1924), 558.
4.43　　*San Francisco Chronicle,* June 15, 1924.
4.44　　*Saturday Review* [London], CXXXVIII (Nov. 1, 1924), 447.
4.45　　*Springfield Daily Republican,* Mar. 27, 1924, p. 10.
4.46　　*Springfield Sunday Republican,* Mar. 30, 1924, p. 3-A.
4.47　　*Time,* III (May 12, 1924), 14.
4.48　　*Times* [London] *Literary Supplement,* No. 1189 (Oct. 30, 1924),
pp. 673-74.

4.49　　"An Emily Dickinson Letter, Nov. 6, 1847." *Mt. Holyoke Alumnae
Quarterly,* IX (Jan. 1926), 153-55.

The first complete printing of a letter to Abiah Root written
while ED was at Mt. Holyoke Seminary.

4.50　　Margaret Higginson Barney. "Fragments from Emily Dickinson."
Atlantic Monthly, CXXXIX (June 1927), 799-801.

T.W. Higginson's daughter prints letters of ED to her father.

[5.35]   MacGregor Jenkins. *Emily Dickinson, Friend and Neighbor* (1930).

4.51   "Two Unpublished Autograph Letters of Emily Dickinson." *Yale University Library Gazette,* VI (Oct. 1931), 42-43.
First printing of two letters to Eudocia C. Flynt.

[15.31]   Kate Dickinson Sweetser. "Emily Dickinson, A Girl of Genius," in *Great American Girls* (1931).

4.52   *Letters of Emily Dickinson.* Edited by Mabel Loomis Todd. *New and Enlarged Edition.* N.Y. and London: Harper, 1931. 457 pp. $4.00.
An enlarged edition of the 1894 volume (4.3) with a new introduction by Mrs. Todd (6.1000a), pp. xii-xxiv. A third edition was published in 1951 (4.80).
Reviewed:

Allen (6.28)	Jack (6.534)	Schappes (6.890)
C., S.C. (6.167)	Jordan (6.555)	Taggard (6.976)
Deutsch (6.277)	Moore (6.723)	Untermeyer (6.1020)
Gannett (6.391)	Moran (6.727)	Walton (6.1065)
Hicks (6.464)	Rourke (6.865)	Whicher (6.1115)

Unsigned reviews:
4.53   *Amherst Record,* Nov. 25, 1931, p. 8.
4.54   *Boston Transcript,* Nov. 18, 1931, p. 2.
4.55   *Springfield Sunday Union and Republican,* Nov. 1, 1931, p. 7-E.
4.56   *Springfield Sunday Union and Republican,* Dec. 6, 1931, pp. 1-E, 10-E.
4.57   *Times* [London] *Literary Supplement,* No. 1559 (Dec. 17, 1931), p. 1023.

4.58   John Howard Birss. "A Letter of Emily Dickinson." *Notes and Queries,* CLXIII (Dec. 17, 1932), 441.
Partial reprint of a letter to Perez Cowan that was first published in the *Libbie Auction Catalogue* (of the Edward Abbott collection), Feb. 25-26, 1909. 6 pp.

4.59   Martha Dickinson Bianchi. *Emily Dickinson Face to Face: Unpublished Letters with Notes and Reminiscences.* Boston and New York: Houghton Mifflin, 1932. 290 pp. Published at $3.50.
A volume of reminiscences containing ED's early notes with letters and poems. Preface by Alfred Leete Hampson, pp. ix-xx.
Reviewed:

Bartlett (6.71)	H., R. (6.433)	Sessions (6.908-
Deutsch (6.274)	Hutchison (6.528)	909)
Farrell (6.331)	Pollitt (6.812)	Taggard (6.977)
Gannett (6.387)	Schappes (6.882,	Untermeyer (6.1029)
	6.888)	

Unsigned reviews:
4.60   *Christian Science Monitor,* Jan. 14, 1933, p. 6.
4.61   *Commonweal,* XVII (April 12, 1933), 671.
4.62   *Nation,* CXXXVI (Jan. 18, 1933), 71.
4.63   *New Republic,* LXXIII (Jan. 4, 1933), 223.
4.64   *New York Sunday Telegram,* Jan. 15, 1933.
4.65   *Springfield Sunday Union and Republican,* Jan. 15, 1933, p. 7-E.

4.66   Thomas F. Madigan's catalog, *Autograph Album,* I (Dec. 1933),
        50.
        The first printing of excerpts of a letter dated Jan. 13, 1854,
        to Edward Everett Hall. The first full printing was in *Ameri-
        can Literature,* VI (Mar. 1934), 5.

4.67   *Scribner's Magazine,* XCV (April 1934), 290.
        First printing of a letter to Prof. Richard H. Mather on the
        death of his wife. The letter was submitted for inclusion in
        William Lyon Phelps' column, "As I Like It," by Mrs. William
        Tyler, nee Elizabeth Mather.

[6.740] *Hartford Daily Times* (Mar. 7, 1936), p. 9.

4.68   Mary Adèle Allen. "The Boltwood House. Memories of Amherst
        Friends and Neighbors." *Amherst Graduates' Quarterly,*
        XXVI (Aug. 1937), 297-307.
        Includes the first printing of three brief notes to Mrs. Lucius
        Boltwood.

4.69   Helen H. Arnold. "'From the Garden We Have Not Seen': New
        Letters of Emily Dickinson." *New England Quarterly,* XVI
        (Sept. 1943), 363-75.
        Fourteen brief notes written to Henry Vaughan Emmons before
        his graduation from Amherst in 1854.

4.70   Frank Davidson. "Some Emily Dickinson Letters." *Indiana
        Quarterly for Bookmen,* I (Oct. 1945), 113-18.
        The first printing of three letters to Mrs. Joseph Haven, writ-
        ten probably in 1858-59.

[6.237] Annie Louise Crowell. "Emily Dickinson — An Heritage of
        Friendship" (Feb. 1946).

4.71   "Letters from Emily Dickinson." *The Month at Goodspeeds,*
        XVII (May 1946), 251-54.
        Describes an ED letter to Rev. and Mrs. J.L. Jenkins and a
        second manuscript note of two sentences.

4.72   Carl J. Weber. "Two Notes from Emily Dickinson." *Colby Col-
        lege Quarterly,* XV (June 1946), 239-40.
        Announces the addition to the Colby College Library of two ED
        holograph notes addressed to Mrs. Julius H. Seelye. Both are
        here printed for the first time.

4.73   *The Collector, A Magazine for Autograph and Historical Collec-
        tors,* LXI (Oct. 1948), 230-31.
        Description and partial first printing of a note to Eugenia Hall;
        see *Letters,* 1958 (4.90), II, 550.

4.74   *The Collector, A Magazine for Autograph and Historical Collec-
        tors,* LXIII (May 1950), 107.
        Partial first printing of a second and presumably later note to
        Eugenia Hall; see *Letters,* 1958 (4.90), III, 881.

4.75   *Amherst Alumni News,* IV (July 1951), 14.
        First printing of three letters to Kendall Emerson; see *Let-
        ters,* 1958 (4.90), III, 804-05, 853, 894-95.

4.76   *Emily Dickinson's Letters to Dr. and Mrs. Josiah Gilbert Hol-
        land.* Edited by Theodora Van Wagenen Ward. Cambridge,
        Mass.: Harvard Univ. Press; Toronto: S.J.R. Saunders, 1951.
        252 pp. $4.00.

Of the 93 letters included in this volume, 64 are published for the first time. An introductory essay discusses ED's friendship with the Holland family; see also 5.97.

Reviewed:

Bishop (6.105)	Greever (6.422)	Sherrer (6.920)
Case (6.188)	Harding (6.444)	Wells (6.1098)
Chase (6.196)	Johnson (6.542)	Whicher (6.1132)
	Newcomer (6.743)	

Unsigned reviews:

4.77   *New Yorker,* XXVII (Sept. 29, 1951), 123.

4.78   *Springfield Republican,* April 29, 1951, p. 8-C.

4.79   *United States Quarterly Book Review,* VII (Sept. 1951), 224.

4.80   *Letters of Emily Dickinson.* Edited by Mabel Loomis Todd, with an Introduction by Mark Van Doren. Cleveland: World Publishing Co., 1951. 389 pp. $3.75.

     Toronto: McClelland; London: Gollancz, 1952. Softcover ed.: N.Y.: Grosset and Dunlap (The Universal Library), 1962.

A reissue of the 1931 Todd edition (4.52) with an introduction by Mark Van Doren, pp. v-xv.

Reviewed:

C., R.A. (6.165)	Fausset (6.335)	Schirmer-Imhoff
Case (6.188)	M., P. (6.635)	(10.70)
Chase (6.196)	Nicolson (6.748)	Wells (6.1103)
Clarke (6.217)	Nims (6.750)	Whicher (6.1137)
	Raine (6.829)	

Unsigned reviews:

4.81   *Listener,* XLVIII (Nov. 27, 1952), 903.

4.82   *New Yorker,* XXVII (Sept. 29, 1951), 123.

4.83   *San Francisco Chronicle,* April 8, 1951, p. 14.

4.84   *Times* [London] *Literary Supplement,* No. 2613 (Feb. 29, 1952), p. 158.

4.85   *Hampshire Daily Gazette* [Northampton, Mass.], Dec. 18, 1952.

     First printing of a letter to Susan Gilbert Dickinson; see *Letters,* 1958 (4.90), II, 465.

[6.283]   Elizabeth Dickerman. "Portrait of Two Sisters, Emily and Lavinia Dickinson" (Feb. 1954).

[5.9]   Millicent Todd Bingham. *Emily Dickinson: A Revelation* (1954).

4.86   *Emily Dickinson's Home: Letters of Edward Dickinson and His Family.* With Documentation and Comment by Millicent Todd Bingham. N.Y.: Harper; Toronto: Musson, 1955. 600 pp.

     Reissued in softcover with slight corrections as *Emily Dickinson's Home; The Early Years as Revealed in Family Correspondence and Reminiscences.* N.Y.: Dover, 1967.

An extensive gathering of the Dickinson family letters and papers with biographical sketches of persons mentioned and appendices that collect material relating to Edward Dickinson's election and brief term in Congress. A number of ED letters and notes make their first appearance.

Reviewed:

Ball (6.64)	Ciardi (6.213)	Ferguson (6.339)

Greever (6.423)	Voiles (6.1054)	White (6.1153,
Meredith (6.692)	Wells (6.1100)	6.1161a)
Munn (6.737)	Whitbread (6.1147)	Wilson (6.1185)
Sherrer (6.923)		Wilson (6.1187)

Unsigned reviews:

4.87   *New Yorker*, XXXI (Sept. 10, 1955), 159.

4.88   *United States Quarterly Book Review*, XI (Sept. 1955), 307.

4.89   Millicent Todd Bingham. "Prose Fragments of Emily Dickinson." *New England Quarterly*, XXVIII (Sept. 1955), 291-318.
        A first printing of fragments, many written toward the end of ED's life.

4.90   *The Letters of Emily Dickinson*. Edited by Thomas H. Johnson and Theodora Ward. 3 vols. Cambridge, Mass.: Belknap Press of Harvard Univ. Press; Toronto: S.J.R. Saunders; London: Oxford Univ. Press, 1958. Paged continuously, 999 pp.
        Prints the full text of all known letters, notes, and prose fragments, with complete manuscript and publication information for each item. Includes biographical sketches of recipients and persons mentioned and an index.

Reviewed:

Åhnebrink (6.16)	Hillyer (6.486)	Sale (6.872)
Anderson (6.32)	Laing (6.588)	Sewall (6.914)
Bradbrook (6.131)	Maurin (6.672)	Spiller (6.945)
Craig (6.235)	Miller (6.711)	Turner (6.1014)
Cunliffe (6.243)	Nordell (6.754)	Voiles (6.1056)
Ferguson (6.337)	Reeves (6.842)	White (6.1154)
Gregory (6.424)		Willy (6.1182)

Unsigned reviews:

4.91   *College English*, XXI (Mar. 1960), 356.

4.92   *Listener*, LIX (June 12, 1958), 987.

4.93   *New Yorker*, XXXIV (Dec. 6, 1958), 242-43.

[6.842]   *Times* [London] *Literary Supplement*, No. 2935 (May 30, 1958), p. 296.

[3.205]   *Selected Poems and Letters of Emily Dickinson,* ed. Robert N. Linscott (1959).

[6.221]   Earl E. Coleman. "Emily Dickinson" (Spring 1964).

[5.76]   Richard B. Sewall. "The Lyman Letters..." (Autumn 1965).

BOOKS AND ARTICLES
ABOUT EMILY DICKINSON

Separate Publications

5.1   Alexander, Charlotte. *The Poetry of Emily Dickinson. Monarch Notes and Study Guides,* No. 780-7. N.Y.: Monarch Press, 1965. 108 pp.
A guide for students. Summarizes critical comment on ED's poetic techniques and briefly analyzes about forty poems.

5.2   Anderson, Charles R. *Emily Dickinson's Poetry, Stairway of Surprise.* N.Y.: Holt, Rinehart and Winston; London: Heinemann, 1960. 334 pp.
     Softcover ed.: Garden City, N.Y.: Doubleday, 1966.
Close readings, arranged thematically, of about one hundred of ED's best poems. Examines her wit and belief in the potency of language and explores her verbal resourcefulness in rendering both the outer world and the conscious self.
Reviewed:

Arvin (6.55)	Hicks (6.466)	Miller (6.705)
Bradbrook (6.132)	Hollis (6.502)	Miller (6.709)
Feidelson (6.336)	Hughes (6.521)	Nordell (6.753)
Ferguson (6.343)	Le Breton (9.26)	Perrine (6.788)
Fussell (6.376)	Lindberg (6.618)	Wells (6.1101)
Harding (6.448)	Lynen (6.630)	Willy (6.1183)
	Matchett (6.667)	

Unsigned reviews:

5.3   *Times* [London] *Literary Supplement,* No. 3234 (Feb. 20, 1964), p. 148.

5.4   *Times* [London] *Weekly Review,* No. 592 (May 30, 1963), p. 13.

5.5   Bingham, Millicent Todd. *Ancestors' Brocades: The Literary Debut of Emily Dickinson.* N.Y. and London: Harper, 1945. 464 pp.
     Softcover ed.: *Ancestors' Brocades: The Literary Discovery of Emily Dickinson; The Editing and Publication of Her Letters and Poems.* N.Y.: Dover, 1967.
The daughter of Mabel Loomis Todd recounts in detail the story of the first editing of ED, with special attention to family back-

ground and to the feuds which developed over publication of the
manuscripts. Early reviews of the poems and letters listed in
an appendix (see 1.14) are incorporated in the present work.
Reviewed:

Aiken (6.19)	Hillyer (6.483)	Rand (6.832)
Beal (6.81)	Jakeman (6.535)	Raymund (6.837)
Bogan (6.122-123)	Kennedy (6.566)	Scott (6.900)
C., S.C. (6.168)	Laycock (6.602)	Spiller (6.943)
Deutsch (6.276)	Linscott (6.621)	Swallow (6.963)
DeVoto (6.281)	M., M. (6.634)	Whicher (6.1126, 6.1128,
Erskine (6.319)	Matthiessen (6.670)	6.1131, 6.1135)
Fletcher (6.353)	Maynard (6.673)	Wilson (6.1188)
Gannett (6.393)	McLean (6.685)	Winterich (6.1199)
Hackett (6.434)	Middleton (6.701)	

Unsigned reviews:

5.6   *Boston Daily Globe*, April 5, 1945, p. 10.
5.7   *Scholastic*, XLVII (Oct. 8, 1945), 20.
5.8   *Time*, XLV (April 16, 1945), 100, 102, 104.
5.9   Bingham, Millicent Todd. *Emily Dickinson: A Revelation*. N.Y.:
        Harper; Toronto: Musson, 1954. 109 pp.
        Argues that ED's correspondence with Judge Otis Lord attests
        to the emotional strength of their friendship. Over twenty let-
        ters are published for the first time.
        Reviewed:

Chase (6.195)	Hillyer (6.488)	Merrill (6.698)
Ferguson (6.345)	Joost (6.552)	Voiles (6.1053)
Gibson (6.399)	Leyda (6.611)	White (6.1152, 6.1163)

Unsigned reviews:

5.10   *Amherst Alumni News*, VIII, No. 3 (Jan. 1955).
5.11   *New Yorker*, XXXI (Mar. 5, 1955), 120.
5.12   *United States Quarterly Book Review*, XI (Mar. 1955), 3.
5.13   Blake, Caesar R., and Carlton F. Wells, eds. *The Recognition of
        Emily Dickinson, Selected Criticism Since 1890*. Ann Arbor:
        Univ. of Michigan Press; Toronto: Ambassador Books, 1964.
        314 pp.
            Soft cover ed.: Ann Arbor, Mich.: Ann Arbor Paperbacks,
            1968.
        Collects representative critical essays to document the growth
        of ED's reputation. Thirty of the forty-five selections were
        published before 1931.
        Reviewed:

Arp (6.50)	Robbins (6.851; *ALS*,
Galloway (6.386)	*1964*, p. 132)
Miller (6.706)	White (6.1150)

5.14   Capps, Jack L. *Emily Dickinson's Reading 1836-1886*. Cambridge,
        Mass.: Harvard Univ. Press; London: Oxford Univ. Press,
        1966. 230 pp.
        A full-scale discussion of the influence of ED's reading on her
        mind and art. Includes an annotated bibliography of her read-
        ing based in large part on literary allusions in her poems and
        letters. For other guides to ED's reading, see 1.33-34.

Reviewed:

Anderson (6.39)   Miller (5.54, pp. 217, 439)
Clements (6.218)   Robbins (6.851; *ALS, 1966,*
Davidson (6.265)   pp. 139-40)
Marcus (6.655)   Sewall (6.910a)

Unsigned reviews:

5.15   *Times* [London] *Literary Supplement,* No. 3368 (Sept. 15, 1966),
        p. 860.

5.16   *Virginia Quarterly Review,* XLII (Autumn 1966), p. cxliv.

5.17   Chase, Richard Volney. *Emily Dickinson. American Men of Let-*
        ters Series. N.Y.: William Sloane Associates, 1951. 328 pp.
        London: Methuen; Toronto: McLeod, 1952. Softcover ed.:
        N.Y.: Dell; Toronto: Saunders, 1965.
        A critical biography stressing the psychology which ED reveals
        in her poems. Chase believes that her chief stratagem is the
        "achievement of status through crucial experiences" and his
        argument proceeds principally through close attention to indi-
        vidual poems.

Reviewed:

Allen (6.27)   Daiches (6.255)   Manent (11.30)
Barrett (6.68)   Dobrée (6.287)   Mercier (6.691)
Blackmur (6.109)   Engle (6.317)   Ochshorn (6.760)
Brégy (6.139)   Farrelly (6.332)   Perrine (6.798)
Carruth (6.187)   Ferguson (6.342)   Sale (6.871)
Comfort (6.226)   Mandel (6.643)   Sherrer (6.922)

Unsigned reviews:

5.18   *Books In Dunedin* [Dunedin (Scotland) Public Library Assn.], V
        (Mar. 1953), 25.

5.19   *Creative Writing,* V (Oct. 1954), 9-12.

5.20   *Listener,* XLVIII (Nov. 27, 1952), 903.

5.21   *New Statesman and Nation,* XLIV (Sept. 6, 1952), 272.

5.22   *Times* [London] *Literary Supplement,* No. 2637 (Aug. 15, 1952,
        p. 528.

5.23   Davis, Thomas M., ed. *14 by Emily Dickinson, with Selected*
        Criticism. Chicago: Scott, Foresman, 1964. 178 pp.
        Critical analyses of fourteen ED poems are collected and ar-
        ranged for classroom use. Includes study questions and a se-
        lected bibliography.

Reviewed:

White (6.1159)

5.24   Duncan, Douglas. *Emily Dickinson.* Writers and Critics Series.
        Edinburgh: Oliver and Boyd, 1965. 110 pp.
        An introduction to ED's life and work, with a chapter on her
        critical reception. The book discusses several poems in de-
        tail but its primary aim is to provide a succinct assessment
        of her achievement as a whole.

Reviewed:

Robbins (6.851; *ALS, 1965,* p. 154)
Tugwell (6.1011a)

Unsigned reviews:

5.25   *Contemporary Review,* CCVI (June 1965), 334.

5.26   *Times* [London] *Literary Supplement*, No. 3301 (June 3, 1965), p. 456.

5.27   Ford, Thomas W. *Heaven Beguiles the Tired: Death in the Poetry of Emily Dickinson.* University, Alabama: Univ. of Alabama Press, 1966. 208 pp.

After close examination of the major poems on death, Ford concludes that the act of writing poetry itself became for ED a way of probing and understanding the enigma of finitude.

Reviewed:
Capps (6.178)
Robbins (6.851; *ALS, 1966,* p. 141)

5.28   Franklin, R[alph] W[illiam]. *The Editing of Emily Dickinson: A Reconsideration.* Madison: Univ. of Wisconsin Press, 1967. 187 pp.

Shows that the chronology of the early editing can be corrected, that it is possible to establish more accurately ED's own arrangement of the poems and their subsequent rearrangement, and that examination of the printer's copy of *Poems,* 1886, reveals errors and omissions in the 1955 Johnson edition. The final chapter discusses problems in preparing a reader's edition of the poems.

Reviewed:

Blake (6.112a)	Porter (6.815)
Mudge (6.734a)	Sewall (6.910a)

Unsigned reviews:

5.28a   *Times* [London] *Literary Supplement*, No. 3421 (Sept. 1967), p. 840.

5.29   Gelpi, Albert J. *Emily Dickinson, the Mind of the Poet.* Cambridge, Mass.: Harvard Univ. Press; London: Oxford Univ. Press, 1965. 201 pp.

The book attempts a comprehensive internal biography of ED by drawing from a number of passages rather than by explicating individual poems. Describes her adjustment to contrary cultural influences and her pivotal place in the history of American letters, and defines her notion of "double consciousness" and of her role as poet.

Reviewed:

Fields (6.348)	Miller (5.54, p. 435	Thomas (6.990)
Marcus (6.654a)	note 38)	Wells (6.1088)
McAllister (6.674b)	Robbins (6.851; *ALS, 1965*, pp. 153-54)	White (6.1151)

Unsigned reviews:

5.30   *Times* [London] *Literary Supplement*, No. 3366 (Sept. 1, 1966), p. 782.

5.31   Griffith, Clark. *The Long Shadow: Emily Dickinson's Tragic Poetry.* Princeton, N.J.: Princeton University Press, 1964.

Explicatory and psychoanalytic in method, this study focuses on the motif of dread in ED's poetry — dread of change and deprivation, of commitment and masculinity — and shows how the poet's type of personal despair shaped her thought and technique.

Reviewed:

Arsenault (6.51)	Blake (6.112)	Cambon (6.170)

Davis (6.270a)   Sergeant (6.905)   Wehmeyer (6.1080a)
Le Breton (9.28)   Sewall (6.911)   Wells (6.1087)
Porter (6.818)   Spector (6.935)   White (6.1159)
Robbins (6.851; *ALS,* Waggoner (6.1059)
    1964, pp. 132-33)

Unsigned review:

5.32   *Virginia Quarterly Review,* XL (Spring 1964), lxiv-lxv.

5.33   Herring, Emily Louise. *Domestic Imagery in the Poetry of Emily Dickinson.* Kentucky Microcards, Series A; Modern Languages Series, No. 161 [Lexington, Ky.: Univ. of Kentucky Press, 1964). 2 cards, 96 pp.

Discusses the frequency and importance of ED's domestic imagery. Includes explications of relevant poems and a frequency table in the appendix.

5.34   Higgins, David. *Portrait of Emily Dickinson: The Poet and Her Prose.* New Brunswick, N.J.: Rutgers Univ. Press, 1967. 266 pp.

A biographical portrait documented principally by close study of ED's correspondence. Argues that Samuel Bowles rather than Wadsworth was the object of the love poems and the "Master" letters and that her only other amatory attachment was to Judge Otis Lord.

Reviewed:

Gelpi (6.397)

5.35   Jenkins, MacGregor. *Emily Dickinson, Friend and Neighbor.* Boston: Little, Brown, 1930; reissued 1939. 150 pp.

Born across the street from ED in 1869, the author records his childhood impressions of "Miss Emily" and the Dickinson household. A number of ED letters and notes are published for the first time.

Reviewed:

Aiken (6.18)   Green (6.420a)   S., C.E. (6.867a)
Beck (6.83)   Hardy (6.449)   Taggard (6.973)
Carpenter (6.185)   Lapidus (6.596)   Untermeyer (6.1026)
Deutsch (6.275)   Price (6.824)   Wells (6.1086)
Grattan (6.415)   Robbins (6.849)   Wilson (6.1186)

Unsigned reviews:

5.36   *Bookman* [N.Y.], LXXI (June 1930), 336.
5.37   *Boston Evening Transcript,* Part III, Aug. 13, 1930, p. 2.
5.38   *Christian Science Monitor,* May 10, 1930, p. 5.
5.39   *Christian Science Monitor,* June 11, 1930, p. 9.
5.40   *Commonweal,* XII (Sept. 3, 1930), 449.
5.41   *Nation,* CXXX (June 4, 1930), 657.
5.42   *New York Times Book Review,* May 18, 1930, p. 2.
5.43   *Springfield Republican,* May 4, 1930, p. 7-E.

5.44   Johnson, Thomas H. *Emily Dickinson, An Interpretive Biography.* Cambridge, Mass.: Belknap Press of Harvard Univ. Press; London: Oxford Univ. Press; Toronto: S.J.R. Saunders, 1955. 276 pp.

Softcover ed.: N.Y.: Atheneum, 1967.

A biographical and critical study of ED's chief recent editor

stressing the emotional forces within her family and her friend-
ships with Higginson, Wadsworth, and Helen Jackson. Giving
many poems close attention, Johnson also discusses such themes
as circumference, death, and immortality.

Reviewed:

Blackmur (6.108)	Hillyer (6.484)	Wagenknecht (6.1057)
Childs (6.203)	Miller (6.713)	Wells (6.1095)
Ciardi (6.212)	Ransom (6.835)	White (6.1153)
Ferguson (6.344)	Sessions (6.907)	Williams (6.1180)
Fredeman (6.366)	Voiles (6.1055)	Wilson (6.1187)

Unsigned reviews:

5.45   *New Yorker*, XXXII (Mar. 31, 1956), 111-12.
5.46   *Times* [London] *Literary Supplement*, No. 2811 (Jan. 13, 1956),
            pp. 13-15.
5.47   *United States Quarterly Book Review*, XII (Mar. 1956), 3.
5.48   *Yale Review*, XLV (Spring 1956), x.

5.49   Leyda, Jay. *The Years and Hours of Emily Dickinson.* 2 vols.
            New Haven: Yale Univ. Press; London: Oxford Univ. Press;
            Toronto: Burns and MacEachern, 1960. Vol. I, 400 pp. Vol.
            II, 528 pp.
            An exhaustive compilation of biographical materials and docu-
            ments chronologically arranged and fully indexed. Biographical
            sketches of the Dickinson family and friends, I, xxvii-lxxxi.

Reviewed:

Anderson, C.R. (6.38)	Harding (6.447)	Lynn (6.632)
duPont (6.303)	Hicks (6.466)	Miller (6.708-709)
Ferguson (6.338)	Hillyer (6.487)	Shepard (6.918)
G., C. (6.379)	Hollis (6.502)	Thomas (6.988)
Grant (6.413)	Howes (6.517)	White (6.1155)
	Lauter (6.598)	

Unsigned reviews:

[6.413]   *Times* [London] *Literary Supplement*, No. 3094 (June 16, 1961),
                p. 372.
5.50   *Times* [London] *Weekly Review*, No. 485 (May 11, 1961), p. 12.
5.51   *Yale Review*, n.s. L (Summer 1961), vi, viii.

[5.113]   Lindberg-Seyersted, Brita. *The Voice of the Poet: Aspects of
                Style in the Poetry of Emily Dickinson.*
[5.114]   Lubbers, Klaus. *Emily Dickinson: The Critical Revolution.*
5.52   MacLeish, Archibald, Louise Bogan, and Richard Wilbur. *Emily
                Dickinson: Three Views.* Amherst, Mass.: Amherst College
                Press, 1960. 46 pp.
                An anniversary volume of critical essays on ED by three con-
                temporary poets. The essays are listed separately in this bib-
                liography: Bogan (6.119); MacLeish (6.639); Wilbur (6.1174).
                See also 6.367.

5.53   McNaughton, Ruth Flanders. *The Imagery of Emily Dickinson.*
                University of Nebraska Studies, New Series, No. 4. Lincoln:
                Univ. of Nebraska, January 1949. 66 pp.
                Discussion of the sources of ED's imagery and ways it appeals
                to the senses is followed by chapters on the poet's imagery of
                nature, death and life, love and immortality.

5.54   Miller, Ruth. *The Poetry of Emily Dickinson.* Middletown, Conn.:
       Wesleyan Univ. Press, 1968. 480 pp.
       Argues that the substance and manner of ED's poetry grew out
       of her frustrated search for publication and her unfulfilled love
       for Samuel Bowles. This quest caused her to perceive experi-
       ence as confrontation, suffering, and resolution, and to employ
       this paradigm as a dramatic structure governing arrangement
       of poems in the fascicles. The author's method is to make
       connections in imagery and feeling between the poems and let-
       ters, especially the "Master" letters and those addressed to
       Bowles and Higginson. One appendix reconstructs the fasci-
       cles, another groups poems according to themes and clusters
       of metaphors and personae, and a third discusses ED's read-
       ing and suggests several new sources for her poems.
       Reviewed:
       Herron (6.458a)

5.55   Patterson, Rebecca. *The Riddle of Emily Dickinson.* Boston:
       Houghton Mifflin; Toronto: Thomas Allen, 1951; London:
       Gollancz, 1953. 434 pp.
       Excerpt reprinted:
       "Who Was Emily Dickinson's Lover?" *Harper's Bazaar,*
       LXXXV (Nov. 1951), 132, 192, 196-99, 203-04.
       A study of ED's attachment to Susan Gilbert and Kate Scott
       Anthon. The latter is assumed to be the object of the love
       poems and to have caused ED's anguish in 1861.
       Reviewed:

Bishop (6.106)	Gohdes (6.407)	Ochshorn (6.760)
Blackmur (6.109)	Johnson (6.548)	Perrine (6.794)
Chase (6.198)	Joost (6.553)	Sherrer (6.921)
Ciardi (6.211)	Jordan-Smith (6.557)	Voiles (6.1052)
Georges (6.398)	Merrifield (6.696)	Whicher (6.1143)
	Nims (6.751)	

       Unsigned reviews:
5.56   *Nation,* CLXXIII (Dec. 29, 1951), 573.
5.57   *New Yorker,* XXVII (Nov. 3, 1951), 86.
5.58   *Springfield Republican,* Nov. 18, 1951, p. 12-C.

5.59   Phi Delta Gamma, Zeta Chapter [28 W. 44th St., N.Y.]. *Guests In
       Eden, Emily Dickinson* [and] *Martha Dickinson Bianchi.* Edited
       by Winnifred Brown and Alma G. Watson. N.Y.: 1946. 44 pp.
       A commemorative pamphlet honoring ED and Martha Dickinson
       Bianchi, the poet's niece and editor. For contributions in trib-
       ute to ED, see Ginsburg (18.60), Pollitt (6.811), Reeves (19.21),
       Root (6.858), Troubetzkoy (18.128), C. Van Doren (6.1036), and
       Vernon (18.133).

5.60   Pickard, John B. *Emily Dickinson, An Introduction and Interpre-
       tation.* American Authors and Critics Series. N.Y.: Barnes
       & Noble (hardcover); Holt, Rinehart and Winston (softcover),
       1967. 140 pp.
       A general assessment of ED's life and work designed as an in-
       troduction for college students. The first few chapters are
       biographical; the remainder examine her characteristic themes
       through close analysis of the major poems.

5.61   Pollitt, Josephine. *Emily Dickinson: The Human Background of Her Poetry*. N.Y.: Harper, 1930. 350 pp.
The first full-length biography, this book is notable mainly for advancing the thesis that ED secretly loved Major Edward Hunt, the first husband of her friend Helen Hunt Jackson.
Reviewed:

Aiken (6.18)	Grattan (6.415)	Root (6.859)
Bartlett (6.70)	Hardy (6.449)	S., C.E. (6.867a)
Beck (6.83)	Hicks (6.462)	Schappes (6.887)
Bennett (6.93)	Hutchison (6.527)	Shuster (6.925)
Blunden (6.117)	Lemon (6.607)	Untermeyer (6.1026)
Carpenter (6.185)	Libaire (6.615)	Wallace (6.1061)
Case (6.187a)	Linscott (6.620)	Wells (6.1086)
Catel (9.17)	Maynard (6.674)	Welshimer (6.1105)
Church (6.208)	Merchant (6.690)	Whicher (5.104,
Daingerfield (6.258)	Odell (6.764)	p. 321; 6.1129)
Deutsch (6.273)	Paterson (6.772)	Yust (6.1210)
Fairbank (6.328)	Pollitt (6.810)	

Unsigned reviews:

5.62   *Bookman* [N.Y.], LXXI (April-May 1930), 228.
5.63   *Chicago Evening Post*, June 27, 1930, p. 8.
5.64   *Indianapolis News*, April 5, 1930, p. 9.
5.65   *John O'London's Weekly*, XXIII (Aug. 30, 1930), 724.
5.66   *Outlook and Independent*, CLIV (Feb. 19, 1930), 309-11.
5.67   *Saturday Review* [London], CXLIX (Mar. 29, 1930), 391-92.
5.68   *Times* [London] *Literary Supplement*, No. 1430 (April 3, 1930), p. 293.

5.69   Porter, David T. *The Art of Emily Dickinson's Early Poetry*. Cambridge, Mass.: Harvard Univ. Press, 1966. 206 pp.
Explores the growth of ED's mind and the development of her poetic techniques through close examination of the early poems, those written before 1862.
Reviewed:

Anderson (6.39)	Lindberg (6.618a)
Clements (6.218)	Marcus (6.655)
Higgins (6.468)	Robbins (6.851; *ALS, 1966*, p. 140)
King (6.574a)	Sewall (6.910a)

Unsigned reviews:
5.70   *Times* [London] *Literary Supplement*, No. 3366 (Sept. 1, 1966), p. 782.
5.71   *Virginia Quarterly Review*, XLII (Summer 1966), p. c.
5.72   Power, Sister Mary James. *In the Name of the Bee: The Significance of Emily Dickinson*. N.Y.: Sheed and Ward, 1943. 138 pp.
Discusses the themes of renunciation, death, and immortality in ED's poetry and interprets them from the perspective of Christian mysticism. Argues that ED deliberately chose a life of Christian contemplation. Foreword by Alfred Barrett, pp. ix-xi.
Reviewed:

Connors (6.232)	Reilly (6.845)
Crowell (6.239)	Varley (6.1047)
Kennedy (6.565)	Whicher (6.1134)

Unsigned reviews:
5.73   *Pilot* [Boston], Jan. 15, 1944, p. 4.
5.74   *Springfield Sunday Union and Republican,* April 2, 1944, p. 5-B.
5.75   Sewall, Richard B., ed. *Emily Dickinson, A Collection of Critical Essays.* Twentieth Century Views [Series]. Englewood Cliffs, N.J.: Prentice-Hall, 1963. 183 pp.
This volume reprints sixteen of the most distinguished critical essays on ED published between 1924 and 1961.
Reviewed:

C., J.M. (6.164)	Robbins (6.851; *ALS, 1963,* pp. 126-27)
Ferguson (6.341)	Spector (6.936)
Porter (6.817)	White (6.1157)

5.76   Sewall, Richard B. *The Lyman Letters, New Light on Emily Dickinson and Her Family.* Amherst, Mass.: Univ. of Massachusetts Press, 1966. 86 pp.
First published in *The Massachusetts Review,* VI (Autumn 1965), 693-780.
Prints and discusses letters of Joseph B. Lyman which record his impressions of the Dickinson family, especially Lavinia, whom he at one time courted. One item headed "EMILY," an idealized pen-portrait of the poet, is of special interest. In letters to his fiancé, Laura Baker, he quotes portions of letters he had received from Emily and Lavinia.
Reviewed:
Anderson, C.R. (6.39)
Robbins (6.851; *ALS, 1965,* pp. 154-55)
Unsigned reviews:
5.76a   *American Literature,* XXXVIII (Nov. 1966), 428.
5.77   *Virginia Quarterly Review,* XLII (Summer 1966), civ.
5.78   *Yale Review,* LV (Summer 1966), xviii, xxii, xxiv.
5.79   Sherwood, William R[obert]. *Circumference and Circumstance: Stages in the Mind and Art of Emily Dickinson.* N.Y.: Columbia Univ. Press, 1968. 302 pp.
Argues that ED's work falls into four periods: a period of questioning in which she unsuccessfully scrutinized nature for evidence of immortality; a heretical period in which she elevated a male figure into a god; a period of despair and emotional paralysis; and a final period of religious commitment, inaugurated in 1862 by a conversion experience and accompanied by a decision to dedicate her life to major poetic achievement.
Reviewed:
Gross (6.428b)
Porter (6.817a)
5.80   Tabb, John Banister. *John Bannister* [sic] *Tabb on Emily Dickinson.* N.Y.: Seven Gables Bookshop, 1950. 7 unnumbered pages. 500 copies.
Facsimile of a letter from Father Tabb to Frederick M. Hopkins, Sept. 20, 1897, expressing admiration for ED. T. H. Johnson notes similarities between Father Tabb and ED in a brief foreword.

5.81   Taggard, Genevieve. *The Life and Mind of Emily Dickinson.*
              N.Y.: Knopf; London: G. Allen, 1930. 378 pp.
              Also issued in 1930 by Knopf in a limited, autograph edition.
              Reissued by Knopf as an Alblabook, 1934. Also Toronto: Ry-
              erson Press, 1934. Softcover ed.: N.Y.: Cooper Square, 1967.
              More fully documented than Miss Pollitt's biography (5.61),
              this volume emphasizes the influence of New England culture
              on ED's poetic temperament. Argues that ED loved George
              Gould but that her father discouraged the romance.
              Reviewed:

Aiken (6.18)	Hardy (6.449)	Schriftgiesser (6.896)
Beck (6.83)	Hicks (6.463)	Spencer (6.941)
Bellamann (6.88)	Hutchison (6.530)	Sunne (6.962)
Burton (6.162)	L., H. (6.587)	Taggard (6.974)
Carpenter (6.185)	Lane (6.590)	Thomas (6.985)
Case (6.187b)	Lawrence (6.601)	Thorton (6.995)
Catel (9.17)	Leslie (6.608)	Todd (6.1002)
Caughey (6.190)	Merchant (6.690)	Untermeyer (6.1026)
Church (6.208)	Merrill (6.697)	Van Doren, C. (6.1037)
Crowell (6.238)	Morgrage (6.728)	Van Doren, M. (6.1040)
Crowley (6.241)	Paterson (6.773)	Van Vuren (6.1045)
Deutsch (6.275)	Price (6.824)	Wallace (6.1062)
Field (6.346b)	Robbins (6.850)	Welby (6.1082)
Ford (6.361)	S., C.E. (6.867a)	Wells (6.1086, 6.1092)
Grattan (6.415)	Salpeter (6.874)	Whicher (6.1121)
Gregory (6.425)	Sandburg (6.876)	Wilson (6.1186)
Hansen (6.440-441)	Schappes (6.889)	Yust (6.1210)

              Unsigned reviews:
5.82   *Baltimore Observer*, July 12, 1930.
5.83   *Chicago Evening Post*, June 27, 1930, p. 8.
5.84   *Fort Worth* [Texas] *Star-Telegram*, July 13, 1930.
5.85   *Honolulu Star-Bulletin*, July 19, 1930, p. 10.
5.86   *John O'London's Weekly*, XXIII (Aug. 30, 1930), 724.
5.87   *Minneapolis Tribune*, July 6, 1930, p. 4.
5.88   *New York American*, June 29, 1930.
5.89   *San Francisco Chronicle*, July 13, 1930, p. 4-D.
5.90   *Saturday Review*, VI (June 7, 1930), 1118.
5.91   *Springfield Daily Republican*, Aug. 2, 1930, p. 8.
5.92   *Springfield Union*, June 11, 1930, p. 13.
5.93   *Time*, XV (June 30, 1930), 56.
5.94   *Times* [London] *Literary Supplement*, No. 1496 (Oct. 2, 1930),
              p. 775.
5.95   Thackrey, Donald E. *Emily Dickinson's Approach to Poetry.*
              University of Nebraska Studies, New Series, No. 13. Lincoln:
              Univ. of Nebraska, November 1954. 82 pp.
              Discusses ED's attitude toward poetic creation in the light of
              her belief in the power of language and her mystical tendencies.
5.96   Tusiani, Giuseppe. *Two Critical Essays on Emily Dickinson.*
              N.Y.: Venetian Press, 1951. 35 pp.
              Includes two essays in English entitled "The Love Poetry of
              Emily Dickinson," pp. 7-27, and "Rhythm and Rhyme in Emily

Dickinson's Letters," pp. 28-35. The first essay was originally published in Italian (8.29).

5.97 Ward, Theodora. *The Capsule of the Mind, Chapters in the Life
of Emily Dickinson.* Cambridge, Mass.: Harvard Univ. Press;
London: Oxford Univ. Press, 1961. 205 pp.
The first half of the book discusses ED's inner life at different
periods of her development and the second deals with her friend-
ships with Dr. and Mrs. Holland, Samuel Bowles, and T. W.
Higginson.
Reviewed:

Bradbrook (6.132)	Le Breton (9.27)
Hicks (6.467)	Miller (6.707)
Holmes (6.503)	Thomas (6.989)
King (6.574)	Wells (6.1096)

Unsigned reviews:
5.98 *Dalhousie Review* [Halifax] XLII (Autumn 1962), 415.
5.99 *Times* [London] *Literary Supplement,* No. 3130 (Feb. 23, 1962),
p. 122.
5.100 *Yale Review,* n.s. LI (Spring 1962), vi, x, xii.

5.101 Wells, Henry W. *Introduction to Emily Dickinson.* Chicago:
Hendricks House, 1947. 286 pp.
An overall view of ED's art, both in its form and technique and
in its relation to her personality and to her cultural and social
environment.
Reviewed:

Allen (6.25)	Downey (6.300)
Dauner (6.262)	Taggard (6.978)

Unsigned reviews:
5.102 *Springfield Republican,* Oct. 5, 1947, p. 10-B.
5.103 *Times* [London] *Literary Supplement,* No. 2392 (Dec. 6, 1947), p. 628.
5.104 Whicher, George Frisbie. *This Was a Poet, A Critical Biography
of Emily Dickinson.* N.Y.: Scribners, 1938.
Reissued, Philadelphia: Albert Saifer (Dufour Editions),
1952. Softcover ed.: Ann Arbor: Univ. of Michigan Press,
1957. 337 pp. Also published in braille, 3 vols., Mt. Healthy,
Ohio: Clovernook Printing House for the Blind, 1939.
The first fully reliable biographical study. Considers ED in
relation to her New England background with chapters on her
reading and literary friends, her humor, and her poetic method.
Includes a useful bibliographical postscript.
Reviewed:

Boynton (6.127)	Ellis (6.313)	Noda (12.24)
C., S.A. (6.166)	Elting (6.314)	Rand (6.833)
Cameron (6.175)	Gannett (6.392)	Root (6.855)
Canby (6.177)	Gibson (6.400)	Rose Marie (6.860)
Cestre (9.18)	Hawkins (6.456)	Scudder (6.901)
Clark (6.216)	Hillyer (6.481)	Shephard (6.919)
Daly (6.261)	Holmes (6.506)	Spencer (6.939)
Doty (6.295)	Hutchison (6.531)	Taggard (6.966)
Edfelt (13.7)	Moore (6.725)	Tate (6.981)

Thompson (6.994)   Van Doren, M (6.1042)
Untermeyer (6.1019) Vestdijk (10.83)
Unsigned reviews:

5.105 *Book Buyer*, n.s. IV (Nov. 1938), unpaged.
5.106 *Christian Science Monitor*, Dec. 21, 1938, Magazine Section, p. 12.
5.107 *More Books, Bulletin of the Boston Public Library*, XIV (Feb. 1939), 69.
5.108 *New Yorker*, XIV (Nov. 5, 1938), 72.
5.109 *North American Review*, CCXLVI (Winter 1938-1939), 404.
5.110 *Springfield Republican*, Oct. 30, 1938, p. 7-E.
5.111 *Times* [London] *Literary Supplement*, No. 1924 (Dec. 17, 1938), p. 800.

5.112 Wood, Clement. *Emily Dickinson: The Volcanic Heart*. Privately printed, n.p., 1945. 32 pp.
A psychological interpretation which argues that ED's poetry expresses an unusual attraction for her father or for such father-figures as Newton and Wadsworth. Her poems construct a fantasy system by which forbidden passion is sublimated. A copy is owned by the Beinecke Library, Yale University.

ADDENDA

5.113 Lindberg-Seyersted, Brita. *The Voice of the Poet: Aspects of Style in the Poetry of Emily Dickinson*. Cambridge, Mass.: Harvard Univ. Press, 1968. 290 pp.
Also published in Sweden (in English) as Acta Universitatis Upsaliensis, Studia Anglistica Upsaliensia, 6. Upsala: Printed by Almqvist & Wiksells Boktryckeri AB, 1968.
An examination of ED's poetic language, especially the several speakers and kinds of address presented in the poems, speech rhythms and metrical schemes, and the poetic effects of various syntactic structures. Recent linguistic concepts and terminology are employed to show how the poet's verbal techniques bear upon three themes: "colloquialness," "slantness," and "privateness."

5.114 Lubbers, Klaus. *Emily Dickinson: The Critical Revolution*. Ann Arbor: Univ. of Michigan Press, 1968. 335 pp.
Originally published in German as *Der literarische Ruhm Emily Dickinsons: Das erste Jahrhundert amerikanischer und britischer Kritik von Werk und Mensch*. Thesis. Mainz, 1967.
A detailed, largely chronological survey of ED's reputation from 1862-1962. Closely documented with considerable quotation from reviews and literary histories. The appendix contains an extensive list of sources totaling more than 1000 items. This list supplements the present volume in four areas: (1) anthologies published before 1930 in which Dickinson poems appear; (2) musical settings to 1951; (3) literary histories in which ED is *not* discussed; (4) encyclopedias and biographical dictionaries published between 1900 and 1930 in which ED is mentioned.
Reviewed:
White (6.1160)

6.

Parts of Books and Signed Articles

6.1   A., J.B. "The Home of Emily Dickinson." *Packer Alumna* [Packer Collegiate Institute, Brooklyn, N.Y.], VII (Dec. 1891), 143.
Describes a visit with Lavinia in the Dickinson home.

6.2   A., M. *New York World,* July 6, 1924, p. 6-E.
Rev. of *Complete Poems,* 1924 (3.123).

6.3   Abbott, Lawrence F. "Emily Dickinson." *Outlook,* CXL (June 10, 1925), 211-13.
Prompted by the death of Amy Lowell, this essay includes a summary of ED's life and an appreciation of her poetry.

6.4   Abbott, Mary. "Emily Dickinson's Letters." *Chicago Herald,* Dec. 8, 1894, p. 11.
Rev. of *Letters,* 1894 (4.3).

6.5   ———. "Emily Dickinson's Poems." *Chicago Times-Herald,* Sept. 26, 1896, p. 9.
Rev. of *Poems,* 1896 (3.89).

6.6   ———. "Emily Dickinson's Rare Genius." *Chicago Evening Post,* Oct. 6, 1891, p. 4.
Discusses Higginson's *Atlantic* essay (6.473).

6.7   Abernethy, Julian W. *American Literature.* N.Y.: Merrill, 1902, p. 206.
Mentions ED as the only rival of Helen Hunt Jackson among American women poets.

6.8   Adair, Virginia H. "Dickinson's 'One Day is there of the Series.'" *American Notes and Queries,* V (Nov. 1966), 35.
Replies to Paul O. Williams' explication (6.1177). Noted by Robbins, *ALS, 1966* (6.851), p. 144.

6.9   Adams, M. Ray. *New England Quarterly,* XXXII (Dec. 1959), 555-58.
Rev. of Reeves, ed., *Selected Poems* (3.202).

6.10   Adams, Richard P. "Dickinson Concrete." *Emerson Society Quarterly,* No. 44 (III Quarter, 1966), pp. 31-35.
Argues that "ED's poems are generally concerned with moments

of change or motion and with tensions associated with such
moments."
Rev. by Robbins, *ALS, 1966* (6.851), pp. 141-42.

6.11   Adams, Richard P. "Pure Poetry: Emily Dickinson." *Tulane
Studies in English,* VII (1957), 133-52.
Rather than abstracting or simplifying experience, ED's
poems convey the fullness of experience itself.

6.12   Addison, Daniel Dulany. *Lucy Larcom, Life, Letters, and Diary.*
Boston: Houghton, 1894, p. 285.
An 1893 letter records Lucy Larcom's impression of ED's
poems.

6.13   Adelman, Joseph. "Emily Dickinson" in *Famous Women.* N.Y.:
Pictorial Review, 1928, p. 200.

6.14   Agrawal, Ishwar Nath. "Emily Dickinson and the Living Word."
Literary Criterion, VI (Summer 1965), 52-55.
Discusses ED's view of words as living things and the aptness
and variety of her diction.

6.15   ———. "Emily Dickinson: A Study of Diction." *Literary Criterion,* V (Winter 1962), 95-100.
On the exactness of ED's vocabulary and her use of suspended
rhyme. Compares her precision with Poe's and Whitman's
sometimes fuzzy use of words.

6.16   Åhnebrink, Lars. *American Quarterly,* XII (Fall 1960), 425-26.
Rev. of *Letters,* 1958 (4.90).

6.17   Aïdé, Hamilton. "Poems by Emily Dickinson." *Nineteenth Century,* XXXI (April 1892), 703-06.
Rev. of *Poems, 1890* (3.9).

6.18   Aiken, Conrad Potter. "The Dickinson Myth." *Yale Review,* XX
(Winter 1931), 393-96.
Rev. of Jenkins, *Friend and Neighbor* (5.35); Pollitt, *Human
Background* (5.61); and Taggard, *Life and Mind* (5.81).

6.19   ———. "The Dickinson Scandal." *New Republic,* CXIII (July 2,
1945), 25-26.
Rev. of *Bolts of Melody,* 1945 (3.177) and Bingham, *Ancestors'
Brocades* (5.5).

6.20   ———. "Emily Dickinson." *Dial,* LXXVI (April 1924), 301-08.
Reprinted, with minor revisions:
"Introduction" to *Selected Poems,* 1924 (3.127), pp. 5-22.
Bookman [London], LXVII (Oct. 1924), 8, 11-12.
"Introduction" to *Selected Poems,* 1948 (3.193), pp. vii-xvi.
Conrad Aiken. *Reviewer's ABC,* ed. Rufus Blanshard. N.Y.:
    Meridian Books, 1958, pp. 156-63.
Sewall, *Critical Essays* (5.75), pp. 9-15.
Blake and Wells, *Recognition* (5.13), pp. 110-17.
Discusses ED's characteristic themes and notes the influence
of Emersonian individualism upon her life and work. Trans-
lated into Spanish (11.27).

6.21   ———. "Emily Dickinson and Her Editors." *Yale Review,* XVIII
(Summer 1929), 796-98.
Rev. of *Further Poems,* 1929 (3.138).

6.22   Aiken, Conrad Potter. *Modern American Poets.* N.Y.: Random
          House (Modern Library), 1927, pp. vii-viii.
          Brief praise of ED's poetry.

6.23   ———. *New York Evening Post,* Mar. 16, 1929, p. 11-M.
          Rev. of *Further Poems,* 1929 (3.138).

6.24   Aldrich, Thomas Bailey. *"In Re* Emily Dickinson." *Atlantic
          Monthly,* **LXIX** (Jan. 1892), 143-44.
          Reprinted:
          Blake and Wells, *Recognition* (5.13), pp. 54-56.
          Davis, *14 by ED* (5.23), pp. 11-13.
              Also reprinted, with revisions, as "Un Poete Manqué" in
              Ponkapog Papers (Boston: Houghton Mifflin, 1903), pp. 107-11.
          Finds ED's poetry disjointed and shallow.

6.25   Allen, Gay Wilson. "Amherst Parnassus." *New York Times Book
          Review,* July 4, 1948, p. 4.
          Rev. of Wells, *Introduction* (5.101).

6.26   ———. "Emily Dickinson" in *American Prosody,* N.Y.: American
          Book Co., 1935, pp. 307-20.
          Reprinted:
          Blake and Wells, *Recognition* (5.13), pp. 176-86.
          Discusses ED's versification, especially her irregular meter
          and half-rhymes. Describes her as the link between Emerson's
          gnomic style and the suggestive, ejaculatory quality of Imagist
          verse.

6.27   ———. "The Life and Work of Emily." *New York Times Book
          Review,* Dec. 30, 1951, p. 4.
          Rev. of Chase, *ED* (5.17).

6.28   Allen, Hervey. "Emily Dickinson's Editors." *New York Sun,* Nov.
          7, 1931, p. 27.
          Rev. of *Letters,* 1931 (4.52).

6.29   Allen, Mary Adèle. *Around a Village Green, Sketches of Life in
          Amherst.* Northampton, Mass.: Kraushar Press, 1939.
          Reprinted:
          "The Dickinsons Had the Best Woodpile in Amherst." *Christian
          Science Monitor,* Oct. 17, 1942, p. 9.
          A brief reminiscence of the Dickinson family.

[4.68]   ———. "The Boltwood House — Memories of Amherst Friends and
          Neighbors."

6.30   ———. "The First President's House — A Reminiscence."
          Amherst Graduates' Quarterly, **XXVI** (Feb. 1937), p. 93.

6.31   Alling, Kenneth Slade. "Declaration." *The Measure, A Journal of
          Poetry,* No. 22 (Dec. 1922), pp. 15-16.
          Praises the "depth and incandescence" of ED's poetry as an
          example for modern poets.

6.32   Anderson, Charles R. *American Literature,* **XXX** (Nov. 1958),
          371-76.
          Rev. of *Letters,* 1958 (4.90).

6.33   ———. "The Conscious Self in Emily Dickinson's Poetry."
          American Literature, **XXXI** (Nov. 1959), 290-308.
          Close examination of those poems in which ED treats of the

mind, of consciousness, and of the self. The substance of these poems is personal rather than philosophical; they reveal the poet's self-mastery based on "her absolute loyalty to mind."

6.34   Anderson, Charles R. "Dickinson's 'Reverse Cannot Befall.'" *Explicator*, XVIII (May 1960), Item 46.

634a   ——. "Emily Dickinson" in *American Literary Masters*, ed. C. R. Anderson, et. al. 2 vols. N.Y.: Holt, Rinehart and Winston, 1965, I, 967-87.
This introduction to a college textbook selection of ED's poems gives special consideration to the poet's use of language (wit, words, and the province of poetry), to her attitude toward nature (perception, evanescence, and process), and to several of her major themes — ecstasy and despair, death and immortality.

6.35   ——. "From a Window in Amherst: Emily Dickinson Looks at the American Scene." *New England Quarterly*, XXXI (June 1958), 147-71.
ED as a detached and amused satirist of American life.

6.36   ——. *Modern Language Notes*, LXX (Nov. 1955), p. 535.
Rev. of Jean Simon, ed., *ED, Poĕms*, 1954 (9.2).

6.37   ——. *Modern Language Notes*, LXXI (May 1956), 386-90.
Rev. of *Poems*, 1955 (3.197).

6.38   ——. *Modern Language Notes*, LXXVI (Dec. 1961), 904-07.
Rev. of Leyda, *Years and Hours* (5.49).

6.39   ——. *New England Quarterly*, XXXIX (Dec. 1966), 522-28.
Rev. of Capps, *ED's Reading* (5.14); Porter, *Early Poetry* (5.69); and Sewall, *Lyman Letters* (5.76).

6.40   ——. "The Trap of Time in Emily Dickinson's Poetry." *Journal of English Literary History*, XXVI (Sept. 1959), 402-24.
Examines a group of poems which illustrate ED's concept that man's mind is imprisoned in time.

6.41   Anderson, John Q. "Emily Dickinson's Butterflies and Tigers." *Emerson Society Quarterly*, No. 47 (II Quarter, 1967), pp. 43-48.
Contrasts ED's use of butterflies with her use of panthers, leopards, and tigers.

6.42   ——. "The Funeral Procession in Dickinson's Poetry." *Emerson Society Quarterly*, No. 44 (III Quarter, 1966), pp. 8-12.
Close reading of six poems employing the funeral procession theme.

6.43   Anderson, Paul W. "The Metaphysical Mirth of Emily Dickinson." *Georgia Review*, XX (Spring 1966), 72-83.
Examines ED's humor, especially her use of satire and metaphysical wit. Discusses the question of her relation to Donne.
Rev. by Robbins, *ALS, 1966* (6.851), p. 143.

6.44   Angela Carson, Mother. "Dickinson's 'Safe in their Alabaster Chambers.'" *Explicator*, XVII (June 1959), Item 62.
Reprinted:
Davis, *14 by ED* (5.23), p. 24.

6.45   Angoff, Charles. "Emily Dickinson and Religious Poetry." *Tomorrow*, VII (Dec. 1947), 24.
Questions, in a brief note, whether ED wrote any but religious poetry.

6.46   Archibald, R. C. "Emily Dickinson: A Song." *Notes and Queries,*
        CLXVI (Jan. 27, 1934), 71.
        Notes an early musical setting for "Have you got a Brook in
        your little heart."

6.47   Arlott, John. *Nineteenth Century,* CXLIII (Jan. 1948), 59.
        Rev. of *Bolts of Melody,* 1947 (3.182) and *Poems,* 1947 (3.183).

6.47a   Armour, Richard. "Emily Dickinson" in *American Lit Relit.*
        N.Y.: McGraw-Hill, 1964, pp. 96-99.
        A spoof of some of the legends that surround ED.

[6.324] Arms, George. "Dickinson's 'These are the days when Birds
        come back.'"

6.48   Armstrong, Martin. "Emily Dickinson." *Week End Review* [Lon-
        don], VIII (Nov. 4, 1933), 467-68.
        Rev. of *Poems,* 1933 (3.158).

6.49   ——. "The Poetry of Emily Dickinson." *Spectator* [London],
        CXXX (Jan. 6, 1923), 22-23.
        Reprinted:
        Blake and Wells, *Recognition* (5.13), pp. 105-09.
        An introductory article, brief but appreciative, by an English
        critic.

6.50   Arp. Thomas Roscoe. *New England Quarterly,* XXXVIII (Mar.
        1965), 108-10.
        Rev. of Blake and Wells, *Recognition* (5.13).

6.51   Arsenault, Anne. *Dalhousie Review,* XLV (Autumn 1965), 383, 385.
        Rev. of Griffith, *Long Shadow* (5.31).

6.52   Arvin, Newton. *American Literature,* XXVIII (May 1956), 232-36.
        Rev. of *Poems,* 1955 (3.197).

6.53   ——. *Commonweal,* I (Mar. 25, 1925), 552-53.
        Rev. of Bianchi, *Life and Letters* (4.36).

6.54   ——. "Emily Dickinson" in *American Pantheon,* ed. Daniel
        Aaron and Sylvan Schendler. N.Y.: Delacorte Press (A Sey-
        mour Lawrence Book), 1967, pp. 167-73.
        An essay-review of *Further Poems,* 1929 (3.138). Stresses the
        richness and the range of ED's poetry, as well as its intensity.

6.55   ——. "The Great Among the Many." *New York Times Book
        Review,* Sept. 11, 1960, p. 14.
        Rev. of Anderson, *Stairway of Surprise* (5.2).

6.56   [Ash, Lee, ed.] "Editor's Notes and Reading." *American Notes
        and Queries,* I (May 1963), 138.
        Mentions a letter from William White noting ED's exclusion
        from the *Concise Dictionary of American History.*

6.56a   Atkins, Elizabeth. *The Poet's Poet: Essays on the Character and
        Mission of the Poet as Interpreted in English Verse of the Last
        One Hundred and Fifty Years.* Boston: Marshall Jones Co.,
        1922, pp. 205, 284-85.
        Quotes briefly from ED.

6.57   Austin, H. Russell. "Emily Dickinson — Woman or Phantom?"
        The Milwaukee Journal, July 26, 1950, p. 24.

6.58   Avery, Christine. "Science, Technology, and Emily Dickinson."
        Bulletin of the British Association for American Studies [Man-
        chester, Eng.], n.s. IX (Dec. 1964), 47-55.

ED's negative and positive reactions to science maintain a "strenuous balance of attitude."

6.59   B., F. *Boston Evening Transcript Book Section*, Dec. 22, 1934, p. 3.
Rev. of *Poems for Youth*, 1934 (3.159).

6.60   B., H. *New York Evening Post*, June 11, 1924, p. 14.
Rev. of Bianchi, *Life and Letters* (4.36).

6.61   Babbitt, Irving. *On Being Creative and Other Essays*. Boston: Houghton, Mifflin, 1932, p. 111.
Quotes the first four lines of "I never hear the word 'escape'" as an example of romantic, Transcendental poetry.

6.62   Babler, Otto F. "Emily Dickinson: A Bibliographical Note." *Notes and Queries*, CLXV (July 15, 1933), 29.
Notes a 1907 Czech anthology containing three ED poems; see 13.16.

6.62a   Backus, Joseph M. "Two 'No-Name' Poets." *Names*, XV (Mar. 1967), 1-7.
Discusses ED's poem, "I'm Nobody! Who are you?" and compares its use of a "no-name" to E. E. Cummings' "anyone lived in a pretty how town."

[8.36] Baldi, Sergio. "The Poetry of Emily Dickinson (1956)." *Sewanee Review*, LXVIII (July-Sept. 1960), 438-49.
Translated from Italian (8.36).

6.63   Baldwin, Eleanor. "Emily Dickinson." *El Palenque* [San Diego, Calif.], IV (Jan. 1931), 32-33.

6.64   Ball, Lewis F. "Between Book Ends." *Richmond* [Va.] *Times Dispatch*, June 19, 1955, p. F-5.
Rev. of Bingham, *ED's Home* (4.86).

6.65   Ballanger, Martha. "The Metaphysical Echo." *English Studies in Africa*, VIII (Mar. 1965), 71-80.
The metaphysical tradition links ED to Edward Taylor and Elinor Wylie.

6.66   Banzer, Judith. "'Compound Manner': Emily Dickinson and the Metaphysical Poets." *American Literature*, XXXII (Jan. 1961), 417-33.
Shows that ED's verse has much in common with that of Donne, Herbert, and other metaphysicals and documents her reading of their poetry. For comment, see Miller, *Poetry of ED* (5.54), p. 214.

6.67   Barbot, Mary Elizabeth. "Emily Dickinson Parallels." *New England Quarterly*, XIV (Dec. 1941), 689-96.
Notes verbal similarities between ED's poems and the published writings of Wadsworth and T. W. Higginson.

6.68   Barrett, William. "Death and the Maiden." *Partisan Review*, XIX (May-June 1952), 364-67.
Rev. of Chase, *ED* (5.17).

6.69   Bartlett, Alice Hunt. "Dynamics of American Poetry: CXVIII." *Poetry Review* [London], XXXVIII (July-Aug. 1947), 289.
Places the poetry of Melville Cane in "the lyric tradition of Emily Dickinson."

6.70   Bartlett, Frances. "The Human Aspect of Emily Dickinson."

Boston Evening Transcript, Book Section, Mar. 29, 1930, p. 4.
Rev. of Pollitt, *Human Background* (5.61).

6.71   Bartlett, Frances. "Emily Dickinson Seen Face to Face." *Boston Evening Transcript,* Book Section, Jan. 14, 1933, p. 2.
Rev. of Bianchi, *Face to Face* (4.59).

6.72   Bartlett, Phyllis. *Poems in Process.* N.Y.: Oxford Univ. Press, 1951, pp. 84-87, *passim.*
Notes that ED evidently wrote with great speed, but lingered over alternative word choices.

6.73   Bass, Althea. "A Classmate of Emily Dickinson." *Colophon,* V, Part 19 (Dec. 1934), 8 unnumbered pages.
Discusses the student essays of Sarah Worcester, a classmate of ED's at Mount Holyoke Seminary.

6.74   Batchelder, Ann. "If I Know What I Mean." *Delineator,* CXXIV. (April 1934), 26.
Reports a visit to ED's home.

6.75   Bates, Arlo. "Literary Affairs in Boston." *Book Buyer,* n.s. VIII (Nov. 1891), 417.
Notes Higginson's *Atlantic* essay (6.473) and compares ED with Walt Whitman.

6.76   ——. "Literary Topics in Boston." *Book Buyer,* n.s. VIII (Feb. 1891), 10.
Notes the popularity of *Poems,* 1890 (3.9).

6.77   ——. "Literary Topics in Boston." *Book Buyer,* n.s. VIII (May 1891), 153.
Discusses the critical reception of ED's first book of poems and notes the preparation of a second.

6.78   ——. "Miss Dickinson's Poems." *Boston Courier,* Nov. 23, 1890.
Rev. of *Poems,* 1890 (3.9).
Reprinted:
Blake and Wells, *Recognition* (5.13), pp. 12-18.

6.79   Bates, Katharine Lee. *American Literature.* N.Y.: Macmillan, 1898, pp. 178-79.
Brief mention of ED as a minor poet.

6.80   ——. "A House of Rose." *Yale Review,* XIV (Jan. 1925), 396-99.
Rev. of *Complete Poems,* 1924 (3.123) and Bianchi, *Life and Letters* (4.36).

6.81   Beal, George Brinton. "Love Mystery in Life of Poet Emily Dickinson Revived." *Boston Sunday Post,* Magazine Section, May 27, 1945, p. 5.
Rev. of *Bolts of Melody,* 1945 (3.177) and Bingham, *Ancestors' Brocades* (5.5).

6.82   Beaty, Jerome, and William H. Matchett. *Poetry: From Statement to Meaning.* N.Y.: Oxford Univ. Press, 1965, pp. 28-34, 130-31, *passim.*
Contains explications of "After great pain, a formal feeling comes" and "Belshazzar had a Letter."

6.83   Beck, Clyde. "New Light On the Life of a Peculiar Genius." *Detroit News,* June 29, 1930, p. 4.
Rev. of Jenkins, *Friend and Neighbor* (5.35); Pollitt, *Human. Background* (5.61); and Taggard, *Life and Mind* (5.81).

6.83a   Beck, Ronald. "Dickinson's 'I heard a Fly buzz — when I died.'"
          Explicator, XXVI (Dec. 1967), Item 31.

6.84   Beck, Warren. "Poetry's Chronic Disease." *English Journal,*
          XXXIII (Sept. 1944), 357-64.
          Contains an explication of "Go not too near a House of Rose,"
          pp. 362-63.

6.85   Becker, May Lamberton. "The Reader's Guide." *New York Her-
          ald Tribune Book Week,* X, No. 8 (Oct. 29, 1933), p. 25.
          Comments on the historical accuracy of Susan Glaspell's play,
          Alison's House (17.14), and on recent biographies of ED.

6.85a   ———. "The Reader's Guide." *Saturday Review,* VI (May 10,
          1930), 1030.
          Notes the Hampshire Bookshop observance of the ED Centenary,
          May 1930; see also 22.8-13.

6.86   ———. *New York Herald Tribune Books,* Jan. 6, 1935, p. 7.
          Rev. of *Poems for Youth,* 1934 (3.159).

6.87   ———. *New York Herald Tribune Books,* April 26, 1936, p. 4.
          Rev. of *Unpublished Poems,* 1935 (3.167).

6.88   B[ellamann], H[enry]. *The State* [Columbia, S.C.], July 27, 1930,
          p. 31.
          Rev. of Taggard, *Life and Mind* (5.81).

6.89   Benét, Stephen Vincent. *Bookman* [N.Y.], LIX (Aug. 1924), 732-35.
          Rev. of Bianchi, *Life and Letters* (4.36).

6.90   Benét, William Rose. "Dear Me, Emily." *Saturday Review,* IX
          (June 3, 1933), 632.
          Discusses some reactions to ED's definition of poetry ("If I
          feel physically as if the top of my head were taken off....").

6.91   ———. *Saturday Review,* VI (Nov. 30, 1929), 488.
          Comment concerning Joseph Auslander's poem, "Letter to ED,"
          in his *Letters to Women* (18.9).

6.92   Benn, Caroline Wedgwood. *New Statesman and Nation,* XLIII (May
          3, 1952), 527.
          Letter to the editor critical of a review by Kathleen Raine; see
          6.829.

6.93   Bennett, Mary A. "A Note on Josephine Pollitt's *Emily Dickinson:
          The Human Background of Her Poetry.*" *American Literature,*
          II (Nov. 1930), 283-86.
          Notes discrepancies in Miss Pollitt's use of sources.

6.94   Berenson, Adrienne. "Emily Dickinson's Social Attitudes: A
          Dissenting View." *Western Humanities Review,* VI (Autumn
          1952), 351-62.
          Argues that "ED's poems, and indeed her life itself, dramatize
          her protest against social and religious convention."

6.95   Bianchi, Martha Dickinson. "Emily Dickinson." *Saturday Review,*
          I (Aug. 2, 1924), 20.
          Letter to the editor defending her *Life and Letters* (4.36).

6.96   ———. "To the Editors of the Smith College Monthly." *Smith
          College Monthly,* II (Nov. 1941), 2, 26-27.
          Notes ED's friendship with Clark Seelye and Mary Jordan.

6.97   Bingham, Millicent Todd. "Emily Dickinson's Earliest Friend."

American Literature, VI (May 1934), 191-92. A rejoinder by
George F. Whicher, pp. 192-93.
Criticizes Whicher's article on Benjamin F. Newton; see
6.1127.

6.98   Bingham, Millicent Todd. "Emily Dickinson's Handwriting — A
Master Key." *New England Quarterly,* XXII (June 1949),
229-34.
Suggests that ED's handwriting provides clues for dating the
poems.

6.99   ———. "A Friend of Amherst." *Amherst Record,* Nov. 9, 1932,
p. 7.
A tribute to Mabel Loomis Todd.

6.100   ———. *Mabel Loomis Todd, Her Contributions to the Town of
Amherst. A Paper.... Nov. 1, 1934.* N.Y.: George Grady
Press, 1935. 60 pp.

6.101   ———. "A Moment of Drama." *Radcliffe Quarterly,* XLIII (Feb.
1959), 13-17.
Mrs. Bingham discusses her work in publishing the poems.

6.102   Birdsall, Virginia Ogden. "Emily Dickinson's Intruder in the
Soul." *American Literature,* XXXVII (Mar. 1965), 54-64.
House imagery and the motif of intrusion in the poetry of ED.
Rev. by Robbins, *ALS, 1965* (6.851), p. 158.

6.103   Birss, John Howard. "Emily Dickinson: A Bibliographical
Note." *Notes and Queries,* CLXIV (June 17, 1933), 421.
Notes publication of "If I can stop one Heart from breaking" in
Silver Linings, ed. E.T. Brown, Chicago, 1912.

6.104   ———. "Emily Dickinson: Portraits Wanted." *Notes and
Queries,* CLXIV (Feb. 25, 1933), 141.
Calls attention to a portrait of ED appearing in 1894. See also
Notes and Queries, CLXIV (Jan 28, 1933), 66, and (Feb. 11,
1933), 105.

6.105   Bishop, Elizabeth. "Love from Emily." *New Republic,* CXXV
(Aug. 27, 1951), 20-21.
Rev. of *Letters to Holland,* 1951 (4.76).

6.106   ———. "Unseemly Deductions." *New Republic,* CXXVII (Aug. 18,
1952), 20.
Rev. of Patterson, *Riddle* (5.55).

6.107   Blackmur, Richard P. "Emily Dickinson: Notes on Prejudice
and Fact." *Southern Review,* III (Autumn 1937), 323-47.
Reprinted:
R.P. Blackmur. *Language As Gesture.* N.Y.: Harcourt,
Brace, 1937 (reprinted 1952), pp. 25-50.
R.P. Blackmur. *The Expense of Greatness.* N.Y.: Arrow
Editions, 1940, pp. 106-38.
American Harvest, ed. Allen Tate and John Peale Bishop.
N.Y.: L.B. Fischer, 1942, pp. 229-56. Translated into
Spanish; see 11.17.
Blake and Wells, *Recognition* (5.13), pp. 201-23.
A critical evaluation which dismisses some prevailing as-
sumptions about ED and looks closely at her use of language
in several poems. Finds that most, though not all, of her

poems are "so many exercises in self-expression"; like Whitman, her craft was not always equal to her *élan.*

6.108 Blackmur, Richard P. "Emily Dickinson's Notation." *Kenyon Review,* XVIII (Spring 1956), 224-37.
Reprinted:
Sewall, *Critical Essays* (5.75), pp. 78-87.
An essay-review of *Poems,* 1955 (3.197) and Johnson, *Interpretive Biography* (5.44). Examines the "deeper forms of [ED's] notation, both in verse and in the movements of her psyche." Remarks on her "nuptial" celebration of intimacy, her fear of the contingent world, and her "protestant self-excruciation in life's name."

6.109 ———. "A Plea for the Essay." *Kenyon Review,* XIV (Summer 1952), 530-34.
Rev. of Chase, *ED* (5.17) and Patterson, *Riddle* (5.55).

6.110 ———. "Religious Poetry in America." *University — A Princeton Magazine,* IX (Summer 1961), 14-19.
Reprinted:
Religious Perspectives in American Culture, ed. James Ward Smith and A. Leland Jamison, in *Religion in American Life,* Vol. II, Princeton Studies in American Civilization, No. 5. Princeton, N.J.: Princeton Univ. Press, 1961, pp. 273-87.
Devotes a paragraph to ED's type of religious poetry.

6.111 Blair, Walter, and W.K. Chandler, eds. *Approaches to Poetry,* 2nd ed. N.Y.: Appleton-Century-Crofts, 1953, pp. 258-60.
This college textbook includes a brief discussion of "A narrow Fellow in the Grass."

6.112 Blake, Caesar R. *New England Quarterly,* XXXVII (Dec. 1964), 552-54.
Rev. of Griffith, *Long Shadow* (5.31).

6.112a ———. *New England Quarterly,* XLI (Sept. 1968), 475-76.
Rev. of Franklin, *Editing* (5.28).

6.113 Blankenship, Russell. "Emily Dickinson," in *American Literature as an Expression of the National Mind.* N.Y.: Holt, 1931, pp. 576-79.
ED was not aware of current literature and philosophy but she wrote with the "imagination of a great poet."

6.114 Bliss, Frederick Jones, and Mrs. Daniel Bliss [nee Abby Wood], eds. *The Reminiscences of Daniel Bliss.* N.Y.: Fleming H. Revell Co., 1920, p. 62.
A reminiscence of ED noted in Whicher, *This Was a Poet* (5.104), pp. 139, 326.

6.115 Block, Louis J. "A New England Nun." *Dial,* XVIII (Mar. 1, 1895), 146-47.
Rev. of *Letters,* 1894 (4.3). Notes that ED broke with the Puritan tradition but was not at home in the new world.

6.116 Bloom, Margaret. "Emily Dickinson and Dr. Holland." *University of California Chronicle,* XXXV (Jan. 1933), 96-103.
Contains information on ED's friendship with the Holland family and an evaluation of Dr. Holland as a writer.

6.117   Blunden, Edmund. "Emily Dickinson." *Nation and Athenaeum*,
XLVI (Mar. 22, 1930), 863.
Reprinted:
Blake and Wells, *Recognition* (5.13), pp. 134-37.
Rev. of *Complete Poems*, 1928 (3.123); *Further Poems*, 1929
(3.138); and Pollitt, *Human Background* (5.61). An apprecia-
tion based chiefly on the newly published poems. Includes a
brief comparison of ED with Christina Rossetti.

6.118   ——. "Nineteenth Century Poetry." *Nation and Athenaeum*,
XLVIII (Jan. 31, 1931), 574.
Sees ED as a mystic.

6.118a   Bogan, Louise. *Achievement in American Poetry*. Chicago:
Henry Regnery, 1951, pp. 26-27; Gateway Edition [1963], pp.
22-23.
Describes the impact of ED's first appearance in print in the
1890's.

6.119   ——. "A Mystical Poet," in *Emily Dickinson: Three Views*
(5.52), pp. 27-34.
Reprinted:
Sewall, *Critical Essays* (5.75), pp. 137-43.
Notes resemblances between ED and mystical poets, especially Blake, but stresses that her imagination is "of this
world."

6.120   ——. "The Poet Dickinson." *Poetry*, XLVIII (June 1936), 162-
66.
Rev. of *Unpublished Poems*, 1935 (3.167).

6.121   ——. "The Poet Dickinson Comes to Life." *New Yorker*, XXXI
(Oct. 8, 1955), 190-91.
Rev. of *Poems*, 1955 (3.197).

6.122   ——. "The Summers of Hesperides Are Long." *Tomorrow*, IV
July 1945), 61-62.
Reprinted:
Louise Bogan. *Selected Criticism*. N.Y.: Noonday, 1955, pp.
289-94.
Rev. of *Bolts of Melody*, 1945 (3.177) and Bingham, *Ancestors'
Brocades* (5.5).

6.123   ——. "Verse." *New Yorker*, XXI (April 21, 1945), 84-86.
Rev. of *Bolts of Melody*, 1945 (3.177) and Bingham, *Ancestors'
Brocades* (5.5).

6.124   Bolin, Donald W. "Dickinson's 'A Clock Stopped.'" *Explicator*,
XXII (Dec. 1963), Item 27.

6.125   ——. "Emily Dickinson and the Particular Object." *Forum*
[Houston], III (Fall 1962), 28-31.
ED was interested in the particular, observable object, not in
nature in general.

6.126   Bond, C.C.J. "A Haunting Echo." *Canadian Literature*, No. 16
(Spring 1963), pp. 83-84.
Compares ED to Sarah Binks, "the Sweet Songstress of Sas-
katchewan."

6.127   Boynton, Percy H. "The Book Table." *Amherst Graduates'
Quarterly*, XXVIII (Feb. 1939), 203-04.

Rev. of Whicher, *This Was a Poet* (5.104).

6.128   Boynton, Percy H. "Emily Dickinson," in *Literature and American Life*. Boston: Ginn, 1936, pp. 690-99, *passim*.
A general introduction which discusses ED's relationship to Emerson.

6.129   ——. "A New England Nun." *New Republic*, XXXIX (June 25, 1924), 130-31.
Rev. of Bianchi, *Life and Letters* (4.36).

6.130   Brackett, Anna Callander. *The Technique of Rest*. N.Y.: Harpers, 1892, p. 25.
Arguing that we should not be bothered by lapses of memory, the author quotes ED: "Is it oblivion or absorption when things pass from our minds?" The quotation is from the poet's conversation with T.W. Higginson as reported in the latter's *Atlantic* essay (6.473), p. 453.

6.131   Bradbrook, Muriel Clara. *Modern Language Review*, LIV (April 1959), 269-70.
Rev. of *Letters*, 1958 (4.90).

6.132   ——. *Modern Language Review*, LVII (Oct. 1962), 599-600.
Rev. of Anderson, *Stairway of Surprise* (5.2) and Ward, *Capsule of the Mind* (5.97).

6.133   Bradford, Gamaliel. *The Letters of Gamaliel Bradford, 1918-1931*, ed. Van Wyck Brooks. Boston: Houghton, 1934.
The index cites eleven brief references to ED.

6.134   ——. *Atlantic Monthly*, CXXXII (April 1924), 10.
Reprinted:
The Piper [Boston: Houghton Mifflin], May 1924, pp. 3-4.
Rev. of Bianchi, *Life and Letters* (4.36).

6.135   ——. "Portraits of American Women: Emily Dickinson." *Atlantic Monthly*, CXXIV (Aug. 1919), 216-26.
Reprinted:
Gamaliel Bradford. "Emily Dickinson" in *Portraits of American Women*. Boston: Houghton, 1919, pp. 227-57.
Gamaliel Bradford. "Emily Dickinson" in *Portraits and Personalities*, ed. Mabel A. Bessey. Boston: Houghton, 1933, pp. 189-212.
Discusses ED's character and personality.

6.136   Braithwaite, William Stanley. *Boston Evening Transcript*, Book Section, Mar. 30, 1929, p. 7.
Rev. of *Further Poems*, 1929 (3.138).

6.137   ——. "Poems of a Lifetime." *Boston Evening Transcript*, Sept. 30, 1914, p. 24.
Rev. of *Single Hound*, 1914 (3.114).

6.138   Breed, Paul F. "'Boanerges' a Horse?" *American Notes and Queries*, I (Feb. 1963), 86.
Finds no horses with this name in mythology. For replies, see 6.179 and 6.637.

6.139   Brégy, Katherine. *Catholic World*, CLXXV (July 1952), 319.
Rev. of Chase, *ED* (5.17).

6.140   ——. "Emily Dickinson: A New England Anchoress." *Catholic World*, CXX (Dec. 1924), 344-54.

Rev. of *Complete Poems*, 1924 (3.123) and Bianchi, *Life and Letters* (4.36).

6.141   Breit, Harvey. "Traveler." *New York Times Book Review*, July 7, 1957, p. 8.
Notes ED's growing reputation in Italy.

6.142   Breitmeyer, Eleanor. "Parke Family Recalls Life in Emily Dickinson Home." *Detroit News*, Feb. 21, 1965, p. 5-E.
A brief reminiscence by the Rev. Hervey C. Parke, former rector of the Amherst Episcopal Church, who purchased the Dickinson home in 1916.

6.143   Brenner, Rica. "Emily Dickinson," in *Twelve American Poets Before 1900*. N.Y.: Harcourt, 1933, pp. 267-95.
A general introduction to ED's life and work.

6.144   Brickell, Herschel. "The Literary Landscape." *North American Review*, CCVII (May 1929), among front advertising pages.
Rev. of *Further Poems*, 1929 (3.138).

6.145   [Bridges, Robert.] "Droch," pseud. "Bookishness." *Life* [N.Y.], XVIII (Dec. 3, 1891), 326.
Rev. of *Poems*, 1891 (3.52).

6.146   ———. "The Poems of Emily Dickinson." *Life* [N.Y.], XVI (Nov. 27, 1890), 304.
Rev. of *Poems*, 1890 (3.9).

6.147   Brigdman, Richard. "Emily Dickinson: A Winter Poet in a Spring Land." *Moderna Språk* [Stockholm], LVI (1962), 1-8.
Reviews recent ED scholarship and discusses her imagery and preoccupation with death. In English.

[3.206]   Brinnin, John Malcolm. "Introduction" to *Emily Dickinson*, Laurel Poetry Series (1960), pp. 7-20.

6.148   Britt, George. "Behind the Back of Books and Authors." *New York Telegram*, Dec. 10, 1930, p. 14.
Rev. of *Poems*, 1930 (3.151).

6.149   Bronson, Walter C. *American Poems (1625-1892)*. Chicago: Univ. of Chicago Press, 1912 (reprinted 1931), pp. 533-36.
Includes, without comment, seven poems by ED.

6.150   ———. *A Short History of American Literature*. Boston: Heath, 1900, p. 285; rev. & enl. ed., 1919, p. 324.
"A rare vein is that of Emily Dickinson (1830-1886), whose condensed little poems on nature and life startle and stab by their erratic originality of thought and phrase." Comment complete.

6.150a   Brooks, Cleanth. *Modern Poetry and the Tradition*. Chapel Hill: Univ. of North Carolina Press, 1939, pp. 76n., 241.
Briefly notes ED's place in the metaphysical tradition.

6.151   ———, and Robert Penn Warren. *Understanding Poetry: An Anthology for College Students*. N.Y.: Holt, 1938, pp. 468-71.
Rev. [2nd] ed., 1950, pp. 325-27.
Reprinted:
Davis, *14 by ED* (5.23), pp. 49-51.
Explication of "After great pain, a formal feeling comes."
See also 6.880.

6.152   Brooks, Noah. "Books of the Christmas Season." *Book Buyer*,
           n.s. VII (Dec. 1890), 521.
           Rev. of *Poems*, 1890 (3.9).

6.153   Brooks, Philip. "Notes On Rare Books." *New York Times Book
           Review*, April 21, 1935, p. 20.
           Notes an auction catalog description of 21 manuscript letters
           and notes by ED to Mrs. J. Howard Sweetser.

6.154   Brooks, Van Wyk. "End of an Era." *Saturday Review*, XXII (June
           22, 1940), 3-4, 16.
           Reprinted:
           Van Wyk Brooks. *New England Indian Summer, 1865-1915*.
              N.Y.: Dutton, 1940, pp. 316-29.
           Scholastic, XXXVIII (Mar. 10, 1941), 17-19, 22.
           Van Wyk Brooks. *This Is My Best*, ed. Whit Burnett. N.Y.:
              Dial, 1942, pp. 260-70.
           American Authors Today, ed. Whit Burnett and Charles Eli
              Slatkin. Boston: Ginn, 1947, pp. 241-52.
           Van Wyk Brooks. *A Chilmark Miscellany*. N.Y.: Dutton,
              1948, pp. 219-31.
           For a Spanish translation, see 11.21.
           A biographical study of ED and her milieu.

6.155   Brown, John Howard, ed. "Dickinson, Emily Elizabeth" in
           Lamb's Biographical Dictionary of the United States. Boston:
           James H. Lamb, 1900.

6.156   Brown, Rollo Walter. "A Sublimated Puritan." *Saturday Review*,
           V (Oct. 6, 1928), 186-87.
           Reprinted:
           Rollo Walter Brown. *Lonely Americans*. N.Y.: Coward-
              McCann, 1929, pp. 235-57.
           A biographical interpretation stressing ED's personal quali-
           ties, especially her renunciation and courage.

6.157   Bruère, Martha B. *Laughing Their Way: Women's Humor in
           America*, ed. Martha B. Bruère and Mary R. Beard. N.Y.:
           Macmillan, 1934, pp. 97-99.
           Quotes four poems to show that ED had her lighter moments.

6.158   Burgess, John William. "How I Found Amherst College and What
           I Found." *Amherst Graduates' Quarterly*, XVII (Nov. 1927),
           3-13.
           Discusses the Dickinson home, p. 10.

6.159   ——. *Reminiscences of an American Scholar*. N.Y.: Columbia
           Univ. Press, 1934, pp. 60-62.
           A brief description, based on personal reminiscence, of ED
           and her family.

6.159a   Burlingame, Robert. "Marsden Hartley's *Androscoggin:* Return
           to Place." *New England Quarterly*, XXXI (Dec. 1958), 447-62.
           Notes Hartley's indebtedness to ED, especially her influence
           on his poetry. Cites an unpublished letter to Mrs. Charles P.
           Kuntz, July 1933, in which he says the "voices of Emerson,
           Thoreau, Emily Dickinson belong to my space, my innate
           areas." For a reply, see Meredith, 6.694a.

6.159b   ——. *Of Making Many Books: A Hundred Years of Reading*,

Writing, and Publishing. N.Y.: Scribner's, 1946, pp. 72, 272-74.

Notes W.C. Brownell's letter to Burlingame [of Scribner's] proposing a Dickinson broadside. Also includes excerpts of letters regarding the August 1890 printing of "Renunciation" in *Scribner's Magazine* (3.8).

6.160 Burnshaw, Stanley. "The Three Revolutions of Modern Poetry." *Sewanee Review,* LXX (Summer 1962), 427-28.
Reprinted:
Stanley Burnshaw. *Varieties of Literary Experience.* N.Y.: New York Univ. Press, 1962, p. 147.
Cites "Further in Summer than the Birds" as "non-syntactical" like Mallarmé's poem, "Sainte."

6.161 Burrows, Frederick W. "The Single Hound." *New England Magazine.* LII (Dec. 1914), 165-66.
Rev. of *Single Hound,* 1914 (3.114).

6.162 Burton, Richard. "Discussion of Genevieve Taggard's *The Life and Mind of Emily Dickinson."* *Creative Reading,* V (Aug. 1930), 445-52.
Rev. of Taggard, *Life and Mind* (5.81).

6.163 C., E.R. "Emily Dickinson: Notes on Her Personality and Her Latest Poems." *Sun,* no date or page. Clipping in the Jones Library, Amherst.
Rev. of *Poems,* 1896 (3.89).
My search did not locate this item in the *New York Sun* for Aug.-Oct. 1896.

6.164 C., J.M. "Paperback Sampler." *Christian Science Monitor,* Aug. 22, 1963, p. 11.
Rev. of Sewall, *Critical Essays* (5.75).

6.165 C., R.A. "Again Emily." *Christian Science Monitor,* Mar. 15, 1951, p. 10.
Rev. of *Letters,* 1951 (4.80).

6.166 C., S.A. "The Reviewer's Quill." *Wings,* IV (Spring 1939), 23-24.
Rev. of Whicher, *This Was a Poet* (5.104).

6.167 C., S.C. "Emily's House." *Christian Science Monitor,* Jan. 16, 1932, p. 5.
Rev. of *Letters,* 1931 (4.52).

6.168 ———. "The Secret Dickinsonian Treasure." *Christian Science Monitor,* April 16, 1945, p. 14.
Rev. of *Bolts of Melody,* 1945 (3.177) and Bingham, *Ancestors' Brocades* (5.5).

6.169 Cairns, William B. *A History of American Literature.* N.Y.: Oxford Univ. Press, 1912, p. 466; rev. ed., 1930, pp. 515-16.
"Though uneven ... [ED's verses] show unquestionable genius. The author had humor, insight, and an unusual power of terse and well rounded expression. Her *Letters* are interesting, but are disappointing in that they give so little clue to her personality" (p. 516).

6.170 Cambon, Glauco. *College English,* XXVI (Mar. 1965), 491.
Rev. of Griffith, *Long Shadow* (5.31).

6.171 ———. "Emily Dickinson and the Crisis of Self-Reliance" in

Transcendentalism and Its Legacy, ed. Myron Simon and
Thornton H. Parsons. Ann Arbor: Univ. of Michigan Press,
1966, pp. 123-33.
ED shared with Emerson an attitude of openness to experience;
unlike him, she experienced the universe as a radical otherness. In the face of cosmic alienation, hers was a "desperate"
self-reliance. Rev. by Robbins, *ALS, 1966* (6.851), p. 143.

6.172   Cambon, Glauco. "Emily Dickinson: Confrontation of the Self
with Otherness in the Inner Space," in *The Inclusive Flame:
Studies in Modern American Poetry.* Bloomington, Ind.: Indiana Univ. Press, 1963, pp. 27-49, 232-34.
ED's spatial imagination allows her to vivify the existential
boundaries of experience — death, eternity, "circumference."
The poet's "totally internalized spiritual vastness" is mani-
fested in her sense of identity as a perpetual crisis and ad-
venture. Notes connections with other poets. See also the
author's similar study of ED in Italian (8.46).

6.173   ——. "On Translating Dickinson." *Chelsea Review* [N.Y.], No.
7 (May 1960), pp. 77-79.
A review essay on the translations of Guido Errante (8.3, 8.6).
Eight poems are reprinted in parallel English-Italian columns,
pp. 80-87.

6.173a   ——. *Recent American Poetry.* University of Minnesota Pam-
phlets on American Writers, No. 16. Minneapolis: Univ. of
Minnesota Press, 1962, p. 40.
Briefly compares ED to the poet John Logan.

6.174   ——. "Violence and Abstraction in Emily Dickinson." *Sewanee
Review,* LXVIII (July-Sept. 1960), 450-64.
Argues that ED's boldly experimental use of language is paral-
leled in the drive toward an "absolute" poetry characteristic of
Mallarmé, Rilke, and Valéry.

6.175   Cameron, May. "Books On Our Table." *New York Post,* Nov. 1,
1938, p. 10.
Rev. of Whicher, *This Was a Poet* (5.104).

6.176   Campbell, Harry Modean. "Dickinson's 'The last Night that She
lived.'" *Explicator,* VIII (May 1950), Item 54.

6.177   Canby, Henry Seidel. *Book-of-the-Month Club News* [N.Y.], Nov.
1939, unpaged.
Rev. of Whicher, *This Was a Poet* (5.104).

6.178   Capps, Jack L. *American Literature,* XXXIX (May, 1967), 227-
28.
Rev. of Ford, *Heaven Beguiles the Tired* (5.27).

6.179   ——. "'Boanerges' a Horse?" *American Notes and Queries,* II
(Dec. 1963), 57-58.
Replies to an inquiry by Paul F. Breed (6.138). See also 6.637.

6.180   Carlson, Eric W. "Dickinson's 'I started Early — Took my Dog.'"
Explicator, XX (May 1962), Item 72.
Reprinted:
Davis, *14 by ED* (5.23), pp. 89-90.

6.181   Carmen, Bliss. "A Note on Emily Dickinson." *Boston Evening
Transcript,* Nov. 21, 1896, p. 15.

Reprinted:

Blake and Wells, *Recognition* (5.13), pp. 61-68.

Excerpt reprinted in *American Life in Literature,* ed. J. B.
    Hubbell. N.Y.: Harper, 1936, II, 266.

Rev. of *Poems,* 1896 (3.89).

6.182 Carpenter, Edward Wilton, and Charles F. Morehouse. *The His-*
    tory of the Town of Amherst, Mass.
    Amherst, Mass.: Press of Carpenter and Morehouse, 1896.
    Published in two parts. Part I: General history of the town.
    Part II: Town Meeting records. Complete in one volume.

6.183 Carpenter, Frederic I. "Dickinson's 'Farther in Summer than
    the Birds.'" *Explicator,* VIII (Mar. 1950), Item 33.
    Reprinted:
    Davis, *14 by ED* (5.23), pp. 120-21.

6.184 ———. "Emily Dickinson and the Rhymes of Dream." *University*
    of Kansas City Review, XX (Winter 1953), 113-20.
    Excerpt reprinted in Davis, *14 by ED* (5.23), pp. 58-59.
    ED's poetry deals with the tragic reality of daily life, the
    transcendental beauty of imaginative life, and the relationship
    between them.

6.185 ———. *New England Quarterly,* III (Oct. 1930), 753-57.
    Rev. of Jenkins, *Friend and Neighbor* (5.35); Pollitt, *Human*
    Background (5.61); and Taggard, *Life and Mind* (5.81).

6.186 Carpenter, Margaret Haley. *Sarah Teasdale, A Biography.* N.Y.:
    Schulte, 1960, p. 276.
    In a note to Sarah Teasdale, Carl Sandburg links ED and po-
    etry of silence.

6.187 Carruth, Hayden. "A Peculiar Genius." *Nation,* CLXXIV (May
    10, 1952), 456-57.
    Rev. of Chase, *ED* (5.17).

6.187a C[ase], E[lizabeth] N. *Hartford Sunday Courant,* Mar. 2, 1930,
    p. 8-E.
    Rev. of Pollitt, *Human Background* (5.61).

6.187b ———. "Literary Topics." *Hartford Daily Courant,* July 9, 1930,
    p. 10.
    Rev. of Taggard, *Life and Mind* (5.81).

6.188 Case, Josephine Young. *New England Quarterly,* XXIV (Dec.
    1951), 546-48.
    Rev. of *Letters,* 1951 (4.80) and *Letters to Holland,* 1951 (4.76).

6.189 Cate, Hollis L. "Emily Dickinson and 'The Prisoner of Chillon.'"
    American Notes and Queries, VI (Sept. 1967), 6-7.
    On the significance of ED's allusions to Byron's poem.

6.190 Caughey, M. L. "Emily Dickinson — The Solitary Poet." *Cincin-*
    nati Times Star, July 15, 1930.
    Rev. of Taggard, *Life and Mind* (5.81).

6.191 Chadwick, Helen Cary. "Emily Dickinson: A Study." *Personal-*
    ist, X (Oct. 1929), 256-69.
    Biographical rather than interpretative. Seeks to "present the
    reality of a very human person."

6.192 Chadwick, John W. "Emily Dickinson." *Unity* [Chicago], XXVI
    (Jan. 22, 1891), 171.

6.193   Chadwick, John W. "Poems by Emily Dickenson [sic]." *Christian
            Register* [Boston], LXIX (Dec. 18, 1890), 828.
            Rev. of *Poems*, 1890 (3.9). This review is defended in a later
            issue of the *Christian Register;* see 7.3.

6.193a   Chamberlain, Arthur. "Emily Dickinson — Poet and Woman."
            Boston Commonwealth, XXXI (Feb. 20, 1892), 6-7.
            Notes Mrs. Todd's lectures on ED.

6.194   ——. "The Poems of Emily Dickinson." *Boston Commonwealth*
            XXX (Dec. 26, 1891), 7.
            Rev. of *Poems*, 1891 (3.52).

6.195   Chase, Richard. "Amatory Jottings of a Pure Spirit." *Saturday
            Review*, XXXVII (Nov. 20, 1954), 19-20.
            Rev. of Bingham, *Revelation* (5.9).

6.196   ——. *Nation*, CLXXII (April 21, 1951), 380-81.
            Rev. of *Letters*, 1951 (4.80) and *Letters to Holland*, 1951 (4.76).

6.197   ——. "A Poet's Economy." *Hopkins Review*, V (Fall 1951),
            34-37.
            Discusses Constance Rourke's estimation of ED in *American
            Humor* (6.864) and argues that disinterested critical assess-
            ment of the poet should cancel "ideal visions." See also the
            author's *ED* (5.17), pp. 133-37.

6.198   ——. "Seeking a Poet's Inspiration." *Saturday Review*, XXXIV
            (Dec. 1, 1951), 26.
            Rev. of Patterson, *Riddle* (5.55).

6.199   ——. *Walt Whitman Reconsidered*. N.Y.: William Sloan Asso-
            ciates, 1955, pp. 74, 79, 118, 123, 127.
            Discusses wit and American humor characteristic of ED,
            among others.

6.200   Chew, Samuel C. "Emily Dickinson." *Guardian*, I (Dec. 1924),
            23-24.
            Rev. of *Complete Poems*, 1924 (3.123) and Bianchi, *Life and
            Letters* (4.36).

6.201   C[hickering], J[oseph] K. "The Late Lavinia Dickinson; Friend's
            Admiring Tribute to a Unique Personality." *Springfield Re-
            publican*, Nov. 30, 1899, p. 5.
            Reprinted:
            Bingham, *ED's Home* (4.86), pp. 490-92.
            Appearing shortly after Lavinia's death, this tribute noted her
            devotion to Emily and several other personal qualities.

6.202   Child, Clarence Griffin. *Citizen* [Philadelphia], III (May 1897),
            61-62.
            Rev. of *Poems*, 1896 (3.89).

6.203   Childs, Herbert Ellsworth. *Arizona Quarterly*, XII (Spring 1956),
            82-83.
            Rev. of Johnson, *Interpretive Biography* (5.44).

6.204   ——. "Emily Dickinson and Sir Thomas Browne." *American
            Literature*, XXII (Jan. 1951), 455-65.
            Parallels, similarities, possible borrowings.

6.205   ——. "Emily Dickinson, Spinster." *Western Humanities Re-
            view*, III (Oct. 1949), 303-09.
            ED was already psychologically a spinster at age twenty-three.

6.206   Chmaj, Betty E. "The Metaphors of Resurrection." *Universitas; A Journal of Religion and the University* [Detroit], II (Fall 1964), 91-109.
Mentions ED and Edward Taylor in a discussion of Finnish-American hymns.

6.207   Christie, John A. "A New Chapter in American Literature." *Vassar Alumnae Magazine*, XLII (Oct. 1956), 2-6, 10.
On the history of ED's reputation and editing.

6.208   Church, Richard. "The Life-Story of Emily Dickinson." *Spectator* [London], CXLV (Sept. 6, 1930), 316.
Rev. of Pollitt, *Human Background* (5.61) and Taggard, *Life and Mind* (5.81).

6.209   Ciardi, John. "Dickinson's 'I heard a Fly buzz — when I died.'" *Explicator*, XIV (Jan. 1956), Item 22.
Reprinted:
Davis, *14 by ED* (5.23), p. 67.

6.210   ———. *How Does a Poem Mean?* Part III of *An Introduction to Literature* by H. Barrows, John Ciardi, *et. al.* Boston: Houghton, Mifflin, 1959, pp. 798-99, 801-02.
Contains a few study questions on "A narrow Fellow in the Grass."

6.211   ———. *New England Quarterly*, XXV (Mar. 1952), 93-98.
Rev. of Patterson, *Riddle* (5.55).

6.212   ———. "Out of the Top Drawer." *Nation*, CLXXXI (Nov. 5, 1955), 397-98.
Rev. of *Poems*, 1955 (3.197) and Johnson, *Interpretive Biography* (5.44).

6.213   ———. "The Poet's Family Circle." *New York Times Book Review*, May 29, 1955, pp. 4, 17.
Rev. of Bingham, *ED's Home* (4.86).

6.214   Clark, Harry Hayden, ed. "Emily Dickinson" in *Major American Poets*. N.Y.: American Book Co., 1936, pp. 893-902.
The section devoted to ED in this college anthology includes 28 poems, a brief introductory essay, and an annotated bibliography (pp. 894-97).

6.215   ———, ed. *Transitions in American Literary History*. Durham, N.C.: Duke Univ. Press, 1953, pp. 325, 376, 383, *passim*.

6.216   ———. Three Spokesmen of Nineteenth-Century America." *Yale Review*, XXVIII (Mar. 1939), 633-37.
Rev. of Whicher, *This Was a Poet* (5.104).

6.217   Clarke, Clorinda. *Catholic World*, CLXXIII (May 1951), 157-58.
Rev. of *Letters*, 1951 (4.80).

6.218   Clements, R. J. "Poetry on the Campus." *Saturday Review*, XLIX (June 11, 1966), 68.
Rev. of Capps, *ED's Reading* (5.14) and Porter, *ED's Early Poetry* (5.69).

6.219   Clendenning, John. "Cummings, Comedy, and Criticism." *Colorado Quarterly*, XII (Summer 1963), 44-53.
ED as one of Cummings' literary ancestors, p. 49.

6.220   Clough, Wilson O. "Dickinson's 'When I hoped I feared.'" *Explicator*, X (Nov. 1951), Item 10.

6.220a   Cody, John. "Emily Dickinson and Nature's Dining Room."
         Michigan Quarterly Review, VII (Fall 1968), 249-54.
         "Throughout her life, Emily Dickinson retained the character-
         istics of the unloved child, and saw in her mother the total
         failure of maternal functions."

6.220b   ———. "Emily Dickinson's Vesuvian Face." *American Imago*,
         XXIV (Fall 1967), 161-80.
         A line-by-line psychoanalytic interpretation of "My Life had
         stood — a Loaded Gun."

6.221   C[oleman], E[arle] E. "Emily Dickinson." *Princeton University
         Library Chronicle*, XXV (Spring 1964), 230-31.
         Notes two additions to the Princeton collection of ED manu-
         scripts.

6.222   Collins, John Churton. *Studies in Poetry and Criticism*. London:
         George Bell and Sons, 1905, p. 75.
         "Emily Dickinson is, in her jerky transcendentalism and
         strained style, too faithful a disciple of Emerson, but much of
         her work has real merit." Comment complete.

6.223   Colson, Ethel M. *Chicago Herald*, Oct. 10, 1914, p. 9.
         Rev. of *Single Hound*, 1914 (3.114).

6.224   Colton, Aaron Merrick. "Letter Read at the One Hundred and
         Fiftieth Anniversary of the First Congregational Church of
         Amherst, Mass." in *The Old Meeting House and Vacation Pa-
         pers*. N.Y.: Worthington, 1890, pp. 144-69.
         Personal reminiscences include memories of Edward Dickin-
         son, *circa* 1840. No mention of ED.

6.225   Colton, Arthur W. "The Enchanting Emily." *New York Evening
         Post Literary Review*, IV (May 31, 1924), 788.
         Rev. of Bianchi, *Life and Letters* (4.36).

6.226   Comfort, Ann. *San Francisco Chronicle*, Jan. 27, 1952, p. 11.
         Rev. of Chase, *ED* (5.17).

6.227   Comings, Lois Leighton. "Emily Dickinson." *Mount Holyoke
         Alumnae Quarterly*, VIII (Oct. 1924), 133-39.
         A general appreciation.

6.228   Connelly, James T. "Dickinson's 'I heard a Fly buzz — when I
         died.'" *Explicator*, XXV (Dec. 1966), Item 34.

6.229   ———. "Dickinson's 'Wild Nights.'" *Explicator*, XXV (Jan. 1967),
         Item 44.

6.230   Connely, Willard. "Emily Dickinson in Her Life, Letters, and
         Poetry" in *Essays By Divers Hands*, ed. Harold Nicolson.
         *Transactions of the Royal Society of Literature of the United
         Kingdom*, n.s. XXIII (London: Oxford Univ. Press, 1947), 1-19.
         A biographical study stressing ED's friendships with Benjamin
         Newton, Charles Wadsworth, T. W. Higginson, and Samuel Bowles.

6.231   Connors, Donald F. "The Significance of Emily Dickinson." *Col-
         lege English*, III (April 1942), 624-33.
         Stresses ED's dependence on introspection.

6.232   ———. *Thought*, XIX (1944), 544-46.
         Rev. of Power, *In the Name of the Bee* (5.72).

6.233   Corke, Hilary. *Listener*, LXI (April 2, 1959), 606.
         Rev. of *Selected Poems*, 1959 (3.202).

6.234 Coursen, Herbert R., Jr. "Nature's Center." *College English,*
XXIV (Mar. 1963), 467-69.
On the views of nature held by ED, Melville, and Henry Adams.

6.235 Craig, G. Armour. *American Scholar,* XXVII (Autumn 1958), 518,
520.
Rev. of *Letters,* 1958 (4.90).

6.236 Crawford, Bartholow, Alexander C. Kern, and Morriss H. Needle-
man. "Emily (Elizabeth) Dickinson," in *American Literature,*
3rd. ed., *College Outline Series,* No. 49. N.Y.: Barnes and
Noble, 1953, pp. 231-34.
Contains a summary of suggested merits and defects of ED's
poetry.

6.237 Crowell, Annie Louise. "Emily Dickinson — An Heritage of
Friendship." *Mt. Holyoke Alumnae Quarterly,* XXIX (Feb.
1946), 129-30.
The author relates reminiscences of her mother, daughter of
Aaron Warner, Prof. of English at Amherst and friend of the
Dickinson family. She describes the Dickinson home as open
and friendly. Includes the first printing of two notes from ED
to Mary Warner (Crowell) and one from Lavinia.

6.238 ——. "'Where Loveliness Keeps a House.'" *Mt. Holyoke Alumnae Quarterly,* XIV (Jan. 1931), 239-41.
The author's mother, Mary Warner, girlhood friend of ED,
reports that ED's father was no Puritan tyrant.

6.239 Crowell, Jane C. "Emily Dickinson and Catholicism." *Springfield Sunday Union and Republican,* Mar. 12, 1944, p. 7-E.
Letter to the editor regarding Power, *In the Name of the Bee*
(5.72).

6.240 Crowell, Mary W. "Emily Dickinson's Letters." *Springfield Republican,* April 1, 1933, p. 6.
A reply to 7.28 minimizing the importance of Mrs. Todd's
1894 edition of ED's letters (4.3). For a rejoinder praising
the work of Mrs. Todd, see 6.884.

6.241 Crowley, Paul. "The Dickinson Mystery Again." *Commonweal,*
XII (Oct. 1, 1930), 557-58.
Rev. of Taggard, *Life and Mind* (5.81).

6.242 Cunliffe, Marcus. "Minor Key (Emily Dickinson and Others)," in
The Literature of the United States. Baltimore: Penguin
Books, 1959 (rev ed., 1961), pp. 180-84. Translated into Ger-
man, see 10.46.
Praises ED's originality, although she is "technically a poor
poet," and notes her interest in death and immortality.

6.243 ——. *Review of English Studies,* n.s. XII (Nov. 1961), 434-36.
Rev. of *Letters,* 1958 (4.90).

6.243a Cunningham, Donald H. "Emily Dickinson's 'I heard a Fly buzz —
when I died.'" *American Notes and Queries,* VI (June 1968),
150-51.

6.244 Cunninghma, Nora B. "Emerson and Emily Dickinson." *Christian Science Monitor,* XLIX (May 6, 1957), 8.
ED's poetry would have pleased Emerson.

6.245   Cunningham, Walter W. "The Importance of Being a 'Nobody.'"
        Christian Science Monitor, XXIV (May 14, 1932), 11.
        Reprinted:
        "Their Early Essays," *Christian Science Monitor,* XLIX (July
           10, 1957), 8.
        ED's poem is used as a point of departure in this essay prais-
        ing "being a nobody."

6.246   Curran, George. "Emily Dickinson and Religion." *Smith College
        Monthly,* II (Nov. 1941), 7-9.

6.247   Curtis, Jared R. "Edward Taylor and Emily Dickinson: Voices
        and Visions." *Susquehanna University Studies,* VII (June 1964),
        159-67.
        Both ED and Edward Taylor employ surprise and juxtaposition
        and revel in paradox and the grotesque. Rev. by Robbins, *ALS,
        1965* (6.851), p. 156.

6.248   Cutler, Bruce. "An American Heart of Darkness." *Poetry,* CVII
        (Mar. 1966), 401-03.
        The comment that Frederick Goddard Tuckerman ranks with
        ED among American poets is occasioned by a review of his
        Complete Poems, ed. N. Scott Momaday (N.Y.: Oxford Univ.
        Press, 1965).

6.249   Cutting, Mary D. "Letters of Emily Dickinson." *Christian In-
        quirer* [N.Y.], VII (Dec. 27, 1894), 7.
        Rev. of *Letters,* 1894 (4.3).

6.250   ———. "Literature." *Christian Inquirer* [N.Y.], IV (April 9,
        1891).
        Rev. of *Poems,* 1890 (3.9).

6.251   D., H. E. "Dickinson's 'The Soul selects her own Society.'" *Ex-
        plicator,* III (Dec. 1944), Query 7.
        Asks whether there is a precise anatomical or zoological ref-
        erence in the last two lines.

6.252   ———. "Dickinson's 'Truth — is as old as God.'" *Explicator,* II
        (Nov. 1943), Query 11.
        Reprinted:
        Explicator, IV (April 1946), Query 14.
        Questions whether the poem has an ironic connotation.

6.253   D., J. J. *America,* XII (Jan 2, 1915), 299-300.
        Rev. of *Single Hound,* 1914 (3.114).

6.254   D., M. E. "The Bookshop and Emily Dickinson — Anniversary
        Celebration, May 1930." *Book Scorpion Miscellany.* Pub. by
        The Hampshire Bookshop, Northampton, Mass. No date or
        page.
        Rev. of *Further Poems,* 1929 (3.138) and notice of the forth-
        coming ED celebration (22.8-13).

6.254a Dabney, J[ulia] P[arker]. *The Musical Basis of Verse: A Scien-
        tific Study of the Principles of Poetic Composition.* N.Y.:
        Longmans, Green, 1901, p. 107.
        ED's "startling tonal combinations" exemplify a poetic cadence
        that is satisfying though imperfect.

6.255   Daiches, David. *Manchester Guardian,* Aug. 26, 1952, p. 4.
        Rev. of Chase, *ED* (5.17).

6.256 Daiches, David, and William Charvat, eds. *Poems in English, 1530-1940*. N.Y.: Ronald Press, 1950, pp. 727-28.
Brief explications are contained in notes to Dickinson poems.

6.257 Dailey, Mary Ann. "The Locomotive as Visualized by Walt Whitman and Emily Dickinson." *Lit*, No. 6 (Spring 1965), pp. 23-25.
Contrasts ED's feminine conception of a train in "I like to see it lap the Miles" with Whitman's masculine picture of a locomotive.

6.258 Daingerfield, Elizabeth and Juliet. *Lexington* [Mass.] *Herald,* Mar. 23, 1930.
Rev. of Pollitt, *Human Background* (5.61).

6.259 Dalgliesh, Alice. *Saturday Review*, XLVII (May 16, 1964), 58.
Rev. of *Poems*, sel. Poltz, 1964 (3.210).

6.260 Dall, Caroline Healey. "Two Women's Books." *Boston Evening Transcript*, Dec. 22, 1894, p. 16.
Rev. of *Letters*, 1894 (4.3).

6.261 Daly, James. "A Little Plain Woman with Two Smooth Bands of Reddish Hair." *Poetry*, LIII (Mar. 1939), 312-20.
Rev. of Whicher, *This Was a Poet* (5.104).

6.261a Damon, Samuel Foster. *Amy Lowell: A Chronicle*. Boston: Houghton Mifflin, 1935, pp. 295-96, 331-32, 443-44, 611, *passim*.
Notes some of Amy Lowell's lectures on poetry in which she spoke of ED as a precursor of Imagism. Also prints her letter to Mabel Loomis Todd, who had expressed appreciation for Miss Lowell's poem "The Sisters" (18.86) in which ED is mentioned.

6.262 Dauner, Louise. *New England Quarterly*, XXI (June 1948), 267-70.
Rev. of Wells, *Introduction* (5.101).

6.263 D'Avanzo, Mario L. "'Came a Wind Like a Bugle': Dickinson's Poetic Apocalypse." *Renascence*, XVII (Fall 1964), 29-31.
Notes Biblical sources for this poem in Revelation and Ecclesiastes. Noted by Robbins, *ALS, 1964* (6.851), p. 135.

6.264 ———. "Emily Dickinson's Dying Eye." *Renascence*, XIX (Winter 1967), 110-11.
Argues that the poem "I've seen a Dying Eye" records ED's skepticism concerning Emersonian thought.

6.265 Davidson, Frank. *American Literature*, XXXVIII (Nov. 1966), 399.
Rev. of Capps, *ED's Reading* (5.14).

6.266 ———. "A Note on Emily Dickinson's Use of Shakespeare." *New England Quarterly*, XVIII (Sept. 1945), 407-08.
The concluding thought in "A Route of Evanescence" derives from *The Tempest*.

6.267 ———. "'This Consciousness': Emerson and Dickinson." *Emerson Society Quarterly*, No. 44 (III Quar., 1966), pp. 2-7.
Discusses echoes of Emerson in ED's poems.

6.268 Davidson, James. "Emily Dickinson and Isaac Watts." *Boston Public Library Quarterly*, VI (July 1954), 141-49.
Compares themes and metrics. See also 6.316.

6.269   Davis, Lloyd M. "Dickinson's 'I taste a liquor never brewed.'"
          Explicator, XXIII (Mar. 1965), Item 53.
6.270   Davis, Dr. and Mrs. Ozora S. "Emily Dickinson." *Zion's Herald*
          [Boston, Mass.], CVIII (Dec. 10, 1930), 1584.
          "Her great gift to our age is her interpretation of the meaning
          of deathless love."
6.270a   Davis, William F., Jr. *Thought,* XL (Winter 1965), 604-07.
          Rev. of Griffith, *Long Shadow* (5.31).
6.271   Dawson, William James. "American Books That Have Moved
          Me." *Congregationalist and Christian World,* Dec. 4, 1909,
          pp. 779-80.
          An English appreciation of Emerson, Hawthorne, Poe, and ED.
6.271a   ———. *The Makers of English Poetry.* Rev. ed., N.Y.: F.H.
          Revell, 1906, pp. 403-04.
          Mentions ED as "wonderful in native power."
6.272   deFord, Sara. "Emily Dickinson" in *Lectures on Modern Ameri-
          can Poetry.* Tokyo: Hokuseido Press, 1957, pp. 1-26.
          An introductory discussion of ED for college students. In
          English.
6.273   Deutsch, Babette. "A Beam of Light." *New Republic,* LXII (May
          7, 1930), 332.
          Rev. of Pollitt, *Human Background* (5.61).
6.274   ———. "A Dickinson, Not Emily." *New York Post,* Dec. 9, 1932.
          Rev. of Bianchi, *Face to Face* (4.59). My search was unable to
          locate this item cited in the Jones Library handlist (1.16),
          p. 36.
6.275   ———. "Emily Dickinson Again." *New Republic,* LXIII (July 9,
          1930), 211-12.
          Rev. of Jenkins, *Friend and Neighbor* (5.35) and Taggard, *Life
          and Mind* (5.81).
6.276   ———. "Miracle and Mystery." *Poetry,* LXVI (Aug. 1945), 274-
          80.
          Rev. of *Bolts of Melody,* 1945 (3.177) and Bingham, *Ancestors'
          Brocades* (5.5).
6.277   ———. *New York Post,* Nov. 7, 1931, p. 9.
          Rev. of *Letters,* 1931 (4.52).
6.278   ———. "Poetry at the Midcentury." *Virginia Quarterly Review,*
          XXVI (Winter 1950), 69-70.
          Brief comparison of Whitman and Dickinson.
6.278a   ———. *Poetry in Our Time: A Critical Survey of Poetry in the
          English-speaking World, 1900-1960.* 2nd ed., N.Y.: Doubleday
          (Anchor Books), 1963, *passim.*
          Alludes to ED as a precursor of a number of modern poets.
6.279   ———. "A Sojourn In Infinity." *Bookman* [N.Y.], LXIX (May 1929),
          303-06.
          Rev. of *Further Poems,* 1929 (3.138).
6.280   ———. *This Modern Poetry.* N.Y.: Norton, 1935, pp. 21-23
          passim.
6.281   [De Voto, Bernard.] "The Easy Chair." *Harper's Magazine,*
          CXC (June 1945), 602-05.

Rev. of Bingham, *Ancestors' Brocades* (5.5). George F. Whicher replies; see 6.1131.

6.282 [De Witt, Gene.] "On Dynamics in Poems." *Blue Guitar, The Journal of Esthetics* [Solvang, Calif.], No. 12 (Winter 1956), pp. 1-9.

Contains a discussion of kinetic and sequential movement in "Because I could not stop for Death."

6.283 Dickerman, Elizabeth. "Portrait of Two Sisters, Emily and Lavinia Dickinson." *Smith Alumnae Quarterly*, XLV (Feb. 1954), 79.

Personal recollection of ED. Includes the first printing of a letter to Mrs. George S. Dickerman.

6.284 Dickinson, Ellen E. "Emily Dickinson." *Brooklyn Eagle*, April 28, 1892.

Reprinted:

Boston Evening Transcript, Sept. 28, 1894, p. 4.

Mrs. Bingham notes in *Ancestors' Brocades* (5.5), pp. 263-66, that this article was widely reprinted in newspapers, including the Chicago *Inter Ocean*, Dec. 1, 1894. Mrs. Bingham also mentions a second article, "Emily Dickinson: Her Personality and Surroundings in Her Home," a "rehash" of the first, printed in the *Boston Transcript*, Oct. 12, 1895. Both articles contain recollections and anecdotes by Mrs. Dickinson, wife of one of ED's cousins. Excerpts are reprinted in Leyda, *Years and Hours* (5.49), II, 482.

6.285 [Dickinson, Susan.] "Miss Emily Dickinson of Amherst." *Springfield Daily Republican*, May 18, 1886, p. 4.

Reprinted:

Amherst Record, May 18, 1886, p. 4.

Leyda, *Years and Hours* (5.49), II, 472-74.

An admiring tribute written as an obituary by the poet's sister-in-law. Unsigned.

6.285a Dickinson, Thomas Herbert. *The Making of American Literature*. N.Y.: Century, 1932, pp. 599-605, 644, 691.

An introduction to ED's life and a brief, appreciative discussion of her poetry.

6.286 Dietrick, Ellen Battelle. "One-Sided Criticism." *Woman's Journal* [Boston], XXIII (Jan. 16, 1892), 18.

6.287 Dobrée, Bonamy. "The Secluded Poet." *Spectator* [London], CLXXXIX (Aug. 1, 1952), 165.

Rev. of Chase, *ED* (5.17).

6.288 Dods, Agnes M. "Emily Dickinson House Still Stands, Serene and Aloof." *Amherst Journal Record*, Oct. 20, 1964, p. 12.

6.289 ———. "Famous Amherst Names Inscribed on West Cemetery Monuments." *Amherst Journal Record*, July 9, 1964, p. 11.

6.290 Dole, Nathan Haskell. "Literary Topics in Boston." *Book Buyer*, n.s. VII (Dec. 1890), 546.

Rev. of *Poems*, 1890 (3.9).

6.291 ———. "Mabel Loomis Todd." *Saturday Review*, IX (Nov. 19, 1932), 260.

Obituary and appreciation.

6.292   Dole, Nathan Haskell. "Notes From Boston." *Book News* [Philadelphia], X (Mar. 1892), 307-08.
          Reprinted:
          "Emily Dickinson's Personality." *Book Buyer*, n.s. IX (May 1892), 157-58.
          Taggard, *Life and Mind* (5.81), pp. 375-77.
          Discusses a paper given by Mabel Loomis Todd on ED. Reprints excerpts from Mrs. Todd's reminiscences of the poet and notes that "at least 1200 poems" have been cataloged in addition to the 1890 volume, then in its eleventh edition.

6.292a   Donaldson, Scott. "Minding Emily Dickinson's Business." *New England Quarterly*, XLI (Dec. 1968), 574-82.
          Examines those poems in which the word "Circumference" occurs in an effort to show that it "came to stand for the unreachable goal she was always questing toward — the goal of perfect perception and ideal comprehension."

6.293   Donoghue, Denis. "Emily Dickinson" in *Connoisseurs of Chaos: Ideas of Order in Modern American Poetry*. N.Y.: Macmillan, 1965, pp. 100-28.
          Takes issue with Allen Tate on the importance of New England Puritan doctrines in understanding ED (see 6.980) and argues that by conceiving of the universe as centered in the poet's soul, ED could bind herself with cordiality and tact to the external world. This essay was originally delivered as a lecture at the Univ. of Cincinnati; see 21.10.

6.294   Dorinson, Zahava Karl. "'I taste a liquor never brewed': A Problem in Editing." *American Literature*, XXXV (Nov. 1963), 363-65.

6.295   Doty, John H. *Touchstone* [Amherst College], IV (Nov. 1938), 22.
          Rev. of Whicher, *This Was a Poet* (5.104).

6.296   Doubleday, Neal Frank. *Studies in Poetry*. N.Y.: Harper, 1949, pp. 39-40, 89-91 *passim*.
          Contains study questions for a number of Dickinson poems.

6.297   Douglas, Emily Taft. *Remember the Ladies, The Story of the Women Who Helped Shape America*. N.Y.: Putnam, 1966.
          ED is discussed in Chapter 9, "Storming Parnassus: A Poet, A Painter, A Dancer," pp. 172-81.

6.298   Douglas, George W. "Life of a Notable Woman Poet." *Philadelphia Public Ledger*, April 8, 1924.
          Rev. of Bianchi, *Life and Letters* (4.36).

6.299   Douglas, Wallace W. *English "A" Analyst* [Northwestern Univ., Evanston, Ill.], No. 4, pp. 1-3.
          Reprinted:
          The Critical Reader, ed. Wallace Douglas, Roy Lamson, and Hallett Smith. N.Y.: Norton, 1949.
          Contains an explication of "I taste a liquor never brewed."

6.300   Downey, Harris. *American Literature*, XX (Jan. 1949), 465-66.
          Rev. of Wells, *Introduction* (5.101).

6.300a   Drew, David P. "Emily Brontë and Emily Dickinson as Mystic Poets." *Brontë Society Transactions*, XV, No. 3 (1968), pp. 227-32.

ED maintained a more academic approach to mystical experience than did Emily Brontë.

6.301   Drew, Elizabeth. *Poetry: A Modern Guide to Its Understanding and Enjoyment,* N.Y.: Norton, 1959, pp. 53-54, 73, 84, 124-25.
Includes an explication of "After great pain, a formal feeling comes."

6.302   Duncan, Joseph Ellis. *The Revival of Metaphysical Poetry.* Minneapolis, Minn.: Univ. of Minnesota Press, 1959.
Metaphysical themes and techniques in ED's poetry, pp. 5, 77-88, 189, 204.

6.303   duPont, M. M. "The Endless Study." *New Republic,* CXLIII (Nov. 28, 1960), 30-32.
Rev. of *Complete Poems,* 1960 (3.207), and Leyda, *Years and Hours* (5.49).

6.304   E., C. M. "Letters to the Editors." *Critic,* XX (Feb. 13, 1892), 105.
The author mentions ED in her reply to an article on "The Absence of the Creative Faculty in Women" by Milly Elliott Seawell, which appeared in *Critic,* Nov. 29, 1891.

6.305   E., R. D. "Dickinson's 'Safe in their Alabaster Chambers.'" *Explicator,* XVI (Feb. 1958), Query 6.

6.306   Earle, Genevieve B. "'Some Watcher of the Skies.'" *Book Collector's Packet,* III (Mar. 1939), 11-12.
Reports the author's quest for poems in tribute to ED and quotes from Edwin Markham's letter to Charles Warren Stoddard dated Jan. 13, 1892: "A new name has recently come into this kingly company. I refer to the poems of Emily Dickinson, the Queen of the Quaint. Do you know her? If not, arise at midnight and go forth to find her books. She is quainter, if not stronger than Thoreau — than Landor — than Blake." Two photostatic copies of this letter are at the Jones Library, Amherst. See also 6.657.

6.306a   Early, Eleanor. "The Enigma of Emily Dickinson." *New York Times,* Oct. 13, 1968, Section 10, p. 1.
This illustrated article, written for the travel section of the *Times,* describes the Dickinson house and deals briefly with several other topics, chiefly the question regarding ED's suitors. For a reply, see J. Richard Phillips, 6.801.

6.307   Eaton, Anne T. *New York Times Book Review,* Dec. 23, 1934, p. 9.
Rev. of *Poems For Youth,* 1934 (3.159).

6.308   Eberhart, Richard. "Some New Light Shed on Emily Dickinson." *Washington* [D.C.] *Sunday Star,* Nov. 20, 1960.

6.309   Eby, Cecil D. "'I taste a liquor never brewed': A Variant Reading." *American Literature,* XXXVI (Jan. 1965), 516-18.
Rev. by Robbins, *ALS, 1965* (6.851), p. 158.

6.309a   Edelstein, Tilden G. *Strange Enthusiasm, A Life of Thomas Wentworth Higginson.* New Haven, Conn.: Yale Univ. Press, 1968, pp. 342-352, *passim.*
Discusses Higginson's response to ED's poetry and his editing of some of her poems. Suggests that Higginson's poem, "Astra Castra" (pub. 1889) is about ED, p. 345, and that two of

Higginson's fictional characters are based in part upon ED,
pp. 308, 313.

6.310   Edwards, Louise B. "Emily Dickinson." *Housekeeper's Weekly*,
III, No. 15 (April 9, 1892), pp. 2-3.
An appreciation that quotes excerpts from ED's letters as
published in Higginson's *Atlantic* essay (6.473).

6.311   Elias, Robert H. and Helen L. "Dickinson's 'Farther in Summer
than the Birds.'" *Explicator*, XI (Oct. 1952), Item 5.
Reprinted:
Davis, *14 by ED* (5.23), pp. 125-26.

6.312   Elliott, G. R. *American Literature*, I (Jan. 1930), 439-42.
Rev. of *Further Poems*, 1929 (3.138).

6.313   Ellis, [Harold] Milton. *New England Quarterly*, XII (Sept. 1939),
604-08.
Rev. of Whicher, *This Was a Poet* (5.104).

6.314   Elting, M. L. *Forum* [N.Y.], CI (Jan. 1939), p. v.
Rev. of Whicher, *This Was a Poet* (5.104).

6.315   Emblen, D. L. "A Comment on 'Structural Patterns in the Poetry
of Emily Dickinson.'" *American Literature*, XXXVII (Mar.
1965), 64-65.
Replies to Suzanne M. Wilson's article; see 6.1191.

6.316   England, Martha Winburn. "Emily Dickinson and Isaac Watts:
Puritan Hymnodists." *Bulletin of the New York Public Li-
brary*, LXIX (Feb. 1965), 83-116.
Reprinted:
Martha Winburn England and John Sparrow. *Hymns Unbidden:
Donne, Herbert, Blake, Emily Dickinson and the Hymnogra-
phers.* N.Y.: New York Public Library, 1966, pp. 113-47.
Both ED and Isaac Watts modify the metrical conventions of
hymnody; ED, however, parodies the religious orthodoxy of
Watts. The peculiar quality of humor in her poetry derives
not from metaphysical wit but from Puritan iconoclasm.
Rev. by Robbins, *ALS, 1965* (6.851), pp. 156-57.

6.317   Engle, Paul. "Evaluating Poems of the Remote, Ecstatic, Baf-
fling Emily Dickinson." *Chicago Sunday Tribune Magazine of
Books*, Jan. 6, 1952, p. 4.
Rev. of Chase, *ED* (5.17).

6.318   ———. "The Ever-Echoing Avenues of Song." *New York Times
Book Review*, May 10, 1964, Children's Book Section, pp. 2,
33.
Rev. of *Poems*, sel. Plotz, 1964 (3.210).

6.319   Erskine, John. "The Dickinson Saga." *Yale Review*, XXXV (Sept.
1945), 74-83.
Reprinted:
John Erskine. *In Memory of Certain Persons: An Autobiog-
raphy.* Philadelphia: Lippincott, 1947, pp. 128-38.
A sidelight on the Dickinson family feud and review of Bingham, *Ancestors' Brocades* (5.5).

6.320   ———. "Reading and Writing" in *The Complete Life: A Guide to
the Active Enjoyment of the Arts and of Living.* N.Y.: Mess-
ner, 1943, p. 50.

Although ED's poetry is occasionally poignant, "the range of her thought and feeling" is "extremely narrow."

6.321 Eshleman, Lloyd Wendell. "'Gossamer and Gold,' Unpublished Poems of Emily Dickinson." *New York Sun*, Feb. 29, 1936, p. 30.
Rev. of *Unpublished Poems*, 1935 (3.167).

6.322 Essig, Erhardt, H. "Dickinson's 'One dignity delays for all.'" *Explicator*, XXIII (Oct. 1964), Item 16.
Noted in Robbins, *ALS, 1964* (6.851), p. 135.

6.323 Everett, Barbara. *Critical Quarterly*, I (Summer 1959), 159-60, 162.
Rev. of *Selected Poems*, 1959 (3.202).

6.324 *The Explicator*, Editors of. "Dickinson's 'These are the days when Birds come back.'" *Explicator*, II (Feb. 1944), Item 29.
Reprinted:
Davis, *14 by ED* (5.23), pp. 2-3.
In a rejoinder to this article (6.1034), Marshall Van Deusen refers to its author as George Arms, one of the editors of *The Explicator*.

6.325 F., J. F. "The Bookshelf." *Woman's Journal* [N.Y.], n.s. XV, No. 8 (August 1930), p. 24.
Rev. of Bianchi, *Life and Letters* (4.36).

6.326 Fadiman, Clifton. "Party of One." *Holiday*, XVI (Sept. 1954), 6, 8-9.
Briefly recounts ED's "freakish post-mortem success story."

6.327 Fain, John Tyree. "The 'New Poems' of Emily Dickinson." *Modern Language Notes*, LXVIII (Feb. 1953), 112-13.
Poems may be quarried from her "prose" letters.

6.328 Fairbank, J. Wilder. "Mysterious Emily Dickinson." *Boston Herald*, July 6, 1930, p. 10.
In a letter to the editor, the author replies to a review (see 6.1105) of Pollitt, *Human Background* (5.61) and defends Helen Hunt's love for her husband.

6.329 Faris, Paul. "Dickinson's 'The Soul selects her own Society.'" *Explicator*, XXV (April 1967), Item 65.

6.330 ——. "Eroticism in Emily Dickinson's 'Wild Nights.'" *New England Quarterly*, XL (June 1967), 269-274.
Argues that "Wild Nights — Wild Nights!" is a poem of despair rather than sexuality.

6.331 Farrell, James T. "The Book of the Day. With Some Thoughts on Cultism, Giggling and Guessing Games." *New York Sun*, Dec. 12, 1932, p. 25.
Rev. of Bianchi, *Face to Face* (4.59).

6.332 Farrelly, John. "Emily Dickinson." *Scrutiny*, XIX (Oct. 1952), 76-78.
Rev. of Chase, *ED* (5.17).

6.333 Fasel, Ida. "'Called Back': A Note on Emily Dickinson." *Iowa English Yearbook*, No. 8 (Fall 1963), p. 73.
Notes similarities between ED and the heroine of Hugh Conway's novel, *Called Back*.

6.334   Fasel, Ida. "Emily Dickinson's Walden." *Iowa English Yearbook*, No. 7 (Fall 1962), pp. 22-28.
ED's seclusion was probably influenced by Thoreau's *Walden*.

6.335   Fausset, H. I'A. *Manchester Guardian*, Feb. 26, 1952, p. 4.
Rev. of *Letters*, 1951 (4.80).

6.336   Feidelson, Charles. *Modern Language Notes*, LXXVI (Dec. 1961), 908-10.
Rev. of Anderson, *Stairway of Surprise* (5.2).

6.337   Ferguson, J. DeLancey. "All Evidence In, She Remains an Enigma." *New York Herald Tribune Books*, XXXIV, No. 49 (July 13, 1958), p. 3.
Rev. of *Letters*, 1958 (4.90).

6.338   ———. "Emily Dickinson: All of Her Poems and Most of Her Life." *New York Herald Tribune Books*, XXXVII, No. 17 (Nov. 27, 1960), p. 26.
Rev. of *Complete Poems*, 1960 (3.207) and Leyda, *Years and Hours* (5.49).

6.339   ———. "Emily Dickinson as the Family Saw Her." *New York Herald Tribune Books*, XXXI, No. 42 (May 29, 1955), p. 3.
Rev. of Bingham, *ED's Home* (4.86).

6.340   ———. "Emily Dickinson With Her Poems as She Wrote Them." *New York Herald Tribune Books*, XXXII, No. 7 (Sept. 25, 1955), p. 10.
Rev. of *Poems*, 1955 (3.197).

6.341   ———. "Her Disorder Is Her Own." *New York Times Book Review*, Nov. 17, 1963, p. 67.
Rev. of Sewall, *Critical Essays* (5.75).

6.341a   ———. "Highlights in the Scholarly Journals." Clipping dated June 2, 1934, from an unidentified newspaper in the Beinecke Library, Yale Univ.
Notes an article by George F. Whicher, "Emily Dickinson's Earliest Friend" (6.1127).

6.342   ———. "Landscapes of a New England Poet's Mind." *New York Herald Tribune Books*, XXVIII, No. 20 (Dec. 30, 1951), p. 4.
Rev. of Chase, *ED* (5.17).

6.343   ———. "A New and Thoughtful Reading of Emily Dickinson." *New York Herald Tribune Books*, XXXVII, No. 2 (Aug. 14, 1960), p. 1.
Rev. of Anderson, *Stairway of Surprise* (5.2).

6.344   ———. "A New England Poet's Life: Mystery and Meaning." *New York Herald Tribune Books*, XXXII, No. 14 — Part I (Nov. 13, 1955), p. 11.
Rev. of Johnson, *Interpretive Biography* (5.44).

6.345   ———. "Yet One More Emily Dickinson Mystery." *New York Herald Tribune Books*, XXXI, No. 14 — Part I (Nov. 14, 1954), p. 6.
Rev. of Bingham, *Revelation* (5.9).

6.346   Fern, Dale Edward. "Knowing How and Learning How." *The Living Church*, CXXI, No. 13 (Sept. 24, 1950), pp. 16-17.
Compares ED and T.S. Eliot.

6.346a Field, Eugene. "Sharps and Flats," *Chicago Daily News* [Morning Edition], 1891?
        A brief note on ED mentioning some of her alleged peculiarities. A clipping of this item in the Jones Library, Amherst, is erroneously dated by hand May 3, 1891. My search of Field's column, "Sharps and Flats," was unable to locate the reference in issues of the *News* published within a few months of May 1891.

6.346b Field, Louise Maunsell. "Biography Boom." *North American Review,* CCXXX (Oct. 30, 1930), 438-39.
        Rev. of Taggard, *Life and Mind* (5.81).

6.347   Field, Walter Taylor. "Another Glimpse of Emily Dickinson." *Amherst Graduates' Quarterly,* XXIV (Nov. 1934), 44-45.

6.348   Fields, Kenneth. *Southern Review,* n.s. II (Autumn 1966), 971-72.
        Rev. of Gelpi, *Mind of the Poet* (5.29).

6.349   Finch, John. "Poet of the Thing Missed." *Smith College Monthly,* II (Nov. 1941), 10, 27.
        On the theme of deprivation in ED's poetry.

6.350   Finch, Wallace H. "The Poetry of Emily Dickinson." *Religion In Life,* II (Spring 1933), 194-202.
        A general introduction and appreciation.

6.351   Fish, Kenneth E., Jr. *The Case for Poetry,* ed. Frederick L. Gwynn, Ralph W. Condee, and Arthur O. Lewis, Jr. See 6.430.
        Mr. Fish writes an explication of "A Route of Evanescence" especially for inclusion in the second (1965) edition of this anthology, p. 94.

6.351a Fisk[e], Fidelia. *Recollections of Mary Lyon, with Selections from Her Instructions to the Pupils in Mount Holyoke Female Seminary.* Boston: American Tract Society, 1866.
        Publishes a number of Miss Lyon's chapel talks and "afternoon exercises." In one, she is quoted as saying, "Economy should be strict, and based on principle. It should extend to the smallest things" (p. 239).

6.352   Fitts, Dudley. *Saturday Review,* XLII (July 25, 1959), 14.
        Rev. of *Selected Poems,* 1959 (3.202).

6.352a Flaccus, Kimball. "Lyric Telegrams." *Voices,* No. 86 (Summer 1936), 49-50.
        Rev. of *Unpublished Poems,* 1935 (3.167).

6.353   Fletcher, John Gould. "The Ablative Estate." *Sewanee Review,* LIII (Oct.-Dec. 1945), 661-70.
        Rev. of *Bolts of Melody,* 1945 (3.177) and Bingham, *Ancestors' Brocades* (5.5).

6.354   ———. "Woman and Poet." *Saturday Review,* I (Aug. 30, 1924), 77-78.
        Rev. of *Complete Poems,* 1924 (3.123) and Bianchi, *Life and Letters* (4.36).

6.355   Fletcher, Robert S., and Malcolm O. Young. *Amherst College Biographical Record of the Graduates and Non-Graduates 1821-1921.* Centennial Edition. Amherst, Mass.: Amherst College, 1927 (rev. 1939, 1963).

6.356   Fletcher, William I. "The Amherst Dickinsons and the College."
          Amherst Graduates' Quarterly, VI (May 1917), 179-85.
          Summarizes the careers of ED's grandfather, father, brother,
          and nephew.

6.357   ———. "A Gifted Family," *Critic*, XXIX (May 28, 1898), 359.
          The death of Edward Dickinson prompts this tribute to the
          Dickinson family. Brief mention of ED.

6.358   Flores, Kate. "Dickinson's 'I started Early — Took my Dog.'"
          Explicator, IX (May 1951), Item 47.
          Reprinted:
          Davis, *14 by ED* (5.23), 87-88.

6.359   Fodaski, Martha. "Dickinson's ''Twas like a Maelstrom.'" *Ex-
          plicator*, XIX (Jan. 1961), Item 24.

6.360   Foerster, Norman. "Later Poets: Emily Dickinson" in *Cam-
          bridge History of American Literature*, ed. W.P. Trent, S.P.
          Sherman, and C. Van Doren. N.Y.: Macmillan, 1921 (1936),
          III, 31-34.
          Reprinted:
          Blake and Wells, *Recognition* (5.13), pp. 94-97.

6.360a   Ford, Mrs. Gordon Lester (nee Emily Ellsworth Fowler). Recol-
          lection of ED in Leyda, *Years and Hours*, (5.49), II, 478.

6.361   Ford, Lillian C. "Emily Dickinson Unveiled." *Los Angeles
          Times*, June 22, 1930.
          Rev. of Taggard, *Life and Mind* (5.81).

6.362   Ford, Thomas W[ellborn]. "Emily Dickinson and the Civil War."
          University of Kansas City Review, XXXI (Mar. 1965), 199-203.
          The Civil War heightened ED's awareness of death. Rev. by
          Robbins, *ALS, 1965* (6.851), pp. 158-59.

6.363   ———. "Emily Dickinson and Death." *Midwest Quarterly*, IV
          (Autumn 1962), 33-44.
          Considers death as the major motivating force behind ED's
          creativity. See 5.27.

6.364   Forrester, Richard Merryfield. "Emily of Amherst." *Yankee*,
          XII (Aug. 1948), 32-33, 41, 64-67.
          Reviews the theories concerning ED's "romance."

6.365   Françon, Marcel. *Books Abroad*, XXXII (Spring 1958), 216-17.
          Rev. of Errante, ed., *Poesie*, 1956 (8.3).

6.366   Fredeman, William E. *Books Abroad*, XXX (Autumn 1956), 444.
          Rev. of Johnson, *Interpretive Biography* (5.44).

6.367   French, Reginald F. "Foreword" to *Emily Dickinson: Three
          Views* (5.52), pp. 7-9.

6.368   French, Yvonne. "Chronicles: Poetry." *London Mercury*, XXIX
          (Dec. 1933), 161-63.
          Rev. of *Complete Poems*, 1933 (3.158).

6.369   Friar, Kimon, and John Malcolm Brinnin, eds. *Modern Poetry,
          American and British*. N.Y.: Appleton, Century, Crofts, 1951.
          Explication of "Wonder — is not precisely Knowing," pp. 456-
          57.
          For a reply, see 6.762.

6.370   Friedlaender, V. H. "Emily Dickinson." *Country Life* [London],
          LXVI (Oct. 26, 1929), 565.

Rev. of *Further Poems*, 1929 (3.138).

6.371 Friedman, Norman, and Charles A. McLaughlin. *Poetry: An Introduction to Its Form and Art.* N.Y.: Harper, 1961, rev. ed. 1963, pp. 47-48, 75-76 *passim.*
A college text; contains an explication of "To lose one's faith — surpass."

6.372 Friedrich, Gerhard. "Dickinson's 'I heard a Fly buzz — when I died.'" *Explicator*, XIII (April 1955), Item 35.
Reprinted:
Davis, *14 by ED* (5.23), pp. 65-67.

6.373 Frohock, Wilbur Merrill. "Emily Dickinson: God's Little Girl" in *Strangers to This Ground: Cultural Diversity in Contemporary American Writing.* Dallas, Texas: Southern Methodist Univ. Press, 1961, pp. 98-110.
Discusses ED's isolation and her use of "masks," especially the *persona* of a child.

6.374 Frump, Timothy. "Emily Dickinson: A Song." *Notes and Queries*, CLXV (Dec. 2, 1933), 386.
Notes a 1913 musical setting for "I'll tell you how the Sun rose."

6.375 Frye, [Herman] Northrup. "Emily Dickinson" in *Major Writers of America*, ed. Perry Miller, *et. al.*, 2 vols. N.Y.: Harcourt, Brace, 1962, II, 4-16.
Reprinted:
Northrup Frye. *Fables of Identity; Studies in Poetic Mythology.* N.Y.: Harcourt, Brace, 1963, pp. 193-217.
A wide-ranging biographical and critical introduction.

6.376 Fussell, Edwin. *American Literature,* XXXIII (May 1961), 234-35.
Rev. of Anderson, *Stairway of Surprise* (5.2).

6.377 ———. "The Meter-Making Argument" in *Aspects of American Poetry, Essays Presented to Howard Mumford Jones,* ed. Richard M. Ludwig. Columbus: Ohio State Univ. Press, 1962, p. 22.
Alludes to ED in a discussion of metrical dissonance in American poetry.

6.378 G. "A Connecticut Valley Poet." *Homestead* [Springfield, Mass.], XVI (Oct. 6, 1894), 11.

6.379 G., C. *American Literature,* XXXIII (Mar. 1961), 104.
Rev. of *Complete Poems*, 1960 (3.207) and Leyda, *Years and Hours* (5.49). The review may be attributed to Clarence L. Gohdes.

6.380 ———. *San Francisco Sunday Chronicle "This World" Magazine,* Dec. 18, 1960, p. 21.
Rev. of *Complete Poems*, 1960 (3.207).

6.381 G., H. "Editing Emily." *Politics and Letters,* I (Winter-Spring 1947), 123-24.
Rev. of *Bolts of Melody*, 1947 (3.182) and *Poems*, 1947 (3.183).

6.382 G., J. R. "Dickinson's 'I dreaded that first Robin, so.'" *Explicator,* V (Oct. 1946), Query 3.

6.383 ———. "Dickinson's 'I'll tell you how the Sun rose.'" *Explicator,* V (Feb. 1947), Query 12.

6.384   G., W. M. "Identity of Emily Dickinson's Friend." *Springfield
          Sunday Union and Republican,* May 20, 1934, p. 7-E.
          Discusses two articles by Prof. George Whicher of Amherst
          College; see 6.1119 and 6.1127.

6.385   ——. "Whicher Writes Essay on Emily Dickinson." *Amherst
          Record,* May 9, 1934, p. 9.
          Notes the publication of two articles by Prof. George Whicher;
          see 6.1119 and 6.1127.

6.386   Galloway, David D. "The Perils of Emily." *Spectator* [London],
          CCXIII (Dec. 11, 1964), 820.
          Rev. of Blake and Wells, *Recognition* (5.13).

6.387   Gannett, Lewis. "Emily Dickinson." *New York Herald Tribune,*
          Dec. 5, 1932, p. 11.
          Rev. of Bianchi, *Face to Face* (4.59).

6.388   ——. "Emily Dickinson Mysteries." *New York Herald Tribune,*
          Feb. 7, 1936, p. 13.
          Rev. of *Unpublished Poems,* 1935 (3.167).

6.389   ——. "Emily Dickinson's 'Sweet Christmas.'" *New York Her-
          ald Tribune,* Dec. 25, 1931, p. 23.
          Quotes ED's statements on Christmas from her letters.

6.390   ——. "A Glimpse of Emily Dickinson." *New York Herald Tri-
          bune,* Jan. 27, 1934, p. 9.
          Quotes a reminiscence of ED from J. W. Burgess, *Reminis-
          cences of an American Scholar* (6.159).

6.391   ——. *New York Herald Tribune,* Nov. 4, 1931, p. 21.
          Rev. of *Letters,* 1931 (4.52).

6.392   ——. *New York Herald Tribune,* Nov. 1, 1938, p. 19.
          Rev. of Whicher, *This Was a Poet* (5.104).

6.393   ——. *New York Herald Tribune,* April 5, 1945, p. 19.
          Rev. of *Bolts of Melody,* 1945 (3.177) and Bingham, *Ancestors'
          Brocades* (5.5).

6.394   Gardner, Maude. "Two Famous Girls of Amherst, Mass." *Ave
          Maria* [Notre Dame, Ind.], XXXVI (Oct. 29, 1932), 561-63.
          On ED and Helen Hunt Jackson.

6.394a   Garland, Hamlin. *Companions on the Trail; A Literary Chroni-
          cle.* N.Y.: Macmillan, 1931, p. 121.
          An account of an imaginary meeting with ED in the form of a
          diary entry (dated Jan. 30, 1902): "To-day at Stedman's I met
          Emily Dickinson, a tall, slender, graceful creature in a very
          smart gown. She turned out to be a long time acquaintance of
          Richard Burton, and on the basis of this mutual friendship we
          reached an almost instant understanding. She professed to
          like some of my writing and I could honestly reciprocate. I
          admire her singularly concise verse. Her work is related to
          Emerson, but must not be counted a poor relation." Comment
          complete.

6.395   Garlington, Jack. "Emily Dickinson's Curious Biographers."
          Colorado Quarterly, VI (Autumn 1957), 170-77.
          Reviews theories advanced by ED's biographers concerning
          the identity of her "lover."

6.396   Garrow, A. Scott. "A Note on Manzanilla." *American Litera-
         ture,* XXXV (Nov. 1963), 366.
         Discusses the possible reference of "Manzanilla" in "I taste a
         liquor never brewed." Rev. by Robbins, *ALS, 1963* (6.851),
         p. 128.
6.397   Gelpi, Albert J. *American Literature,* XXXIX (Jan. 1968), 569-
         71.
         Rev. of Higgins, *Portrait of ED* (5.34).
6.398   Georges, Justine Flint. *New Hampshire Profiles,* I (Mar. 1952),
         56.
         Rev. of Patterson, *Riddle* (5.55).
6.399   Gibson, Walter. "Amherst Authors." *Amherst Alumni News,*
         VII, No. 3 (Jan. 1955), p. 31.
         Rev. of Bingham, *Revelation* (5.9).
6.400   Gibson, Wilfrid. "Dabbling in the Dark." *London Mercury,*
         XXXIX (Dec. 1938), 231-32.
         Rev. of Whicher, *This Was a Poet* (5.104).
6.401   Gilchrist, Beth Bradford. *The Life of Mary Lyon.* Boston:
         Houghton, Mifflin, 1910.
         A biography of ED's teacher and founder of Mount Holyoke Fe-
         male Seminary. See also 6.493.
6.402   Gipson, Richard M. "Emily Dickinson's Furniture Portrayed for
         First Time." *New York Sun,* May 16, 1936, p. 30.
         Discusses the Hallet & Davis piano that ED used. Illustrated.
6.403   Gleason, Madeline. "Emily's Love of Words." *Christian Science
         Monitor,* Mar. 24, 1943, p. 9.
         ED's love for words led to her frequent use of the pathetic
         fallacy.
6.404   Glenn, Eunice. "Emily Dickinson's Poetry: A Revaluation."
         Sewanee Review, LI (Oct.-Dec. 1943), 574-88.
         Excerpt reprinted:
         Davis, *14 by ED* (5.23), pp. 107-09.
         Discussion of ED as a metaphysical poet.
6.405   Goffin, Robert. "Emily Dickinson." *New Hungarian Quarterly*
         [N.Y.], V (Autumn 1964), 181-86.
         Notes similarities between ED and the French Symbolists.
         Includes explications.
6.406   Gohdes, Clarence L. "New Voices in Verse" in *Literature of the
         American People, An Historical and Critical Survey,* ed. Ar-
         thur Hobson Quinn. N.Y.: Appleton, 1951, pp. 729-36.
         A general introduction to ED's life and poetry.
6.407   ———. *South Atlantic Quarterly,* LI (April 1937), 335-36.
         Rev. of Patterson, *Riddle* (5.55).
6.407a   Golden, Samuel A. *Frederick Goddard Tuckerman.* N.Y.:
         Twayne, 1966, pp. 140-41, 151-52, *passim.*
         Compares ED and Tuckerman.
6.408   Goldsmith, Joseph Hannele. "Inspired, Half-Educated, Puritan,
         and Feminine." *Partisan Review,* XII (Summer 1945), 402-04.
         Rev. of *Bolts of Melody,* 1945 (3.177).
6.409   Gorman, Herbert Sherman. "Emily Dickinson" in *The Proces-
         sion of Masks.* Boston: B.J. Brimmer, 1923, pp. 43-54.

Discusses aspects of ED's use of language: exactness, abrupt-
ness, and concentration of meaning.

6.410   Gorman, Herbert Sherman. "Life and Letters of a Gentle New
England Poet." *New York Times Book Review*, XXIX, No. 14
(April 13, 1924), p. 7.
Rev. of Bianchi, *Life and Letters* (4.36).

6.411   Graham, Bessie. "Emily Dickinson" in *Bookman's Manual*. N.Y.:
R.R. Bowker, 1924, pp. 172-73.
Notes the popularity of ED's poems.

6.412   Grant, Douglas. "The American Lyric" in *Purpose and Place,
Essays on American Writers*. N.Y.: St. Martin's Press,
1965, pp. 99-111.
Places ED in the lyric tradition of American poetry, pp. 105-
107. In finding in nature symbols, not emblems, she builds
upon the principles of her New England poet-predecessors.

6.413   [———]. "The Woman in White." *Times* [London] *Literary Sup-
plement*, No. 3094 (June 16, 1961), p. 372.
Reprinted:
Douglas Grant. "Emily Dickinson: The Woman in White" in
Purpose and Place. N.Y.: St. Martin's Press, 1965, pp.
92-98.
This essay reviews Leyda, *Years and Hours* (5.49), and dis-
cusses ED's preoccupation with death and renunciation.

6.414   Grasberger, George. "What Is So Rare." *Philadelphia Inquirer
Magazine*, Nov. 20, 1949, p. 41.

6.415   Grattan, C. Hartley. "Emily Dickinson: Her Life, Mind, Poems
and Lovers." *New York World*, Aug. 10, 1930, p. 5-M.
Rev. of Pollitt, *Human Background* (5.61), Jenkins, *Friend
and Neighbor* (5.35), Taggard, *Life and Mind* (5.81), Bianchi,
Life and Letters (4.36), and Hampson, *ED: A Bibliography*
(1.6).

6.416   ———. "Wanted: Unemployed Writers to Study American Literary Problems." *Bookman* [N.Y.], LXXIII (Mar. 1931), 48-55.
Mentions ED (p. 53) as one writer whose "mystery is as much
a mystery as ever and there is still room for a good detective
to exercise his talents."

6.417   Graves, Gertrude Montague. "A Cousin's Memories of Emily
Dickinson." *Boston Sunday Globe*, Jan. 12, 1930, p. 41.
Excerpt reprinted:
Letters, 1958 (4.90), II, 589-90.
Leyda, *Years and Hours* (5.49), II, 275-76.
A reminiscence.

6.418   Graves, Louise B. "The Likeness of Emily Dickinson." *Harvard
Library Bulletin*, I (Spring 1947), 248-51.
Discusses seven attempts by artists to convey in picture the
poet's elusive charm.

6.419   Green, Clara Bellinger. "Emily Dickinson. Further Thoughts on
Her Further Poems." *Boston Evening Transcript*, Book Sec-
tion, July 13, 1929, p. 3.
Rev. of *Further Poems*, 1929 (3.138). Answered by Alfred
Leete Hampson; see 6.438.

6.420   Green, Clara Bellinger. "Further Poems of Emily Dickinson."
         Outlook and Independent, CLI (Mar. 27, 1929), 504-05.
         Rev. of *Further Poems,* 1929 (3.138). See also 6.767.

6.420a   ———. "The Lover of Emily." *Boston Herald,* Sept. 27, 1930,
         p. 13.
         Rev. of Jenkins, *Friend and Neighbor* (5.35).

6.421   ———. "A Reminiscence of Emily Dickinson." *Bookman* [N.Y.],
         LX (Nov. 1924), 291-93.
         A personal reminiscence in the context of a review of Bianchi,
         Life and Letters (4.36). The author recalls, as a young girl,
         singing for ED; see *Letters,* 1958 (4.90), II, 599-600.

6.422   Greever, Garland. *Personalist,* XXXIII (Spring 1952), 215.
         Rev. of *Letters to Holland,* 1951 (4.76).

6.423   ———. *Personalist,* XXXVII (Autumn 1956), 421-24.
         Rev. of Bingham, *ED's Home* (4.86).

6.424   Gregory, Horace. "The Real Emily Dickinson." *Commonweal,*
         LXVIII (Aug. 1, 1958), 449-50.
         Rev. of *Letters,* 1958 (4.90).

6.425   ———. "The Real Emily Dickinson." *New Freeman,* II (Nov. 12,
         1930), 212-13.
         Rev. of Taggard, *Life and Mind* (5.81).

6.426   Griffith, Clark. "Emily and 'Him': A Modern Approach to Emily
         Dickinson's Love Poetry." *Iowa English Yearbook,* No. 6 (Fall
         1961), pp. 13-22.
         Dread of the possessive male can be seen throughout ED's
         poetry. See also Griffith, *Long Shadow* (5.31), especially pp.
         149-84.

6.427   ———. "Emily Dickinson's Love Poetry." *University of Kansas
         City Review,* XXVII (Dec. 1960), 93-100.
         Excerpt reprinted:
         Davis, *14 by ED* (5.23), pp. 44-45.
         Dread of generalized masculinity is the real subject of ED's
         love poetry.

6.428   ———. *New England Quarterly,* XXXVIII (Sept. 1965), pp. 405-07.
         Rev. of Rosenbaum, *A Concordance* (2.3).

6.428a   Gross, Harvey. *Sound and Form in Modern Poetry.* Ann Arbor:
         Univ. of Michigan Press, 1964, pp. 15-16.
         Discusses the rhythmic structure of "After great pain, a for-
         mal feeling comes."

6.428b   Gross, Theodore L. *Yale Review,* LVII (Summer 1968), 619.
         Rev. of Sherwood, *Circumference* (5.79).

6.429   Guitar, Mary Anne, and Constance Urdang. "Baroque — 1941."
         Smith College Monthly, II, No. 2 (Nov. 1941), p. 12.
         On ED's home.

6.430   Gwynn, Frederick L., Ralph W. Condee, and Arthur D. Lewis,
         Jr., eds. *The Case for Poetry.* Englewood Cliffs, N.J.:
         Prentice-Hall, 1954, pp. 105-06, 109; 2nd ed., 1965, pp. 90-94.
         Reprints explications by various authors of "Because I could
         not stop for Death" and "A Route of Evanescence." See also
         6.351.

6.431   H., A. C. "Illuminating View of Family of Illustrious Woman
          Poet." *Savannah* [Ga.] *Morning News*, May 29, 1955, p. 56.
6.432   H., A. R. "Poet, Mystic, Martyr." *Christian Register,* CVIII
          (May 2, 1929), 370-371.
          Rev. of *Further Poems,* 1929 (3.138).
6.432a   H., C. *New York Sun,* April 4, 1945, p. 20.
          Rev. of *Bolts of Melody,* 1945 (3.177).
6.433   H., R. *New England Quarterly,* VI (June 1933), 417.
          Rev. of Bianchi, *Face to Face* (4.59).
6.434   Hackett, Francis. *New York Times,* April 5, 1945, p. 21.
          Reprinted:
          Francis Hackett. On *Judging Books, In General and In Partic-
          ular.* N.Y.: Day, 1947, pp. 226-28.
          Rev. of *Bolts of Melody,* 1945 (3.177) and Bingham, *Ancestors'
          Brocades* (5.5).
6.435   Halleck, Reuben Post. *History of American Literature.* N.Y.:
          American Book Co., 1911.
          ED is mentioned in this history only as an "author of unique
          short lyrics," p. 404.
6.436   ——. "Emily Dickinson, 1830-1886." *The Romance of Ameri-
          can Literature.* N.Y.: American Book Co., 1934, pp. 257-63.
          A biographical and critical introduction.
6.437   Hammond, William Gardiner. *Remembrance of Amherst: An
          Undergraduate's Diary, 1846-1848,* ed. George F. Whicher.
          N.Y.: Columbia Univ. Press, 1946.
          Although ED is not mentioned in it, Hammond's diary (as
          Whicher says) "well serves to convey an idea of the college
          town where her mind took shape."
6.438   Hampson, Alfred Leete. "Emily Dickinson: Evidence of the Au-
          thenticity of Her *Further Poems." Boston Evening Transcript,*
          Book Section, Aug. 3, 1929, p. 3.
          Replies to a review by Clara Bellinger Green, see 6.419.
6.438a   Haney, John Louis. *The Story of Our Literature: An Interpreta-
          tion of the American Spirit.* N.Y.: Scribner's, 1923, pp. 210-
          11.
          Briefly praises ED's charm, emotional intensity, and unusual
          insight.
6.439   Hansen, Harry. "Emily Dickinson — 1930." *New York World,*
          Dec. 10, 1930, p. 9.
          Rev. of *Poems,* 1930 (3.151).
6.440   ——. "The First Reader." *New York World,* June 20, 1930, p.
          12.
          Rev. of Taggard, *Life and Mind* (5.81).
6.441   ——. *Harper's Magazine* CLXI (Aug. 1930), among front ad-
          vertising pages.
          Rev. of Taggard, *Life and Mind* (5.81).
6.442   Hansen, Waldemar. "Land Ho! Infinity! Emily Dickinson As a
          Protestant Telescope." *Horizon,* XVII (Jan. 1948), 71-76.
          Rev. of *Bolts of Melody,* 1947 (3.182) and *Poems,* 1947 (3.183).
6.443   Haraszti, Zoltan. "An Emily Dickinson Collection." *Boston
          Evening Transcript,* Book Section, Dec. 8, 1923, p. 6.

Describes and comments on Higginson's collection of ED
manuscripts exhibited at the Boston Public Library.

6.444   Harding, Walter. "'Dazzling Snapshots of the Human Spirit.'"
Chicago Sunday Tribune Magazine of Books, May 6, 1951, p. 5.
Rev. of *Letters to Holland,* 1951 (4.76).

6.445   ——. "Dickinson's Letters Found Rewarding." *Richmond* [Va.]
News Leader, June 11, 1955, p. 8.

6.446   ——. "A Literary Accomplishment." *Chicago Sunday Tribune
Magazine of Books,* Sept. 25, 1955, p. 3.
Rev. of *Poems,* 1955 (3.197).

6.447   ——. "On Poets and Poetry: Collected Data and Collections of
Verse." *Chicago Sunday Tribune Magazine of Books,* Nov. 13,
1960, p. 10.
Rev. of *Complete Poems,* 1960 (3.207) and Leyda, *Years and
Hours* (5.49).

6.448   ——. "Overdue Dickinson Critique." *Chicago Sunday Tribune
Magazine of Books,* July 31, 1960, p. 2.
Rev. of Anderson, *Stairway of Surprise* (5.2).

6.449   Hardy, Warren F. "As I View the Thing." *Decatur* [Ill.] *Herald,*
July 13, 1930, p. 6.
Reprinted:
Amherst Record, Jan. 9, 1935, p. 2.
Describes a visit to ED's home and a conversation with Mme.
Bianchi. Briefly reviews Taggard, *Life and Mind* (5.81), Pol-
litt, *Human Background* (5.61), and Jenkins, *Friend and Neigh-
bor* (5.35).

6.450   Harris, George. "Newly Found Poems by Emily Dickinson Are
Intimate Lyrics." *Richmond* [Va.] *Times-Dispatch,* Mar. 31,
1929, p. 16.
Rev. of *Further Poems,* 1929 (3.138).

6.451   ——. "A Niece's Biography of Emily Dickinson." *Richmond*
[Va.] *Times-Dispatch,* Jan. 18, 1931.
Rev. of 1930 reissue of Bianchi, *Life and Letters* (4.36).

6.452   Harris, Sarah B. "Emily Dickinson." *The Courier* [Lincoln,
Neb.], X, No. 16 (April 6, 1895), p. 3.
A brief appreciation emphasizing the poet's seclusion.

6.453   Hartley, Marsden. "Emily Dickinson." *Dial,* LXV (Aug. 15,
1918), 95-97.
Revised and reprinted:
Marsden Hartley. *Adventures in the Arts.* N.Y.: Boni &
Liveright, 1921, pp. 198-206.
An impressionistic appreciation. For a note on Hartley's in-
debtedness to ED, see Burlingame, 6.159a; McBride, 6.674c;
Merideth, 6.694a.

6.454   Hasley, Lois. "Meteors in December." *CEA Critic,* XIII, No. 8
(Nov. 1951), pp. 7-8.
Describes an imaginary, posthumous visit to ED.

6.455   Hastings, William T[hompson]. *Syllabus of American Literature.*
Chicago: Univ. of Chicago Press, 1923, p. 77.
Describes ED as a cloistered poet who composed "whimsical

meditations on life in brief poems of startling and naïve originality, vivid, pungent, subtle, and imaginative...."

6.456   Hawkins, Desmond. "Emily Dickinson." *New Statesman and Nation*, XVII (May 13, 1939), 752.
Rev. of Whicher, *This Was a Poet* (5.104).

6.457   Heath, Monroe. "Emily Dickinson" in *Great Americans At a
Glance: Authors*, Vol. III. Redwood City, Calif.: Pacific
Coast Publishers, 1956, p. 19.
Reprinted:
Monroe Heath. *Great Americans At a Glance: Wor.en*, Vol.
IV. Menlo Park, Calif.: Pacific Coast Publishers, 1957, p.
17.

6.458   Herbert, T. Walter. "Near-rimes and Para-phones." *Sewanee
Review*, XLV (Oct.-Dec. 1937), 433-52.
Includes ED in a discussion of types of near-rhymes, pp. 446-
49.

6.458a Herron, Ima Honaker. "A Tough-Minded Craftsman." *CEA
Critic*, XXXI (Nov. 1968), 15.
Rev. of Miller, *Poetry of ED* (5.54).

6.459   Hewlett, Horace W. "'This Was a Poet' — Emily Dickinson," in
In Other Words — Amherst in Prose and Poetry, ed. Horace
W. Hewlett. Amherst, Mass.: Amherst College Press, 1964,
pp. 123-46.
Reprints two articles by George F. Whicher (6.1125, 6.1141)
and an article and a poem by Richard Wilbur (6.1174, 18.136).

6.460   Hiatt, David. "Dickinson's 'Of Bronze — and Blaze.'" *Explicator*,
XXI (Sept. 1962), Item 6.

6.461   Hicks, Granville. "Emily Dickinson" in *The Great Tradition, An
Interpretation of American Literature Since the Civil War*.
N.Y.: Macmillan, 1933 (rev. ed. 1935), pp. 124-30.
Reprinted:
Blake and Wells, *Recognition* (5.13), pp. 167-72.
This introduction to ED's life and poetry describes her as a
"fugitive" from the settled orthodoxy of Amherst.

6.462   ——. "The Mind of Emily Dickinson." *Nation*, CXXX (Mar. 19,
1930), 329.
Rev. of Bianchi, *Life and Letters* (4.36) and Pollitt, *Human
Background* (5.61).

6.463   ——. "Mystery and Mystification." *Nation*, CXXX (June 25,
1930), 735-36.
Rev. of Taggard, *Life and Mind* (5.81).

6.464   ——. "The Mystic and Bizarre Emily." *Nation*, CXXXIV (Jan.
27, 1932), 119.
Rev. of *Letters*, 1931 (4.52).

6.465   ——. *New York World*, Mar. 24, 1929, p. 10-M.
Rev. of *Further Poems*, 1929 (3.138).

6.466   ——. "Recluse and Rebel." *Saturday Review*, XLIII, No. 44
(Oct. 29, 1960), p. 16.
Rev. of *Complete Poems*, 1960 (3.207); Anderson, *Stairway of
Surprise* (5.2); and Leyda, *Years and Hours* (5.49).

6.467   ——. *Saturday Review*, XLV (June 23, 1962), 26.

Rev. of Ward, *Capsule of the Mind* (5.97).

6.468   Higgins, Davis J. M. *American Literature*, XXXVIII (Jan. 1967), 567-68.

Rev. of Porter, *Early Poetry* (5.69).

6.469   ———. "Emily Dickinson's Prose" in Sewall, *Critical Essays* (5.62), pp. 162-67.

Reprinted as the introductory chapter to the author's *ED: The Poet and Her Prose* (5.34), pp. 3-24.

Describes the singularity of ED's prose style.

6.470   ———. "In Praise of Emily." *Saturday Review*, XXXVI (May 30, 1953), 21.

Defends ED's craftsmanship in a reply to Burges Johnson; see 6.540.

6.471   ———. "Twenty-five Poems by Emily Dickinson: Unpublished Variant Versions." *American Literature*, XXXVIII (Mar. 1966), 1-21.

Comment on some unpublished variants; see 3.211.

6.472   Higginson, Mary Thacher. *Thomas Wentworth Higginson: The Story of His Life*. Boston: Houghton Mifflin, 1914, pp. 312-13, 368-69.

Discusses Higginson's acquaintance with ED and his role as her literary executor. Includes the first printing of Higginson's account in his diary of ED's funeral.

6.473   Higginson, Thomas Wentworth. "Emily Dickinson's Letters." *Atlantic Monthly*, LXVIII (Oct. 1891), 444-56.

Revised and reprinted:

T. W. Higginson, *Carlyle's Laugh, and Other Surprises*. Boston: Houghton, Mifflin, 1909, pp. 249-83.

Reprinted:

Atlantic Monthly Jubilee: One Hundred Years of the Atlantic, ed. Edward Weeks and Emily Flint. Boston: Little, Brown, 1957, pp. 184-99.

Reprinted, slightly abridged:

Selected Poems and Letters of Emily Dickinson, 1959, ed. Linscott (3.205), pp. 5-24.

Higginson recounts the history of his friendship with ED and prints, for the first time, seventeen poems and about twenty letters. For a recording of excerpts from this article, see 20.4.

Reviewed:

Abbott (6.6)	Whiting (6.1170)
Bates (6.75)	Wingate (6.1194)
Edwards (6.310)	

Unsigned reviews:

6.473a   *Independent*, XLIII (Sept. 10, 1891), 1355.
6.473b   *Independent*, XLIII (Sept. 24, 1891), 1421.
6.473c   *Review of Reviews* [N.Y.], IV (Nov. 1891), 459.
6.473d   *Springfield Sunday Republican*, Sept. 27, 1891, p. 6.

6.473e   ———. "Helen Jackson ('H.H.')" in *Contemporaries*. Boston: Houghton Mifflin, 1900, p. 162.

"The poetry of Mrs. [Helen Hunt] Jackson unquestionably takes

rank above that of any American woman, and its only rival
would be found, curiously enough, in that of her early school-
mate, Emily Dickinson." Comment complete.

6.474   Higginson, Thomas Wentworth. "Letter to a Young Contributor."
Atlantic Monthly, IX (April 1862), 401-11.
Reprinted:
T.W. Higginson. *Atlantic Essays*. Boston: Osgood, 1871, pp.
    71-92. Reissued: N.Y.: Longmans, Green, 1894.
Massachusetts Review, VI (Spring-Summer 1965), [570-80].
This article prompted ED's first letter to Higginson. It was
reviewed in the *Springfield Daily Republican*, Mar. 29, 1892,
p. 2.

6.475   ———. *Letters and Journals of Thomas Wentworth Higginson,
1846-1906*, ed. Mary Thacher Higginson. Boston: Houghton
Mifflin, 1921.
Letter and journal entries relating to ED, pp. 268, 331-32.
Four boxes of Higginson's letters and journals in manuscript
are owned by the Houghton Library, Harvard University.
Some of his correspondence regarding ED is at the Robert
Frost Library, Amherst College.

6.476   ———. "An Open Portfolio." *Christian Union*, XLII (Sept. 25,
1890), 392-93.
Reprinted:
American Poetry and Poetics, ed. Daniel G. Hoffman. Garden
    City, N.Y.: Doubleday Anchor Original, 1962, pp. 417-26.
Blake and Wells, *Recognition* (5.13), pp. 3-10.
The earliest essay about ED's poetry. Includes the first print-
ing of thirteen poems and a variant version of "Safe in their
Alabaster Chambers."

6.477   ———. "Preface" to *Poems*, 1890 (3.9), pp. [iii]-vi.
Reprinted:
Bingham, *Ancestors' Brocades* (5.5), pp. 416-17.
Blake and Wells, *Recognition* (5.13), pp. 10-12.
Poems (1890-1896), introd. Monteiro (3.212), pp. [iii]-vi.
In sketching some of the qualities of ED's poetry, Higginson
notes similarities with William Blake and anticipates the ob-
jection of certain critics with the remark: "After all, when a
thought takes one's breath away, a lesson on grammar seems
an impertinence."

6.477a   [———]. "Recent American Poetry." *Nation*, LX (May 23, 1895),
402.
A review of John Banister Tabb's *Poems* which compares his
verse with ED's and quotes poems by each on the hummingbird.

6.477b   [———]. "Recent American Poetry." *Nation*, LXX (April 5,
1900), 265.
Notes that Mrs. Louise Chandler Moulton's poetry is inferior
to ED's in "imagination." Attributed to Higginson by Edelstein, *Strange Enthusiasm* (6.309a), p. 352.

6.477c   [———]. "Recent Poetry." *Nation*, LI (Nov. 27, 1890), 422-23.
Rev. of *Poems*, 1890 (3.9). As Mary Thacher Higginson points

out in *T.W. Higginson* (6.472), p. 414, poetry reviews for the *Nation* were written by Higginson from 1879-1904. However, John White Chadwick and Mary Augusta Jordon also wrote reviews for the *Nation* during this period. Whether Higginson chose to review those Dickinson volumes with which he was closely associated is uncertain.

6.477d   [————]. "Recent Poetry." *Nation*, LIII (Oct. 15, 1891), 297. Rev. of *Poems*, 1891 (3.52). Attributed to Higginson by Edelstein, *Strange Enthusiasm* (6.309a), p. 350.

6.477e   [————]. "Recent Poetry." *Nation*, LV (Dec. 15, 1892), 453. Describes Anne Reeve Aldrich as a poet "whose whole existence dwells, like Emily Dickinson's, in the dim twilight...."

6.477f   [————]. "Recent Poetry." *Nation*, LXI (Oct. 24, 1895), 296. Compares the terseness of ED and Stephen Crane. Attributed to Higginson by Edelstein, *Strange Enthusiasm* (6.309a), p. 352.

6.477g   [————]. "Recent Poetry." *Nation*, LXIII (Oct. 8, 1896), 274-75. Reprinted:
New York Evening Post, Oct. 10, 1896, p. 14.
Rev. of *Poems*, 1896 (3.89). Attributed to Higginson by Edelstein, *Strange Enthusiasm* (6.309a), p. 352.

6.477h   [————]. "Recent Poetry." *Nation*, LXXV (Dec. 11, 1902), 465. Of E.A. Robinson's poetry: "... when there is obscurity, it is often like that of Emily Dickinson when she piques your curiosity through half a dozen readings and suddenly makes all clear." Attributed to Higginson by Edelstein, *Strange Enthusiasm* (6.309a), p. 352.

6.477i   ————, and Henry Walcott Boynton. *A Reader's History of American Literature*. Boston: Houghton Mifflin, 1903, pp. 126, 130-31, 264, 281.
Although ED's "irregular" poetry is not likely ever to appeal to a wide audience, it "preserves a lyrical power almost unequaled in her generation."

6.478   Hill, Frank E. "Emily Dickinson." *New York Sun*, July 26, 1924, p. 5.
Rev. of *Complete Poems*, 1924 (3.123).

6.479   Hillyer, Robert S. "'Ah, Necromancy Sweet!' Beauty Out of the Past." *Boston Herald*, Mar. 16, 1929, p. 17.
Rev. of *Further Poems*, 1929 (3.138).

6.480   ————. *Atlantic Monthly*, CXLIII, No. 4 (April 1929), pp. 16, 18.
Rev. of *Further Poems*, 1929 (3.138).

6.481   ————. "Biography at Close Range." *Atlantic Monthly*, CLXII, No. 6 (Dec. 1938), among front advertising pages.
Rev. of Whicher, *This Was a Poet* (5.104).

6.482   ————. "Emily Dickinson." *The Freeman*, VI (Oct. 18, 1922), 129-31.
Reprinted:
Robert S. Hillyer. *Essays of Our Times*, ed. Sharon Osborne Brown. Chicago: Scott, Foresman, 1928, pp. 203-11.
Blake and Wells, *Recognition* (5.13), pp. 98-104.
A critical appreciation. The essay emphasizes that although ED divorced herself from the orthodoxy of her day, she was

neither eccentric nor perverse. Hillyer discusses this essay in his book, *In Pursuit of Poetry* (6.484a), pp. 166-67.

6.483   Hillyer, Robert S. "Emily Dickinson's Unpublished Poems — and Their Genesis." *New York Times Book Review*, April 15, 1945, pp. 3, 20, 22, 24.
Rev. of *Bolts of Melody*, 1945 (3.177) and Bingham, *Ancestors' Brocades* (5.5).

6.484   ———. "Here Is Emily." *New York Times Book Review*, Nov. 27, 1955, pp. 40-41.
Rev. of Johnson, *Interpretive Biography* (5.44).

6.484a   ———. *In Pursuit of Poetry.* N.Y.: McGraw-Hill, 1960, pp. 58-59, 114, 166-67, *passim*.
Discusses ED's reputation and her influence on Conrad Aiken.

6.485   ———. "The Later Emily Dickinson." *Hound and Horn*, II (July-Sept. 1929), 423-25.
Rev. of *Further Poems*, 1929 (3.138).

6.485a   ———. *A Letter to Robert Frost and Others.* N.Y.: Knopf, 1937, p. 4.
In a poem of friendship to Robert Frost, Hillyer mentions Frost's and his own reaction to ED.

6.486   ———. "On the Letter-Writer Was the Indelible Mark of the Poet." *New York Times Book Review*, Mar. 16, 1958, p. 3.
Rev. of *Letters*, 1958 (4.90).

6.487   ———. "'Pardon My Sanity in a World Insane.'" *New York Times Book Review*, Nov. 27, 1960, pp. 4, 30.
Rev. Leyda, *Years and Hours* (5.49).

6.488   ———. "Phantom Lovers." *New York Times Book Review*, Nov. 7, 1954, p. 18.
Rev. of Bingham, *Revelation* (5.9).

6.489   ———. "What Emily Really Wrote." *New York Times Book Review*, Sept. 11, 1955, p. 7.
Rev. of *Poems*, 1955 (3.197).

6.490   Hindus, Milton. "Emily's Prose: A Note." *Kenyon Review*, II (Winter 1940), 88-91.
"Random reactions to some of Miss Dickinson's letters."

6.490a   ———. "In Literature, Too, Fame is Fickle." *New York Times Book Review*, Sept. 2, 1962, pp. 1, 17.
Devotes a paragraph to fluctuations in ED's critical reputation, p. 17.

6.491   Hinshaw, Edna Bangs. "Some Early Recollections of Emily Dickinson." *Boston Herald*, Magazine Section, Dec. 18, 1927, p. 3.
A reminiscence.

6.492   Hirsch, David H. "Emily Dickinson's 'Presentiment.'" *American Notes and Queries*, I (Nov. 1962), 36-37.
ED's use of "presentiment" should not be taken to suggest complete despair. For Hirsch's rejoinder to a rebuttal by Laurence Perrine (6.793), see *American Notes and Queries*, III (April 1965), 120.

6.493   Hitchcock, Edward. *The Power of Christian Benevolence Illustrated in the Life and Labors of Mary Lyon.* Northampton,

Mass.: Hopkins and Bridgman, 1851; Bridgman and Childs, 1860.

A biography of ED's teacher and founder of Mount Holyoke Female Seminary. See also 6.401.

6.494   Hoagland, Marjorie. "To Preserve Dickinson Home." *New York Times,* Nov. 21, 1964, p. 28.

Letter to the editor criticizing the announced plan to sell the Dickinson home; see 7.55.

6.495   Hoepfner, Theodore C. "'Because I could not stop for Death.'" *American Literature* XXIX (Mar. 1957), 96.

Reprinted:

Davis, *14 by ED* (5.23), p. 113.

Takes issue with Richard Chase's comment on this poem.

6.496   Hoffman, Frederick J. "The Technological Fallacy in Contemporary Poetry." *American Literature,* XXI (Mar. 1949), 97.

Reprinted:

Poetry as Experience, ed. Norman C. Stageberg and Wallace Anderson. N.Y.: American Book Co., 1952, p. 460.

This article contains an explication of "I like to see it lap the Miles" in a footnote on the page cited.

6.497   Hogan, William. *San Francisco Chronicle,* Jan. 9, 1962, p. 39.

Rev. of *Final Harvest,* 1962 (3.208).

6.498   Hogue, Caroline. "Dickinson's 'I heard a Fly buzz — when I died.'" *Explicator,* XX (Nov. 1961), Item 26.

Reprinted:

Davis, *14 by ED* (5.23), pp. 68-69.

6.499   ——. "Dickinson's 'There Came a Day at Summer's Full.'" *Explicator,* XI (Dec. 1952), Item 17.

Reprinted:

Davis, *14 by ED* (5.23), p. 42.

6.500   ——. "Dickinson's 'When I hoped I feared.'" *Explicator,* X (May 1952), Item 49.

6.501   Hollahan, Eugene. "Dickinson's 'I heard a Fly buzz — when I died.'" *Explicator,* XXV (Sept. 1966), Item 6.

Rev. by Robbins, *ALS, 1966* (6.851), p. 144.

6.502   Hollis, C. Carroll. "Last Word on Our Greatest Woman Poet." *America,* CIV (Mar. 11, 1961), 762-63.

Rev. of *Complete Poems,* 1960 (3.207); Anderson, *Stairway of Surprise* (5.2); and Leyda, *Years and Hours* (5.49).

6.503   Holmes, John. "A Bomb, Not a Brown Wren." *Christian Science Monitor,* Mar. 8, 1962, p. 6.

Rev. of *Final Harvest,* 1962 (3.208) and Ward, *Capsule of the Mind* (5.97).

6.504   ——. *Boston Transcript,* Dec. 14, 1935, p. 4.

Rev. of *Unpublished Poems,* 1935 (3.167).

6.505   ——. *Boston Transcript,* May 8, 1937, p. 5.

Rev. of *Poems,* 1937 (3.173).

6.506   ——. *Boston Transcript,* Dec. 17, 1938, p. 1.

Rev. of Whicher, *This Was a Poet* (5.104).

6.506a   Houghton, Donald E. "Dickinson's 'The butterfly obtains.'" *Explicator,* XXVII (Sept. 1968), Item 5.

6.507   Howard, Leon. "The Search for Reality" in *Literature and the American Tradition.* N.Y.: Macmillan, 1955, pp. 164-69. Garden City, N.Y.: Doubleday, 1960 [1963], pp. 188-89. Notes that although ED was influenced by Emerson, she was largely unaffected by external events of public interest. Her verse suggests "private communication."

6.508   Howard, Mabel, William Howard, and Emily Harvey. "Dickinson's 'My wheel is in the dark!'" *Explicator,* XVII (Nov. 1958), Item 12.

6.509   Howard, William. "Dickinson's 'I can wade Grief.'" *Explicator,* XIV (Dec. 1955), Item 17.

6.510   ———. "Dickinson's 'I never saw a Moor.'" *Explicator,* XXI (Oct. 1962), Item 13.

6.511   ———. "Dickinson's 'Safe in their Alabaster Chambers.'" *Explicator,* XVII (June 1959), Item 62.
Reprinted:
Davis, *14 by ED* (5.23), pp. 23-24.

6.512   ———. "Dickinson's 'There came a Day at Summer's full.'" *Explicator,* XII (April 1954), Item 41.
Reprinted:
Davis, *14 by ED* (5.23), pp. 43-44.

6.513   ———. "Emily Dickinson's Poetic Vocabulary." *PMLA,* LXXII (Mar. 1957), 225-48.
Compares ED's vocabulary with those of other poets and concludes that it is "not in the words she uses but in the way she uses them that ED is most original."

6.514   Howe, Mark Anthony DeWolfe. "Emily Dickinson: Enigma" in *Who Lived Here? A Baker's Dozen of Historic New England Houses and Their Occupants.* Photographs by Samuel Chamberlain. Boston: Little, Brown, 1952, pp. 57-68.
Includes a biographical essay and photographs of the Dickinson home and of the ED room in the Houghton Library, Harvard.

6.515   ———. "Literary Affairs in Boston." *Book Buyer,* n.s. XI (Oct. 1894), 425.
Prepublication notice of *Letters,* 1894 (4.3). Includes the first printing of "They might not need me — yet they might"; see 3.84.

6.516   [Howells, William Dean.] "The Poems of Emily Dickinson." *Harper's Magazine,* LXXXII (Jan. 1891), 318-21.
Reprinted:
American Poetry and Poetics, ed. Daniel G. Hoffman. Garden City, N.Y.: Doubleday Anchor Original, 1962, pp. 426-31.
Blake and Wells, *Recognition* (5.13), pp. 18-24.
Excerpt reprinted:
Davis, *14 by ED* (5.23), pp. 9-11.
This influential appreciation touches on ED's seclusion, her new England character, and the imaginative force of her poetry.

6.516a   ———, and Mark Twain. *Mark Twain — Howells Letters: The Correspondence of Samuel L. Clemens and William Dean Howells,* ed. Henry Nash Smith and William M. Gibson. 2

vols. Cambridge, Mass.: Harvard Univ. Press, 1960, II, 681.

In a letter to Twain dated Oct. 23, 1898, Howells quotes the second quatrain of "The Bustle in a House" as expressing the "awful despair" of the death of a loved one.

6.517   Howes, Barbara. "Emily, Day By Day." *Virginia Quarterly Review*, XXXVII (Spring 1961), 286-90.
Rev. of Leyda, *Years and Hours* (5.49).

6.518   Hoyt, Florence S. "Intelligent Sociability." *Congregationalist*, LXXVIII (Mar. 2, 1893), 337-38.
Shows how ED's poems may be used as a "mixer" for a literary evening. Each guest gets half a poem.

6.519   [Hughes, Rupert.] Chelifer, pseud. "The Ideas of Emily Dickinson." *Godey's Magazine*, CXXXIII (Nov. 1896), 541-43.
Rev. of *Poems*, 1890 (3.9), 1891 (3.52), and 1896 (3.89) and *Letters*, 1894 (4.3).

6.520   ———. "Sappho and Other Princesses of Poetry." *Godey's Magazine*, CXXXII (Jan. 1896), 94-95.
Brief comment on ED notes her "pantheism."

6.521   Hughes, Ted. "Emily Dickinson's Poetry." *The Listener*, LXX (Sept. 12, 1963), 394.
Rev. of Anderson, *Stairway of Surprise* (5.2).

6.522   Humphries, Rolfe. "A Retouched Portrait." *The Measure, A Journal of Poetry*, No. 39 (May 1924), pp. 13-15.
Rev. of Bianchi, *Life and Letters* (4.36).

6.523   ———. "'Too Difficult a Grace.'" *New Republic*, LIX, No. 755, Part II, "Spring Review Section" (May 22, 1929), pp. 38-40.
Rev. of *Further Poems*, 1929 (3.138).

6.524   Hunt, Percival. "Emily Dickinson," Talk No. VII in *A Series of Eight Radio Talks on Some Writers of Older New England*, Radio Publication No. 36. Pittsburg: Univ. of Pittsburg, 1928, pp. 48-56.
A general introduction to ED's poetry; notes her music, intensity, individuality, homely words, and humor. Transcript of a radio broadcast by Percival Hunt, Feb. 18, 1928.

6.525   Hurd, Pearl Strachan. "All the Difference." *Christian Science Monitor*, May 15, 1956, p. 10.
An account of an interview with Mme. Bianchi is included in this brief appreciation.

6.526   Hutchison, Percy. "Further Poems of That Shy Recluse, Emily Dickinson." *New York Times Book Review*, Mar. 17, 1929, p. 3.
Rev. of *Further Poems* (3.138).

6.527   ———. "The Mystery of Emily Dickinson." *New York Times Book Review*, Feb. 23, 1930, p. 5.
Rev. of Bianchi, *Life and Letters* (4.36) and Patterson, *Riddle* (5.55).

6.528   ———. "New Letters and Memories of Emily Dickinson." *New York Times Book Review*, Dec. 11, 1932, pp. 4, 21.
Review of Bianchi, *Face to Face* (4.59).

6.529   ———. *New York Times Book Review*, Nov. 24, 1935, p. 2.

Rev. of *Unpublished Poems,* 1935 (3.167).

6.530 Hutchison, Percy. "That Unsolved Enigma in the Life of Emily Dickinson." *New York Times Book Review,* June 22, 1930, p. 3.
Rev. of Taggard, *Life and Mind* (5.81).

6.531 ———. "A Fine Study of Emily Dickinson." *New York Times Book Review,* Nov. 13, 1938, p. 4.
Rev. of Whicher, *This Was a Poet* (5.104).

6.532 Hyde, Marietta, ed. "School Days" in *Modern Biography.* [1st ed.] N.Y.: Harcourt, 1926, pp. 90-102.
Reprints an excerpt from Bianchi, *Life and Letters* (4.36), having to do with ED's childhood. The editor provides an introduction, pp. 90-91. The reprinting, with its introduction, is omitted from later editions of this volume, an anthology intended mainly for young people.

6.533 Ives, Ella Gilbert. "Emily Dickinson: Her Poetry, Prose and Personality." *Boston Evening Transcript,* Oct. 5, 1907, Part 3, p. 3.
Reprinted:
Blake and Wells, *Recognition* (5.13), pp. 71-78.
A general introduction and appreciation.

6.534 Jack, P. M. "A Not Abnormal Woman." *New York Sun,* Nov. 21, 1931, p. 27.
Rev. of *Letters,* 1931 (4.52).

6.535 Jakeman, Adelbert M. "Emily Dickinson Books Give New Poems, Insights." *Springfield Union-Republican,* April 8, 1945, p. 4-D.
Rev. of *Bolts of Melody,* 1945 (3.177) and Bingham, *Ancestors' Brocades* (5.5).

6.536 James, Alice. *Alice James, Her Brothers — Her Journal,* ed. Anna Robeson Burr. N.Y.: Dodd, Mead, 1934, pp. 248-49.
Reprinted:
The Diary of Alice James, ed. Leon Edel. N.Y.: Dodd, Mead, 1964, p. 227.
A January 1892 diary entry comments on ED's reputation in England: "It is reassuring to hear the English pronouncement that ED is fifth-rate — they have such a capacity for missing quality."

6.537 Jenkins, MacGregor. "A Child's Recollections of Emily Dickinson." *Christian Union,* XLIV (Oct. 24, 1891), 776-77.
See also the author's book-length reminiscence, *Emily Dickinson: Friend and Neighbor* (5.35).

6.538 Jennings, Elizabeth. "Emily Dickinson and the Poetry of the Inner Life." *Review of English Literature* [Leeds], III (April 1962), 78-87.
The sources of ED's universal appeal lie in the artful exploration of her inner world.

6.539 ———. "Idea and Expression in Emily Dickinson, Marianne Moore and Ezra Pound" in *American Poetry,* ed. Irvin Ehrenpreis. *Stratford-Upon-Avon Studies,* No. 7. N.Y.: St. Martin's Press; London: Edward Arnold, 1965, pp. 96-113.
A wide-ranging critical essay touching upon, among other

matters, the richness of ED's inner life, her artistry, and her intellectual depth. Concludes that the three poets share a contemplative "watchful" attitude toward the world.

6.540 Johnson, Burges. "Inspired and Uninspired Writers." *Saturday Review,* XXXVI (April 25, 1953), 12-13, 44-46.
Brief mention of ED (p. 45) as a gifted writer who lacked technique. For reply by David J.M. Higgins, see 6.470.

6.541 Johnson, Rossiter, and John Howard Brown, eds. "Dickinson, Emily Elizabeth" in *The Twentieth Century Biographical Dictionary of Notable Americans.* 10 vols. Boston: The Biographical Society, 1904, III, unpaged.

6.542 Johnson, Thomas H. "Affectionately, Emily." *New York Times Book Review,* April 22, 1951, p. 6.
Rev. of *Letters to Holland,* 1951 (4.76).

6.543 ———. "Dickinson's 'Immured in Heaven.'" *Explicator,* XI (Mar. 1953), Item 36.

6.544 ———. "Emily Dickinson: Creating the Poems." *Harvard Library Bulletin,* VII (Autumn 1953), 257-70.
On the variant states of poems among the Dickinson manuscripts.

6.545 ———. "Emily Dickinson: The Prisms of a Poet." *Saturday Review,* XXXIII (June 30, 1950), 16-17.
Reprinted:
Blake and Wells, *Recognition* (5.13), pp. 261-64.
On the need to determine the Dickinson canon.

6.546 ———. "Establishing a Text: The Emily Dickinson Papers." *Studies in Bibliography,* V (1952-1953), 21-32.
Discusses problems in editing the manuscripts.

6.547 ———. "The Great Love in the Life of Emily Dickinson." *American Heritage,* VI (April 1955), 52-55.
About ED and Charles Wadsworth.

6.548 ———. "Kate Scott and Emily Dickinson." *New York Times Book Review,* Nov. 4, 1951, pp. 3, 34.
Rev. of Patterson, *Riddle* (5.55).

6.549 ———. "Speaking of Books." *New York Times Book Review,* Aug. 20, 1950, p. 2.
Briefly suggests stages in ED's artistic apprenticeship and notes the need for exact transcription of her poems and letters.

6.550 ———. "The Vision and Veto of Emily Dickinson" in *Final Harvest,* 1962 (3.208), pp. vii-xiv.
In this introduction to his edition of selected ED poems, Johnson emphasizes her achievement as a prosodist and her "tragic vision."

6.551 Jones, Howard Mumford. "Great American Poetess." *The New Student,* VII (Jan. 4, 1928), 12.
Rev. of *Complete Poems,* 1924 (3.123).

6.552 Joost, Nicholas. "Emily Dickinson: A Revelation." *Poetry,* LXXXVI (May 1955), 119-20.
Rev. of Bingham, *Revelation* (5.9).

6.553   Joost, Nicholas. "The Pain That Emily Knew." *Poetry*, LXXX
          (July 1952), 242-45.
          Rev. of Patterson, *Riddle* (5.55).

6.554   [Jordan, Mary Augusta]. "Letters of Emily Dickinson." *Nation*,
          LIX (Dec. 13, 1894), 446-47.
          Reprinted:
          Blake and Wells, *Recognition* (5.13), pp. 57-61.
          Rev. of *Letters*, 1894 (4.3).

6.555   ———. "A Valuable Record." *Yale Review*, XXI (Spring 1932),
          625-26.
          Rev. of *Letters*, 1931 (4.52).

6.556   Jordan, Raymond J. "Dickinson's 'The Bustle in a House.'" *Ex-
          plicator*, XXI (Feb. 1963), Item 49.

6.557   Jordan-Smith, Paul. "Riddle of Dickinson Seclusion Explored."
          Los Angeles Times, Nov. 4, 1951, Part 4, p. 6.
          Rev. of Patterson, *Riddle* (5.55).

6.558   Josephson, Matthew. "Those Who Stayed" in *Portrait of the Art-
          ist as American*. N.Y.: Harcourt, 1930 (reissued Octagon
          Books, 1964), pp. 139-98.
          Describes ED as living in splendid spiritual isolation from the
          material world, pp. 173-78.

6.559   Judd, Sylvester. *History of Hadley, Including the Early History
          of Hatfield, South Hadley, Amherst and Granby, Mass.* by Syl-
          vester Judd *with Family Genealogies* by Lucius M. Boltwood.
          Northampton, Mass.: Metcalf, 1863.
          Genealogy of Samuel Fowler Dickinson, p. 485.

6.560   K., B. M. "New Books." *Catholic World*, CXXX (Oct. 1929),
          115-16.
          Rev. of *Further Poems*, 1929 (3.138).

6.561   K., W. S. "A Fresh Reading of Emily Dickinson." *Boston Even-
          ing Transcript*, July 11, 1895, p. 5.
          An appreciation.

6.562   Kazin, Alfred. "Called Back." *The Griffin* [N.Y.], IX (1960), No.
          11, pp. 2-9.
          Reprinted:
          Alfred Kazin. *Contemporaries*. Boston: Little, Brown, 1962,
          pp. 50-56.
          Comments on the history of ED editing and includes a brief
          critical appreciation of ED's precision and depth of feeling.

6.563   Keleher, Julia. "The Enigma of Emily Dickinson." *New Mexico
          Quarterly*, II (Nov. 1932), 326-32.
          The author discounts ED's alleged love affair and argues that
          she can be placed "in the stream of mystic poets who wooed
          the creations of their minds...."

6.564   Kelley, William Valentine. "Emily Dickinson: The Hermit
          Thrush of Amherst" in *Down the Road and Other Essays of
          Nature, Literature and Religion*. N.Y.: Eaton and Mains,
          1911, pp. 214-83.
          An introduction and appreciation. The author includes bio-
          graphical material, mostly anecdotes, and speculates about
          the quality of ED's inner life.

6.565   Kennedy, John S. "Emily Dickinson Interpreted." *The Catholic Transcript* [Hartford, Conn.], Jan. 13, 1944, p. 5.
Rev. of Power, *In the Name of the Bee* (5.72).

6.566   Kennedy, Leo. *Chicago Sun Book Week*, April 15, 1945, p. 8.
Rev. of *Bolts of Melody*, 1945 (3.177) and Bingham, *Ancestors' Brocades* (5.5).

6.567   Kenny, Virginia. "Was Emily Dickinson Short of Hearing?" *Highlights, Bulletin of the New York League for the Hard of Hearing*, XXXIX (Fall 1960), 5, 11, 15.
Argues that ED may have suffered hearing loss.

6.568   Kerman, Joseph. "American Music: The Columbia Series (II)." *Hudson Review*, XIV (Fall 1961), 408-18.
Describes the "excruciating" nature of ED's poetry in a discussion of Aaron Copeland's musical settings to twelve ED poems (19.9).

6.569   Keyes, Rowena Keith. "Alumnae Conference Impressions." *Mount Holyoke Alumnae Quarterly*, XIII (Jan. 1930), 188-90.
Reports the ED Poetry Conference held in conjunction with the Founder's Day Celebration, Mount Holyoke, Nov. 1929. See also 22.1-7.

6.570   Keys, F. V. "The Poet in Time and Space." *North American Review*, CCXIX (June 1924), 905-12.
Rev. of Bianchi, *Life and Letters* (4.36), pp. 911-12.

6.571   Kahn, Salamatullah. "The Love Poetry of Emily Dickinson." *Literary Criterion*, VI (Summer 1964), 37-51.
Argues that ED's unrequited love for Wadsworth taught her patience, fortitude, and self-understanding.

6.571a Kher, Inder Nath. "'An Abyss's Face': The Structure of Emily Dickinson's Poem." *Pluck* [Univ. of Alberta, Edmonton], II Fall 1968), 12-14.
An explication of "What mystery pervades a well!"

6.572   Kilgour, Raymond L. *Messrs. Roberts Brothers, Publishers*. Ann Arbor, Mich.: Univ. of Michigan Press, 1952, pp. 236-46, *passim*.
An account of the early publishing history of ED's poems and letters.

6.573   Kindilien, Carlin T. *American Poetry in the Eighteen Nineties*. Providence, R.I.: Brown Univ. Press, 1956, pp. 2, 25, 87-88, *passim*.
Discusses ED's influence on poets of the Nineties, including Lizette Reese, Gertrude Hall Brownell, John Banister Tabb (see also 5.80), Martha Dickinson Bianchi, Harry Lyman Koopman, and others.

6.574   King, Carlyle. *Queen's Quarterly*, LXIX (Autumn 1962), 486.
Rev. of Ward, *Capsule of the Mind* (5.97).

6.574a ———. *Queen's Quarterly*, LXXIII (Autumn 1966), 454.
Rev. of Porter, *Early Poetry* (5.69).

6.575   [Kirby, John Pendy]. "Dickinson's 'A Bird came down the Walk.'" *Explicator*, II (June 1944), Item 61.

6.576   Kirkland, Caroline. "Emily Dickinson's Poems." *Chicago Figaro*, II (Feb. 12, 1891), 428.

Rev. of *Poems,* 1890 (3.9).

6.577 Klett, Ada M. "Doom and Fortitude: A Study of Poetic Metaphor in Annette von Droste-Hülshoff (1797-1848) and Emily Dickinson (1830-1886)." *Monatshefte für deutschen Unterricht,* XXXVII (Jan. 1945), 37-54.

Annette von Droste-Hülshoff is a poet of doom, ED of fortitude. In English.

6.578 Knapp, Lewis M. "The Lover's Mother Goose." *Saturday Review,* XII (Oct. 26, 1935), 9.

Describes a 1905 anthology containing two ED poems.

6.578a Knight, Grant Cochran. *American Literature and Culture.* N.Y.: Ray Long and Richard R. Smith, Inc., 1936, pp. 182, 292, 303-06, *passim.*

Regards ED as a "brilliant exception to the decaying romanticism" of her period.

6.578b ———. *The Critical Period in American Literature.* Chapel Hill: Univ. of North Carolina Press, 1951 (reissued, Cos Cob, Conn.: John E. Edwards, 1968), pp. viii, 7, 21, 109.

Notes differences between the poetry of ED and Stephen Crane.

6.579 [Knox, John B.]. "And Now She Is Known to Millions." *Springfield Sunday Republican,* Dec. 4, 1955, pp. 1, 8.

"Written by John B. Knox, Associated Press representative in Boston. Appeared in part in *Boston Herald,* Dec. 4, 1955 and perhaps in other papers." — Annotation by Charles R. Green, Librarian, Jones Library, Amherst.

6.580 ———. "Previously Unpublished Emily Dickinson Poems in 3-Vol. Edition." *Hampshire Daily Gazette* [Northampton, Mass.], Sept. 16, 1955, p. 7.

Rev. of *Poems,* 1955 (3.197).

6.580a Koehler, Stanley. "The Art of Poetry VI: William Carlos Williams." *Paris Review,* VIII, No. 32 (Summer-Fall 1964), 111-51.

William Carlos Williams discusses ED, especially her use of American speech, pp. 122-23.

6.581 Koopman, Harry Lyman. "Emily Dickinson." *Brown Magazine,* VIII (Dec. 1896), 82-92.

An introduction and appreciation. Includes an anonymous reminiscence not elsewhere printed.

6.582 Korg, Jacob. *The Force of Few Words.* N.Y.: Holt, Rinehart, Winston, 1966, pp. 31, 65, 143-44.

6.582a Kramer, Aaron. *The Prophetic Tradition in American Poetry, 1839-1900.* Rutherford, N.J.: Fairleigh Dickinson Univ. Press, 1968, pp. 136-37, 208, *passim.*

"The imagery of [ED's] poems remains consistently sympathetic to the defeated, the imprisoned, the hunted . . . ," p. 137.

6.583 Kreymborg, Alfred. "Emily Dickinson. A New Book by the Immortal Tippler." *New York Sun,* Mar. 16, 1929, p. 11.

Rev. of *Further Poems,* 1929 (3.138).

6.584 ———. "The Tippler Leaning Against the Sun" in *Our Singing Strength: An Outline of American Poetry (1620-1930).* N.Y.: Coward McCann, 1929, pp. 193-205.

A general introduction to ED's life and poetry.

6.585   Kunitz, Stanley J., and Howard Haycraft. "Emily Dickinson," in *American Authors 1600-1900, A Biographical Dictionary of American Literature*. N.Y.: Wilson, 1938, pp. 215-217.

6.586   Kurth, Paula. "Emily Dickinson in Her Letters." *Thought*, IV (Dec. 1929), 430-439.
Rev. of Bianchi, *Life and Letters* (4.36).

6.587   L., H. "Genevieve Taggard's Angle on the Emily Dickinson Legend." *Philadelphia Inquirer*, July 12, 1930, p. 14-A.
Review of Taggard, *Life and Mind* (5.81).

6.588   Laing, Dilys. "The Non-Corporeal Friend." *Nation*, CLXXXVI (April 26, 1958), 368-69.
Rev. of *Letters*, 1958 (4.90).

6.589   Lair, Robert L. "Dickinson's 'As by the dead we love to sit.'" *Explicator*, XXV (Mar. 1967), Item 58.

6.590   Lane, James W. "A New England Solitary." *New York Sun*, July 5, 1930, p. 5.
Rev. of Taggard, *Life and Mind* (5.81).

6.591   Lane, Lauriat, Jr. *The Fiddlehead* [Frederickton, N.B.], No. 48 (Spring 1961), p. 57.
Rev. of *Complete Poems*, 1960 (3.207).

6.592   Lang, Andrew. "A Literary Causerie." *The Speaker* [London], III (Jan. 31, 1891), pp. 135-36.
Rev. of *Poems*, 1890 (3.9).

6.593   ———. "A Patriotic Critic." *Illustrated London News*, C (Jan. 2, 1892), 14-15.
Criticizes ED's grammar in a review of T. W. Higginson's *The New World and the New Book*.

6.594   ———. "Some American Poets." *Illustrated London News*, XCVIII (Mar. 7, 1891), 307.
Reprinted:
Blake and Wells, *Recognition* (5.13).
An unfavorable review of *Poems*, 1890 (3.9). For anonymous reviews attributed to Lang, see 3.29-30.

6.595   ———. "The Superior Sex." *Critic*, XXI (Aug. 27, 1892), 112.
Brief reference to ED's "bad rhymes and bad grammar."

6.596   Lapidus, Ben. "A Made-to-Measure Emily." *New Freeman*, II (Oct. 29, 1930), 164.
Rev. of Jenkins, *Friend and Neighbor* (5.35).

6.597   Larrabee, Ankey. "Three Studies in Modern Poetry: The Use of Death and Puritan Theology in Emily Dickinson's Poetry...." *Accent*, III (Winter, 1943), 115-17.
Excerpt reprinted:
Davis, *14 by ED* (5.23), pp. 105-07.
In a reply to Allen Tate's essay (6.980), the author argues that, for ED, reality is personally rather than doctrinally conceived.

6.598   Lauter, Paul. "Beyond the Doric Mode." *New Leader*, XLIII (Dec. 12, 1960), 18-19.
Rev. of *Complete Poems* (3.207) and Leyda, *Years and Hours* (5.49).

6.599   Laverty, Carroll D. "Structural Patterns in Emily Dickinson's
           Poetry." *Emerson Society Quarterly*, No. 44 (III Quar., 1966),
           pp. 12-17.
           ED's use of eight basic rhetorical patterns (definition, analogy,
           etc.) suggests a continuing effort to intellectualize her thoughts
           and emotions through poetry.

6.600   Lavin, J. A. "Emily Dickinson and Brazil." *Notes and Queries*,
           n.s. VII (July 1960), 270-71.
           Discusses the reference to Brazil in "I asked no other thing"
           and criticizes George Monteiro's explication of the poem; see
           6.719-720.

6.601   Lawrence, Rockwell. "The Life and Mind of Emily Dickinson."
           Bookman [N.Y.], LXXI (July 1930), 445-46.
           Rev. of Taggard, *Life and Mind* (5.81).

6.602   Laycock, E. A. *Boston Globe*, April 18, 1945, p. 19.
           Rev. of *Bolts of Melody*, 1945 (3.177) and Bingham, *Ancestors'
           Brocades* (5.5).

6.603   Leary, Lewis. "The Poems of Emily Dickinson." *Thought*, XXXI
           (Summer 1956), 282-86.
           Rev. of *Poems*, 1955 (3.197).

6.604   Lee, Anna Phillips. "Emily Dickinson and Her Family Tree."
           Daughters of the American Revolution Magazine, LXV (Aug.
           1931), 471-77.

6.605   Leisy, Ernest Erwin. *American Literature*, VIII (Mar. 1936),
           102-03.
           Rev. of *Unpublished Poems*, 1935 (3.167).

6.606   ——. *American Literature: An Interpretive Survey*. N.Y.:
           Crowell, 1929, pp. 218-19.
           Describes ED as a precursor of the Imagist School.

6.607   Lemon, Mary Dyer. "New Emily Dickinson Book Reveals Se-
           cret." *Indianapolis Sunday Star*, Mar. 30, 1930, Part 5, p. 11.
           Rev. of Pollitt, *Human Background* (5.61).

6.608   Leslie, Shane. "A New England Poetess." *Saturday Review*
           [London], CL (Sept. 20, 1930), 346-47.
           Rev. of Taggard, *Life and Mind* (5.81).

6.609   Lewis, Benjamin Roland. *Creative Poetry*. Stanford, Calif.:
           Stanford Univ. Press, 1931, pp. 60, 330-31.
           Cites "The Mountain sat upon the Plain" as an example of the
           "projected concrete picture."

6.610   Lewisohn, Ludwig. *Expression in America*. N.Y.: Harper, 1932,
           pp. 356-63.
           Surveys ED's defects and virtues and concludes that although
           she was overrated in the 1890's, she remains one of the few
           great women poets.

6.611   Leyda, Jay. *American Literature*, XXVII (Nov. 1955), 436-37.
           Rev. of Bingham, *Revelation* (5.9).

6.612   ——. "Late Thaw of a Frozen Image." *New Republic*, CXXXII
           (Feb. 21, 1955), 22-24.
           Surveys mistaken ideas about ED.

6.613   ——. "Miss Emily's Maggie" in *New World Writing — Third*

Mentor Selection. N.Y.: New American Library of World Literature, 1953, pp. 255-67.

The Dickinson home as seen through the letters of their maid, Margaret Maher. The letters are reprinted in Leyda, *Years and Hours* (5.49).

6.614   ———. *New England Quarterly,* XXIX (June 1956), 239-45.

Rev. of *Poems,* 1955 (3.197).

Notes that in three instances poems numbered separately by Johnson are actually variant versions of other poems. On recent changes in the canon, see Rosenbaum, *Concordance* (2.3), pp. xvii-xviii, and Franklin, *Editing of ED* (5.28).

6.615   Libaire, George. "Tersely Yours." *New Freeman,* I (May 10, 1930), 211-12.

Rev. of Bianchi, *Life and Letters* (4.36) and Pollitt, *Human Background* (5.61).

6.616   Lind, Sidney E. "Emily Dickinson's 'Further in Summer than the Birds' and Nathaniel Hawthorne's 'The Old Manse.'" *American Literature,* XXXIX (May 1967), 163-69.

Notes parallels between the two texts.

6.617   Lindberg, Brita. "Emily Dickinson's Punctuation." *Studia Neophilologica,* XXXVII, No. 2 (1965), pp. 327-59.

Surveys, in detail, various editors' attempts to render ED's punctuation in print. For a more recent discussion, see Franklin, *Editing of ED* (5.28), pp. 117-28. Rev. by Robbins, *ALS, 1966* (6.851), p. 142.

6.617a   ———. "Further Notes on a Poem by Emily Dickinson." *Notes and Queries,* XV (May 1968), 179-80.

Suggests another reading of "Superfluous were the Sun."

6.618   ———. *Studia Neophilologica,* XXXV, No. 1 (1963), pp. 170-72.

Rev. of Anderson, *Stairway of Surprise* (5.2).

6.618a   ———. *Studia Neophilologica,* XXXVIII, No. 2 (1966), pp. 383-86.

Rev. of Porter, *Early Poetry* (5.69).

6.619   ———. "The Theme of Death in ED's Poetry." *Studia Neophilologica,* XXXIV, No. 2 (1962), pp. 269-81.

Accounts for ED's fascination with death and with the questions it poses.

6.620   Linscott, Robert N. "Emily Dickinson: The Human Background of Her Poetry." *Bookman* [N.Y.], LXXI (April-May 1930), 228.

Rev. of Pollitt, *Human Background* (5.61).

6.621   ———. "Literary Footnote and Literary Event." *Saturday Review,* XXVIII (April 21, 1945), 10.

Rev. of *Bolts of Melody,* 1945 (3.177) and Bingham, *Ancestors' Brocades* (5.5).

6.622   Loggins, Vernon. "Unpremeditated Art: Emily Dickinson and Stephen Crane" in *I Hear America ... Literature in the United States Since 1900.* N.Y.: Crowell, 1937, pp. 9-31.

A general introduction and appreciation. ED discussed, pp. 14-23.

6.623   Long, E. Hudson. "Tom Sawyer's 'Pitchiola.'" *Twainian,* XX (Sept.-Oct. 1961), 4.

Notes that ED read *Picciola, the Prisoner of Fenestrella* by Joseph Xavier Saintine.

6.624   Long, William J. *American Literature: A Study of the Men and the Books that in the Earlier and Later Times Reflect the American Spirit.* Boston, Ginn, 1913, p. 456.
Refers in passing to "the glittering fragments of poetry that strew the pages of Emily Dickinson."

6.625   Love, Cornelia Spencer. "A Northern Poet and a Southern One." *University of North Carolina Extension Bulletin,* XII (Sept. 1932), 27-29.
Discusses methods of individual and group study. The Southern poet is Lizette Woodworth Reese.

6.626   Lowell, Amy. "Emily Dickinson" in *Poetry and Poets: Essays.* Boston: Houghton, 1930, pp. 88-108.
Pictures the disappointments and loneliness of ED's life and makes general comments on her versification, imagery, sense of sound, and other aspects of her art.

6.627   ——. "Introduction" to *The Black Riders and Other Lines,* in *The Work of Stephen Crane,* ed. Wilson Follett. 12 vols. N.Y.: Knopf, 1926 (reissued, N.Y.: Russell & Russell, 1963), IV, p. xviii.
Notes ED's influence on Crane, especially her "use of suggestion."

6.628   Lubbock, Percy. "Emily Dickinson." *Nation and Athenaeum,* XXXVI (Oct. 18, 1924), 114.
Reprinted:
Blake and Wells, *Recognition* (5.13), pp. 118-120.
Rev. of *Selected Poems,* 1924 (3.127) and Bianchi, *Life and Letters* (4.36).

6.629   Luskin, John. "Emily Dickinson, Empress of Calvary." *The Idol, A Literary Review Published by Students of Union College,* II (May 17, 1929), 81-84.
Rev. of *Further Poems,* 1929 (3.138).

6.630   Lynen, John F. *Journal of English and Germanic Philology,* LXII (April 1963), 421-26.
Rev. of Anderson, *Stairway of Surprise* (5.2).

6.631   ——. "Three Uses of the Present: the Historian's, the Critic's, and Emily Dickinson's." *College English,* XXVIII (Nov. 1966), 126-36.
Discusses the relation of "consciousness" to time and eternity in ED's poems. Compares her with Whitman. Noted by Robbins, *ALS, 1966* (6.851), p. 143.

6.632   Lynn, Kenneth S. "'To Compare Original With Refraction.'" *Christian Science Monitor,* Dec. 1, 1960, p. 15.
Rev. of Leyda, *Years and Hours* (5.49).

6.633   M., F. "Emily Dickinson's Poems." *Christian Science Monitor,* July 21, 1924, p. 11.
Rev. of *Complete Poems,* 1924 (3.123).

6.634   M., M. "Dickinson Fans Will Welcome New Collection." *Washington* [D.C.] *Post,* April 22, 1945, p. 16-S.

Rev. of *Bolts of Melody*, 1945 (3.177) and Bingham, *Ancestors' Brocades* (5.5).

6.635   M., P. *Spectator* [London], CLXXXVIII (May 30, 1952), 726.
Rev. of *Letters*, 1951 (4.80).

6.636   M., W. "Emily Dickinson's Poems." *Housekeeper's Weekly*, III (April 9, 1892), 4.
Review of *Poems*, 1890 (3.9) and 1891 (3.52).

6.637   Mabbott, Thomas O. "'Boanerges' a Horse?" *American Notes and Queries*, II (Dec. 1963), 57.
Reply to a query by Paul F. Breed; see 6.138.

6.638   MacLean, Kenneth. "The Mail From Tunis." *University of Toronto Quarterly*, XX (Oct. 1950), 27-32.
Suggests that ED's disappointment in love caused her to identify herself with Shakespeare's Cleopatra and notes parallels in diction and imagery.

6.639   MacLeish, Archibald. "The Private World" in *Emily Dickinson: Three Views* (5.52), pp. 13-26.
Reprinted:
Blake and Wells, *Recognition* (5.13), 301-14.
Revised and reprinted:
Archibald MacLeish. "The Private World: Poems of Emily Dickinson" in *Poetry and Experience*. Boston: Houghton Mifflin, 1961 (reissued, Baltimore, Md.: Penguin Books, 1964), pp. 91-111.
Reprinted as revised:
Sewall, *Critical Essays* (5.75), pp. 150-61.
Argues that voice rather than form supplies the key to ED's achievement.

6.640   Maguire, C. E. "Two Poets: Compared and Contrasted." *Thought*, VIII (Dec. 1933), 396-409.
Compares ED and Katherine Tynan and notes that ED lacks religious faith.

6.641   Main, C. F., and Peter J. Seng. *Poems. Wadsworth Handbook and Anthology*. San Francisco: Wadsworth, 1961, pp. 87-88, 219-20.
Contains explications of "It dropped so low — in my Regard" and "To hear an Oriole sing."

6.642   Malbone, Richard. "Dickinson's 'I taste a liquor never brewed.'" *Explicator*, XXVI (Oct. 1967), Item 14.

6.643   Mandel, Siegfried. *Saturday Review*, XXXV (June 21, 1952), 42-43.
Rev. of Chase, *ED* (5.17).

6.644   Manierre, William R. "Emily Dickinson: Visions and Revisions." *Texas Studies in Literature and Language*, V (Spring 1963), 5-16.
Comparison of the various versions of three poems suggests that the ED manuscript version is always better than subsequent editorial revisions.

6.645   Manley, Francis. "An Explication of Dickinson's 'After great pain, a formal feeling comes.'" *Modern Language Notes*, LXXIII (April 1958), 260-64.

Reprinted:
Davis, *14 by ED* (5.23), pp. 52-55.

6.646   Marcellino, Ralph. "Cato and Emily Dickinson." *Classical Out-
         look*, XXXV (Feb. 1958), 55-56.
         "The rainbow never tells me" suggests that ED knew and
         valued Cato.

6.647   ———. "Correspondence — Emily Dickinson." *New York Herald
         Tribune Books*, May 3, 1936, p. 22.
         Corrects the reading of "vast" to "least" in the poem "Her
         Grace is all she has" as printed in *Poems*, 1930 (3.151).

6.648   ———. "Dickinson's 'The Snow that never drifts.'" *Explicator*,
         XIII (April 1955), Item 36.

6.649   ———. "Emily Dickinson." *College English*, VII (Nov. 1945),
         102-03.
         Discusses ED's use of the word *immortality*, especially as a
         synonym for *death*.

6.650   ———. "Emily Dickinson's 'Ablative Estate.'" *Classical Journal*,
         LIII (Feb. 1958), 231-32.
         Examines ED's use of the word "ablative."

6.651   ———. "Horace and Emily Dickinson." *Classical Journal*, L
         (Dec. 1954), 126.
         Notes an Horatian echo in "It is an honorable Thought." See
         also next entry.

6.652   ———. "Horace and Emily Dickinson." *Classical Journal*, LII
         (Feb. 1957), 221-22.
         Argues that language and imagery in "An honest Tear" as well
         as in "It is an honorable Thought" (see above entry) demon-
         strate ED's acquaintance with Horace *Odes* 3. 30: *exegi mo-
         numentum aere perennius.*

6.653   ———. "Simonides and Emily Dickinson." *Classical Journal*,
         XLII (Dec. 1946), 140.
         "'Go tell it' — What a Message" uses an epigram by Simonides
         on the Spartans who fell at Thermopylae.

6.654   Marcus, Mordecai. "Dickinson's 'Not with a Club, the Heart is
         broken.'" *Explicator*, XX (Mar. 1962), Item 54.

6.654a   ———. "Emily Dickinson: A Balanced View." *Massachusetts
         Review*, VII (Winter 1966), 183-84.
         Rev. of Gelpi, *Mind of the Poet* (5.29).

6.655   ———. *Prairie Schooner*, XL (Fall 1966), 279.
         Rev. of Capps, *ED's Reading* (5.14) and Porter, *Early Poetry*
         (5.69).

6.656   ———. "Walt Whitman and Emily Dickinson." *Personalist*, XLIII
         (Autumn 1962), 497-514.
         Notes similarities in their lives and ideas.

6.657   Markham, Edwin. *American Writers on American Literature*,
         ed. John Macy. N.Y.: Liveright, 1931, p. 143.
         In an essay on Poe, Markham briefly compares his "wayward,
         wind-vying music" to ED's "crabbed cryptic verse" which
         nevertheless "sometimes plunges to the quick of things, and
         leaves one gasping at the daring of her phrase and the marvel
         of her idea." See also 6.306.

6.658   Martin, Jay. "Emily Dickinson," in *Harvests of Change, Ameri-can Literature, 1895-1914*. Englewood Cliffs, N.J.: Prentice-Hall, 1967, pp. 285-96, *passim*.
Discusses the question of ED's isolation from her community and culture. "In private poetry she celebrated her loss of a public usefulness" but "she was sustained by her personal myth of final victory."

6.659   Martz, Louis L. "Donne and the Meditative Tradition." *Thought*, XXXIV (Summer 1959), pp. 269-78.
Mentions ED as one among several modern poets for whom meditation is the "central action" of their poems, p. 275.

6.660   ———. "In 'Being's Centre.'" *University of Toronto Quarterly*, XXVI (July 1957), 556-65.
Review-essay of *Poems*, 1955 (3.197). Some passages re-printed in "Whitman and Dickinson: Two Aspects of the Self"; see next entry.

6.661   ———. "Whitman and Dickinson: Two Aspects of the Self" in *The Poem of the Mind: Essays on Poetry, English and Ameri-can*. N.Y.: Oxford Univ. Press, 1966, pp. 82-104.
Discusses the significance of variants and of the textual changes made by early editors. Compares ED with Whitman and places her within the meditative tradition, noting her de-velopment of a poised and creative self, an inner meditative being. For comment on this essay, see 6.1148.

6.662   Mary Angela, Sister. "What May Vista Be?" *Annals of Saint Anthony's Shrine* [Worchester, Mass.], II (1959), 61-65.

6.663   Mary Anthony, Mother. "Emily Dickinson's Scriptural Echoes." *Massachusetts Review*, II (Spring 1961), 557-61.
Reprinted:
Davis, *14 by ED* (5.23), pp. 45-48.
Notes Biblical allusions in "There came a Day at Summer's full."

6.664   Mary Humiliata, Sister. "Emily Dickinson — Mystic Poet?" *College English*, XII (Dec. 1950), 144-49.
Excerpt reprinted:
Davis, *14 by ED* (5.23), pp. 75-81.
Argues that the term "mystic" is misapplied to ED.

6.665   Mary Irmina, Sister. "Fire and Frailty." *Commonweal*, XXIII (April 3, 1936), 639.
Rev. of *Unpublished Poems*, 1935 (3.167).

6.666   Matchett, William H. "Dickinson's Revision of 'Two Butterflies went out at Noon.'" *PMLA*, LXXVII (Sept. 1962), 436-41.

6.667   ———. *Modern Language Quarterly*, XXII (Mar. 1961), 91-94.
Rev. of *Complete Poems*, 1960 (3.207) and Anderson, *Stairway of Surprise* (5.2).

6.668   ———. "The 'Success' by Emily Dickinson." *Boston Public Li-brary Quarterly*, VIII (July 1956), 144-47.
Two of the changes indicated by Johnson (*Poems*, 1955, I, 53) in "Success is counted sweetest" do not occur in *A Masque of Poets*, 1878 (3.7).

6.669   Matthiessen, Francis Otto. "'Midsummer in the Mind.'" *Satur-day Review*, XIII (Jan. 18, 1936), 12.
         Rev. of *Unpublished Poems*, 1935 (3.167). Finds the Emer-sonian concept of compensation in ED's poetry.

6.670   ——. "The Problem of the Private Poet." *Kenyon Review*, VII (Autumn 1945), 584-97.
         Reprinted:
         F. O. Matthiessen. "Private Poet: Emily Dickinson" in *The Responsibilities of the Critic, Essays and Reviews*, ed. John Rackliffe. N.Y.: Oxford Univ. Press, 1952, pp. 80-92.
         Blake and Wells, *Recognition* (5.13), pp. 225-35.
         A review-essay of *Bolts of Melody*, 1945 (3.177) and Bingham, *Ancestors' Brocades* (5.5). Discusses editing problems and cites other "vexing questions" in ED scholarship that have yet to be resolved.

6.671   Maugham, W. Somerset. *Books and You*. N.Y.: Doubleday, 1940, pp. 102-04.
         ED "has been accorded more praise than she deserves."

6.672   Maurin, Mario. *New England Quarterly*, XXXII (Mar. 1959), 99-102.
         Rev. of *Letters*, 1958 (4.90).

6.673   Maynard, Theodore. "More Books of the Week." *Commonweal*, XLII (May 4, 1945), 75-76.
         Rev. of *Bolts of Melody*, 1945 (3.177) and Bingham, *Ancestors' Brocades* (5.5).

6.674   ——. "The Mystery of Emily Dickinson." *Catholic World*, CXXXIV (Oct. 1931), 70-81.
         Rev. of *Poems*, 1930 (3.151) and Pollitt, *Human Background* (5.61).

6.674a   McAleer, John J. "Transcendentalism and the Improper Boston-ian." *Emerson Society Quarterly*, No. 39 (Second Quarter 1965), pp. 73-78.
         Notes a Boston College thesis on ED's relation to transcenden-talism, p. 78; see 14.80.

6.674b   McAllister, Lester G. *Encounter* [Butler Univ., College of Reli-gion, Indianapolis], XXVI (1965), 533-34.
         Rev. of Gelpi, *Mind of the Poet* (5.29).

6.674c   McBride, Henry. "Artist and Critics: Shifting Artistic Evalua-tions in an Evershifting World." Clipping dated Dec. 22, 1945, from an unidentified newspaper in the Beinecke Library, Yale Univ.
         Notes publication of Marsden Hartley's *Selected Poems*, one of which, entitled "Eight Words," "is so close to Emily Dickinson that it is almost plagiarism." Comment complete.

6.675   McCarthy, Desmond. *London Sunday Times*, Oct. 19, 1947, p. 3.
         Rev. of *Poems*, 1947 (3.183) and *Bolts of Melody*, 1947 (3.182).

6.676   McCarthy, Paul. "An Approach to Emily Dickinson's Poetry." *Emerson Society Quarterly*, No. 44 (III Quar., 1966), pp. 22-31.
         On teaching ED's poetry.

6.677   McCarthy, William H., Jr. "'We Temples Build.'" *Yale Review*, XXV (Mar. 1936), 615-16.

Rev. of *Unpublished Poems,* 1935 (3.167).

6.678   [McCausland, Elizabeth]. "Emily Dickinson as Revealed in
          Poems Withheld by Her Sister." *Springfield Sunday Union and
          Republican,* Mar. 17, 1929, p. 3-E.
          Rev. of *Further Poems,* 1929 (3.138). Attributed to Elizabeth
          McCausland in Hampson, *ED: A Bibliography* (1.6), p. 24.

6.679   [————]. "Old House Solves Not This Literary Mystery." *Spring-
          field Sunday Union and Republican,* Mar. 31, 1929, p. 2-E.
          Rev. of *Further Poems,* 1929 (3.138). Attributed to Elizabeth
          McCausland in Hampson, *ED: A Bibliography* (1.6), p. 25.

6.680   [————]. "A Poet's Qualities as Gleaned in New Emily Dickinson
          Volume." *Springfield Sunday Union and Republican,* Mar. 24,
          1929, p. 7-E.
          Rev. of *Further Poems,* 1929 (3.138). Attributed to Elizabeth
          McCausland in Hampson, *ED: A Bibliography* (1.6), p. 25.

6.681   [————]. "They Will Gather at Amherst in Homage to Emily
          Dickinson." *Springfield Sunday Union and Republican,* May 4,
          1930, p. 3-E.
          Reprinted:
          Elizabeth McCausland. "Emily Dickinson Born One Hundred
              Years Ago" in Hampson, *ED: A Bibliography* (1.6), pp. 29-
              36.
          Notes the Hampshire Bookshop observance of the ED Cente-
          nary, May 1930; see also 22.8-13.

6.682   McElderry, Bruce Robert, Jr. "Emily Dickinson" in *The Realis-
          tic Movement in American Writing,* ed. B. R. McElderry, Jr.
          N.Y.: Odyssey Press, 1965, pp. 412-15.

6.683   ————. "Emily Dickinson: Viable Transcendentalist." *Emerson
          Society Quarterly,* No. 44 (III Quar., 1966), pp. 17-21.
          Notes the predominance of Transcendental feeling and ideas in
          ED's poems, especially those published in the 1890, 1891, and
          1896 editions.

6.683a   McLaughlin, Richard. *Springfield Republican,* Dec. 11, 1960, p.
          4-D.
          Rev. of *Complete Poems* (3.207).

6.684   McLean, Sydney Robertson. "Alumnae Conference Impressions."
          Mt. Holyoke Alumnae Quarterly, XIII (Jan. 1930), p. 190.
          See also 22.1-7.

6.685   ————. *American Literature,* XVII (Jan. 1946), 363-65.
          Rev. of Bingham, *Ancestors' Brocades* (5.5) and *Bolts of Mel-
          ody,* 1945 (3.177).

6.686   ————. "Emily Dickinson." *Mt. Holyoke Alumnae Quarterly,* XIX
          (Feb. 1936), 221-23.
          Rev. of *Unpublished Poems,* 1935 (3.167).

6.687   ————. "Emily Dickinson at Mt. Holyoke." *New England Quar-
          terly,* VII (Mar. 1934), 25-42.
          An account of ED's spiritual crisis at Mt. Holyoke Seminary.
          G. F. Whicher comments on this article in "Emily Dickinson
          at Mount Holyoke" (6.1124) and *This Was a Poet* (5.104), p.
          319. See also 14.51.

6.688   McNally, James. "Perspectives in Movement — A Poem by
         Emily Dickinson." *CEA Critic*, XXVI (Nov. 1963), 9-10.
         A study of "I like to see it lap the Miles."

6.689   McNaughton, Ruth Flanders. "Emily Dickinson on Death." *Prai-
         rie Schooner*, XXIII (Summer 1949), 203-14.
         Discusses ED's fascination with death as an aspect of her
         constant ambivalence between skepticism and faith.

6.690   Merchant, Frank. "The Dickinson Mystery." *Town & Gown*, I
         (Oct. 1930), 34-39.
         Rev. of Pollitt, *Human Background* (5.61) and Taggard, *Life
         and Mind* (5.81).

6.691   Mercier, Vivian. *Commonweal*, LV (Jan. 18, 1952), 379-80.
         Rev. of Chase, *ED* (5.17).

6.692   Meredith, William. *New England Quarterly*, XXIX (June 1956),
         252-54.
         Rev. of Bingham, *ED's Home* (4.86).

6.693   Merideth, Robert. "Dickinson's 'I had not minded — Walls.'"
         Explicator, XXIII (Nov. 1964), Item 25.
         Noted by Robbins, *ALS, 1964* (6.851), p. 135.

6.694   ———. "Emily Dickinson and the Acquisitive Society." *New
         England Quarterly*, XXXVII (Dec. 1964), 435-52.
         Notes the frequency of the language of economics in ED's po-
         etry and argues that she was highly critical of the materialis-
         tic values of her culture. Rev. by Robbins, *ALS, 1965* (6.851),
         pp. 157-58.

6.694a   ———. "A 'Maine-iac' in Search of a Tradition." *Colby Library
         Quarterly*, Series VII, No. 1 (Mar. 1965), pp. 27-29.
         In a rejoinder to Robert Burlingame's article on Marsden
         Hartley's indebtedness to ED (6.159a), Prof. Merideth argues
         that ED was less a poetic influence than a carrier of cultural
         tradition for Hartley.

6.695   Merriam, George S. *The Life and Times of Samuel Bowles*. 2
         vols. N.Y.: Century, 1885.
         No mention of ED but tells of visits to the home of Austin
         Dickinson, II, 79.

6.696   Merrifield, Richard. *Yankee*, XV (Dec. 1951), 41-42, 44.
         Rev. of Patterson, *Riddle* (5.55).

6.697   Merrill, Phyllis. *Hadley Book Shop* [South Hadley, Mass.], VI,
         No. 1, Dec. 1930, unpaged.
         Rev. of Taggard, *Life and Mind* (5.81).

6.698   Merrill, Walter McIntosh. *New England Quarterly*, XXVIII (June
         1955), 283-84.
         Rev. of Bingham, *Revelation* (5.9).

6.699   Mesick, Jane. "Alumnae Conference Impressions." *Mt. Holyoke
         Alumnae Quarterly*, XII (Jan. 1930), 190.
         See also 22.1-7.

6.700   Metzger, Charles R. "Emily Dickinson's Sly Bird." *Emerson
         Society Quarterly*, No. 44 (III Quar., 1966), pp. 21-22.
         Explicates "A Bird came down the Walk."

6.700a   Meyer, Howard N. *Colonel of the Black Regiment. The Life of*

Thomas Wentworth Higginson. N.Y.: W.W. Norton, 1967, pp. 158-66, 270-72, 294-99, *passim.*
Briefly reviews the history of Higginson's friendship with ED and his role in the first publication of her poems.

6.701 Middleton, J. E. "Emily Dickinson and Her Work; New Light on a Shy Poet." *Saturday Night* [Toronto], LX (June 16, 1945), 30.
Rev. of *Bolts of Melody,* 1945 (3.177) and Bingham, *Ancestors' Brocades* (5.5).

6.702 Miles, Josephine, ed. *The Poem. A Critical Anthology.* Englewood Cliffs, N.J.: Prentice-Hall, 1959, pp. 36-37.
Contains an explication of "I stepped from Plank to Plank."

6.703 Miles, Susan. "The Irregularities of Emily Dickinson." *London Mercury,* XIII (Dec. 1925), 145-58.
Reprinted:
Blake and Wells, *Recognition* (5.13), pp. 123-29.
A reply to Harold Monro (see 6.717) which argues that ED's irregularities serve to express a sense of fracture in her world.

6.704 Miller, Betty. "Elizabeth and Emily Elizabeth." *Twentieth Century,* CLIX (June 1956), 574-83.
On ED and Elizabeth Barrett Browning.

6.705 Miller, F. DeWolfe. *New England Quarterly,* XXXIV (Mar. 1961), 114-16.
Rev. of Anderson, *Stairway of Surprise* (5.2).

6.706 ———. *Western Humanities Review,* XIX (Spring 1965), 186.
Rev. of Blake and Wells, *Recognition* (5.13).

6.707 Miller, James E., Jr. *College English,* XXIII (Feb. 1962), 415.
Rev. of Ward, *Capsule of the Mind* (5.97).

6.708 ———. *College English,* XXIII (Mar. 1962), 516.
Rev. of Leyda, *Years and Hours* (5.49).

6.709 ———. "Emily Dickinson's Bright Orthography." *Hudson Review,* XIV (Summer 1961), 301-06.
Reprinted:
James E. Miller, Jr. *Quests Surd and Absurd.* Chicago: Univ. of Chicago Press, 1967, pp. 137-44.
Rev. of *Complete Poems,* 1960 (3.207); Anderson, *Stairway of Surprise* (5.2); and Leyda, *Years and Hours* (5.49).

6.710 ———. "Emily Dickinson: The Thunder's Tongue." *Minnesota Review,* II (Spring 1962), 289-304.
Reprinted:
James E. Miller, Jr. *Quests Surd and Absurd.* Chicago: Univ. of Chicago Press, 1967, pp. 145-58.
Shows how sudden changes in syntax and form contribute to the element of surprise in ED's poetry.

6.711 Miller, Perry. "Emily Dickinson: The Shunning of Joy." *Reporter,* XVIII (May 29, 1958), 34-36.
Rev. of *Letters,* 1958 (4.90).

6.712 ———. "From Edwards to Emerson." *New England Quarterly,* XIII (Dec. 1940), 617.
Refers to ED's phrase "Debauchee of Dew" (in "I taste a liquor

never brewed") as an example of one of the heresies of New
England Puritanism, "the heresy of power."

6.713   ———. *New England Quarterly*, XXIX (Mar. 1956), 101-03.
Rev. of Johnson, *Interpretive Biography* (5.44).

6.713a   Miller, Ruth. "Through the Mist of Tears" in *Banasthali Patrika*
[Banasthali, Bengal], No. 11 (July 1968), Special Number on
American Literature, ed. Rameshwar Gupta, pp. 16-19.

6.714   Mills, Rosamund. "Emily Dickinson." *Interludes* [Baltimore,
Md.], VII (Winter 1930-1931), 80-84.
An account of ED's "romance" based on Bianchi's *Life and
Letters* (4.36).

6.715   Miner, Earl Roy. "Dickinson's 'A Clock stopped — Not the Man-
tel's.'" *Explicator*, XIII (Dec. 1954), Item 18.

6.716   Moldenhauer, Joseph J. "Emily Dickinson's Ambiguity: Notes on
Technique." *Emerson Society Quarterly*, No. 44 (III Quar.,
1966), pp. 35-44.
Through a close reading of "She lay as if at play" and "The
last Night that She lived," the author examines the poetic
strategies by which ED renders her sense of ambiguity. Rev.
by Robbins, *ALS, 1966* (6.851), p. 142.

6.717   Monro, Harold. "Books of the Quarter." *The Criterion*, III (Jan.
1925), 322-24.
Reprinted:
Blake and Wells, *Recognition* (5.13), pp. 121-22.
Rev. of *Selected Poems*, 1924 (3.127). Monro's charge that
ED's poetry is "overrated" is answered by Susan Miles' "The
Irregularities of ED" (6.703).

6.718   Monroe, Harriet. "The Single Hound by Emily Dickinson." *Poetry*, V (Dec. 1914), 138-40.
Rev. of *Single Hound*, 1914 (3.114).

6.719   Monteiro, George. "Emily Dickinson and Brazil." *Notes and
Queries*, n.s. IX (Aug. 1962), 312-13.
Replies to J. A. Lavin, who, in "Emily Dickinson and Brazil,"
(6.600) is critical of Monteiro's reading of "I aksed no other
thing"; see next entry.

6.720   ———. "Emily Dickinson's Merchant God." *Notes and Queries*,
n.s. VI (Dec. 1959), 455-56.
Argues that "I asked no other thing" uses humor to mock the
deities of later Puritan orthodoxy.

6.721   ———. "Traditional Ideas in Dickinson's 'I felt a Funeral, in my
Brain.'" *Modern Language Notes*, LXXV (Dec. 1960), 656-63.
This poem embodies ideas of Pascal, Milton, and Emerson to
express the redemptive power of grace.

6.722   Moore, Geoffrey. "American Literature." *Times* [London] *Literary Supplement*, June 13, 1958, p. 329, and July 4, 1938, p.
377.
Replies to a review attributed to James Reeves; see 6.842.

6.723   Moore, Marianne. "Emily Dickinson." *Poetry*, XLI (Jan. 1933),
219-26.
Rev. of *Letters*, 1931 (4.52).

6.724   Moore, Virginia. "Emily Dickinson" in *Distinguished Women Writers*. N.Y.: Dutton, 1934, pp. 145-60.
A biographical introduction.

6.725   ———. "The Poetic Mind." *Virginia Quarterly Review*, XV (Summer 1939), 452-56.
Rev. of Whicher, *This Was a Poet* (5.104).

6.726   ———. "Women Poets." *Bookman* [N.Y.], LXXI (July 1930), 388-95.
Describes ED (p. 392) as one of "ten or twelve women lyricists who are great in all but the first sense."

6.727   Moran, Helen. "Queens Now." *London Mercury*, XXVI (June 1932), 138-46.
ED is included in a discussion of various women authors of the nineteenth century. Rev. of *Letters*, 1931 (4.52).

6.728   Morgrage, Louise. "The Immortal Emily." *California Arts and Architecture*, XXXIX (Aug. 1930), 49.
Rev. of Taggard, *Life and Mind* (5.81).

6.729   Morison, Samuel Eliot. *Builders of Bay Colony*. Boston: Houghton, Mifflin, 1930, pp. 323, 336.
Anne Bradstreet's genius is reincarnated in ED, whose "elfin, almost *gamin* attitude" she prefigures.

6.730   Morley, Christopher. "College Highway." *Saturday Review*, XII (Sept. 28, 1935), 12, 15.
A traveler's impression of the Dickinson house and barn.

6.731   Moseley, Edwin. "The Gambit of Emily Dickinson." *University of Kansas City Review*, XVI (Autumn 1949), 11-19.
ED's characteristic poetic strategy is to treat grand things from a distance and to pretend humility before them.

6.732   Mottram, E. N. W. "Emily Dickinson" in *The Concise Encyclopedia of English and American Poetry*, ed. Stephen Spender and Donald Hall. N.Y.: Hawthorne Books, 1963, pp. 115-16.
"Her weaknesses are those of a too neatly repeated range, probably arising from that lack of discipline in writing for an audience of her peers, and an almost total reluctance to resist habits of metre, vocabulary and tone."

6.733   Moulton, Louise Chandler. "With the Poets." *Boston Sunday Herald*, Nov. 22, 1891, p. 24.
Rev. of *Poems*, 1891 (3.52).

6.734   ———. "A Very Remarkable Book." *Boston Sunday Herald*, Nov. 23, 1890, p. 24.
Excerpt reprinted:
Poems (1890-1896), ed. Monteiro, 1967 (3.212), pp. xiv-xv.
Rev. of *Poems*, 1890 (3.9).

6.734a   Mudge, Jean McClure. *Papers of the Bibliographical Society of America*, LXII (Second Quarter 1967), 272-75.
Rev. of Franklin, *Editing* (5.28).

6.735   Muirhead, James Fullarton. *The Land of Contrasts: A Briton's View of His American Kin*. Boston: Lamson, Wolffe, 1898; N.Y.: John Lane, 1900, pp. 178-86.
A generally appreciative introduction to ED, stressing that "her defects are easily paralleled" in English literature.

6.735a   Mullican, James S. "Dickinson's 'Water makes many Beds.'"
         Explicator, XXVII (Nov. 1968), Item 23.

6.736   Mumford, Lewis. "Pan's Sister." *New York Herald Tribune
         Books*, Mar. 17, 1929, pp. 1, 6.
         Rev. of *Further Poems*, 1929 (3.138).

6.737   Munn, L. S. "Emily Dickinson's Home — Rich in Family Back-
         ground." *Springfield Sunday Republican*, Oct. 9, 1955, p. 10-C.
         Rev. of Bingham, *ED's Home* (4.86).

6.738   Murdock, Kenneth B. *New England Quarterly*, X (Sept. 1937),
         613.
         Rev. of *Poems*, 1937 (3.173).

6.738a   Muri, John T. "A Study Guide to Poems of Emily Dickinson."
         N.C.T.E. Studies in the Mass Media [National Council of
         Teachers of English, Champaign, Ill.], I (May 1961), 3-20.
         Contains text and study questions designed for high school use
         to accompany the N.C.T.E. recording of ED's poems (20.5).

6.739   Murphy, Esther. "The Curious History of Emily Dickinson."
         New York Herald Tribune Book News and Reviews, April 20,
         1924, pp. 25, 30.
         Rev. of Bianchi, *Life and Letters* (4.36).

6.740   Murray, Marian. "Emily Dickinson's Handwriting Here. Mrs.
         A. L. Gillett Has Notes Written to Her as Girl." *Hartford
         Daily Times*, Mar. 7, 1936, p. 9.
         An article featuring material supplied by Mrs. Sara Colton
         Gillett which reproduces an ED letter allegedly sent to Mrs.
         Gillett when she was a girl; see *Letters*, 1958 (4.90), III, 886-
         87.

6.741   Musser, Grace S. "Emily Dickinson. Letters and Poems of a
         Lonely New England Woman Who Believed in 'Art for Truth.'"
         San Francisco Call, Sept. 20, 1896.
         Rev. of *Poems*, 1896 (3.89).

6.742   N., I. O. "Dickinson's 'I like to see it lap the Miles.'" *Explica-
         tor*, II (May 1944), Query 31.
         Questions whether a dragon rather than a horse is implicated
         in this poem and whether "Boanerges" suggests a "loud vocif-
         erous preacher" rather than merely the Biblical "sons of
         thunder."

6.742a   Narasimhiah, C. D., ed. *Indian Response to American Literature.*
         New Delhi: U.S. Educational Foundation in India, 1967.
         Includes two essays on ED.

6.742b   Newcomer, Alphonso G. *American Literature.* Chicago: Scott,
         Foresman, 1901, pp. 283-84, 288-89.
         A literary history with qualified praise for ED's poems:
         "... stamped though they be with the celestial signature, they
         are but fragments, and in the temple of art, which keeps its
         riches for the perfect statue, they must shine obscurely."

6.743   Newcomer, James. "Emily's Obliquities." *Southwest Review*,
         XXXVII (Winter 1952), 78-79.
         Rev. of *Letters to Holland*, 1951 (4.76).

6.744   Newell, Kenneth B. "Dickinson's 'Aurora is the effort.'" *Expli-
         cator*, XX (Sept. 1961), Item 5.

6.745 Newell, Kenneth B. "Dickinson's 'We should not mind so small a flower.'" *Explicator,* XIX (June 1961), Item 65.

6.746 Newman, Charles. "Candor is the Only Wile: The Art of Sylvia Plath." *Tri-Quarterly,* No. 7 (Fall 1966), pp. 39-64.
       Makes several comparisons between ED and Sylvia Plath, noting, for example, that both poets are driven from the abstraction of myth back to the concrete.

6.747 Nichols, Frances A. "New Literature." *Boston Sunday Globe,* Dec. 14, 1890, p. 25.
       Rev. of *Poems,* 1890 (3.9).

6.748 Nicolson, Harold. "Shy Bobolink." *Observer* [London], No. 8384, (Feb. 10, 1952), p. 7.
       Rev. of *Letters,* 1951 (4.80).

6.749 Niemeyer, Carl A. "The Gentleman With the Deep Voice." *Union College Review,* XLVII (Jan. 1958), 6-8.
       On ED and Charles Wadsworth.

6.750 Nims, John Frederick. "'Dazzling Snapshots of the Human Spirit.'" *Chicago Sunday Tribune Magazine of Books,* May 6, 1951, p. 5.
       Rev. of *Letters,* 1951 (4.80).

6.751 ———. "Solution of a 90 Year Old Love Mystery." *Chicago Sunday Tribune Magazine of Books,* Nov. 11, 1951, p. 3.
       Rev. of Patterson, *Riddle* (5.55).

6.752 Nist, John. "Two American Poets and a Spider." *Walt Whitman Birthplace Bulletin,* IV (Jan. 1961), 8-11.
       Originally published in Portuguese; see 11.45.
       Compares ED's "A Spider sewed at Night" with Whitman's "A noiseless patient spider" and finds that ED, unlike Whitman, is "more New England than American." "His [Whitman's] vision probes the universe; hers, the front parlor" (p. 9).

6.753 Nordell, Rod. "The Art and Artist Become Freshly Accessible." *Christian Science Monitor,* Dec. 1, 1960, p. 15.
       Rev. of *Complete Poems,* 1960 (3.207) and Anderson, *Stairway of Surprise* (5.2).

6.754 ———. "A Poet's Letters." *Christian Science Monitor,* April 10, 1958, p. 11.
       Rev. of *Letters,* 1958 (4.90).

6.755 North, Helen Marshall. "Emily Dickinson's Letters." *Home Journal* [N.Y.], Jan. 2, 1895.
       Rev. of *Letters,* 1894 (4.3).

6.756 North, Jessica Nelson. "Building a Legend." *Poetry,* XXXV (Dec. 1929), 164-67.
       Rev. of *Further Poems,* 1929 (3.138).

6.757 Nyren, Dorothy, ed. and comp. "Dickinson, Emily" in *A Library of Literary Criticism.* N.Y.: Ungar, 1960, pp. 132-36.
       Reprints brief excerpts from thirteen critics on ED.

6.758 O'Brien, Anthony. "Emily Dickinson: The World, the Body, and the Reflective Life." *Critical Review* [Univ. of Melbourne], No. 9 (1966), pp. 69-80.
       Explores connections between ED's ways of imagining thought and the bodily life through close study of seven poems.

6.759   Ochshorn, Myron. "Dickinson's 'I know some lonely Houses off
        the Road.'" *Explicator,* XI (Nov. 1952), Item 12.
6.760   ———. "In Search of Emily Dickinson." *New Mexico Quarterly,*
        XXIII (Spring 1953), 94-106.
        A review-essay of Chase, *ED* (5.17) and Patterson, *Riddle*
        (5.55). Argues that critics have overlooked the theme of in-
        tense suffering in ED's poetry.
6.761   [O'Connor, William Van]. "Emily Dickinson: The Domestication
        of Terror." *Times* [London] *Literary Supplement,* No. 2793
        (Sept. 9, 1955), p. 532.
        Revised and expanded in William Van O'Connor, *The Gro-*
            tesque: An American Genre and Other Essays. Carbon-
            dale, Ill.: Southern Illinois Univ. Press, 1962, pp. 98-108.
        ED tried to domesticate and make beautiful a terrifying cos-
        mos.
6.762   ———. "The Responsibilities of Editors." *Poetry,* LXXIX (Feb.
        1952), 291-92.
        Criticizes an explication of "Wonder — is not precisely Know-
        ing"; see 6.369.
6.763   ———. *Sense and Sensibility in Modern Poetry.* Chicago: Univ.
        of Chicago Press, 1948, pp. 156-57 *passim.*
        Briefly notes ED's influence on modern poetry and includes an
        explication of "The Brain — is wider than the Sky."
6.764   Odell, Ruth. *Helen Hunt Jackson.* N.Y.: Appleton-Century, 1939.
        ED discussed, pp. 56-69 *passim.*
        Criticizes Josephine Pollitt's hypothesis that ED fell in love
        with Major Hunt.
6.765   O'Halloran, Elspeth. "A Gallant Woman." *Springfield Union,*
        Mar. 22, 1929, p. 18.
        Rev. of *Further Poems,* 1929 (3.138).
6.766   Orr, Clifford. *Boston Evening Transcript,* Book Section, Mar.
        29, 1924, p. 14.
        Rev. of Bianchi, *Life and Letters* (4.36).
6.767   *The Outlook and Independent,* Editors of. *Outlook and Indepen-*
        dent, CLI (April 24, 1929), 669, 680.
        Clara Bellinger Green's intimation that some of the poems
        printed in *Further Poems* may not be authentic elicited an
        editorial disclaimer of responsibility for statements made in
        her review; see 6.420.
6.768   Parker, Barbara N. "The Dickinson Portraits by Otis A. Bul-
        lard." *Harvard Library Bulletin,* VI (Winter 1952), 133-37.
        Describes portraits of the Dickinson family by Otis Bullard
        and includes a brief sketch of the painter's life.
6.769   Parks, Edd Winfield. "The Public and the Private Poet." *South
        Atlantic Quarterly,* LVI (Autumn 1957), 480-85.
        Compares ED and Walt Whitman.
6.770   Parsons, Thornton H. "The Indefatigable Casuist." *University
        Review* [formerly *University of Kansas City Review*], XXX
        (Oct. 1963), 19-25.
        ED makes a variety of connections between ultimate fulfill-
        ment and immediate denial.

6.771 Parton, Ethel. "Emily Dickinson: A Review." *Outlook*, CXXXVI (April 23, 1924), 701-02.
Rev. of Bianchi, *Life and Letters* (4.36).

6.772 Paterson, Isabel. "Emily Dickinson's Mysterious Love Affair." *New York Herald Tribune*, Feb. 21, 1930, p. 11.
Rev. of Pollitt, *Human Background* (5.61).

6.773 ———. "The New England Sappho." *New York Herald Tribune*, June 20, 1930, p. 17.
Rev. of Taggard, *Life and Mind* (5.81).

6.774 Pattee, Fred Lewis. *Century Readings for a Course in American Literature*. N.Y.: Century, 1926, p. 700.

6.775 ———. "Gentian, Not Rose: The Real Emily Dickinson." *Sewanee Review*, XLV (April-June 1937), 180-97.
A reappraisal of the work of ED, deploring the myths that have grown up around her. Argues that much of her work has been too highly praised and that its future will depend on better editing.

6.776 ———. *A History of American Literature Since 1870*. N.Y.: Century, 1915, pp. 340-41, *passim*.
A brief, unfavorable evaluation.

6.777 ———. "The Transition Poets," in *The New American Literature: 1890-1930*. N.Y.: Century, 1930, pp. 196-99.
A brief introduction. Emphasizes ED's dismissal of conventional poetic techniques, especially versification, and concludes that her "final place among the poets is still open to question." See 6.883.

6.778 Patterson, Rebecca. "Elizabeth Browning and Emily Dickinson." *Educational Leader*, XX (July 1956), 21-48.
Discusses ED's reading of Elizabeth Barrett Browning, especially *Aurora Leigh*.

6.779 ———. "Emily Dickinson's Debt to Günderode." *Midwest Quarterly*, VII (July 1967), 331-54.
Notes resemblances between ED's relationship to her sister-in-law, Sue Dickinson, and that between Karoline von Günderode (1780-1806), a minor German poet, and her friend, Elizabeth Brentano (1785-1859). A book of Günderode's poems, known to have been in the Dickinson household, may have influenced ED's thought and language.

6.780 ———. "Emily Dickinson's Hummingbird." *Educational Leader*, XXII (July 1958), 12-19.
Excerpt reprinted:
Davis, *14 by ED* (5.23), pp. 140-48.
A close reading of "A Route of Evanescence" with reference to related poems.

6.781 ———. "Emily Dickinson's Palette." *Midwest Quarterly*, V (Summer 1964), 271-91; VI (Autumn 1964), 97-117.
Discusses the frequency and significance of ED's use of color. Compares her in this respect with her favorite poet-models.

6.782 Payne, William Morton. "Recent Books of Poetry." *Dial*, XI (Feb. 1891), 313.
Rev. of *Poems*, 1890 (3.9).

6.783   Payne, William Morton. "Recent Poetry." *Dial*, XXII (Feb. 1, 1897), 90.
        Rev. of *Poems*, 1896 (3.89).

6.784   Pearce, Roy Harvey. "On the Continuity of American Poetry." *Hudson Review*, X (Winter 1957-58), 518-39.
        ED discussed, pp. 531-36.
        Revised and expanded in Pearce, *The Continuity of American Poetry*. Princeton, N.J.: Princeton Univ. Press, 1961, pp. 174-86, *passim*.
        ED's concern with being herself exemplifies an egocentricism basic to nineteenth century American style. In her work "life [is] being made even as it is being lived through. . . . Writing poems she writes herself."

6.785   Pearson, Edmund Lester. "Two Poets." *Outlook*, CXXXVII (July 23, 1924), 479.
        Rev. of *Complete Poems*, 1924 (3.123).

[3.117] Peattie, Elia W. *Chicago Daily Tribune*, Oct. 10, 1914, p. 10.
        Rev. of *Single Hound*, 1914 (3.114).

6.786   Peckham, Morse, and Seymour Chatman, eds. *Word, Meaning, Poem*. N.Y.: Crowell, 1961, pp. 302-12.

6.787   Pellew, George. "Ten Years of American Literature." *Critic*, XVIII (Jan. 17, 1891), 29.
        Rev. of *Poems*, 1890 (3.9).

6.788   Perrine, Laurence. "All of Emily Dickinson." *Southwest Review*, XLVI (Spring 1961), 178-79.
        Rev. of *Complete Poems*, 1960 (3.207) and Anderson, *Stairway of Surprise* (5.2).

6.789   ———. "Dickinson's 'A Clock stopped.'" *Explicator*, XIV (Oct. 1955), Item 4.

6.790   ———. "Dickinson's 'I started Early — Took my Dog.'" *Explicator*, X (Feb. 1952), Item 28.
        Reprinted:
        Davis, *14 by ED* (5.23), pp. 88-89.

6.791   ———. "Dickinson's 'My Life had stood — a Loaded Gun.'" *Explicator*, XXI (Nov. 1962), Item 21.

6.792   ———. "Dickinson's 'There's a certain Slant of light.'" *Explicator*, XI (May 1953), Item 50.
        Reprinted:
        Davis, *14 by ED* (5.23), pp. 34-35.

6.793   ———. "Emily Dickinson's 'Presentment' [sic] Again." *American Notes and Queries*, III (April 1965), 119.
        A reply to David Hirsch's "Emily Dickinson's 'Presentiment'"; see 6.492.

6.794   ———. "Emily's Beloved Friend." *Southwest Review*, XXXVII (Winter 1952), 81-83.
        Rev. of Patterson, *Riddle* (5.55).

6.795   ———. "The Importance of Tone in the Interpretation of Literature." *College English*, XXIV (Feb. 1963), 389-95.
        Contains an explication of "Two Butterflies went out at Noon," pp. 389-90.

6.796   Perrine, Laurence. "The Nature of Proof in the Interpretation of
         Poetry." *English Journal,* LI (Sept. 1962), 393-98.
         Contains an explication of "Where Ships of Purple — gently
         toss," pp. 394-96.

6.796a   ———. "Sea and Surging Bosom." *CEA Critic,* XXX (Nov. 1967),
         9.
         Takes exception to one detail of Prof. White's explication of
         "The thought beneath so slight a film;" see 6.1149. White's
         rejoinder follows on the same page.

6.797   ———. *Sound and Sense: An Introduction to Poetry.* N.Y.: Har-
         court, 1956; 2nd ed., 1963.
         Contains explications of "There is no Frigate like a Book," p.
         32; "Apparently with no surprise," p. 86; "My life closed twice
         before its close," pp. 126-27 (1st ed. pagination).

6.798   ———. "Woman of Letters." *Southwest Review,* XXXVII (Sum-
         mer 1952), 258.
         Rev. of Chase, *ED* (5.17).

6.799   Perry, Ernestine C. "Anecdotes of Noted Amherst Women Re-
         lated." *Springfield Union,* Mar. 23, 1929.
         Reports a Women's Club program on ED, Mary Heaton Vorse,
         and Helen Hunt.

6.800   ———. "Mme. M. D. Bianchi Tells of a Vivid Emily Dickinson."
         Springfield Union, Oct. 24, 1930, p. 10.
         Reports a reminiscence by ED's niece, Martha Dickinson
         Bianchi.

6.801   Phillips, J. Richard. "Amherst Exception." *The New York
         Times,* Nov. 10, 1968, Section 10, p. 9.
         Letter to the editor replying to an article by Eleanor Early;
         see 6.306a.

6.802   Pitkin, Walter B. "Introduction" to *As We Are, Stories of Here
         and Now.* N.Y.: Harcourt, Brace, 1923, p. xi.
         Quotes "I never saw a Moor" as an example of an "unrealis-
         tic" attitude toward life.

6.803   Plummer, Myrtes-Marie. "Emily Dickinson." *Kansas City Po-
         etry Magazine,* II (Mar. 1942), 12.
         A brief introduction to ED's life.

6.804   Poe, Elizabeth Ellicott. "Half-Forgotten Romances of American
         History." *Washington Post,* Mar. 25, 1935.
         About ED and Leonard Humphrey.

6.805   Poetry Workshop, Columbus, Georgia. "Dickinson's 'My Life
         had stood — a Loaded Gun.'" *Explicator,* XV (May 1957), Item
         51.

6.806   Pohl, Frederick J. "Dickinsoniana." *Saturday Review,* VII (Jan.
         10, 1931), 522.
         A letter to the editor critical of Taggard's explanation (see
         Life and Mind, 5.81) for ED's choice of Higginson as her lit-
         erary preceptor. Also discusses possible sources for refer-
         ences in "Our lives are Swiss," "Pigmy seraphs — gone
         astray" and "The Flower must not blame the Bee."

6.807   ———. "The Emily Dickinson Controversy." *Sewanee Review,*
         XLI (Oct.-Dec. 1933), 467-82.

Contends that Edward Hunt provided the inspiration for the love poems.

6.808　　Pohl, Frederick J. "The Poetry of Emily Dickinson." *Amherst Monthly*, XXV (May 1910), 47-50.

6.809　　Pollitt, Josephine. "Emily and Major Hunt." *Saturday Review*, VI (July 5, 1930), 1180.
A letter to the editor summarizing evidence for ED's romantic interest in Edward Hunt.

6.810　　——. "Emily Beyond the Alps." *Saturday Review*, XXIX (April 13, 1946), 20.
Rev. of a French translation by Félix Ansermoz-Dubois, 1945 (9.1).

6.811　　——. "In Lands I Never Saw" in *Guests In Eden* (5.59), pp. 34-37.
Discusses foreign publication of ED.

6.812　　——, and Lewis Gannett. "Whom Did Emily Dickinson Love?" *New York Herald Tribune*, Dec. 31, 1932, p. 11.
Mr. Gannett publishes a letter from Josephine Pollitt noting inaccuracies in Mme. Bianchi's volume, *ED Face to Face* (4.59).

6.813　　Pommer, Henry F. "Dickinson's 'The Soul Selects Her Own Society.'" *Explicator*, III (Feb. 1945), Item 32.

6.813a　——. "The Mysticism of Eugene O'Neill." *Modern Drama*, IX (May 1966), 26-39.
Briefly notes that ED's mysticism is more intense than O'Neill's (p. 37).

6.814　　Porter, Alan. "Emily Dickinson." *Spectator* [London], CXXXIII (Oct. 18, 1924), 549-50.
Rev. of Bianchi, *Life and Letters* (4.36) and *Selected Poems*, 1924 (3.127).

6.815　　Porter, David T. *American Literature*, XL (Mar. 1968), 91-92.
Rev. of Franklin, *Editing of ED* (5.28).

6.816　　——. "Emily Dickinson: The Formative Years." *Massachusetts Review*, VI (Summer 1965), 559-69.
Revised and reprinted as the first chapter of the author's *The Art of Emily Dickinson's Early Poetry* (5.69), pp. 1-15.
Contrasts ED's artistic self-assurance with her pose of artlessness at the time of her early letters to Higginson.
Rev. by Robbins, *ALS, 1965* (6.851), p. 157.

6.817　　——. *New England Quarterly*, XXXVI (Dec. 1963), 522-24.
Rev. of Sewall, *Critical Essays* (5.75).

6.817a　——. *New England Quarterly*, XLI (Sept. 1968), 459-61.
Rev. of Sherwood, *Circumference* (5.79).

6.818　　——. *New Mexico Quarterly*, XXXIV (Spring 1964), 105-06.
Rev. of Griffith, *Long Shadow* (5.31).

6.819　　Poulet, Georges. "Time and American Writers — Emily Dickinson" in *Studies in Human Time*, trans. Elliott Coleman. Baltimore: Johns Hopkins Univ. Press, 1956, pp. 345-50.
ED's sense of time is dominated by supreme moments, often following in the closest succession, "in one of which everything is given, and in the other everything taken away."

6.820   Powell, Desmond S. "Emily Dickinson." *Colorado College Pub-*
        lications, General Series, No. 200, Study Series, No. 19 (May
        1934), pp. 1-12.
        Argues that ED's reputation will rest chiefly on her love po-
        etry.

6.821   [Power], Sister Mary James. "Emily's Neighborhood." *Catholic*
        World, CLVIII (Nov. 1943), 143-49.
        An excerpt from the author's book-length study of ED, *In the*
        Name of the Bee (5.72). Contends that ED offered herself as
        a "free oblation" to her loved ones and that "her response to
        sacrifice had supernaturalized the natural in her heart."

6.822   Powers, James H. "World Acclaims Emily Dickinson, But She's
        Still 'The Queer Poet' to Amherst." *Boston Sunday Globe*,
        Nov. 23, 1930, pp. 6, 7.
        On the ED Centenary celebration, Amherst, Dec. 10, 1930; see
        also 22.14-19.

6.823   Prescott, Frederick Clarke. "Emily Dickinson's *Further*
        Poems." *American Literature*, I (Nov. 1929), 306-07.
        Questions the editing of *Further Poems*, 1929 (3.138), espe-
        cially with reference to the line divisions.

6.824   Price, James. "Genevieve Taggard Reveals Mysterious Love
        Affair of Emily Dickinson." *Philadelphia Record*, June 21,
        1930, p. 10-C.
        Rev. of Taggard, *Life and Mind* (5.81) and Jenkins, *Friend and*
        Neighbor (5.35).

6.824a Price, Lawrence Marsden. *The Reception of United States Lit-*
        erature in Germany. Univ. of North Carolina Studies in Com-
        parative Literature, No. 39. Chapel Hill: Univ. of North
        Carolina Press, 1966, p. 79.
        Although German anthologies of American poets, including ED,
        have made little impact on the German public, they have been
        well received by German critics.

6.825   Price, Warwick James. "The Poetry of Emily Dickinson." *Yale*
        Literary Magazine, LIX (Oct. 1893), 25-27.
        An appreciation: ". . . the careful and sympathetic reader soon
        discovers the pearls of the writer's thought, though they be
        strung on a pack thread between common beads."

6.826   ———. "Three Forgotten Poetesses." *Forum* [N.Y.], XLVII
        (Mar. 1912), 361-76.
        Discusses ED, Amy Levy, and Emma Lazarus.

6.827   R., C. C. "Letters from Amherst." *Christian Science Monitor*,
        June 30, 1937, p. 7.
        Notes a change for the worse in ED's letter-writing style in
        1857 and argues that her letters "were the result of a desire
        for perfection in all things."

6.828   Rabe, Olive H. "Emily Dickinson as a Mystic." *Colorado Quar-*
        terly, XIV (Winter 1966), 280-88.
        Many of ED's poems have their source in the experience of
        spiritual illumination and find their analogies in the accounts
        of famous mystics. Rev. by Robbins, *ALS, 1966* (6.851), p.
        143.

6.829   Raine, Kathleen. "The Little Emily." *New Statesman and Nation*, XLIII (April 19, 1952), 470, 472.
          Rev. of *Letters*, 1951 (4.80). The author's rejoinder to Caroline Wedgwood Benn's criticism of this review (see 6.92) appears May 10, 1952, p. 556.

6.830   Rand, Frank Prentice. "Amherst Authors — Mostly Poets" in *The Village of Amherst: A Landmark of Light.* Amherst, Mass.: Amherst Historical Society, 1958, pp. 229-30.
          A brief, biographical entry.

6.831   ———. "More Emily-ana." *Amherst Record,* Jan. 12, 1967, p. 17.
          Discusses ED's possible relationship to Hasket Derby.

6.832   Rand, Jerry. "New Light on the Case of the Poet Emily Dickinson." *New York Sun,* April 4, 1945, p. 20.
          Rev. of Bingham, *Ancestors' Brocades* (5.5).

6.833   ———. "The Opening of a Door On a Woman Poet's World." *New York Sun,* Nov. 5, 1938, p. 34.
          Rev. of Whicher, *This Was a Poet* (5.104).

6.834   [Rand, W. J.] "A Woman of Talent. Mabel Loomis Todd Introduced Emily Dickinson to the World." *New York Sun,* Nov. 23, 1932, p. 10.
          An obituary.

6.835   Ransom, John Crowe. "Emily Dickinson." *Perspectives U.S.A.,* No. 15 (Spring 1956), pp. 5-20.
          <u>Reprinted:</u>
          Sewall, *Critical Essays* (5.75), pp. 88-100.
          Translated into German, see 10.63.
          In this wide-ranging essay, Ransom discusses T.H. Johnson's 1955 edition of the *Poems* (3.197) and his *Interpretive Biography* (5.44) and examines ED's "renunciation" as a way of finding "her poet's mask: the personality which was antithetical to her natural character and identical with her desire."

6.836   Rapin, René. "Dickinson's 'Farther in Summer than the Birds.'" *Explicator,* XII (Feb. 1954), Item 24.
          <u>Reprinted:</u>
          Davis, *14 by ED* (5.23), pp. 127-29.

6.836a   Rascoe, Burton. [Selected essays reprinted from the *New York Herald Tribune*] in *A Bookman's Daybook,* ed. C. Hartley Grattan. N.Y.: Horace Liveright, 1929, pp. 6, 299.
          A 1922 essay includes ED in a list of favorite poets (alongside Adelaide Crapsey and Amory Hare) while another article seven years later describes her as one of America's best poets "on the evidence of two or three lyrics alone."

6.837   Raymund, Bernard. "The Unknown Peninsula." *Rocky Mountain Review,* X (Winter 1946), 109-15.
          Review of *Bolts of Melody,* 1945 (3.177) and Bingham, *Ancestors' Brocades* (5.5).

6.838   Read, Herbert. *Spectator* [London], CLI (Dec. 29, 1933), 971.
          <u>Reprinted:</u>
          Blake and Wells, *Recognition* (5.13), pp. 173-75.
          Rev. of *Poems,* 1933 (3.158).

6.839   Rede, Kenneth. "Emily Dickinson — Poetic Rebel." *Christian
         Science Monitor*, April 9, 1924, p. 10.
         Rev. of Bianchi, *Life and Letters* (4.36).

6.840   R[eeves], J[ames], and L[aura] R[iding]. "Humour and Poetry as
         Related Themes." *Epilogue* [London], III (Spring 1937), 173-
         90.
         Discusses ED (pp. 186-87) as a forerunner of modern poetry
         in which "the words do not arise from the subject; the subject
         is made the frailest of excuses for collecting pretty words. . . ."

6.841   Reeves, James. "Introduction" to *Selected Poems*, 1959 (3.202),
         pp. ix-lii.
         Partially reprinted:
         Sewall, *Critical Essays* (5.75), pp. 117-26.
         An introduction to ED's life and work, giving close attention to
         several poems. Replies to objections raised by R. P. Black-
         mur and deals with some of the recurring problems of Dickin-
         son scholarship, including the poet's alleged lack of technique
         and the irregularity of her rhymes and rhythms. Brief expli-
         cations are contained in the notes, pp. 103-08.

6.842   [———]. "The Primitive Vision." *Times* [London] *Literary Sup-
         plement*, No. 2935, May 30, 1958, p. 296.
         Review of *Letters*, 1958 (4.90). Discounts ED's alleged ec-
         centricity and stresses her difficulty in preserving her iden-
         tity as a woman and her love for life. The author replies to
         Geoffrey Moore's criticism of this article (see 6.722) June 27,
         1958, p. 361, and again July 11, 1958, p. 393.

6.843   ———. *Understanding Poetry*. London: Heinemann, 1965, pp.
         35-36, 88-89, 103-04, *passim*.
         Discusses "Presentiment — is that long Shadow — on the Lawn"
         as an example of surprise and naturalness in poetry.

6.844   Reid, Mary J. "Julia C. R. Dorr and Some of Her Poet Contem-
         poraries." *The Midland Monthly* [Des Moines, Iowa], III (June
         1895), 499-507.
         Includes a brief vignette of ED and the comment that her aph-
         oristic style anticipates a penchant for condensation charac-
         teristic of the end of the century.

6.845   R[eilly], J. J. "New Books." *Catholic World*, CLIX (April 1944),
         89-90.
         Rev. of Power, *In the Name of the Bee* (5.72).

6.846   Reiss, Edmund. "Recent Scholarship on Whitman and Dickinson"
         in *The Teacher and American Literature*, ed. Lewis Leary.
         Champaign, Ill.: National Council of Teachers of English,
         1965, pp. 115-27.

6.847   Riley, Herbert Elihu. *An Amherst Book. A Collection of Stories,
         Poems, Songs, Sketches and Historical Articles by Alumni and
         Undergraduates of Amherst College.* N.Y.: Republic Press,
         1896.

6.848   Roach, Helen. "Emily Dickinson: A Hearing." *Improving Col-
         lege and University Teaching*, XIII (Summer 1965), 185.
         A review of a recording of ED's poems read by Lucyle Hook;
         see 20.5.

6.849   Robbins, Frances Lamont. "Emily Dickinson, Friend and Neigh-
         bor." *Outlook and Independent,* CLV (May 7, 1930), 22, 24.
         Rev. of Jenkins, *Friend and Neighbor* (5.35).

6.850   ——. "The Life and Mind of Emily Dickinson." *Outlook and In-
         dependent,* CLV (June 25, 1930), 307.
         Rev. of Taggard, *Life and Mind* (5.81).

6.851   Robbins, J. Albert. "Nineteenth-Century Poetry — Emily Dickin-
         son" in *American Literary Scholarship, An Annual.* Durham,
         N.C.: Duke Univ. Press, 1965 —.
         Summarizes the most important Dickinson scholarship during
         the year covered in each volume: *1963,* pp. 126-28; *1964,* pp.
         130-36; *1965,* pp. 153-59; *1966,* pp. 139-44.

6.852   Roberts, Richard Ellis. "Uncut Stones" in *Reading For Pleasure
         and Other Essays.* London: Methuen, 1928 (2nd ed., 1931),
         pp. 185-90.
         An appreciation of ED's poetry, noting "... its force, its oddly
         inappropriate roughness, its occasional banality, its frequent
         immaturity, its startling flashes of illumination, its great debt
         to Heine."

6.853   Roller, Bert. *Children in American Poetry 1610-1900.* Nash-
         ville, Tenn.: George Peabody College for Teachers Publica-
         tion No. 72 (1930), pp. 150-52, 185.
         In ED's poetry, the child is presented "as a religious rebel,
         an intellectual being who revolted from the conventional and
         traditional dogma of the past."

6.854   Rollins, Carl Purington. "An Emily Dickinson Catalogue." *Sat-
         urday Review,* VII (Jan. 17, 1931), 542.
         Rev. of *Yale University Library, Emily Dickinson* (1.1).

6.855   Root, E. Merrill. "Ariel Among Puritans." *Christian Century,*
         LVI (Mar. 1, 1939), 284-85.
         Rev. of Whicher, *This Was a Poet* (5.104).

6.856   ——. "Clothes vs. Girl." *The Measure,* No. 39 (May 1924), pp.
         15-18.
         Rev. of Bianchi, *Life and Letters* (4.36).

6.857   ——. "Emily Dickinson: Symbol and Dynamo." *Christian Cen-
         tury,* L (June 14, 1933), 784-86.
         Argues that ED is "our great American poet of exile."

6.858   ——. "'The Soul Unto Itself'" in *Guests In Eden* (5.59), pp. 39-
         41.
         A brief appreciation.

6.859   ——. "Sunlight at Last." *Christian Century,* XLVII (April 2,
         1930), 436-37.
         Rev. of Pollitt, *Human Background* (5.61).

6.860   Rose Marie, Sister. *Commonweal,* XXIX (Nov. 18, 1938), 106.
         Rev. of Whicher, *This Was a Poet* (5.104). Whicher replies;
         see 6.1142.

6.861   Rosenbaum, S. P. "Emily Dickinson and the Machine." *Studies
         in Bibliography,* XVIII (1965), 207-27.
         Recounts the difficulties encountered in preparing the Cornell
         computer concordance to the poems of ED. Rev. by Robbins,
         ALS, 1964 (6.851), p. 131.

6.862   Rosenberger, Coleman. "The Rediscovery of Emily Dickinson."
          Queens Quarterly, LII (Autumn 1945), 352-55.
          Rev. of *Bolts of Melody*, 1945 (3.177).
6.862a   Rossetti, Christina. [Excerpt from a letter to Thomas Niles] in
          Lubbers, *Critical Revolution* (5.114), p. 30.
          Praises ED's genius, but objects to some of her "irreligious"
          poems. MS. owned by the Amherst College Library.
6.863   Rossky, William. "Dickinson's 'A Clock stopped.'" *Explicator*,
          XXII (Sept. 1963), Item 3.
          Rev. by Robbins, *ALS, 1963* (6.851), p. 128.
6.864   Rourke, Constance. *American Humor: A Study of the National
          Character*. N.Y.: Harcourt, Brace, 1931, pp. 266-76.
          Reissued:
          Garden City, N.Y.: Doubleday Anchor Books, 1953, pp. 209-
          212.
          The author argues that ED is not only a lyric poet but a comic
          poet in the American tradition. See also 6.197.
6.865   ———. "Emily Dickinson's Own Story." *New Republic*, LXX
          (April 20, 1932), 279-80.
          Rev. of *Letters*, 1931 (4.52).
6.865a   Rovit, Earl H. "American Literature and 'The American Expe-
          rience.'" *American Quarterly*, XIII (Summer 1961), 120 note
          6, 121 note 8.
          Relates ED's circumference image to Jonathan Edwards' phi-
          losophy and a peculiarly American need for metaphysical
          self-definition.
6.865b   ———. "The Shape of American Poetry." *Jahrbuch für Amerika-
          studien*, VI (1961), 122-133.
          Suggests that ED and Wallace Stevens are similarly concerned
          with the experience of metaphysical isolation.
6.866   Ruland, Richard. *The Rediscovery of American Literature:
          Premises of Critical Taste, 1900-1940*. Cambridge, Mass.:
          Harvard Univ. Press, 1967, pp. 260-61 *passim*.
          Summarizes F. O. Matthiessen's estimate of ED.
6.867   Russell, Robert. "Dickinson's 'At Half past Three, a single
          Bird.'" *Explicator*, XVI (Oct. 1957), Item 3.
6.867a   S., C. E. "Emily Dickinson." *Scribner's Magazine*. LXXXVIII
          (Oct. 1930), 32, 34 (among front advertising pages).
          Rev. of Jenkins, *Friend and Neighbor* (5.35), Pollitt, *Human
          Background* (5.61), and Taggard, *Life and Mind* (5.81).
6.868   S., P. P. "If Not Too Much." *Christian Science Monitor*, Dec. 4,
          1935, Magazine Section, p. 13.
          Rev. of *Unpublished Poems*, 1935 (3.167).
6.869   ———. "Lyrics from Emily." *Christian Science Monitor*, Jan.
          16, 1935, Magazine Section, p. 12.
          Rev. of *Poems For Youth*, 1934 (3.159).
6.870   Sackville-West, Victoria M. "New Poetry." *Nation and Athe-
          naeum*, XLVI (Nov. 2, 1929), 178.
          Rev. of *Further Poems*, 1929 (3.138).
6.870a   Sahal, N. "Emily Dickinson on Renown" in *Banasthali Patrika*
          [Banasthali, Bengal], No. 11 (July 1968).

Special Number on American Literature, ed. Rameshwar
Gupta, pp. 83-85.

6.871   Sale, Arthur. *Cambridge Review* [Cambridge, Eng.], LXXIV
(Jan. 24, 1953), 244-46.
Rev. of Chase, *ED* (5.17).

6.872   ——. *Cambridge Review* [Cambridge, Eng.], LXXX (Feb. 21,
1959), 357-58.
Rev. of *Letters,* 1958 (4.90).

6.873   Salls, Helen Harriet. "The Amherst Ariel." *South Atlantic
Quarterly,* XXXVI (Oct. 1937), 488-89.
Rev. of *Unpublished Poems,* 1935 (3.167).

6.874   Salpeter, Harry. "Genevieve Taggard's Emily." *New York
World,* June 22, 1930, p. 7-M.
Rev. of Taggard, *Life and Mind* (5.81).

6.875   Sanborn, Franklin Benjamin. "The Breakfast Table." *Boston
Daily Advertiser,* Oct. 27, 1891, p. 4.
Reprinted:
Bingham, *Ancestors' Brocades* (5.5), pp. 183-84.
Replies to an unfavorable English review of *Poems,* 1890; see
3.30.

6.876   Sandburg, Carl. "Corner Lots." *The Household Magazine,* XXXI
(May 1931), 6.
An appreciation of ED and a review of Taggard's *Life and
Mind* (5.81).

6.877   Sandeen, Ernest. "Delight Deterred by Retrospect: Emily Dickinson's Late Summer Poems." *New England Quarterly,* XL
(Dec. 1967), 483-500.
Explores ED's interior world through close study of a series
of related poems in which she records her response to Indian
summer. Argues that the poet achieves an enlarged and in-
tensified inner life by means of detached, disciplined analysis
of her immediate experience of the outer world.

6.878   Sapir, Edward. "Emily Dickinson: A Primitive." *Poetry,* XXVI
(May 1925), 97-105.
Rev. of *Complete Poems,* 1924 (3.123) and Bianchi, *Life and
Letters* (4.36).

6.879   Satin, Joseph Henry. *Reading Poetry.* Boston: Houghton Mifflin,
1964, pp. 1090-91, *passim.*

6.880   Satterwhite, Joseph N. "Robert Penn Warren and Emily Dickinson." *Modern Language Notes,* LXXI (May 1956), 347-49.
Notes that ED in "After great pain, a formal feeling comes"
and Robert Penn Warren in *All the King's Men* describe, in
similar ways, the shock that follows severe emotional injury.

6.881   Saunders, Thomas E. *The Discovery of Poetry.* Oakland, N.J.:
Scott, Foresman, 1967, pp. 344-46, *passim.*

6.881a   Savage, D. S. "Death: A Sequence of Poems" in *Master Poems
of the English Language,* ed. Oscar Williams. N.Y.: Trident
Press, 1966, pp. 750-55. Softcover ed.: N.Y.: Washington
Square Press, 1967, pp. 788-94.
ED's sense of unending homelessness informs her vision of
death as the content and meaning of life.

6.882   Schappes, Morris U. *American Literature,* V (Mar. 1933), 82-
           85.
           Rev. of Bianchi, *Face to Face* (4.59).

6.883   ———. "Emily Dickinson." *Saturday Review,* VIII (July 25, 1931),
           10.
           Corrects factual errors concerning ED in F. L. Patee's *The
           New American Literature 1890-1930;* see 6.777.

6.884   ———. "Emily Dickinson's Editors." *Springfield Republican,*
           April 8, 1933, p. 8.
           Letter to the editor critical of Mme. Bianchi's editing of ED's
           letters (4.36) in reply to a letter to the editor by Mary Crowell
           (6.240). Prof. Schappes defends Mrs. Todd's 1894 edition of
           the letters (4.3).

6.885   ———. "Errors in Mrs. Bianchi's Edition of Emily Dickinson's
           Letters." *American Literature,* IV (Jan. 1933), 369-84.
           Finds 68 textual errors in M. D. Bianchi's *Life and Letters*
           (4.36).

6.886   ———. "Notes on the Concrete as Method in Criticism." *Sym-
           posium* [Concord, N.H.], II (July 1931), 315-24.
           Notes richness of connotation in "Love — is anterior to Life,"
           p. 318.

6.887   ———. "An Obvious Error." *Saturday Review,* VII (Oct. 18,
           1930), 256.
           A letter to the editor to explain and apologize for an error in
           Josephine Pollitt's *Human Background* (5.61).

6.888   ———. "Once More." *Poetry,* XLII (Sept. 1933), 345.
           Rev. of Bianchi, *Face to Face* (4.59).

6.889   ———. *Symposium* [Concord, N.H.], I (Oct. 1930), 545-50.
           Rev. of Taggard, *Life and Mind* (5.81).

6.890   ———. *Symposium* [Concord, N.H.], III (April 1932), 260-69.
           Rev. of *Letters,* 1931 (4.52). Notes changes in ED's letter-
           writing style.

6.891   Schauffler, Henry Park. "The Second Series of Emily Dickin-
           son's Poems." *Amherst Literary Monthly,* VI (Nov. 1891),
           175-82.
           Rev. of *Poems,* 1891 (3.52).

6.892   ———. "Suggestions from the Poems of Emily Dickinson." *Am-
           herst Literary Monthly,* VI (June 1891), 87-90.
           An early appreciation. The first stanza of "It struck me —
           every Day" is here printed for the first time.

6.893   Scherman, David E., and Rosemarie Redlich. *Literary America;
           A Chronicle of American Writers From 1607-1952 With 173
           Photographs of the American Scene That Inspired Them.*
           N.Y.: Dodd, Mead, 1952.
           ED, pp. 68-69.

6.893a   Schlauch, Margaret. "Linguistic Aspects of Emily Dickinson's
           Style." *Prace Filologiczne* [*Philological Studies*] [Warsaw],
           XVIII, Part 1 (1963), 201-15.
           Argues that ED's linguistic oddities have historic precedents
           and that they are in accord with her other stylistic techniques.
           In English.

6.894   Schlauch, Margaret. *Modern English and American Poetry:*
         Techniques and Ideologies. London: Watts, 1956, pp. 30-31,
         32.
         Notes ED's use of etymology to achieve poetic effects.

6.895   Schreiber, Flora Rheta. "Emily Is In the House; Emily Dickin-
         son as Revealed Through Her Imagery." *Poet Lore,* XLVI
         (Spring 1940), 76-82.
         Examines the "house — door — prison" cluster of images in
         ED's poetry. For another discussion of house imagery, see
         V. O. Birdsall, "Emily Dickinson's Intruder in the Soul"
         (6.102).

6.896   Schriftgiesser, Karl. "The Life and Mind of Emily Dickinson."
         Boston Evening Transcript, Book Section, July 5, 1930, p. 2.
         Rev. of Taggard, *Life and Mind* (5.81).

6.897   Scott, Aurelia G. "Emily Dickinson's 'Three Gems.'" *New En-
         gland Quarterly,* XVI (Dec. 1943), 627-28.
         ED's reference to "the pearl and then the onyx and then the
         emerald stone" (*Letters,* 1958, I, 303) may have been to a book
         of poems by Poe.

6.898   Scott, Wilbur. "Dickinson's 'I'll tell you how the Sun rose.'"
         Explicator, VII (Nov. 1948), Item 14.

6.899   Scott, Winfield Townley. "Emily Dickinson and Samuel Bowles."
         Fresco [Detroit], X, No. 1 (Fall 1959), pp. 7-17.
         Reprinted:
         Fresco, X, No. 3 (Summer 1960), pp. 3-13.
         W. T. Scott, *Exiles and Fabrications.* Garden City, N.Y.:
             Doubleday, 1961, pp. 11, 40-49.
         Excerpt reprinted:
         "'The Errand from My Heart —.'" *Horizon,* III (July 1961),
             100-05.
         Argues that Samuel Bowles, not Charles Wadsworth, was the
         object of ED's poems of love and renunciation.

6.900   ——. "More of Emily's Letter to the World." *Providence Sun-
         day Journal,* April 8, 1945, Section VI, p. 6.
         Rev. of *Bolts of Melody,* 1945 (3.177) and Bingham, *Ancestors'*
         Brocades (5.5).

6.901   Scudder, V. D. *Living Church* [Milwaukee], XCIX (Dec. 28, 1938),
         698.
         Rev. of Whicher, *This Was a Poet* (5.104).

6.901a   Searles, John R. *English Journal,* LVII (Nov. 1968), p. 1238.
         Reviews a recording of ED's poems read by Julie Harris; see
         20.6.

6.902   Sedgwick, W. E. *New England Quarterly,* IX (Mar. 1936), 143-45.
         Rev. of *Unpublished Poems,* 1935 (3.167).

6.903   de Selincourt, Basil. "Emily Dickinson's Poems: 'The Stars By
         Day.'" *Observer* [London], Oct. 10, 1937, p. 5.
         Rev. of *Poems,* 1937 (3.173).

6.904   Sergeant, Elizabeth Shepley. "An Early Imagist." *New Republic,*
         IV (Aug. 14, 1915), 52-54.
         Reprinted:
         Blake and Wells, *Recognition* (5.13), pp. 88-93.

An appreciation and review of *Single Hound,* 1914 (3.114).

6.905 Sergeant, Howard. *English* [Oxford, Eng.], XV (Autumn 1964), 111.
Rev. of Griffith, *Long Shadow* (5.31).

6.906 Sessions, John A. "Poet For Our Day." *New Leader,* XXXIX (May 7, 1956), 16-17.
Rev. of Johnson, *Interpretive Biography* (5.44).

6.907 Sessions, Ruth Huntington. "Emily Dickinson Face to Face." *Nation,* CXXXVI (Jan. 18, 1933), 65-66.
Urges an end to investigation into the identity of ED's lover.

6.908 ——. "Emily Dickinson No Thwarted Recluse." *Springfield Sunday Union and Republican,* Dec. 25, 1932, p. 7-E.
Rev. of Bianchi, *Face to Face* (4.59).

6.909 ——. "A Review." *Amherst Record,* Dec. 21, 1932, p. 6.
Rev. of Bianchi, *Face to Face* (4.59).

6.910 Sewall, Richard B. "Dickinson's 'To undertake is to achieve.'" *Explicator,* VI (June 1948), Item 51.

6.910a ——. "Emily Dickinson: New Looks and Fresh Starts." *Modern Language Quarterly,* XXIX (Mar. 1968), 84-90.
A review-essay of Capps, *ED's Reading* (5.14), Franklin, *Editing* (5.28), and Porter, *Early Poetry* (5.69).

[5.76] ——. "The Lyman Letters: New Light on Emily Dickinson and Her Family."

6.911 ——. *Modern Language Quarterly,* XXVI (June 1965), 351-53.
Rev. of Griffith, *Long Shadow* (5.31).

6.912 ——. *New England Quarterly,* XVIII (Sept. 1945), 409-11.
Rev. of *Bolts of Melody,* 1945 (3.177).

6.913 ——. "On Teaching Emily Dickinson." *English Leaflet* [New England Association of Teachers of English], LXIII (Spring 1964), 3-14.
Suggestions on reading and teaching ED from a paper given at the 1963 Yale Conference on English.

6.914 ——. "A Poet All the Time." *Saturday Review,* XLI (Mar. 22, 1958), 21.
Rev. of *Letters,* 1958 (4.90).

6.915 Sexton, Carol. "The Relation of Emily Dickinson to God." *Aspects* [North Carolina Wesleyan College], II (Jan. 1965), 30-43.
Since her father would not let her love a man, ED addressed her poems to God as if he were her lover. In this way she satisfied her need for poetic expression and for someone acceptable to love.

6.916 Shackford, Martha Hale. "The Poetry of Emily Dickinson." *Atlantic Monthly,* CXI (Jan. 1913), 93-97.
Reprinted:
Martha Hale Shackford. *Studies of Certain Nineteenth Century Poets.* Natick, Mass.: Suburban Press, 1946, pp. 75-82.
Blake and Wells, *Recognition* (5.13), pp. 79-88.
Revised and reprinted:
"Emily Dickinson: 1830-1886" in *Talks on Ten Poets, Wordsworth to Moody.* N.Y.: Bookman Associates, 1958, pp. 112-20.

An introduction addressed to the general reader. The author cites ED's "intensity of feeling," "sensitivity to irony and paradox," and "courageous acceptance of life."

6.917   Shaw, John MacKay. *Childhood in Poetry.* 5 vols. Tallahassee: Florida State Univ. Press, 1962. Reissued, Detroit: Gale Research Co., [1967].

An annotated catalogue of English and American poets included in the Shaw Childhood in Poetry Collection in the Library of Florida State University. Lists 21 books and periodicals in which appear poems by ED relating to childhood, vol. II, pp. 742-46.

6.917a   Sheffler, R. A. "Emily Dickinson's 'A Clock Stopped.'" *Massachusetts Studies in English,* I (1967), 52-54.

6.918   Shepard, Odell. "Bringing Emily Downstairs." *Nation,* CXCI (Dec. 17, 1960), 478-79.

Rev. of *Complete Poems,* 1960 (3.207) and Leyda, *Years and Hours* (5.49).

6.919   ———. "Witch-Hazel Blossom." *Nation,* CXLVII (Dec. 10, 1938), 635-36.

Rev. of Whicher, *This Was a Poet* (5.104).

6.920   Sherrer, Grace B. *American Literature,* XXIII (Nov. 1951), 380-82.

Rev. of *Letters to Holland,* 1951 (4.76).

6.921   ———. *American Literature,* XXIV (May 1952), 255-58.

Rev. of Patterson, *Riddle* (5.55).

6.922   ———. *American Literature,* XXIV (Nov. 1952), 407-10.

Rev. of Chase, *ED* (5.17).

6.923   ———. *American Literature,* XXVII (Jan. 1956), 598-600.

Rev. of Bingham, *ED's Home* (4.86).

6.924   ———. "A Study of Unusual Verb Constructions in the Poems of Emily Dickinson." *American Literature,* VII (Mar. 1935), 37-46.

Notes ED's use of archaic subjunctives and omission of verbal auxiliaries.

6.925   Shuster, George N. "Emily Dickinson." *Commonweal,* XII (May 7, 1930), 23-24.

Rev. of Pollitt, *Human Background* (5.61).

6.925a   Simon, Myron. "'Self' in Whitman and Dickinson." *CEA Critic,* XXX (Dec. 1967), 8.

"Emily Dickinson's rather limiting conception of the self [in contrast to Whitman's] places her in the position of discovering most knowledge to be tentative."

6.926   Skard, Sigmund. *American Studies in Europe, Their History and Recent Organization.* 2 vols. Philadelphia: Univ. of Pennsylvania Press, 1958, II, 452, 489, 541.

Mentions ED studies in Sweden and Italy and a doctoral thesis written on ED at the University at Istanbul.

6.927   Skeel, Esther Elizabeth. "Alumnae Conference Impressions." *Mt. Holyoke Alumnae Quarterly,* XII (Jan. 1930), 191-92.

On the ED Poetry Conference held in connection with the Founder's Day Celebration, Mt. Holyoke College, Dec. 1929. See also 22.1-7.

6.928   Skinner, Edna L. "Poems for Youth." *Amherst Record*, Nov. 21, 1934, p. 3.
        Rev. of *Poems for Youth*, 1934 (3.159).

6.929   Smith, Grover. "Dickinson's 'A Route of Evanescence.'" *Explicator*, VII (May 1949), Item 54.
        Reprinted:
        Davis, *14 by ED* (5.23), pp. 138-39.

6.930   Smith, Lucy Humphrey. "The Mystery of Emily Dickinson's Life." *Literary Digest International Book Review*, II (July 1924), 587-88.
        Rev. of *Life and Letters*, 1924 (4.36).

6.931   Smith, Russell St. Clair. "Dickinson's 'I dreaded that first Robin, so.'" *Explicator*, V (Feb. 1947), Item 31.

6.932   ———. "Emily Dickinson: A Bibliographical Note." *Notes and Queries*, CXCIII (May 1, 1948), 188-89.
        Notes early printings of "If I can stop one Heart from breaking" and "They might not need me — yet they might."

6.933   *Smith College Monthly, Emily Dickinson Issue*, Vol. II, No. 2 (Nov. 1941), 30 pp.
        Contributions are listed separately by author in this bibliography; see Anon., 19.13; Bianchi, 6.96; Curran, 6.246; Finch, 6.349; Guitar and Urdang, 6.429; Taggard, 6.975. Reprints a poem mistakenly ascribed to ED, "A Clamor in the Treetops," p. 11; see White, 6.1162.

6.934   Southworth, James Granville. "Emily Dickinson," in *Some Modern American Poets*. N.Y.: Macmillan; Oxford: Blackwell, 1950, pp. 14-27.
        Emily Dickinson's self-willed isolation from life and the pointless obscurity of much of her poetry limit her otherwise considerable achievement.

6.935   Spector, Robert D. "'How Dreary to Be Somebody.'" *Saturday Review*, XLVII (May 30, 1964), 43.
        Rev. of Griffith, *Long Shadow* (5.31).

6.936   ———. *Saturday Review*, XLVII (Feb. 1, 1964), 36.
        Rev. of Sewall, *Critical Essays* (5.75).

6.937   Speight, Harold E. B. "Emily Dickinson." *Christian Leader*, Aug. 4, 1934, p. 987.

6.938   Spencer, Benjamin T. "Criticism: Centrifugal and Centripetal." *Criticism*, VIII (Spring 1966), 139-54.
        Includes an explication of "I heard a Fly buzz — when I died," pp. 141-42.

6.939   Spencer, Theodore. "Emily and Her Editors." *New Republic*, XCVII (Dec. 21, 1938), 209.
        Rev. of Whicher, *This Was a Poet* (5.104).

6.940   ———. *New England Quarterly*, II (July 1929), 498-501.
        Reprinted:
        Blake and Wells, *Recognition* (5.13), pp. 131-133.
        Rev. of *Further Poems*, 1929 (3.138).

6.941   ———. "A Search for a Lover. New Guesses and Mystery." *Boston Herald*, Book Section, June 28, 1930, p. 15.
        Rev. of Taggard, *Life and Mind* (5.81).

6.942   Spicer, John L. "The Poems of Emily Dickinson." *Boston Public Library Quarterly*, VIII (July 1956), 135-43.
Addenda to T. H. Johnson's note to "A narrow Fellow in the Grass" in his 1955 edition of the poems (3.197), II, 713-14.

6.943   Spiller, Robert E. *American Historical Review*, LI (Oct. 1945), 171.
Rev. of Bingham, *Ancestors' Brocades* (5.5).

6.944   ———. "Art and the Inner Life: Dickinson, James" in *The Cycle of American Literature, An Essay in Historical Criticism.*
N.Y.: Macmillan, 1955, [ED discussed] pp. 164-69, *passim.*
Softcover ed.: N.Y.: New American Library, 1957, pp. 129-32 *passim.*
ED's choice of poetry as a vocation helps us to understand her recurring themes of renunciation and withdrawal.

6.945   ———. *Modern Language Notes*, LXXIV (Mar. 1959), 270-72.
Rev. of *Letters*, 1958 (4.90).

6.946   S[prague], M[ary] A. "Review of New Emily Dickinson Volume."
Amherst Record, Nov. 27, 1935, p. 6.
Rev. of *Unpublished Poems*, 1935 (3.167).

6.947   Squire, J. C. "Emily Dickinson." *Observer* [London], CXXXVIII (Oct. 13, 1929), 6.
Rev. of *Further Poems*, 1929 (3.138).

6.948   Stamm, Edith Perry. "Emily Dickinson: Poetry and Punctuation." *Saturday Review*, XLVI (Mar. 30, 1963), 26-27, 74.
Excerpt reprinted:
Davis, *14 by ED* (5.23), pp. 59-64.
Argues that ED's "eccentric" punctuation marks are elocutionary symbols meant to direct oral reading of the poems. A reply by Theodora Ward (6.1071) is answered May 25, 1963, p. 23. See also Franklin, *Editing of ED* (5.28), pp. 118-20, 121.
Rev. by Robbins, *ALS, 1963* (6.851), p. 127. For a fuller exposition of the author's argument, see her Ph.D. thesis, 14.33.

6.949   Starke, Aubrey H. "Emily Dickinson as a Great Unknown."
American Book Collector [Plainfield, N.J.], V (Aug.-Sept. 1934), 245-50.
A resumé of ED's publishing career.

6.950   ———. "An Omnibus of Poets." *Colophon*, IV, Part 16, Mar. 1934, 12 unnumbered pages.
Identifies all of the anonymous contributors to *A Masque of Poets* (see 3.7) and discusses the volume's printing history and popular reception. Includes excerpts of reviews.

6.951   Stearns, Alfred Earnest. *An Amherst Boyhood.* Amherst: Amherst College, 1946, p. 72.
Mentions his childhood impression of ED as a "crazy spinster."

6.952   Stedman, Edmund Clarence. *Life and Letters of Edmund Clarence Stedman,* by Laura Stedman and George M. Gould. 2 vols. N.Y.: Moffat, Yard, 1910, II, 472-73.
In a Dec. 1900 letter to H. H. Furness, Stedman defends inclusion of 21 of ED's poems in his *An American Anthology,* N.Y.: Houghton Mifflin, 1900.

6.953   Stephenson, William E. "Emily Dickinson and Watts's Songs for
         Children." *English Language Notes*, III (June 1966), 278-81.
         Suggests that ED must have read Isaac Watts's *Divine Songs
         Attempted in Easy Language for . . . Children* and that Watts's
         children's verse "may be more directly in the background of
         her poetry than his hymns and psalms." Rev. by Robbins,
         ALS, 1966 (6.851), pp. 143-44.

6.954   Stern, Milton R. "Poems for Teaching." *Clearing House*, XXXII
         (Jan. 1958), 314-15.
         A discussion of imagery in "There's a certain Slant of light"
         in an article for secondary school teachers.

6.955   Stewart, Randall. *American Literature and Christian Doctrine*.
         Baton Rouge: Louisiana State Univ. Press, 1958, pp. 69-72
         passim.
         Compares ED with Emerson and Hawthorne.

6.956   Stoddard, Francis H. "Technique in Emily Dickinson's Poems."
         Critic, n.s. XVII (Jan. 9, 1892), 24-25.
         Reprinted:
         Blake and Wells, *Recognition* (5.13), pp. 51-53.
         Defends ED's poetic form in a reply to an anonymous review
         of *Poems,* 1891; see 3.70.

6.957   Stoddard, Richard Henry. "World of Letters — Letters of Emily
         Dickinson." *Mail and Express* [N.Y.], Mar. 2, 1895, p. 20.
         Rev. of *Letters,* 1894 (4.3).

6.958   Stone, Edward. "Emily Dickinson's Collar." *Exercise Exchange*
         [Bennington, Vt.], XII (Nov. 1964), 3-4.
         Notes parallels between "I never lost as much but twice" and
         Herbert's "The Collar."

6.959   Stonier, G. W. "Innocence Without Experience." *New Statesman
         and Nation*, XIV (Oct. 23, 1937), 655-56.
         Rev. of *Poems,* 1937 (3.173).

6.960   Stunz, Arthur N. "Bolts of Melody." *Saturday Review*, XXVIII
         (Aug. 18, 1945), 19.
         Letter to the editor identifying "My God, what is a heart"
         (*Bolts of Melody*, p. 125) as stanzas 2 and 3 of George Her-
         bert's "Mattens."

6.961   Sugden, Emily R. "Emily Dickinson." *Saturday Review*, VII
         (Sept. 13, 1930), 128.
         Letter to the editor discussing the Amherst legend of a lover
         whom ED's father had forbidden her to see.

6.962   Sunne, Richard. *New Statesman*, XXXV (Sept. 13, 1930), 708.
         Rev. of Taggard, *Life and Mind* (5.81), p. 708.

6.963   Swallow, Alan. *New Mexico Quarterly*, XV (Summer 1945), 222-
         24.
         Rev. of Bingham, *Ancestors' Brocades* (5.5) and *Bolts of Mel-
         ody,* 1945 (3.177).

6.964   S[weetser], K[ate] D[ickinson]. "Emily Dickinson." *Magazine of
         Poetry*, VI (Feb. 1894), 108.
         A biographical note accompanying a selection of ED's poetry.

6.965   T., A. "An Edition of the Poems of Emily Dickinson." *Boston
         Daily Traveller*, Nov. 22, 1890, p. 11.-

Rev. of *Poems*, 1890 (3.9).

6.965a   T., J. M. *Vote* [London], Nov. 28, 1924, p. 382.
Rev. of *Selected Poems*, 1924 (3.127).

6.965b   Tabb, John Banister. *Letters — Grave and Gay, and Other Prose*,
ed. Francis E. Litz. Washington, D.C.: Catholic Univ. of
America Press, 1950, pp. 61, 62-63, 72, 93, 94, 96, 140.
Brief allusions to ED among Father Tabb's letters that indi-
cate strong approval of her poetry. See also 5.80.

6.966   Taggard, Genevieve. "The Amherst Genius." *Saturday Review*,
XIX (Nov. 26, 1938), 6.
Rev. of Whicher, *This Was a Poet* (5.104).

6.967   ———, ed. *Circumference: Varieties of Metaphysical Verse*.
N.Y.: Covici-Friede, 1929.
Discusses ED's relation to Donne and metaphysical poetry,
pp. 9-13.

6.968   ———. "A Dickinson Bibliography." *Saturday Review*, VII (Mar.
28, 1931), 698.
Letter to the editor defending the Jones Library bibliography
(1.8); see 6.1008.

6.969   ———. "Emily Dickinson." *Nation*, CXIX (Oct. 8, 1924), 376-78.
Rev. of *Complete Poems*, 1924 (3.123) and Bianchi, *Life and
Letters* (4.36).

6.970   ———. "Emily Dickinson." *New Republic*, LXXXVI (Feb. 26,
1936), 82.
Rev. of *Unpublished Poems*, 1935 (3.167).

6.971   ———. "Emily Dickinson and Her Editor." *Quarterly Review of
Literature*, II (1946), No. 4, pp. 350-53.
Rev. of *Bolts of Melody*, 1945 (3.177).

6.972   ———. "The Little 'Scholar' of 1848." *Journal of Adult Educa-
tion*, II (Jan. 1930), 75-76.
Notes talks by Mrs. Todd and Robert Hillyer at the "Emily
Dickinson Memorial Conference," Mt. Holyoke College, Nov.
8, 1929 and calls for new recognition of ED's achievement.
See also 22.1-7.

6.973   ———. "Memories of Miss Emily." *New York Herald Tribune
Books*, June 1, 1930, p. 2.
Rev. of Jenkins, *Friend and Neighbor* (5.35).

6.974   ———. "A Note from Miss Taggard." *Creative Reading*, V (Oct.
1, 1930), 775.
Replies to a review of *Life and Mind* (5.81) by Richard Burton;
see 6.162.

6.975   ———. "Notes on Emily Dickinson and Emerson." *Smith College
Monthly*, II (Nov. 1941), 3-6.

6.976   ———. "Poet as Letter Writer." *New York Herald Tribune
Books*, Dec. 13, 1931, pp. 1-2.
Rev. of *Letters*, 1931 (4.52).

6.977   ———. "Tantalizing New Facts About Emily Dickinson." *New
York Herald Tribune Books*, Dec. 11, 1932, p. 3.
Rev. of Bianchi, *Face to Face* (4.59).

6.978   ———. "Tu Fu's Kin." *Saturday Review*, XXX (Oct. 4, 1947),
14-15.

Rev. of Wells, *Introduction* (5.101).

6.979   Tasker, J. Dana. *Commonweal*, X (June 26, 1929), 234.
          Rev. of *Further Poems*, 1929 (3.138).

6.980   Tate, Allen. "Emily Dickinson." *Outlook*, CXLIX (Aug. 15, 1928), 621-23.
          This essay appears, substantially revised and expanded, as "New England Culture and Emily Dickinson." *Symposium* [Concord, N.H.], III (April 1932), 206-26.
          Reprinted, with minor revisions:
          Allen Tate. *Reactionary Essays on Poetry and Ideas*. N.Y.: Scribner, 1936, pp. 3-25.
          Reprinted:
          America Through the Essay: An Anthology for English Courses, ed. A. Theodore Johnson and Allen Tate. N.Y.: Oxford Univ. Press, 1938, pp. 312-27.
          Readings from the Americas, ed. Guy A. Cardwell. N.Y.: Ronald Press, 1947, pp. 232-46.
          Allen Tate. *On the Limits of Poetry: Selected Essays 1928-1948*. N.Y.: Swallow Press and William Morrow, 1948, pp. 197-213.
          Allen Tate. *The Man of Letters in the Modern World: Selected Essays 1928-1955*. N.Y.: Meridian Books, 1955, pp. 211-226.
          Literature in America: An Anthology of American Criticism, ed. Philip Rahv. N.Y.: Meridian Books, 1957, pp. 189-201.
          Allen Tate. *Collected Essays*. Denver: Swallow Press, 1959, pp. 197-211.
          Interpretations of American Literature, ed. Charles Feidelson and Paul Brodtkorb. N.Y.: Oxford Univ. Press, 1959, pp. 197-211.
          American Literary Essays, ed. Lewis Leary. N.Y.: Crowell, 1960, pp. 117-26.
          Sewall, *Critical Essays* (5.75), pp. 16-27.
          Blake and Wells, *Recognition* (5.13), pp. 153-67.
          Critical Approaches to American Literature, ed. Roy B. Browne and Martin Light. 2 vols. N.Y.: Crowell, 1965, II, 54-67.
          Translated into Japanese: see 12.6.
          Discusses the historical situation that produced **ED**, especially the decay of Puritan theology as a unified vision of the world. This disintegration made possible in ED's poetry a perfect fusion of sensibility and thought.

6.981   ———. "The Poet and Her Biographer." *Kenyon Review*, I (Spring 1939), 200-03.
          Rev. of Whicher, *This Was a Poet* (5.104).

6.982   Taylor, E. M. M. "Readers' Queries — Emily Dickinson." *Notes and Queries*, n.s. VI (April 1959), 155.
          Asks the significance of "Brazil" in "I asked no other thing."

6.983   Taylor, Walter Fuller. "Emily Dickinson (1830-1886)" in *A History of American Letters*. N.Y.: American Book Co., 1936, pp. 281-82, 553-55, *passim*.

A brief introduction and bibliography.

6.983a   Taylor, Walter Fuller. *The Story of American Letters*. Chicago:
          Henry Regnery, 1956, pp. 255-56, 282, 362.

6.984   T[empleman], W[illiam] D. *Personalist*, XLII (Spring 1961), 255-
          56.
          Rev. of *Selected Poems*, 1959 (3.202).

6.985   Thomas, Gilbert. "Emily Dickinson." *Bookman* [London],
          LXXVIII (Sept. 1930), 326-27.
          Rev. of Taggard, *Life and Mind* (5.81).

6.986   Thomas, Macklin. "Analysis of the Experience in Lyric Poetry."
          College English, IX (Mar. 1948), 317-21.
          Contains an explication of "Go not too near a House of Rose,"
          pp. 320-21.

6.987   Thomas, Owen P., Jr. "Dickinson's 'So glad we are.'" *Explica-
          tor*, XVIII (Nov. 1959), Item 10.

6.988   ——. *New England Quarterly*, XXXIV (Mar. 1961), 106-08.
          Rev. of Leyda, *Years and Hours* (5.49).

6.989   ——. *New England Quarterly*, XXXV (Sept. 1962), 413-15.
          Rev. of Ward, *Capsule of the Mind* (5.97).

6.990   ——. *New England Quarterly*, XXXVIII (Dec. 1965), 527-28.
          Rev. of Gelpi, *Mind of the Poet* (5.29). Notes the definition of
          "circumference" in ED's dictionary (23.1).

6.991   Thompson, David W. "Interpretative Reading as Symbolic Ac-
          tion." *Quarterly Journal of Speech*, XLII (Dec. 1956), 389-97.
          Contains explication of "Go not too near a House of Rose," pp.
          395-96.

6.992   Thompson, Edward. "The Complete Poems of Emily Dickinson."
          Observer [London], Nov. 5, 1933, p. 9.
          Rev. of *Poems*, 1933 (3.158).

6.993   Thompson, Maurice. "Miss Dickinson's Poems." *America*, V
          (Jan. 8, 1891), 425.
          Reprinted:
          Blake and Wells, *Recognition* (5.13), pp. 28-33.
          Rev. of *Poems*, 1890 (3.9).

6.994   Thompson, Ralph. "Books of the Times." *New York Times*, Oct.
          31, 1938), p. 13.
          Rev. of Whicher, *This Was a Poet* (5.104).

6.995   Thornton, James. "Emily Dickinson." *Nation and Athenaeum*,
          XLVII (Sept. 27, 1930), 800.
          Rev. of Taggard, *Life and Mind* (5.81).

6.996   Tiffany, Charles. "Emily Dickinson's Secret Considered."
          Springfield Republican, Sept. 2, 1930, p. 6.
          Letter to the editor suggesting that "she loved no man, but
          loved love."

6.997   Todd, John Emerson. *Modern Language Journal*, XLIX (Nov.
          1965), 459-60.
          Rev. of Rosenbaum, *Concordance* (2.3).

6.998   Todd, Mabel Loomis. "About Authors." *Book Buyer*, n.s. IX
          (Feb. 1892), 7.
          Replies to a request for a portrait of ED. See also Birss,
          6.104.

6.999   Todd, Mabel Loomis. "Emily Dickinson's Letters." *Bachelor of
            Arts*, I (May 1895), 39-66.
            A general discussion of ED's letters based on Mrs. Todd's
            1894 edition (4.3) and from which she here reprints excerpts.
            Argues that the letters, unlike the poems, show a progression
            in thought and expression.

6.1000   ——. "Emily Dickinson's Literary Debut." *Harper's*, CLX
            (Mar. 1930), 463-71.
            Excerpts reprinted:
            Boston Sunday Post, Mar. 2, 1930, p. E-10.
            Recounts the transcribing and publishing of ED's poems for
            the 1890 and 1891 editions.

6.1000a   ——. "Introduction to Second Edition" in *Letters*, 1931 (4.52),
            pp. xii-xxiv.
            Describes how ED's letters first came to be published in 1894.
            For a fuller description, see Bingham, *Ancestors' Brocades*
            (5.5) pp. 189-323.

6.1001   ——. "Introductory" to *Letters*, 1894 (4.3), I, [v]-xii.
            Reprinted:
            Letters, 1931 (4.52), pp. xxv-xxxi.
            Letters, 1951 (4.80), pp. xvii-xxii.
            Mrs. Todd argues that although ED's letters often show a
            "disinclination" for both the dogmas of orthodox religion and
            the pretenses of society, they never express "real irrever-
            ence." In her love of nature, the poet resembles Emily
            Brontë.

6.1002   ——. "Miss Taggard's Emily." *Saturday Review*, VII (Sept. 6,
            1930), 99.
            Rev. of Taggard, *Life and Mind* (5.81).

6.1003   ——. "Preface" to *Poems*, 1891 (3.52), pp. iii-viii.
            Reprinted:
            Bingham, *Ancestors' Brocades* (5.5), pp. 417-19.
            Blake and Wells, *Recognition* (5.13), pp. 42-44.
            Poems (1890-1896), introd. Monteiro (3.212), pp. 161-66.
            Briefly describes the condition of ED's manuscripts and some
            of the editing problems they entailed. Reprints part of a letter
            to ED from Helen Hunt Jackson expressing enthusiasm for her
            poems.

6.1004   ——. "Preface" to *Poems*, 1896 (3.89), pp. vii-viii.
            Reprinted:
            Bingham, *Ancestors' Brocades* (5.5), p. 420.
            Poems (1890-1896), introd. Monteiro (3.212), pp. 395-96.
            Notes that while some of ED's poems had an "obvious personal
            origin," many others "were simply spontaneous flashes of in-
            sight, apparently unrelated to outward circumstance."

6.1005   Tolles, Catherine. "The Fire and Dew of Emily Dickinson." *Mt.
            Holyoke Monthly*, XXXVII (April 1930), 209-22.
            Examines the "metaphysics" of ED and links her with John
            Donne and Emerson.

6.1005a   Towheed, M. O. "The Wit of Emily Dickinson" in *Banasthali Pa-
            trika* [Banasthali, Bengal], No. 11 (July 1968), Special Number
            on American Literature, ed. Rameshwar Gupta, pp. 20-30.

6.1006   Trewin, J. C. "Ancient and Modern." *Observer* [London], Dec.
         28, 1947, p. 3.
         Rev. of *Bolts of Melody*, 1947 (3.182) and *Poems*, 1947 (3.183).
6.1007   Trilling, Lionel. *The Experience of Literature: A Reader With
         Commentaries.* Garden City, N.Y.: Doubleday, 1967, pp. 917-
         19.
         Includes an explication of "'Go tell it' — What a Message."
6.1008   Troxell, Gilbert M. *Saturday Review,* VII (Jan. 10, 1931), 527.
         Rev. of Jones Library, *Emily Dickinson: A Bibliography* (1.8).
         Genevieve Taggard replies: see 6.968.
6.1009   Trueblood, Charles K. "Emily Dickinson." *Dial,* LXXX (April
         1926), 301-11.
         Reprinted:
         American Criticism, ed. William A. Drake. N.Y.: Harcourt,
             1926, pp. 291-307.
         Literary Opinion in America, ed. Morton D. Zabel. N.Y.:
             Harper, 1937, pp. 251-62. Omitted in later editions.
         An essay-review of Bianchi, *Life and Letters* (4.36). Dis-
         cusses ED's inner withdrawal from the world and the "lyric
         incisiveness" of her poetry.
6.1010   Tuckerman, Frederick. *Amherst Academy, A New England
         School of the Past, 1814-1861.* Amherst: 1929.
         Includes biographical sketches of the Dickinson family.
         Discusses ED and prints some of her letters to a schoolmate
         on life at the Academy, pp. 109-13, *passim.* The curriculum
         and textbooks of the Academy (1838-1861) are described, pp.
         99-100.
6.1011   Tugwell, Simon. "Dickinson's 'The Crickets sang.'" *Explicator,*
         XXIII (Feb. 1965), Item 46.
6.1011a ———. *Essays in Criticism,* XVI (Jan. 1966), 111-17.
         Rev. of Duncan, *ED* (5.24) and Rosenbaum, *Concordance* (2.3).
6.1012   ———. "Notes on Two Poems by Emily Dickinson." *Notes and
         Queries,* n.s. XIII (Sept. 1966), 342-43.
         Reinterprets "Portraits are to daily faces" and "Superfluous
         were the Sun." Rev. by Robbins, *ALS, 1966* (6.851), p. 144.
         Brita Lindberg suggests another reading for "Superfluous
         were the Sun"; see 6.617a.
6.1013   Turner, Arlin. "Emily Dickinson Complete." *South Atlantic
         Quarterly,* LV (Oct. 1956), 501-04.
         Rev. of *Poems*, 1955 (3.197).
6.1014   ———. "The Letters of Emily Dickinson." *South Atlantic Quar-
         terly,* LVIII (Winter 1959), 132-34.
         Rev. of *Letters*, 1958 (4.90).
6.1015   Twitchett, E. G. "Further Poems of Emily Dickinson." *London
         Mercury,* XXI (Nov. 1929), 76-77.
         Rev. of *Further Poems*, 1929 (3.138).
6.1016   Tyler, William Seymour. *History of Amherst College During its
         First Half Century, 1821-1871.* Springfield, Mass.: C. W.
         Bryan, 1873.
         Includes an estimate of Edward Dickinson written a year be-
         fore his death, p. 539. Reprinted in Taggard, *Life and Mind*
         (5.81), pp. 377-78.

6.1017 Underhill, Evelyn. "Emily Dickinson." *London Mercury,* **XXXVII**
(Nov. 1937), 72-73.
Rev. of *Poems,* 1937 (3.173).

6.1018 Unger, Leonard, and William Van O'Connor, eds. *Poems for*
Study: A Critical and Historical Introduction. N.Y.: Holt,
Rinehart, Winston, 1953.
Contains an explication of "Because I could not stop for Death,"
pp. 547-48.

6.1019 Untermeyer, Louis B. *American Literature,* X (Jan. 1939), 510-
11.
Rev. of Whicher, *This Was a Poet* (5.104).

6.1020 ———. "At the Source." *Saturday Review,* VIII (Nov. 21, 1931),
307-08.
Rev. of *Letters,* 1931 (4.52).

6.1021 ———. "Colossal Substance." *Saturday Review,* V (Mar. 16,
1929), 769-71.
Rev. of *Further Poems,* 1929 (3.138).

6.1022 ———. "The Compleat Spinster Poet." *Saturday Review,* **XXXVIII**
(Sept. 10, 1955), 37-39.
Rev. of *Poems,* 1955 (3.197).

6.1023 ———. "Contemporary Poetry," in *American Writers on Ameri-*
can Literature, ed. John Macy. N.Y.: Liveright, 1931, pp.
503-16.
Cites ED as a forerunner of contemporary American poetry,
p. 516.

6.1024 ———. "Daughters of Niobe." *American Spectator,* I (Nov. 1932),
4.
In an article on self-pity in women poets, Untermeyer briefly
notes the intensity of personal grief in ED.

6.1025 ———. "Emily Dickinson," in *Lives of the Poets.* N.Y.: Simon
& Schuster, 1959, pp. 578-90.
A general introduction to ED's life and poetry.

6.1026 ———. "Emily Dickinson." *Saturday Review,* VI (July 5, 1930),
1169-71.
Rev. of Jenkins, *Friend and Neighbor* (5.35); Pollitt, *Human*
Background (5.61); and Taggard, *Life and Mind* (5.81).

6.1027 ———. "Emily Dickinson" in *A Treasury of Great Poems.* N.Y.:
Simon & Schuster, 1942, pp. 943-45.
Compares ED to Christina Rossetti in a brief introduction to a
selection from ED's poems.

6.1028 ———. *Modern American Poetry.* 2nd. ed. N.Y.: Harcourt, 1921,
pp. 3-4.
This often-quoted introduction to a selection from ED's poems
was expanded and revised for the 3rd ed., 1925, pp. 31-34, and
further expanded for the 5th ed., 1936, pp. 75-81. The essay
remains unchanged in succeeding editions, the most recent
being the New and Enlarged [8th] Edition, 1962, pp. 88-94.

6.1029 ———. "A More Intimate Emily." *Saturday Review,* IX (Jan. 7,
1933), 363.
Rev. of Bianchi, *Face to Face* (4.59).

6.1030 ———. *Play in Poetry.* N.Y.: Harcourt, 1938, pp. 48-51.

In a chapter entitled "The Religious Conceit," the author discusses the element of playfulness in ED's poetry.

6.1031   Untermeyer, Louis B. "Thoughts After a Centenary." *Saturday Review*, VII (June 20, 1931), 905-06.
Urges further examination of ED's life and art.

6.1032   Van der Vat, D. G. "Emily Dickinson (1830-1886)." *English Studies* [Amsterdam], XXI (1939), 241-60.
A survey of ED's work designed to aid new readers of her poetry. Discusses its relation to metaphysical poetry, to French symbolism, and to Puritan thought, and examines some of her major themes.

6.1033   Van Deusen, Marshall. "Dickinson's 'Farther in Summer than the Birds.'" *Explicator*, XIII (Mar. 1955), Item 33.
Reprinted:
Davis, *14 by ED* (5.23), pp. 129-31.

6.1034   ———. "Dickinson's 'These are the days when Birds come back.'" *Explicator*, XII (April 1954), Item 40.
Reprinted:
Davis, *14 by ED* (5.23), pp. 3-4.

6.1035   Van Doorn, Willem. "How It Strikes a Contemporary — American Poetry." *English Studies* [Amsterdam], VIII (Oct. 1926), 129-42.
Discusses ED, pp. 132-35. Notes her neglect of form and concludes that "even a beloved person's tricks of speech will weary us at last."

6.1036   Van Doren, Carl. *American Literature: An Introduction*. Los Angeles: U.S. Library Assn., Westwood Hills Press, 1933, pp. 67-70.
Reprinted:
Carl Van Doren. *What is American Literature?* N.Y.: William Morrow, 1935, pp. 91-95.
Carl Van Doren. *Carl Van Doren Selected by Himself*. N.Y.: Viking, 1945, pp. 610-12.
"A Secret in White," in *Guests in Eden* (5.59), pp. 42-44.
A brief appreciation. Notes the absence of local color in ED: "Her provincialism is universality."

6.1037   ———. "The Life and Mind of Emily Dickinson." *Wings*, IV (Aug. 1930), 16.
Rev. of Taggard, *Life and Mind* (5.81).

6.1038   Van Doren, Carl, and Mark Van Doren. *American and British Literature Since 1890*. N.Y.: Century, 1925, pp. 7-10.
Appreciative but brief introductory comments on ED's poetry.

6.1039   Van Doren, Mark. *Introduction to Poetry* [also published as *Enjoying Poetry*]. N.Y.: William Sloane Associates, 1951, pp. 12-16, 39-42.
Subsequent editions published as *Introduction to Poetry*. N.Y.: Dryden Press, 1957; N.Y.: Holt, Rinehart, Winston, 1962.
Explication of "I had not minded walls" and "The Soul selects her own Society." Comment on the former is reprinted in Blake and Wells, *Recognition* (5.13), pp. 264-68.

6.1040   Van Doren, Mark. "The Mystery of Emily Dickinson." *Theatre Guild Magazine,* VII (Aug. 1930), 40-41.
Rev. of Taggard, *Life and Mind* (5.81).

6.1041   ———. "Nerves Like Tombs." *Nation,* CXXVIII (Mar. 20, 1929), 348-49.
Reprinted with an additional paragraph in Mark Van Doren, *The Private Reader, Selected Articles and Reviews.* N.Y.: Holt, 1942, pp. 170-74.
Discusses ED's metaphysical wit in a review of *Further Poems,* 1929 (3.138).

6.1042   ———. "The Shining 'Mystery' of Emily Dickinson." *New York Herald Tribune Books,* Nov. 6, 1938, p. 3.
Rev. of Whicher, *This Was a Poet* (5.104).

6.1043   ———. "The Untired Genius." *Nation,* CXLI (Dec. 25, 1935), 746.
Rev. of *Unpublished Poems,* 1935 (3.167).

6.1044   Van Loon, Hendrik Willem. "Emily Dickinson and Frédéric Chopin" in *Van Loon's Lives.* N.Y.: Simon & Schuster, 1942, pp. 731-66.
Describes an imaginary dinner party in which the guests are Dickinson, Chopin, and Rossini.

6.1045   Van Vuren, Floyd. "In Printing House Square." *Milwaukee Journal,* June 14, 1930, p. 4.
Review of Taggard, *Life and Mind* (5.81).

6.1046   Van Wyck, William. "Emily Dickinson's Songs Out of Sorrow." *Personalist,* XVIII (April 1937), 183-89.
Contrasts ED's "wistfulness and simplicity" to the pretentious rhetoric of such poets as Poe, Longfellow, and Swinburne.

6.1047   Varley, Lee. "Emily Dickinson." *Springfield Daily Republican,* Feb. 14, 1944, p. 6.
Rev. of Power, *In the Name of the Bee* (5.72).

6.1048   Vernon, Greenville. *Commonweal,* XIII (Jan. 7, 1931), 275.
Rev. of *Poems,* 1930 (3.151).

6.1049   Vickery, Gertrude. "Emily Dickinson: Famous Poetess." *Amherst Record,* Nov. 27, 1935, p. 2.

6.1050   Vinci-Roman, F. "Emily Dickinson." *New York World,* Mar. 30, 1924, p. 6-E.
Rev. of Bianchi, *Life and Letters* (4.36).

6.1051   Voigt, Gilbert P. "The Inner Life of Emily Dickinson." *College English,* III (Nov. 1941), 192-96.
Sees ED as a mystic.

6.1052   Voiles, Jane. *San Francisco Chronicle,* Dec. 2, 1951, p. 18.
Rev. of Patterson, *Riddle* (5.55).

6.1053   ———. *San Francisco Chronicle,* Nov. 28, 1954, p. 17.
Rev. of Bingham, *Revelation* (5.9).

6.1054   ———. *San Francisco Chronicle,* June 19, 1955, p. 17.
Rev. of Bingham, *ED's Home* (4.86).

6.1055   ———. *San Francisco Chronicle,* Jan. 22, 1956, p. 19.
Rev. of Johnson, *Interpretive Biography* (5.44).

6.1056   ———. *San Francisco Chronicle,* April 13, 1958, p. 24.
Rev. of *Letters,* 1958 (4.90).

6.1056a Wachner, Clarence W., Frank E. Ross, and Eva Marie Van

Houten, eds. *The Changing Years of American Literature.*
N.Y.: Macmillan (Literary Heritage; a Macmillan paperback
series), 1963, p. 133.

6.1057 Wagenknecht, Edward. "The Quiet Spinster of Amherst, Mass."
Saturday Review, XXXIX (Jan. 21, 1956), 45.
Rev. of Johnson, *Interpretive Biography* (5.44).

6.1058 Waggoner, Hyatt H. "Emily Dickinson: The Transcendent Self."
Criticism, VII (Fall 1965), 297-334.
Reprinted:
Hyatt H. Waggoner. "Proud Ephemeral: Emily Dickinson" in
American Poets From the Puritans to the Present. Boston:
Houghton Mifflin, 1968, pp. 181-222.
Documents the importance of Emerson to ED, especially to
her religious thought and her sense of personal growth. His
influence is decisive for her concept of the transcendent self
and of the role of the poet. Nevertheless, Biblical and Puritan
influences were altered, not canceled, by Emersonian principles. The hymn and ballad forms appealed to ED precisely
because they were not "literary" — they suggested "not literature but life." Rev. by Robbins, *ALS, 1965* (6.851), pp. 155-56.

6.1059 ———. *South Atlantic Quarterly,* LXIV (Winter 1965), 151-52.
Rev. of Griffith, *Long Shadow* (5.31).

6.1060 Walcutt, Charles Child, and Edwin Whitesell, eds. "Dickinson"
in *The Explicator Cyclopedia,* Vol. I, *Modern Poetry.* Chicago:
Quadrangle Books, 1966, pp. 55-88.
Reprints articles previously published in *The Explicator.*

6.1061 Wallace, Margaret. *New York Evening Post,* Mar. 1, 1930, p. 7-S.
Rev. of Pollitt, *Human Background* (5.61).

6.1062 ———. "A Plausible Solution of Emily Dickinson's Romance."
New York Evening Post, June 21, 1930, p. 8-M.
Rev. of Taggard, *Life and Mind* (5.81).

6.1063 Walsh, Chad. *Doors Into Poetry.* Englewood Cliffs, N.J.:
Prentice-Hall, 1962, pp. 14-18.
Includes an explication of "I like to see it lap the Miles."

6.1064 Walsh, Thomas. *Commonweal,* V (Feb. 23, 1927), 441.
Rev. of *Complete Poems,* 1924 (3.123).

6.1065 Walton, Eda Lou. "The Letters of Emily Dickinson." *New York
Times Book Review,* Nov. 22, 1931, p. 2.
Rev. of *Letters,* 1931 (4.52).

6.1065a ———. *Nation,* CXXXIII (Sept. 2, 1931), 234-35.
Rev. of *The Sonnets of Frederick Goddard Tuckerman,* ed.
Witter Bynner (N.Y.: Knopf, 1931). Argues that Tuckerman,
like ED, "felt emotion in terms of *homely* experience" (p. 234).

6.1065b Want, M. S. "Emily Dickinson." *Jammu and Kashmir University
Review,* VIII (June 1966), 8-25.

6.1066 Ward, Alfred Charles. "Emily Dickinson" in *American Literature, 1880-1930.* N.Y.: Dial; London: Methuen, 1932, pp. 43-
52.
Reprinted:
Blake and Wells, *Recognition* (5.13), pp. 145-53.

An attempt, by a British critic, to find ED's place in American cultural and literary history. Compares her to Housman.

6.1067   Ward, Samuel G. [Excerpts from a letter to Thomas Wentworth Higginson, dated Oct. 11, 1891] in Mary Loomis Todd, "Introduction to Second Edition," *Letters*, 1931 (6.1000a), p. xxii, and Lubbers, *Critical Revolution* (5.114), p. 33.

Suggests that the Puritan sources of ED's poetry might limit her appeal: "No wonder six editions have been sold; every copy, I should think to a New Englander. She may become world famous, or she may never get out of New England." MS. owned by the Amherst College Library.

[4.76]   Ward, Theodora. "The Background" to *Emily Dickinson's Letters to Doctor and Mrs. Josiah Gilbert Holland*, ed. Theodora Ward, 1951, pp. 3-27.

Revised and reprinted:

Theodora Ward. "Josiah Gilbert Holland and Elizabeth Chapin Holland" in *Capsule of the Mind* (5.97), pp. 115-38.

6.1068   ——. "Emily Dickinson and T. W. Higginson." *Boston Public Library Quarterly*, V (Jan. 1953), 3-18.

Reprinted:

Theodora Ward. "Thomas Wentworth Higginson" in *Capsule of the Mind* (5.97), pp. 178-96.

Had he been more enthusiastic about her poetry, Higginson might have been able to overcome ED's resistence to publication.

6.1069   ——. "The Finest Secret: Emotional Currents in the Life of Emily Dickinson After 1865." *Harvard Library Bulletin*, XIV (Winter 1960), 82-106.

Reprinted:

Theodora Ward. "The Finest Secret" in *Capsule of the Mind* (5.97), pp. 78-112.

The death of her father and many of her friends caused ED to view death not as a fascinating riddle but as "a heavy encroaching shadow."

6.1070   ——. "Ourself Behind Ourself: An Interpretation of the Crisis in the Life of Emily Dickinson." *Harvard Library Bulletin*, X (Winter 1956), 5-38.

Revised and reprinted:

Theodora Ward. "Ourself Behind Ourself" in *Capsule of the Mind* (5.97), pp. 40-77.

Traces the psychic rather than biographical events of 1860-1865 which shaped ED's life as woman and poet.

6.1071   ——. "Poetry and Punctuation." *Saturday Review*, XLVI (April 27, 1963), 25.

Letter to the editor replying to Edith Perry Stamm, "Emily Dickinson: Poetry and Punctuation"; see 6.948.

6.1072   Warren, Austin. "Emily Dickinson." *Sewanee Review*, LXV (Autumn 1957), 565-586.

Reprinted:

American Critical Essays: Twentieth Century, ed. Harold

Lowther Beaver. N.Y.: Oxford Univ. Press, 1959, pp. 105-29.

Sewall, *Critical Essays* (5.75), pp. 101-16.

Blake and Wells, *Recognition* (5.13), pp. 268-86.

A wide-ranging review-essay of *Poems*, 1955 (3.197). Discusses problems in editing and biography and examines ED's poems about death.

6.1073   Warren, Austin. *The New England Conscience.* Ann Arbor: Univ. of Michigan Press, 1966, p. 209.
Brief mention of ED as one of New England's eccentrics.

6.1074   Wasson, Mildred. "Victory Comes Late to Emily Dickinson." *Literary Digest International Book Review*, III (Nov. 1925), 780-81.
Rev. of *Complete Poems*, 1924 (3.123).

6.1075   Waterman, Nixon. "Woman Poets of America. Our 'Feminine Walt Whitman.'" *Boston Globe,* July 1, 1924, p. 16.

6.1076   Waugh, Dorothy. "Dickinson's 'Those not live yet.'" *Explicator,* XV (Jan. 1957), Item 22.

6.1077   ———. "Emily Dickinson — Horticulturist." *Horticulture,* XXXII (Aug. 1954), 367, 388.

6.1078   ———. "Emily Dickinson's Garden." Photographs by Holbrook Clark. *Popular Gardening,* IV (Jan. 1953), 34-35, 68-71.

6.1079   ———. "The Things That Sing." *Quest* [pub. by Montclair, N.J., Women's Club], XXXI (Feb. 1962), 11-13, 27.
An appreciation.

6.1080   Wegelin, Christof. "Dickinson's 'Wild Nights.'" *Explicator,* XXVI (Nov. 1967), Item 25.

6.1080a   Wehmeyer, W. A. *Cithara* [St. Bonaventure Univ.], V (Nov. 1965), 81-82.
Rev. of Griffith, *Long Shadow* (5.31).

6.1081   Weirick, Bruce. *From Whitman to Sandburg in American Poetry.* N.Y.: Macmillan, 1924, pp. 96-97.
Brief but enthusiastic comment notes ED's "Emersonian pith, intellectual and emotional daring."

6.1082   Welby, T. Earle. "Emily Dickinson." *Week End Review* [London], II (Aug. 2, 1930), 164-65.
Rev. of Taggard, *Life and Mind* (5.81). "It is questionable whether she [ED] was in the mass of her work a poet at all."

6.1083   ———. "Four Poets and Many Morals." *Saturday Review* [London], CXLVIII (Sept. 28, 1929), 352-53.
Rev. of *Further Poems*, 1929 (3.138). "She neither boldly flouts rhyme and metre nor respects them; she takes long, careless shots at the right word, and her felicities have about them something fluky. What she really needed was a new art; she did nothing towards creating it, and even a vivid slovenliness is, after all, slovenliness" (p. 352).

6.1084   Welland, Dennis S. R. "The Dark Voice of the Sea, A Theme in Modern American Poetry" in *American Poetry,* ed. Irvin Ehrenpreis, Stratford-Upon-Avon Studies, No. 7, N.Y.: St. Martin's Press; London: Edward Arnold, 1965, pp. 196-219.
Describes ED's use of the sea as "potentiality for annihilation."

6.1085   Welland, Dennis S. R. "Emily Dickinson and Her 'Letter to the
          World'" in *The Great Experiment in American Literature*, ed.
          Carl Bode. N.Y.: Praeger; London: Heinemann, 1961, pp.
          53-78.
          A critical estimate which discusses ED's characteristic
          themes and techniques. Focuses on her experimental use of
          language.

6.1085a   Wellek, René, and Austin Warren. *Theory of Literature*. 3rd ed.
          N.Y.: Harcourt, Brace & World, 1963, pp. 206, 303.
          Notes that ED invokes the experience of death and resurrec-
          tion through the use of "de-animizing, anti-mystic metaphor."

6.1086   Wells, Anna Mary. *American Literature*, II (Jan. 1931), 455-58.
          Rev. of Jenkins, *Friend and Neighbor* (5.35); Pollitt, *Human
          Background* (5.61); Taggard, *Life and Mind* (5.81); and Hamp-
          son, *ED: A Bibliography* (1.6).

6.1087   ———. *American Literature*, XXXVI (Nov. 1964), 374-75.
          Rev. of Griffith, *Long Shadow* (5.31).

6.1088   ———. *American Literature*, XXXVIII (May 1966), 253-54.
          Rev. of Gelpi, *Mind of the Poet* (5.104).

6.1089   ———. *Dear Preceptor: The Life and Times of Thomas Went-
          worth Higginson*. Boston: Houghton Mifflin, 1963, pp. 122-53,
          226-42, 274-94, *passim*.
          A sympathetic treatment of Higginson's dealings with ED and
          his role in the early publication of her poems.

6.1090   ———. "Early Criticism of Emily Dickinson." *American Liter-
          ature*, I (Nov. 1929), 243-59.
          ED fell into obscurity between 1900 and 1915, but during the
          decade before the turn of the century she was quite widely
          discussed.

6.1091   ———. "Further Poems of Emily Dickinson." *Mt. Holyoke
          Alumnae Quarterly*, XIII (July 1929), 78-81.
          Rev. of *Further Poems*, 1929 (3.138).

6.1092   ———. "A Poet's Biography of a Poet." *Mt. Holyoke Alumnae
          Quarterly*, XIV (Oct. 1930), 161-63.
          Rev. of Taggard, *Life and Mind* (5.81).

6.1093   ———. "Was Emily Dickinson Psychotic?" *American Imago*,
          XIX (Winter 1962), 309-21.
          Argues that while there are indications that ED may have been
          psychotic, the poems themselves cannot be used as medical or
          biographical evidence.

6.1094   Wells, Carolyn. "Lavinia Dickinson." *Colophon*, I, Part 3 (Sept.
          1930), 4 unnumbered pages.
          Recollection of a childhood visit to ED's sister.

6.1095   Wells, Henry Willis. *American Literature*, XXVIII (Mar. 1956),
          93-95.
          Rev. of Johnson, *Interpretive Biography* (5.44).

6.1096   ———. *American Literature*, XXXIV (Mar. 1962), 124-25.
          Rev. of Ward, *Capsule of the Mind* (5.97).

6.1097   ———. *Atlantic Monthly*, CLXXVI (July 1945), 129-30.
          Rev. of *Bolts of Melody*, 1945 (3.177).

6.1098   Wells, Henry Willis. "Contradictions of Life and Art." *Saturday Review*, XXXIV (Sept. 29, 1951), 17-18.
Rev. of *Letters to Holland*, 1951 (4.76).

6.1099   ———. "Frugality and Infinity," in *The American Way of Poetry*, Columbia Studies in American Culture, No. 13. N.Y.: Columbia Univ. Press, 1943, pp. 67-77.
Portrays ED in terms of her human and spiritual environment, noting especially the "void in her heart caused by a loveless life and an unlovely God."

6.1100   ———. "A Lyricists's Milieu." *Saturday Review*, XXXVIII (June 11, 1955), 17-18.
Rev. of Bingham, *ED's Home* (4.86).

6.1101   ———. "The Maenad of Amherst." *New Leader* [N.Y.], XLIII (Nov. 14, 1960), 24-25.
Rev. of Anderson, *Stairway of Surprise* (5.2).

6.1102   ———. *New Poets From Old, A Study in Literary Genetics*. N.Y.: Columbia Univ. Press, 1940; Russell & Russell, 1964, pp. 86, 171, *passim*.
Describes ED as the "greatest single force on modern American versification."

6.1103   ———. "To express the Human Heart." *Saturday Review*, XXXIV (May 19, 1951), 18.
Rev. of *Letters*, 1951 (4.80).

6.1103a ———. "A View of Emily Dickinson." *N.C.T.E. Studies in the Mass Media* [National Council of Teachers of English, Champaign, Ill.], II (Nov. 1961), 14-16.
A general introduction and appreciation.

6.1104   ———. *Where Poetry Stands Now*. Toronto: Ryerson Press, 1948, pp. 1-3.

6.1105   Welshimer, Helen. "Emily Dickinson's Real Lover Revealed." *Boston Herald*, May 4, 1930, Section C, p. 3.
Rev. of Pollitt, *Human Background* (5.61). For a reply to this review, see Fairbank, 6.328.

6.1106   West, Edward Sackville. "Keepsake." *New Statesman and Nation*, n.s. XXXIV (Nov. 29, 1947), 435-36.
Rev. of *Bolts of Melody*, 1947 (3.182) and *Poems*, 1947 (3.183). Notes the difficulty in evaluating ED's "genuine, but very limited and capricious, muse."

6.1107   West, H. F. "Forgotten Dartmouth Men: A Founder of Amherst College — Samuel F. Dickinson, 1795." *Dartmouth Alumnae Magazine*, XXVII (Feb. 1935), 60, 62.
A biographical sketch of ED's grandfather.

6.1108   West, Ray B., Jr. "Emily's Forest." *Rocky Mountain Review*, V (Spring-Summer 1941), 1-3.
Examines ED's references to insects and raises the possibility of Freudian interpretation.

6.1109   Westbrook, Perry D. *Acres of Flint: Writers of Rural New England, 1870-1900*. Washington, D.C.: Scarecrow Press, 1951, pp. 70-72, 138.
Brief discussion of ED as a New England eccentric.

6.1110 [Wetcho, W. F.] "Letters of Emily Dickinson." *Boston Daily Advertiser*, Nov. 23, 1894, p. 4.
Rev. of *Letters*, 1894 (4.3).

6.1111 Wetherell, J. E. "Poems by Emily Dickinson," in *Later American Poems*. Toronto: Copp, 1896, pp. 185-86.
A brief selection of poems with an introduction.

6.1112 Wheatcroft, John Stewart. "Emily Dickinson's Poetry and Jonathan Edwards On the Will." *Bucknell Review*, X (Dec. 1961), 102-27.
Edwards' theory of the will as a passive power informs ED's concepts of renunciation and of poetic inspiration and helps us understand her preoccupation with death as the archetype of passive election. See also the author's thesis "ED and the Orthodox Tradition" (14.11).

6.1113 ———. "Emily Dickinson's White Robes." *Criticism*, V (Spring 1963), 135-47.
The image of white robes illustrates the working of the orthodox tradition in ED's poetry and allows her to conceive of eternity and to resolve the problem of death in terms of a consummation of love. Rev. by Robbins, *ALS, 1963* (6.851), p. 127.

6.1114 Wheeler, Charles B. *The Design of Poetry*. N.Y.: Norton, 1966, pp. 172-75, 189-92, *passim*.
Contains explications of "Because I could not stop for Death" and "I heard a Fly buzz — when I died."

6.1115 Whicher, George Frisbie. *American Literature*, IV (Nov. 1932), 318-22.
Rev. of *Letters*, 1931 (4.52).

6.1116 ———. *American Literature*, XII (Mar. 1940), 124-26.
Rev. of Cecchi, *ED* (8.27).

6.1117 ———. "The Book Table." *Amherst Graduates' Quarterly*, XIV (May 1925), 206-07.
Rev. of *Complete Poems*, 1924 (3.123) and Bianchi, *Life and Letters* (4.36).

6.1118 ———. "A Centennial Appraisal" in Jones Library, *Emily Dickinson: A Bibliography* (1.8), pp. 9-15.
Reprinted:
Blake and Wells, *Recognition* (5.13), pp. 137-41.
Comments briefly on the history of ED's reputation and notes some of the main themes of her poetry.

6.1119 ———. "A Chronological Grouping of Some of Emily Dickinson's Poems." *Colophon*, IV, Part 16 (Mar. 1934), 16 unnumbered pages.
Discusses methods of dating the poems and features a chronological list of about one fifth of the poems printed by 1934.
For newspaper articles noting the publication of this essay, see 6.384-385.

6.1120 ———. "The Deliverance of Emily Dickinson." *New York Herald Tribune Weekly Book Review*, Aug. 13, 1950, pp. 2, 12.
Reviews the history of ED editing and applauds both the

transfer of the manuscripts to Harvard and the appointment of
T. H. Johnson as editor of the Dickinson papers.

6.1121   Whicher, George Frisbie. "Emily At Last." *New York Herald
Tribune Books*, June 22, 1930, pp. 1-2.
Rev. of Taggard, *Life and Mind* (5.81).

6.1122   ———. "Emily Dickinson" in *Dictionary of American Biography*.
20 vols. N.Y.: Scribner, 1928-1937, V, 297-98.

6.1123   ———. "Emily Dickinson Among the Victorians" in *Poetry and
Civilization, Essays by George F. Whicher*, ed. Harriet Fox
Whicher. Ithaca: Cornell Univ. Press, 1955, pp. 41-62.
Reprinted:
Blake and Wells, *Recognition* (5.13), pp. 235-50.
Places ED among British and American Poets who were react-
ing against the conventions of the Victorian literary establish-
ment. Discusses her relation to such poets as Lanier, Whit-
man, Donne and the metaphysicals, Keats, Tennyson, and the
Brownings.

6.1124   ———. "Emily Dickinson at Mount Holyoke." *Mt. Holyoke Alumnae Quarterly*, XVIII (May 1934), 27-28.
Reviews Sidney R. McLean's article on this subject; see 6.687.

6.1125   ———. "Emily Dickinson: Centennial Afterthoughts." *Amherst
Graduates' Quarterly*, XX (Feb. 1931), 94-99.
Reprinted:
In Other Words, ed. Horace W. Hewlett (6.459), pp. 123-28.
A brief introduction contrasting ED with the more conventional
poets of her period and stressing her cultivation of the senses.

6.1126   ———. "Emily Dickinson Fifty-Nine Years After. A Third of
Her Entire Body of Poetry Appears For the First Time." *New
York Herald Tribune*, April 8, 1945, pp. 1-2.
Rev. of *Bolts of Melody*, 1945 (3.177) and Bingham, *Ancestors'
Brocades* (5.5).

6.1127   ———. "Emily Dickinson's Earliest Friend." *American Literature*, VI (Mar. 1934), 3-17, 192-93.
Discusses ED's relationship with Benjamin Newton. For a
reply, see Bingham, 6.97. For articles noting the publication
of this essay, see 6.341a and 6.384-385.

6.1128   ———. "Emily Dickinson's Poetry." *Amherst Record*, April 26,
1945, p. 2.
Rev. of *Bolts of Melody*, 1945 (3.177) and Bingham, *Ancestors'
Brocades* (5.5).

6.1129   ———. "Emily's Lover." *New York Herald Tribune Books*, Mar.
2, 1930, p. 2.
Rev. of Pollitt, *Human Background* (5.61).

6.1130   ———. "Emily's Suitors." *Forum* [Philadelphia], CVI (Aug.
1946), 162-66.
Surveys and lays to rest some of the legends surrounding ED.

6.1131   ———. "In Emily Dickinson's Garden." *Atlantic Monthly*,
CLXXVII (Feb. 1946), 64-70.
Argues that Bernard De Voto (see 6.281) and M. T. Bingham
have added new myths to the ED legend and insists that study
of her poetry must begin with her backgrounds.

6.1132   Whicher, George Frisbie. "More Light on Emily." *New York Herald Tribune Books*, April 29, 1951, p. 6.
Rev. of *Letters to Holland*, 1951 (4.76).

6.1133   ——. "New England Poet" in *Mornings at 8:50.*   Northampton, Mass.: The Hampshire Bookshop, 1950, pp. 11-16.
A brief chapel talk on ED.

6.1134   ——. *New England Quarterly*, XVII (Mar. 1944), 130-32.
Rev. of Power, *In the Name of the Bee* (5.72).

6.1135   ——. *New England Quarterly*, XVIII (June 1945), 261-64.
Rev. of Bingham, *Ancestors' Brocades* (5.5).

6.1136   ——. *New England Quarterly*, XXII (Mar. 1949), 110-11.
Rev. of *Poems*, 1890, 1891, reissued 1948 (3.189).

6.1137   ——. *New York Herald Tribune Weekly Book Review*, Mar. 18, 1951, p. 20.
Rev. of *Letters*, 1951 (4.80).

6.1138   ——. "Poetry After the Civil War" in *American Writers on American Literature*, ed. John Macy. N.Y.: Liveright, 1931, 374-88.
Discusses some of the sources of ED's inner life, pp. 384-88.

6.1139   ——. "Poetry in Amherst." *Amherst Record*, July 14, 1937, p. 2.

6.1140   ——, ed. *Poetry of the New England Renaissance 1790-1890.* N.Y.: Rinehart, 1950, pp. xviii-xxi, xxix.
Brief introductory remarks and a bibliographical note for an anthology containing a selection from ED's poems.

6.1141   ——. "Pursuit of the Overtakeless." *Nation,* CLXIX (July 2, 1949), 14-15.
Reprinted:
In Other Words, ed. Horace W. Hewlett (6.459), pp. 141-44.
Poetry and Civilization, ed. Harriet Fox Whicher (6.1123), pp. 63-69.
Describes an interview with a descendant of Charles Wadsworth.

6.1142   ——. "Reply to a Reviewer." *Commonweal,* XXIX (Jan. 6, 1939), 297.
Replies to Sister Rose Marie's review of *This Was a Poet;* see 6.860.

6.1143   ——. "Riddle or Reconstruction." *New York Herald Tribune Books*, Nov. 4, 1951, p. 21.
Rev. of Patterson, *Riddle* (5.55).

6.1144   ——. "Uriel in Amherst." *Amherst Graduates' Quarterly,* XXIII (Aug. 1934), 281-92.
ED may have heard and even met Emerson when he came to Amherst to lecture in 1855 and 1857.

6.1145   Whicher, George M. "Emily Dickinson: A New England Mystic." *The Landmark* [London], XIII (Aug. 1931), 467-70.
The index and table of contents of this journal list the author's initials as "J.M."

6.1146   Whicher, Stephen. "Dickinson's 'Elysium is as far as to.'" *Explicator,* XIX (April 1961), Item 45.

6.1147   Whitbread, Thomas. *Essex Institute Historical Collections* [Salem, Mass.], XCII (July 1956), 290-92.
Rev. of Bingham, *ED's Home* (4.86).

6.1148   White, Gertrude. "Poem of the Mind: Review." *Walt Whitman Review*, XII (Sept. 1966), 71-72.
Rev. of Louis Martz's essay, "Whitman and Dickinson: Two Aspects of the Self"; see 6.661.

6.1149   White, James E. "Emily Dickinson: Metaphysician and Miniaturist." *CEA Critic*, XXIX (Mar. 1967), 17-18.
Explicates "The thought beneath so slight a film" as a metaphysical poem, noting its imagery and its use of irony and paradox. Prof. Perrine replies; see 6.796a.

6.1150   White, William. *American Book Collector*, XV (Dec. 1964), 5.
Rev. of Blake and Wells, *Recognition* (5.13).

6.1151   ———. *American Book Collector*, XV (Summer 1965), 4.
Rev. of Gelpi, *Mind of the Poet* (5.104).

6.1152   ———. *Bulletin of Bibliography*, XXI (Jan.-Apr. 1955), 129.
Rev. of Bingham, *Revelation* (5.9).

6.1153   ———. *Bulletin of Bibliography*. XXI (Sept.-Dec. 1955), 175.
Rev. of Bingham, *ED's Home* (4.86) and Johnson, *Interpretive Biography* (5.44).

6.1154   ———. *Bulletin of Bibliography*, XXII (May-Aug. 1958), 127.
Rev. of *Letters*, 1958 (4.90).

6.1155   ———. *Bulletin of Bibliography*, XXIII (Jan.-Apr. 1961), 80.
Rev. of Leyda, *Years and Hours* (5.49).

6.1156   ———. *Bulletin of Bibliography*, XXIII (May-Aug. 1962), 175-76.
Rev. of *Final Harvest*, 1962 (3.208).

6.1157   ———. *Bulletin of Bibliography*, XXIV (Sept.-Dec. 1963), 31.
Rev. of Sewall, *Critical Essays* (5.75).

6.1158   ———. "The Computer and Emily." *American Book Collector*, XV (Feb. 1965), 9-10.
A review-essay of S. P. Rosenbaum's computer concordance to the Johnson edition of ED's poetry. See also Rosenbaum's article, "Emily Dickinson and the Machine" (6.861).

6.1159   ———. "Emily and '— Ana.'" *American Book Collector*, XV (May 1965), 32.
Rev. of *Poems*, sel. Plotz, 1964 (3.210); Griffith, *Long Shadow* (5.31); and Davis, *14 by ED* (5.23).

6.1159a ———. "Emily on the Stage." *American Book Collector*, XIX (Nov. 1968), 13-16.
An account of the characterizations of ED in the American theatre. Originally delivered as a paper at a meeting of the Michigan Academy of Science, Arts, and Letters, Wayne State University, Detroit, April 20, 1968. See also 17.4.

6.1160   ———. "One-Man Journals, Emily Dickinson, and Two Emily Dickinson Books." *Emily Dickinson Bulletin* (1.21), No. 6 (Dec. 1968), pp. 1-2.
Rev. of *Choice of ED's Verse*, 1968 (3.213) and Lubbers, *Revolution* (5.114).

6.1161   ———. *Papers of the Bibliographical Society of America*, LII (Apr.-June 1958), 157-58.

Describes the Gehenna Press book, *Riddle Poems,* 1957 (3.201).

6.1161a White, William. *Times* [London] *Literary Supplement,* Mar. 2, 1956, p. 133.

Letter to the editor regarding a review of *Poems,* 1955 (3.197) and recommending M. T. Bingham's *ED's Home* (4.86).

6.1162 ———. "Two Unlisted Emily Dickinson Poems." *Colby Library Quarterly,* Series II, No. 5 (Feb. 1948), pp. 69-70.

Notes a brief, anonymous entry in the *Chap-Book* [Chicago], III, No. 11 (Oct. 15, 1895), p. 446, which attributes to ED two poems: "A Clamor in the Treetops" (reprinted, see 6.933) and "If God Upon the Seventh Day." For another poem mistakenly ascribed to ED, see 23.8.

6.1163 ———. "What is a Collector's Item: Emily Dickinson, E. A. Robinson, D. H. Lawrence? An Essay in the Form of a Bibliography." *American Book Collector,* VI (Summer 1956), 6-8.

Includes a review of Bingham, *Revelation* (5.9).

6.1164 ———. "Why Collect Ernest Hemingway — or Anyone?" *Prairie Schooner,* XL (Fall 1966), 232-46.

Argues that a complete bibliography must preceed textual study and that a bibliographer must either be or rely upon a collector. The author mentions his own collection of ED as a case in point.

6.1165 Whiteside, Mary Brent. "Poe and Dickinson." *Personalist,* XV (Autumn 1934), 315-26.

Reprinted:

Muse Anthology of Modern Poetry; Poe Memorial Edition, ed. Dorothy Kissling and Arthur H. Nethercot. N.Y.: Carlyle Straub, 1938, pp. 155-64.

Notes the poets' capacity for self-revelation and compares themes and attitudes toward poetry.

6.1166 Whiting, Lilian. "Life and Imagination of Emily Dickinson." *Springfield Union and Republican,* May 16, 1937, Magazine Section, p. 7-E.

Rev. of *Poems,* 1937 (3.173).

6.1167 ———. "Life in Boston." *Inter Ocean* [Chicago], Dec. 1, 1894, p. 14.

Rev. of *Letters,* 1894 (4.3).

6.1168 ———. "Life in Boston." *Inter Ocean* [Chicago], Sept. 26, 1896, p. 16.

Excerpt reprinted:

Bingham, *Ancestors' Brocades* (5.5), p. 346.

Rev. of *Poems,* 1896 (3.89).

6.1169 ———. "Poems." *Boston Budget,* Nov. 23, 1890.

Excerpt reprinted:

Bingham, *Ancestors' Brocades* (5.5), p. 75.

Rev. of *Poems,* 1890 (3.9).

6.1170 ———. "The Strangely Isolated Life of Emily Dickinson." *Brooklyn Standard Union,* Sept. 26, 1891.

Discusses Higginson's *Atlantic* essay (6.473).

6.1171   Whiting, Lilian. *The World Beautiful in Books*. Boston: Little, Brown, 1901, pp. 85, 185, 189, 227.
Inspirational essays with quotation from ED.

6.1172   Whitman, William. "New Poems by Emily Dickinson." *Boston Sunday Globe*, Feb. 3, 1929, p. 47.
Rev. of *Further Poems* (3.138).

6.1173   Wicks, Frank S. C. "Emily Dickinson's Poems." *Indianapolis News*, Oct. 29, 1924, p. 14.
Rev. of *Complete Poems*, 1924 (3.123).

6.1174   Wilbur, Richard. "Sumptuous Destitution" in *Emily Dickinson: Three Views* (5.52), pp. 35-46.
Reprinted:
In Other Words, ed. Horace W. Hewlett (6.459), pp. 129-40.
Sewall, *Critical Essays* (5.75), pp. 127-36.
Discusses ED's "emotional strategies": self-analysis, renunciation, and beatitude.

6.1175   Wilder, Thornton. "Emily Dickinson." *Atlantic Monthly* CXC (Nov. 1952), 43-48.
ED solved the problem of American loneliness "by loving the particular while living in the universal."

6.1176   ———. "Toward an American Language." *Atlantic Monthly*, CXC (July 1952), 34, 37.
Mentions ED's poetry as illustrating a characteristic American "sense of the boundless" and states that the whole universe is ED's implied audience.

6.1177   Williams, Paul O. "Dickinson's 'One Day is there of the Series.'" *Explicator*, XXIII (Dec. 1964), Item 28.
Reply by Virginia H. Adair; see 6.8. Noted by Robbins, *ALS, 1964* (6.851), p. 135.

6.1178   Williams, Sidney. "The Singular Life and Striking Poetry of Emily Dickinson." *The North American* [Philadelphia], July 19, 1924, p. 5.
Rev. of *Complete Poems*, 1924 (3.123) and Bianchi, *Life and Letters* (4.36).

6.1179   Williams, Stanley T. "Experiments in Poetry: Sidney Lanier and Emily Dickinson" in *Literary History of the United States*, ed. Robert E. Spiller, *et. al.* N.Y.: Macmillan, 1948 (rev. ed., 1963), pp. 899-916. Translated into German, see 10.77.
Reprinted:
Blake and Wells, *Recognition* (5.13), pp. 251-60.
A biographical and critical introduction, pp. 907-16. Stresses dualism in ED's poetry: between the concrete and abstract, the real and unknown, the frail and heroic, the comic and cosmic.

6.1180   ———. *Modern Language Notes*, LXXII (Jan. 1957), 64-66.
Rev. of Johnson, *Interpretive Biography* (5.44).

6.1181   Williams, Talcott. "With the New Books." *Book News* [Philadelphia], XV (Oct. 1896), 42.
Rev. of *Poems*, 1896 (3.89).

6.1181a Williams-Ellis, A. "Poets and Poetry." *Spectator* [London], CXXIX (Nov. 18, 1922), 732-33.

Mentions ED as an example of "the mystical, the exotic, the *macabre.*"

6.1182 Willy, Margaret. *English* [Oxford, Eng.], XII (Spring 1959), 145-46.
Rev. of *Letters*, 1958 (4.90).

6.1183 ——. *English* [Oxford, Eng.], XV (Summer 1964), 68-69.
Rev. of Anderson, *Stairway of Surprise* (5.2).

6.1184 ——. "The Poetry of Emily Dickinson." *Essays and Studies by Members of the English Association*. London: John Murray, 1957, n.s. X, 91-104.
Notes parallels between ED and Emily Brontë and discusses some of ED's poetic innovations.

6.1184a Wilson, Edmund. *Patriotic Gore.* N.Y.: Oxford Univ. Press, 1962, pp. 488-91, 497, *passim.*
Compares ED to Frederick Goddard Tuckerman.

6.1185 Wilson, James R. *Books Abroad*, XXX (Spring 1956), 229-30.
Rev. of Bingham, *ED's Home* (4.86).

6.1186 Wilson, James Southall. "Emily Dickinson and the 'Ghosts.'" *Virginia Quarterly Review,* VI (Oct. 1930), 624-30.
Rev. of Jenkins, *Friend and Neighbor* (5.35) and Taggard, *Life and Mind* (5.81).

6.1187 ——. "Emily Dickinson and Her Poems." *Virginia Quarterly Review,* XXXII (Winter 1956), 154-57.
Rev. of *Poems*, 1955 (3.197); Johnson, *Interpretive Biography* (6.44); and Bingham, *ED's Home* (4.86).

6.1188 ——. "Second Debut of Emily Dickinson." *Virginia Quarterly Review,* XXI (Summer 1945), 447-52.
Rev. of *Bolts of Melody*, 1945 (3.177) and Bingham, *Ancestors' Brocades* (5.5).

6.1189 Wilson, Rufus Rockwell. *New England in Letters.* N.Y.: Wessels, 1904, pp. 304-05.
A brief appreciation.

6.1190 Wilson, Suzanne M. "Emily Dickinson and Twentieth Century Poetry of Sensibility." *American Literature,* XXXVI (Nov. 1964), 349-58.
In her use of sharp, extended images and the technique of free suggestion, ED resembles Ezra Pound, T. S. Eliot, and the American Imagists. Rev. by Robbins, *ALS, 1964* (6.851), pp. 133-34.

6.1191 ——. "Structural Patterns in the Poetry of Emily Dickinson." *American Literature,* XXXV (Mar. 1963), 53-59.
Argues that the structure of ED's poetry (statement, elaboration, and conclusion) and the three variations within this pattern suggest conscious artistry. See also the author's thesis "Structure and Imagery Patterns in the Poetry of Emily Dickinson" (14.8). D. L. Emblem comments on this article; see 6.315.
Rev. by Robbins, *ALS, 1963* (6.851), p. 127.

6.1192 W[ingate, Charles E. L.] "Boston Letter." *Critic,* n.s. XV (April 18, 1891), 212.
Announces an upcoming reading of unpublished ED poems by

Mrs. Todd and T. W. Higginson before the College Club of
Boston.

6.1193   Wingate, Charles E. L. "Boston Letter." *Critic*, n.s. XV (May 9, 1891), 253.
Notes impressions of ED by Mrs. Todd and T. W. Higginson at
the College Club reading; see above entry.

6.1194   ———. "Boston Letter." *Critic*, n.s. XVI (Sept. 19, 1891), 141.
Previews T. W. Higginson's article on ED's letters to appear
in the October issue of the *Atlantic*; see 6.473.

6.1195   ———. "Boston Letter." *Critic*, n.s. XVI (Dec. 5, 1891), 320.
Rev. of *Poems*, 1891 (3.52).

6.1196   Winterich, John Tracy. "The Expansion of an Author Collection"
in *New Paths in Book Collecting, Essays by Various Hands*,
ed. John Carter. N.Y.: Scribner, 1934, pp. 22-29.

6.1197   ———. "Good Second-Hand Condition." *Publisher's Weekly*,
CXVIII (Nov. 15, 1930), 2311-13.
Discusses the text of "Success is counted sweetest" as printed
in *A Masque of Poets* (3.7).

6.1198   ———. "Prosody in Blue." *Saturday Review*, VIII (Feb. 20, 1932), 547.
Notes three ED bibliographies and an early anthology reprinting of "Whose are the little beds, I asked."

6.1199   ———. "Two New Emily Dickinson Books." *Publisher's Weekly*,
CXLVII (May 12, 1945), 1938-42.
Rev. of *Bolts of Melody*, 1945 (3.177) and Bingham, *Ancestors'
Brocades* (5.5).

6.1200   Winters, Yvor. "Emily Dickinson and the Limits of Judgment" in
*Maule's Curse; Seven Studies in the History of American Ob-
scurantism*. Norfolk, Conn.: New Directions, 1938, pp. 149-65.
Reprinted:
Yvor Winters, *In Defense of Reason*. Denver: Swallow Press,
1938, pp. 283-99.
Sewall, *Critical Essays* (5.75), pp. 28-40.
Blake and Wells, *Recognition* (5.13), pp. 187-200.
Excerpts reprinted:
Davis, *14 by ED* (5.23), pp. 31-34, 86.
Translated into French, see 9.35.
Careful scrutiny of ED's poetic techniques with close reading
of several poems, including "Because I could not stop for
Death" and "Farther in summer than the birds."

6.1201   Witham, W. Tasker. *Panorama of American Literature*. N.Y.:
Stephen Daye Press, 1947, pp. 145-50.
A brief introduction to ED's life and poetry.

6.1201a Witherington, Paul. "Dickinson's '"Faith" is a fine invention.'"
Explicator, XXVI (April 1968), Item 62.

6.1202   Wood, Clement. "Emily Dickinson: the Shrinking Seer" in *Poets
of America*. N.Y.: Dutton, 1925, pp. 82-96.
An appreciation with considerable quotation from the poems.
Notes ED's mysticism and modernity. See also 5.112.

6.1203   Woods, Ralph Louis. "Emily Dickinson: A Selection of Ten Love
Poems," in *Famous Poems and the Little Known Stories Behind Them*. N.Y.: Hawthorn, 1961, pp. 66-67.

Sketches ED's attachments to Newton and Wadsworth as a background to a selection from her love poems.

6.1204 Woolsey, Dorothy Bacon. "Tremendous Adventures of a Frail Soul." *Independent,* CXIII (July 5, 1924), 20-21.
Rev. of Bianchi, *Life and Letters* (4.36).

6.1205 W[ortman], D[enis]. "Emily Dickinson's Letters." *Public Opinion* [Washington, D.C.], XVII (Dec. 27, 1894), 952.
Rev. of *Letters,* 1894 (4.3).

6.1206 ———. "The Reading Room." *Christian Intelligencer* [N.Y.], LXII, May 27, 1891, p. 12.
Rev. of *Poems,* 1890 (3.9).

6.1207 Wright, Nathalia. "Emily Dickinson's Boanerges and Thoreau's Atropos: Locomotives on the Same Line?" *Modern Language Notes,* LXXII (Feb. 1957), 101-03.
Reprinted:
Davis, *14 by ED* (5.23), pp. 96-98.
Suggests that ED's description of a train in "I like to see it lap the Miles" was inspired by a similar treatment of the same subject in *Walden.*

[4.34] Wyman, Helen Knight Bullard. "Emily Dickinson as Cook and Poetess."

6.1208 Young, Alexander. *Critic,* n.s. XIV (Dec. 6, 1890), 297.
Notes that *Poems,* 1890 (3.9) has passed into a "second edition."

6.1209 ———. *Critic,* n.s. XIV (Dec. 27, 1890), 340.
Notes that two more ED books are being planned, one of prose and another of poetry.

6.1210 Yust, Walter. "Of Making Many Books." *Philadelphia Public Ledger,* June 2, 1930, p. 11.
Rev. of Taggard, *Life and Mind* (5.81) and Pollitt, *Human Background* (5.61).

6.1211 ———. "A Poet Who Stands Alone." *New York Evening Post Literary Review,* IV (Aug. 9, 1924), 949.
Rev. of *Complete Poems,* 1924 (3.123).

6.1212 Z[abel], M[orton] D[auwen]. "Christina Rossetti and Emily Dickinson." *Poetry,* XXXVII (Jan. 1931), 213-16.
Finds similarities in the two poets' seclusion and in their dedication — Christina Rossetti to Christianity and ED to integrity and self-discovery.

6.1213 Zietlow, Paul. "Teaching Poetry to Students in Grade Ten." *Indiana University English Curriculum Study Center Newsletter,* III (Feb. 1968), 2-5, 7.
Contains suggestions for teaching three ED poems: "The morns are meeker than they were," "An altered look about the hills," and "I dreaded that first Robin, so."

6.1214 Zimmerman, Michael. "Literary Revivalism in America: Some Notes Toward a Hypothesis." *American Quarterly,* XIX (Spring 1967), 71-85.
Attributes the decline of ED's reputation prior to World War II to the influence of anti-intellectual and middlebrow literary ideals (pp. 77-80).

7.

Unsigned Articles

The arrangement of this section is chronological. In the case of anonymous reviews, entries are listed in other sections following the book or
article reviewed. Note that items appearing in periodicals may be found
in the subject index under the title of the periodical in which they are published. For further help in locating unsigned materials, see "Preface," p. xi.

7.1   *Independent,* XLIII (Feb. 5, 1891), 202.
      Of *Poems,* 1890 (3.9): "The volume of 'Poems' by the late
      Emily Dickinson, has gone into the fourth edition, at a popular
      price." Comment complete.

7.2   *Springfield Daily Republican,* Mar. 7, 1891.
      An Amherst correspondent to Mrs. Caroline Healey Dall re-
      calls ED. Reprinted in Leyda, *Years and Hours* (5.49), II,
      483-84.

7.3   "Emily Dickinson's Poems." *Christian Register* [Boston], LXX
      (April 30, 1891), 274.
      Expresses admiration for ED's poetry and defends a review of
      Poems, 1890 by John W. Chadwick for the *Christian Register;*
      see 6.193. This article is attributed to Samuel J. Barrows by
      Lubbers, *Revolution* (5.114), p. 30.

7.4   "Notes." *Nation,* LIII (July 16, 1891), 48.
      Notes that the 8th American edition of *Poems,* 1890 (3.9) is in
      preparation and that an Arabic translation made in Syria has
      gone through several editions. This report of an Arabic trans-
      lation was repeated in the *Critic* two days later; see 7.5.

7.5   "Notes." *Critic,* n.s. XVI (July 18, 1891), 36.
      Reprinted:
      Bingham, *Ancestors' Brocades* (5.5), p. 412.
      "Of the poems of Emily Dickinson, 'an Arabic translation,
      made in Syria,' is said to have passed through several edi-
      tions." Comment complete.

7.6   "The Significance of Emily Dickinson." *Hartford Courant*, Sept.
        24, 1891, p. 4.
        An editorial applauding the popularity of *Poems*, 1890 (3.9)
        and defending their originality. In spite of ED's neglect of
        form, her poetry ought to be appreciated for its treatment of
        the "main themes of human life on its subjective side."

7.7   "Emily Dickinson." *Light* [Worcester, Mass.], IV (Dec. 12, 1891),
        349.
        A brief biographical sketch.

7.8   "Miss Dickinson's Poetry." *Critic*, n.s. XVII (Jan. 23, 1892), 61.
        Quotes a devastating article from an undated *London Daily
        News* on why ED didn't publish.

7.9   "Notes." *Critic*, n.s. XVII (June 11, 1892), 334.
        Quotes from a letter by a "correspondent in Mass." regarding
        a lecture by Mary Loomis Todd at Amherst College in which
        Mrs. Todd quoted from ED's letters. The writer praises the
        charm of ED's letters and predicts that they will be as wel-
        come to the public as the poems have been. In *Ancestors'
        Brocades* (5.5), p. 414, Mrs. Bingham notes that this article
        was reproduced in full as an advertisement for the forthcom-
        ing edition of *Letters*, 1894 (4.3).

7.10   "Americans and Their Books." *Critic*, n.s. XVIII (July 23, 1892),
        48.
        Contains a brief, disparaging allusion to ED in an article re-
        printed from the *London Daily News* for Oct. 27, 1891.

7.11   "A Melancholy Fidelity." *New York Commercial Advertiser*,
        Aug. 23, 1893, p. 5.
        Reports a childhood recollection of ED by Mrs. Luther W.
        Bodman (nee Grace Herbert Smith) and notes that "Amherst
        gossips" have attributed the poet's eccentricities to a ro-
        mance with George Howland which was abruptly ended by her
        father.

7.12   "Literary Notes." *Independent*, XLVI (June 14, 1894), 771.
        Excerpt reprinted:
        Bingham, *Ancestors' Brocades* (5.5), p. 414.
        Notes the forthcoming Todd edition of the letters (4.3) and re-
        ports that "twelve thousand copies of the first volume of Miss
        Emily Dickinson's poems have been issued and seven thousand
        of the second volume."

7.13   "Notes." *Nation*, LIX (Nov. 1, 1894), 325-26.
        Notes the forthcoming publication of ED's letters (4.3).

7.14   "Notes." *Chap-Book* [Chicago], III, No. 11 (Oct. 15, 1895), p. 446.
        This item is discussed by William White; see 6.1162.

7.15   "Six Books of Verse." *Atlantic Monthly*, LXXVII (Feb. 1896), 271.
        Stephen Crane's verse suggests an intellect like ED's.

7.16   "Chronicle and Comment." *Bookman* [N.Y.], III (Aug. 1896), 498.
        Compares the press runs of volumes of poetry by ED and John
        Banister Tabb.

7.17   "Why Was She a Recluse? Two Portland People Talk About
        Emily Dickinson." *Sunday Oregonian* [Portland, Ore.], Mar.
        19, 1899.

Reprinted:
"Appendix V" in Taggard, *Life and Mind* (5.81), pp. 372-75.
Publishes a reminiscence by Mrs. Thomas L. Eliot (nee Henrietta Robins Mack) of her childhood acquaintance with ED.

7.18   "Eleonora Duse Dies in Pittsburgh While on Tour of Country."
New York Evening Post, April 21, 1924.
Excerpt reprinted:
Pollitt, *Human Background* (5.61), pp. 346-47.
Describes the stage presence of Miss Duse as an echo of ED's "sad," "spiritual" poetry.

7.19   "Emily Dickinson." *Hartford Courant,* Feb. 24, 1927, p. 16.
An editorial commenting on ED's gradual increase in popularity and the irony that she appeared to care so little for fame. Quotes Amy Lowell as saying that she would somersault all day if by doing so she might stay with ED.

7.20   *Hampshire Daily Gazette* [Northampton, Mass.], Jan. 30, 1929.
ED's life recalled.

[6.767]   *Outlook and Independent,* CLI (April 24, 1929), 669, 680.

7.21   *Hampshire Daily Gazette* [Northampton, Mass.], Oct. 17, 1929.
Describes ED's home and furnishings.

7.22   "Emily Dickinson's Year at Mt. Holyoke Seminary." *Springfield Sunday Union and Republican,* Nov. 10, 1929, p. 5-E.

7.23   "New Names for the Hall of Fame?" *Publishers' Weekly,* CXVII (Mar. 8, 1930), 1334-36.
ED is among several authors considered for election to the American Hall of Fame located at New York University.

7.24   "Emily Dickinson and Some Early Critics." *Springfield Sunday Union and Republican,* Aug. 3, 1930, p. 5-E.

7.25   "Emily Dickinson Seems to Have Won Fame to Spite the Critics." *San Francisco Chronicle,* Aug. 10, 1930.

7.26   "Emily Dickinson's Poems Discussed." *Hartford Daily Times,* Nov. 13, 1930.

7.27   "Mme. Bianchi Gives Impression of Poet." *Springfield Union,* Nov. 20, 1930.

7.28   "Amherst Poet's First Editor Represented Symbol of an Age. Death of Mabel Loomis Todd Last Fall Removed a True Product of New England." *Springfield Sunday Union and Republican,* Mar. 26, 1933, p. 2-E.
An appreciative survey of Mrs. Todd's life and work. For a reply, see Crowell, 6.240.

7.29   "Valentines, Frowned On by Miss Lyon, Owe Popularity to Mt. Holyoke Girl. Emily Dickinson's Letter Reveals Attitude of Seminary Founder." *Springfield Union,* Feb. 13, 1934.

7.30   "Emily Dickinson Famous Poetess, Outstanding Amherst Personality." *Massachusetts Collegian,* XLVI (Nov. 21, 1935), 2.

7.31   "Sketch of Emily Dickinson." *Jewish Woman's Review,* Feb. 1937.

7.32   "Emily Dickinson, Poet, As Mt. Holyoke Student; One of World's Great Poets Wrote About Seminary to Friends." *Holyoke Daily Transcript and Telegram,* May 7, 1937, "Mt. Holyoke Centennial Supplement," p. 10.

7.33   "Emily Dickinson's Editors and Exploiters Assailed." *Spring-
         field Sunday Union and Republican,* May 23, 1937, p. 7-E.
7.34   "Poet's Letters Held Intact: Emily Dickinson's Niece Leaves
         Strange Will." Clipping from an unidentified newspaper in the
         Beinecke Library, Yale Univ., dated Mar. 14, [1943].
         Reports the disposition of Mme. Bianchi's will regarding her
         collection of ED manuscripts.
7.35   "The World and Emily." *New York Herald Tribune,* April 7,
         1945, 10.
         An editorial on ED's posthumous fame.
7.36   "Emily Dickinson Birth Record." *Springfield Sunday Union and
         Republican,* Dec. 9, 1945, p. 5-D.
         Dr. Isaac G. Cutler entered ED's birth in his record book, now
         owned by the Jones Library, Amherst.
7.37   "Removal of Trains Recalls Poem by Emily Dickinson." *Hamp-
         shire Daily Gazette* [Northampton, Mass.], Jan. 14, 1947, p. 11.
7.38   "Emily Dickinson's Papers Thought Going to Harvard." *Spring-
         field Union,* Mar. 8, 1950, p. 1.
7.39   "Emily Dickinson Exhibit at the Main Library." *Wellesley*
         [Mass.] *Townsman,* May 25, 1950, p. 10.
7.40   "Emily Dickinson's Papers Given to Harvard; 3 Volumes
         Planned." *New York Herald Tribune,* May 31, 1950, p. 17.
7.41   "Key to Genius of Emily Dickinson Seen in Papers Given to Har-
         vard." *New York Times,* May 31, 1950, p. 31.
         Notes G. H. Montague's gift of the Dickinson manuscripts and
         that T. H. Johnson is named as editor.
7.42   "Large Collection of Emily Dickinson Papers Are Given to Har-
         vard." *Amherst Record,* June 1, 1950, pp. 1, 4.
7.43   "The Emily Dickinson Papers." *New York Herald Tribune,* June
         1, 1950, p. 20.
         An editorial noting the Montague gift of Dickinson manuscripts
         to Harvard.
7.44   "Emily Dickinson Papers Given to Harvard." *Publishers' Weekly,*
         CLVII (June 3, 1950), 2456.
7.45   "Out of the Top Drawer." *Time,* LV (June 12, 1950), 91-92.
         On the gift of the Dickinson papers to Harvard.
7.46   "The Dickinson Papers." *Harvard Alumni Bulletin,* LII (June 24,
         1950), 701-02.
         Describes Mr. Montague's gift to Harvard of the ED manu-
         scripts.
7.47   "The Emily Dickinson Room." *Harvard Library Bulletin,* V (Au-
         tumn 1951), 386-87.
         Discusses the "Emily Dickinson Room" located in the Hough-
         ton Library, Harvard.
7.48   "Mt. Holyoke Offers 6 New Scholarships." *New York Times,*
         Nov. 8, 1952, p. 14.
         Mt. Holyoke College names six new scholarships of $1400 in
         honor of ED.
[6.761] "Emily Dickinson: The Domestication of Terror." *Times* [Lon-
         don] *Literary Supplement,* No. 2793 (Sept. 9, 1955), 532.
7.49   "Emily Dickinson Data Freed." *New York Times,* Sept. 12, 1955,

p. 23. Harvard opens its collection of Dickinson papers for research.

7.50   "Amherst Gets Work of Emily Dickinson." *New York Times,* April 30, 1956, p. 26.
Mrs. M. T. Bingham gives 900 manuscripts to Amherst College.

7.51   "Dickinson Gift." *Amherst College Bulletin,* XLVI (Nov. 1956), 45.

7.52   "The Emily Dickinson Papers." *Amherst Alumni News,* X (Oct. 1957), 2-4.
Notes the Bingham bequest of Dickinson manuscripts and related materials to Amherst College.

7.53   "Emily Dickinson Lecture Given at Bowdoin College." *Springfield Union,* Feb. 21, 1958, p. 31. See 7.54.

7.54   "Eminent Lawyer Lauds Poetry of Dickinson. Cites Prolific But Introspective Career." *Bowdoin Orient,* LXXXIX (Feb. 26, 1958), 1.
See 7.53.

[6.413] "The Woman in White." *Times* [London] *Literary Supplement,* No. 3094 (June 16, 1961), p. 372.

7.55   "Dickinson Birthplace Named Historic Site." *New York Times,* Nov. 7, 1964, p. 25.
Notes the dedication of ED's home as a national historic site and that the house is currently for sale. See also 6.494.

7.56   "Amherst Announces Purchase of Emily Dickinson's Birthplace." *New York Times,* Jan. 17, 1965, p. 57.
The home is sold to Amherst College. See also 23.12.

7.57   "Dickinson House." *Amherst Alumni News,* XVIII (Winter 1966), 34-36.

7.58   "Millicent Todd Bingham Dies; Authority on Emily Dickinson." *New York Times,* Dec. 3, 1968, p. 47.

FOREIGN LANGUAGE
MATERIALS

Italian

SEPARATE EDITIONS OF POEMS
AND LETTERS

8.1   *Emily Dickinson, Poesie*. Trans. Marta Bini. Milan: M.A. Denti, n.d. [1947?]. 203 pp.

80 poems in English and Italian, with a preface by Marta Bini. The poems contained in this volume are listed by Russell St. Clair Smith (1.15). Dated "1947 or a little before" by Paola Guidetti; see 8.61, p. 129.

8.2   *Emily Dickinson, Poesie*. Trans. Margherita Guidacci. Florence: Cya, 1947.

Includes a biographical sketch of ED by Margherita Guidacci. See also 8.8.

8.3   *Emily Dickinson, Poesie*. Trans. Guido Errante. Milan: Mondadori, 1956. 621 pp.

First ed., Nov. 1956.

450 poems in English and Italian on opposite pages, based on editions preceding the 1955 Johnson edition. Arrangement of the poems is thematic. A lengthy biographical and critical preface by Guido Errante reconstructs ED's physical and spiritual environment, discusses her fundamental religiousness and her major themes, and analyzes her poetic technique as the source of her wide influence today.

Reviewed:

Breit (6.141)	Guidacci (8.60)
Cambon (6.173)	Guidetti (8.61, pp. 142-43)
Cecchetti (8.47)	Menichini (8.74)
Françon (6.365)	

Unsigned reviews:

8.4   *Libertà*, Aug. 31, 1957.

8.5   *Stechert-Hafner Book News* [N.Y.], XI (Mar. 1957), 76.

8.6   *Emily Dickinson, Poesie*. Trans. Guido Errante. 2 vols. Milan: Mondadori, 1959.

Over 600 poems in English and Italian following the Johnson text
and chronology. The introductory essay (see 8.3) is revised
and expanded.
Reviewed:
     Cambon (6.173)
     Cecchetti (8.48)
     Guidetti (8.61, pp. 152-54)
Unsigned review:
8.7   *Vita*, Dec. 10, 1959.
8.8   *Emily Dickinson, Poesie e Lettere*. Trans. Margherita Guidacci.
         Florence: Sansoni, 1961.
         The translator's critical introduction gives special attention to
         the approximately 300 letters included in this edition. See also
         8.2.
         Reviewed:
         Guidetti (8.61, pp. 158-60)
8.9   *Emily Dickinson*. Trans. Dyna McArthur Rebucci; introd. and
         notes by Sergio Perosa. Milan: Nuova Accademia, 1961.
         In his introduction, Sergio Perosa insists that ED's poetry was
         not an escape from life but rather a way of life, "a spiritual ad-
         venture which is its own justification." Notes ED's affinity with
         Melville and Hawthorne in seeing in natural phenomena symbols
         of ultimate reality and points to connections with European
         poets.
         Reviewed:
         Guidetti (8.61, pp. 155-57)
8.10   *Emily Dickinson, XX Poesie brevi*. Trans. Mario Salvadori.
         Milan: Ferriani, 1961. 96 pp.
         The preface by Mario Salvadori discusses ED's personal
         strength, torment, and rebellion.
         Reviewed:
         Guidetti (8.61, p. 155)
         Simongini (8.94)
8.11   *Emily Dickinson, Selected Poems and Letters*. Ed. Elémire Zolla.
         Milan: Mursia, 1961. 171 pp.
         113 poems and 10 letters in English with introduction and notes
         by Elémire Zolla. Stresses ED's intellectual and literary back-
         ground — from Shakespeare and Hegel to Anne Bradstreet and
         Emily Brontë.
         Reviewed:
         Guidetti (8.61, pp. 157-58)

OTHER PUBLICATION OF POEMS AND LETTERS

8.12   Giocomo Prampolini, trans. *Circoli: Rivista di Poesia* [Genoa],
         III, No. 6 (Nov.-Dec. 1933), pp. 10-15.
         The first Italian translation of ED — includes "If I shouldn't be
         alive," "The Bustle in a House," "There came a Wind like a
         Bugle," "Apparently with no surprise," "Sweet is the swamp
         with its secrets."

Reviewed:
    Guidetti (8.61, p. 121)
8.13   Mario Praz. *Antologia Anglo-Americana*. Milan: Principato,
        1936.
        In Italian.
8.14   "Emilia Dickinson," trans. Gladys Coletti. *Frontespizio* [Flor-
        ence], IX, No. 4 (April 1937), pp. 289-301.
        Translations of 6 poems, with a biographical note, p. 289.
8.15   "Cinque Poesie di E. Dickinson," trans. Luigi Berti. *Meridiano di
        Roma*, April 18, 1937, p. vi.
[8.27] Cecchi, Emilio and Giuditta. *Emily Dickinson* (1939).
8.16   "Tre Poesie di Emilia Dickinson," trans. Vittoria Guerrini. *Meri-
        dano di Roma*, March 7, 1943.
        Includes a biographical sketch.
8.17   Eugenio Montale, trans. *Mondo* [Rome], No. 1 (1945).
        Reprinted:
        Poeti antichi e moderni tradotti da lirici nuovi. Milan: 1945.
        Quaderno di Traduzioni. Milan: 1948.
        Corriere di Informazione, Dec. 15-16, 1956.
        Studi Americani, IX (1963), 128.
        Translation of "There came a Wind like a Bugle." The first
        five lines of this translation are reprinted, with comment, by
        Guidetti (8.61), p. 128.
8.18   "Tre Secoli di Poesia Americana," trans. Gabriele Baldini. *Nuova
        Antologia* [Rome], LXXXII (Dec. 1947), 392-94.
8.19   Gabriele Baldini, and Giorgio Bassani, trans. in *Poeti Americani*.
        Turin: 1949.
        Includes a preface to ED's poems by Gabriele Baldini.
8.20   Carlo Izzo, trans. in *Poesia Americana Contemporanea*. Bologna:
        Guanda, 1949.
        ED poems in English and Italian, pp. 1-24. Includes an intro-
        ductory essay and notes by Carlo Izzo.
8.21   Mario Stefanile, trans. *Fiera Letteraria* [Rome], No. 16, April
        1949.
8.22   Alfredo Rizzardi, trans. *Fiera Letteraria* [Rome], No. 51, Dec.
        1952.
8.23   Alfredo Rizzardi, trans. in *Lirici Americani*. Caltanissetta:
        Sciascia, 1953.
        ED poems in Italian with a preface.
8.24   Don Giuseppe De Luca, trans. *Mater Dei*, Nos. 1-6, Jan.-June,
        1959.
8.25   Guido Errante, trans. *Chelsea Review* [N.Y.], No. 7 (May 1960),
        pp. 80-87.
        8 poems in English and Italian reprinted from *Emily Dickinson,
        Poesie* (Milan: 1959); see 8.6.
8.26   Carlo Izzo, ed., *Le Più Belle Pagine della Letteratura Americana*.
        Milan: Nuova Accademia, 1960.

SEPARATELY PUBLISHED CRITICAL STUDIES

8.27   Cecchi, Emilio and Giuditta. *Emily Dickinson.* Brescia: Morcel-
            liana, 1939. 152 pp.
            A biographical and critical study of ED noting especially her
            relation to other nineteenth-century American writers, the
            modernity of her language, and the suitability of her poetic
            form to her incandescent interior world. About 45 poems or
            parts of poems are translated.
            Reviewed:
               Guidetti (8.61, pp. 122-24)   Vigorelli (8.102)
               Montale (8.77)   Whicher (6.1116)
               Praz (8.83)

8.28   Tedeschini Lalli, Biancamaria. *Emily Dickinson, Prospettive
            critiche.* Florence: F. Le Monnier, 1963. 164 pp.
            Focuses on ED's inner experience, stressing its uncertainty,
            intensity, and desperation. Chapters on ED's immediate en-
            vironment and sense of vocation, her self-willed seclusion, her
            poetic use of the small events of daily life, her "surrealism"
            and connection with the French Symbolists, and her great
            themes of love, death, and eternity.
            Reviewed:
               Guidetti (8.61, p. 164)
               Robbins (6.851; *ALS, 1964* p. 133)

8.29   Tusiani, Giuseppe. *La Poesia Amorosa di Emily Dickinson.* N.Y.:
            Venetian Press, 1950. 35 pp.
            This essay is translated into English and included in the au-
            thor's *Two Critical Essays on Emily Dickinson;* see 5.96.

OTHER CRITICISM AND SCHOLARSHIP

8.30   Alessandrini, Ludovico. "Letture di Ieri e di Oggi." *Osservatore
            della Domenica,* Jan. 17, 1960.

8.31   Altichieri, Gilberto. "Emily Dickinson." *Campo di Marte,* Jan. 1,
            1939.

8.32   Anonymous. "Emily Dickinson. Poesie." *Lucerna,* Sept.-Dec.
            1959.

8.33   Antonini, Giacomo. "Emily Dickinson." *Nazione* [Florence], Feb.
            20, 1960.

8.34   Baldi, Sergio. "Appunti per uno Studio sulla Poesia della Dickin-
            son." *Letteratura,* VI (April-June 1942), 76-88.
            Criticizes ED's affected pose of "prophetess" and notes baroque
            and metaphysical elements in her poetry as well as parallels
            with the Italian "crepuscolari."
            Reviewed:
               Guidetti (8.61), pp. 126-27.

8.35   ———. "Emilia e Margherita." *Nazione* [Florence], Aug. 11, 1962.

8.36   ———. "La Poesia di Emily Dickinson." *Studi Americani,* Vol. II
            No. 2 (1956), pp. 45-66.

This essay, translated into English, appears in *Sewanee Review,*
LXVIII (July-Sept. 1960), 438-49.
Argues that ED's interiorization of reality conditions her poetic
language. Her alleged affinity with metaphysical verse and
other poetic movements is minimized.
Reviewed:
Guidetti (8.61), pp. 137-39.

8.37 Baldini, Gabriele. "Emilia e il Colonnello." *Mondo* [Rome], June
10, 1958.
Discusses ED as revealed in her letters, especially those to
Higginson.

8.38 Bassi, Emma. "Emily Dickinson." *Annali Istituto Universitario
de Napoli, Sezione Germanica,* III (1960), 271-82.

8.39 Berti, Luigi. *Storia della Letteratura Americana.* Milan: 1950.
The introduction to ED in this anthology of American literature
argues that Puritanism was a negative influence on her life and
art.
Reviewed:
Guidetti (8.61), pp. 130-31.

8.40 Bianchi, Ruggero. *La Poetica Dell' Imagismo.* Milan: U. Mursia,
1965, pp. 13-15 *passim.*
Treats ED as an unconscious precursor of imagism.

8.41 Boscardi, Giorgio. "La poetessa reclusa." *Il Secolo XIX,* Jan. 16,
1957.

8.42 Bulgheroni, Marisa. "L'eterno Giardino di Emily." *Studi Americani,* VIII (1962), 77-92.
Discusses ED's synthesis of concrete and abstract, of the personal and the cosmic. This tension became for ED an habitual
way of perceiving the world.
Reviewed:
Guidetti (8.61), pp. 164-65.

8.43 ———. "La Parola di Emily Dickinson." *Mondo* [Rome], April 23,
1963.
On ED's interior journey.

8.44 ———. "Poesia Americana." *Comunita* [Milan], No. 48, Mar. 1957.
Discusses the tension between abstract and concrete in ED's
poetic world.

8.45 Cambon, Glauco. "L'edizione Critica di Emily Dickinson." *Aut-
Aut* [Milan], No. 32 (Mar. 1956), pp. 155-64.
Review-essay of *Poems,* 1955 (3.197). Defends ED's artistry,
especially in her dense and significant vocabulary, and com-
pares her tragic vision to that of Kierkegaard and Pascal.
Reviewed:
Guidetti (8.61), pp. 135-37.

8.46 ———. *Tematica e Sviluppo della Poesia Americana.* Rome:
Edizioni di Storia e Letteratura, 1956, pp. 38-64.
Points out that violent change is a frequent threat in ED's poetry and argues that change and stasis are the two pivotal expe-
riences in her inner world. Discusses her relation to Whitman,
Rilke, and French Symbolism. A similar discussion appeared
subsequently in English; see 6.172.

Reviewed:
    Guidetti (8.61), pp. 143-45.
8.47 Cecchetti, Giovanni. "Emily Dickinson. Poesie. Versioni e prefazione di G. Errante." *Comparative Literature* [Eugene, Ore.],
X (Winter 1958), 73-77.
Rev. of *Poesie*, trans. Errante, 1956 (8.3).
8.48 ———. *Comparative Literature* [Eugene, Ore.], XIII (Winter, 1961),
89-90.
Rev. of *Poesie*, trans. Errante, 1959 (8.6).
8.49 Cecchi, Emilio. "Emilia Dickinson." *Corriere della Sera* [Milan],
Oct. 20, 1936, p. 3.
The first critical article on ED to appear in Italy. Commends
the lucidity with which she renders inner psychological experience and the evocative quality of her diction.
Reviewed:
    Guidetti (8.61), pp. 121-22.
8.50 D'Agostino, Nemi. "Poe, Whitman, Dickinson." *Belfagor* [Flor-
ence], VIII (Sept. 1953), 517-38.
Emphasizes ED's contribution to the creation of a new American poetry.
Reviewed:
    Guidetti (8.61), pp. 133-34.
8.51 Dal Fabbro, Beniamino. "La Lettera al mondo di Emily Dickinson." *Emporium* [Bergamo], Aug. 1946.
8.52 Dall'Arco, Mario. "Emily Dickinson." *Piccolo*, Jan. 1, 1960.
8.53 Da Via, Gualtiero. "Una vita per la poesia." *Quotidiano* [Rome],
July 5, 1957.
8.54 De Dominicis, Annamaria. "Della Poetica di Emily Dickinson."
Itinerari [Genoa], Nos. 9-10, Oct. 1954.
The author, an Italian poet, examines ways ED conceives of the
world but is critical of her artistry.
Reviewed:
    Guidetti (8.61), p. 135.
8.55 Fabiani. "Il Lungo Sogno della Poetessa Reclusa." *Gente*, Oct. 2,
1959.
8.56 Gianturco, Elio. "La Poetessa e il Critico." *Progresso Italo-
Americano*, Oct. 26, 1959.
8.57 Giardini, Cesare. "Il Giardino di Emily." *Il Resto del Carlino*
[Bologna], Mar. 7, 1960.
Reprinted:
La Provincia, Mar. 11, 1960.
Tirreno, Mar. 12, 1960.
Unione Sarda, Mar. 17, 1960.
8.58 Giudici, Giovanni. "Emily Dickinson: dal Mito all Storia." *Mondo
Occidentale*, June 1957.
8.58a Giuliani, Maria Teresa. "Il Vocabolario delle Lettere de Emily
Dickinson." *Studi Americani*, XII (1966), 89-124.
This study of ED's prose vocabulary is arranged by clusters of
words (domestic, religious, legal, etc.) and includes comparison
of word frequencies in the poems and letters. Although primarily a compilation, the essay does contain brief critical discussion of important words and phrases.

8.59   Gorlier, Claudio. "Proposte per una Lettura di Emily Dickinson."
        Aut-Aut [Milan], No. 4, (June 1951), pp. 344-47.
        Urges a more objective evaluation of ED and attempts to define
        her almost "improvised" poetics.
        Reviewed:
            Guidetti (8.61), pp. 131-33.
8.60   Guidacci, Margherita. "Emily Dickinson. Poesie, Versioni e pre-
        fazione di G. Errante." *Il Ponte* [Florence], No. 12 (1956).
        Rev. of *Poesie*, trans. Errante, 1956 (8.3). Notes that although
        ED can look with a clear, disillusioned eye on her own inner
        landscape, she cannot avoid profound fear before the experience
        of love and death.
8.61   Guidetti, Paola. "La Fortuna di Emily Dickinson in Italia (1933-
        1962)." *Studi Americani,* IX (1963), 121-72.
        The history of ED scholarship and criticism in Italy. Its list
        (pp. 167-72) of Italian editions and articles is incorporated in
        the present work.
        Reviewed:
            Robbins, *ALS, 1964* (6.851), p. 135.
8.62   Isotti-Andrei. "Il Mondo Lirico della Dickinson." *L'Osservatore
        Romano,* Jan. 25, 1957.
8.63   Izzo, Carlo. "Emily Dickinson" in *Storia della Letteratura Nord-
        Americana.* Milan: Nuova Accademia, 1957, pp. 490-503.
        Discusses the literary quality of ED's letters and stresses her
        ability to reinvest worn-out words with some of their original
        density and significance.
        Reviewed:
            Guidetti (8.61), pp. 146-47.
8.64   ———. "La poesia di Emily Dickinson." *L'Approdo,* No. 6, April-
        June, 1953.
        An enthusiastic defense of ED's artistry.
8.65   ———. "La Reclusa di Amherst." *Gazzetta del Popolo,* Mar. 20,
        1957.
8.66   Lombardo, Agostino. "La Letteratura Americana in Italia," in
        Ricerca del Vero. Rome: Edizioni Storia e Letteratura, 1961,
        pp. 13-61.
        Brief mention of ED's reputation in Italy.
8.67   ———. "Poesia Americana," in *Spettatore Italiano* [Rome], No. 2,
        Feb. 1954.
        Reprinted:
        Realismo e Simbolismo. Rome: Edizioni Storia e Letteratura,
            1957.
        Links ED to Whitman and Poe in anticipating twentieth-century
        poetic language.
        Reviewed:
            Guidetti (8.61), pp. 134-35.
8.68   ———. "La Poesia di Richard Wilbur." *Criterio,* Aug.-Sept. 1957.
        Reprinted:
        Ricerca del Vero. Rome: Edizioni di Storia e Letteratura,
            1961, pp. 385-96.
        Notes similarities and differences between ED and Richard
        Wilbur's "parnassian art."

Reviewed:
   Guidetti (8.61), pp. 148-50.

8.69   Lombardo, Agostino. "Tradizione Americana." *Studi Americani*, II (1956), 285-301.
Reprinted:
Realismo e Simbolismo. Rome: Edizioni Storia e Letteratura, 1957.
Links ED to other important writers of the American Renaissance in their attempt to scrutinize and record American experience.
Reviewed:
   Guidetti (8.61), pp. 139-40.

8.70   Marniti, Biagia. "Emily Dickinson." *Il Paese* [Bari], May 10, 1957.

8.71   Martini, Carlo. "Emily Dickinson." *Rassegna di Cultura* [Milan], 1940.

8.72   ——. "Tutte le Poesie di Emily Dickinson." *La Voce Republicana* [Rome], April 12, 1957.

8.73   Mauro, Walter. "Il Monologo di Emily Dickinson." *Vie Nuove* [Rome], Mar. 5, 1960.

8.74   Menichini, Dino. "Emily Dickinson. Poesie. Versione e Prefazione di G. Errante." *Il Messaggero Veneto*, Jan. 3, 1957.
Rev. of *Poesie,* trans. Errante, 1956 (8.3).

8.75   Mercuri, Elio. "Poesie e Lettere di Emily Dickinson." *Il Contemporaneo,* Nov. 1962.

8.76   Montale, Eugenio. "Emily." *Il Corriere della Sera* [Milan], May 4, 1957, p. 3.
Describes ED as the Christina Rossetti of New England.
Reviewed:
   Guidetti (8.61), pp. 147-48.

8.77   ——. "La Poesia di Emily Dickinson." *Oggi* [Rome], July 29, 1939.
Rev. of Cecchi, *ED* (8.27). Stresses ED's tough, courageous scrutiny of experience and argues that the roughness of her verse artfully conveys her sense of reality.
Reviewed:
   Guidetti (8.61), p. 124.

8.78   Pagnini, Marcello. "La Poesia di Emily Dickinson." *Studi Americani,* VIII (1962), 35-53.
Sees ED's poems as her attempt to illuminate intuitively the great enigmas of nature, death, and eternity. This search for truth links ED to the main American literary tradition in which poetry is used as a means to decipher the symbolic mystery hidden in reality.
Reviewed:
   Guidetti (8.61), pp. 160-61.

8.79   Pappacena, Enrico. "Emily Dickinson" in *Il Filone d'Oro della Letteratura Americana*. Bari: Edizioni Levante, 1960, pp. 23-24.

8.80   Pisapia, Biancamaria. "La Solitudine nella Letteratura Americana dell'Ottocento." *Studi Americani,* III (1957), 133-70.

This psychological study treats solitude as an existential condition and notes especially ED's sense of tragic fatality and her alarm in the face of an incomprehensible world. ED discussed, pp. 156-68.

Reviewed:
Guidetti (8.61), pp. 140-41.

8.81   Prampolini, Giocomo. *Storia della Letteratura Universale.* Turin: 1951.

The introduction to ED in this anthology praises her art as bare, antirhetorical, and antiliterary.

8.82   ——. *Storia Universale della Letteratura.* Turin: Unione Tipografico-Editrice Torinese, 1936. Vol. III, Part 2, p. 794.

8.83   Praz, Mario. "Emily Dickinson." *La Stampa* [Turin], Aug. 10, 1939.

Reprinted:
Cronache Letterarie Anglosassoni. 2 vols. Rome: Edizioni di Storia e Letteratura, 1951, II, 149-152.
Rev. of Cecchi, *ED* (8.27). Notes parallels between ED and Coventry Patmore, Christina Rossetti, Heine, and the English metaphysicals.

Reviewed:
Guidetti (8.61), p. 125.

8.84   ——. "Voci di Poesia dall'Est e dall'Ovest." *Tempo,* Oct. 9, 1949.

Reprinted:
Cronache Letterarie Anglosassoni. 2 vols. Rome: Edizioni di Storia e Letteratura, 1951.

8.85   Ravegnani, Giuseppe. "La Poetessa dalla Bianca Veste." *Epoca* [Milan], Jan. 20, 1957.

8.86   ——. "La Poetessa Misteriosa." *Epoca* [Milan], Oct. 4, 1959.

8.87   Rizzardi, Alfredo. "Letteratura Anglo-Americana." *Convivium* [Turin], n.s. XXXI (May-June 1963), 368-70.

In a review-essay of Warner Berthoff's *The Example of Melville,* Rizzardi discusses reasons why nineteenth century critics did not understand or ignored such writers as Poe, Melville, and ED. In Italian.

8.88   ——. "La poesia di Melville." *Studi Americani,* I (1955), 159-203.

Reprinted:
La Condizione Americana. Bologna: Cappelli, 1960.
Compares the theme of the sea in Melville and ED (*SA*, pp. 185-86).

8.89   Rosati, Salvatore. "Emily Dickinson." *Il Mondo* [Rome], April 30, 1957.

Reprinted:
L'Ombra dei Padre, Studi sulla Letteratura Americana. Rome: Edizioni de Storia e Letteratura, 1958, pp. 55-61.
Discusses the influence of Puritanism on ED's poetic form and insists that far from being an instinctive artist, she was a masterful literary craftsman.

8.90   Rosati, Salvatore. "Emily Dickinson" in *Storia della Letteratura Americana*. Turin: Edizioni Radio Italiana, 1956, pp. 153-56.

8.91   Scalero, Liliana. "Il Mistero di Emily Dickinson." *La Voce Republicana* [Rome], Mar. 22-23, 1960.
Reprinted:
Il Corriere di Sicilia, Mar. 25, 1960.

8.92   Seppis, Francesco. "La Voce Autentica di una Poetessa nel Rinascimento Letterario Americano." *La Nuova Sardegna*, Dec. 9, 1959.

8.93   Simongini. "Le Colline e i Tramonti Sono i Miei Soli Amici." *La Giustizia*, Nov. 8, 1959.

8.94   ———. *La Giustizia*, May 19, 1961.
Rev. of *XX Poesie brevi*, trans. Mario Salvadori, 1961 (8.10).

8.95   Somma, Luigi. "Gloria del Frammento: Emily Dickinson" in *Storia della Letteratura Americana*. Rome: Casa Editrice Libraria Corso, 1946, pp. 146-48.

8.96   Stefanile, Mario. "Un Ritratto Critico di Emily Dickinson." *Il Mattino* [Naples], Nov. 3, 1957.

8.96a   Stefanini, Ruggero. "Su Alcune Liriche de E. Dickinson." *Rivista di Letteratura Moderne e Comparate*, XIX (Mar. 1966), 46-51. Argues that the following poems express ED's desire to be reconciled with her sister-in-law: "You said that I 'was Great' — one Day," "Ourselves were wed one summer — dear," and "So much Summer."

8.97   Tedeschi, Giuseppe. "Emily Dickinson tra Critica e Leggenda." *La Fiera Letteraria* [Rome], XV, No. 4 (Jan. 31, 1960).

8.98   ———. "Poesie della Dickinson." *Il Popolo* [Rome], July 24, 1962.

8.99   Tedeschini Lalli, Biancamaria. "Emily Dickinson: Dio come Ansia." *Studi Americani*, VIII (1962), 71-76.
Explores ED's characteristic state of anxiety, often described as "awe" in the poems — a state of suspension and fear attended by a sense of personal isolation and the elusiveness of reality.
Reviewed:
Guidetti (8.61), p. 163.

8.100   ———. "Sul Vocabolario Poetico di Emily Dickinson." *Studi Americani*, X (1964), 181-200.
Reviews the findings of William Howard (see 6.513) and insists on the uniqueness of ED's vocabulary, arguing that it must be analyzed not in the abstract but in terms of significant groups of lyrics, e.g., according to chronological "creative periods."
Reviewed:
Robbins, *ALS, 1965* (6.851), p. 158

8.101   Tusiani, Giuseppe. "L'Italia nella Poesia di Emily Dickinson." *La Parola del Popolo* [Chicago], No. 26 (Jan.-Feb. 1957).
Discusses allusions to Italy in ED's poetry.
Reviewed:
Guidetti (8.61), pp. 145-46.

8.102   Vigorelli, Giancarlo. "Emily Dickinson." *L'Italia*, Aug. 8, 1939.
Rev. of Cecchi, *ED* (8.27). Finds parallels between ED and Montale, Baudelaire, and Gianna Manzini.

Reviewed:
> Guidetti (8.61), p. 125.

8.103   Wainstein, Lia. "La Letteratura Americana in Russia." *Studia Americana,* XI (1965), 447-62.
> Comments on the apparent lack of Russian interest in ED, pp. 451, 452-53.

8.104   Zolla, Elémire. "L'Etica Puritana di Emily Dickinson." *Studi Americani,* VIII (1962), 54-70.
> ED participates deeply in the intense spirituality and severe moral discipline of Puritan theology, especially in her "philosophy of sublime emotion."

Reviewed:
> Guidetti (8.61), pp. 161-62.

ED   162

9.

French

SEPARATE EDITIONS OF POEMS AND LETTERS

9.1 *Emily Dickinson, Choix de Poèmes.* Trans. and introd. Félix Ansermoz-Dubois. Geneva: Éditions du Continent, 1945. 125 pp.
Thirty poems in English and French. The biographical and critical preface (pp. 11-25) follows, biographically, Taggard's *Life and Mind* (5.81).
Reviewed:
Pollitt (6.810)

9.2 *Emily Dickinson, Poèmes.* Trans. and introd. Jean Simon. Collection "Autour du Monde," No. 22. Paris: P. Seghers, 1954. 77 pp.
49 poems in English and French on opposite pages. Introduction by Jean Simon, pp. 7-9.
Reviewed:
Anderson (6.36)
Las Vergnas (9.24)
Le Breton (9.25)

9.3 *Emily Dickinson, Poèmes Choisis.* Trans. and introd. P. Messiaen. *Collection Bilingue des Classiques Étrangers.* Aubier: Éditions Montaigne, 1956. 211 pp.
146 poems in English and French following the arrangement and texts of *Poems,* 1937 (3.173) and *Bolts of Melody,* 1945 (3.177). A biographical and critical introduction (pp. 5-60) summarizes ED's attitudes toward nature, love, death, and eternity.

9.4 *Emily Dickinson.* Trans. and introd. Alain Bosquet. *Poètes D'Aujourd'hui,* No. 55. Paris: P. Seghers, 1957. 207 pp.
A collection of 100 poems in English and French based on editions published before the 1955 Johnson edition. Two additional selections of 23 prose and verse aphorisms and 10 letters are in French only. The introduction (pp. 13-59) is mainly biographical.

9.5   *Emily Dickinson. Twenty Poems. Vingt Poèmes.* Introd. Paul
       Zweig, trans. Claude Berger and Paul Zweig, illus. Michèle
       Katz. Paris: Minard, Lettres Modernes, 1963. 63 pp.
       The poems are in English and French and follow the 1955 John-
       son edition. In his suggestive introduction (pp. 3-15), M. Zweig
       stresses ED's use of aristocratic and religious symbols to cre-
       ate a personal sense of coherence and compares her to those
       "'potterers' mentioned by [Claude] Levi-Strauss, who can bring
       together, according to their genius, the disjointed remains of
       various value systems in order to make them function together
       in a precise design."

OTHER PUBLICATION OF POEMS AND LETTERS

9.6   Fernand Bladensperger, trans. *D'Edmond Spenser à Alan Seeger:
       Cent Petits Poèms Anglais.* Cambridge, Mass.: Harvard Univ.
       Press, 1938, pp. 83-85.
       Three poems in French: "I lost a World — the other day,"
       "When Night is almost done," and "It was a quiet way."
[9.29] Pierre Leyris, trans. "Poèmes et Lettres d'Emily Dickinson."
       Mesures, V, No. 3 (July 1939), pp. 125-39.
9.7   Jean Catel. *Quelques Poèmes de l'Amerique Moderne.* Paris:
       Collection Dauphiné, 1945.
9.8   Léonie Villard. *La Poésie Américaine: Trois Siecles de Poésie
       Lyrique et de Poèmes Narratifs.* Paris: Bordas Frères, Les
       Editions Françaises Nouvelles, 1945, pp. 77-84.
       Critical introduction to ED and selected poems in French.
9.9   Maurice Le Breton. *Anthologie de la Poésie Américaine Contem-
       poraine.* Paris: Éditions Denoël, [1948], pp. 35-38, 62-69.
       A critical introduction to ED and three poems in English and
       French: "A narrow Fellow in the Grass," "If I shouldn't be
       alive," and "The Robin's my Criterion for Tune."
9.10   Alain Bosquet. *Anthologie de la Poésie Américaine, des Origines
       à Nos Jours.* Paris: Librairie Stock, Delamain et Boutelleau,
       1956, pp. 94-103.
       Prints 16 poems in English and French with biographical and
       critical notes on ED, pp. 20-21, 285-86.

CRITICISM AND SCHOLARSHIP

9.11   Arnavon, Cyrille. "Emily Dickinson" in *Histoire Littéraire des
       États-Unis.* n.p.: Librairie Hachette, 1953, p. 355.
       A brief introduction.
9.12   Bocquet, Leon. "La Littérature Américaine." *Nouvelle Revue
       Critique* [Paris], XV (April 1931), 162.
9.13   Brown, John. *Panorama de la Littérature Contemporaine aux
       États-Unis.* Paris: Librarie Gallimard, 1954, pp. 47, 250-51.
9.14   Brunel, Pierre. "Le Corbeau (à propos de la transposition par

Claudel d'un poème d'Emily Dickinson)." *Revue des Lettres Modernes*, Nos. 134-136 (1966), pp. 113-18.
Notes the two poets' use of opposition of contraries to create a sense both of confrontation and of indissoluble union. The example from ED is "Water, is taught by thirst."

9.15   Catel, Jean. "Emily Dickinson." Part I: "Essai d'Analyse Psychologique," *Revue Anglo-Américaine,* II (June 1925), 394-405; Part II: "L'Oeuvre," III (Dec. 1925), 105-20.
A general introduction to ED written primarily for French readers previously unacquainted with her life and work. It is one of the earliest full-scale critical essays on ED to be written in a foreign language. See also 10.47.

9.16   ——. "Poésie Moderne aux États-Unis." Part I, *Revue des Cours et Conférences,* XXXIV (May 15, 1933), 210-24; Part II, (May 30, 1933), 345-56.
A brief introduction to ED's life and poetic themes, pp. 345-53. Compares her to Walt Whitman, pp. 353-56.

9.17   ——. "Sur Emily Dickinson, À Propos de Deux Livres." *Revue Anglo-Américaine* [Paris], XIII (Dec. 1935), 140-44.
Rev. of Pollitt, *Human Background* (5.61) and Taggard, *Life and Mind* (5.81).

9.18   Cestre, Charles. *Études Anglaises,* III (July-Sept. 1939), 308-09.
Rev. of Whicher, *This Was a Poet* (5.104).

9.19   ——. "La Poésie" in *La Littérature Américaine.* Paris: Librairie Armand Colin, 1945, pp. 189-91.
A brief characterization of ED's life and poetry.

9.20   ——. *Les Poètes Américains.* Paris: Les Presses Universitaires de France, 1948, pp. 91-103.
This general, critical introduction regards ED as a major modern writer and discusses some of her themes and her relation to other poets.

9.21   Feuillerat, Albert. "La Vie Secrète d'une Puritaine." *Revue des Deux Mondes,* XL (Aug. 1, 1927), 668-91.
A general discussion, chronologically organized, of ED's milieu and personality. Drawing heavily from the letters, M. Feuillerat stresses the "Puritan rigor" of the Dickinson household and the poet's self-discipline and seclusion.

9.22   Goffin, Robert. *Fil d'Ariane pour la Poésie.* Paris: A. G. Nizet, 1964.

9.23   Jacoby, John E. "L'esthétique de la Sainteté: Emily Dickinson" in *Le Mysticisme dans la Pensée Américaine.* Paris: Les Presses Universitaires de France, 1931, pp. 241-76.
Argues that ED's affinities are not with Puritanism but with American mystical thought, especially nature mysticism.

9.24   Las Vergnas, Raymond. "Emily Dickinson." *Hommes et Mondes* [Paris], X (June 1955), 450-52.
Rev. of *Emily Dickinson, Poèmes,* trans. Jean Simon, 1954 (9.2).

9.25   Le Breton, Maurice. *Études Anglaises,* IX (Jan.-Mar. 1956), 90-91.
Rev. of *Emily Dickinson, Poèmes,* trans. Jean Simon, 1954 (9.2).

9.26   ——. *Études Anglaises,* XIV (July-Sept. 1961), 279.
Rev. of Anderson, *Stairway of Surprise* (5.2).

9.27   Le Breton, Maurice. *Études Anglaises*, XVI (Jan.-Mar. 1963), 99.
       Rev. of Ward, *Capsule of the Mind* (5.97).
9.28   ——. *Études Anglaises*, XVIII (Jan.-Mar. 1965), 95-96.
       Rev. of Griffith, *Long Shadow* (5.31).
9.29   Leyris, Pierre. "Poèmes et Lettres d'Emily Dickinson." *Mesures*
       [Paris], V, No. 3 (July 1939), pp. 125-39.
       M. Leyris translates six poems and five letters (to Higginson),
       supplies the English texts of the poems, and provides a brief
       introduction.
9.30   Maurois, André. "Emily Dickinson, Poétesse et Recluse." *Revue
       de Paris*, LXI (Nov. 1954), 1-13.
       Reprinted:
       André Maurois. *Robert et Elizabeth Browning: Portraits
           suivis de Quelques Autres*. Paris: Bernard Grasset, 1955,
           pp. 45-64.
       In this biographical and critical introduction ED is praised as
       "one of the greatest poets of the English language."
9.31   Michaud, Régis. "Dickinson, Emily," in *Dictionnaire Biographique
       des Auteurs*. 2 vols. Paris: Bompiani, 1956, I, 422-23.
9.32   ——. *Panorama de la Littérature Américaine Contemporaine*.
       Paris: Simon Kra, 1926, pp. 128-29.
       Brief notice of ED's poems describes them as "hard to evalu-
       ate": "they emit the odor of a prison but they are nevertheless
       illumined by thought."
9.33   Murciaux, Christian. "Emily Dickinson." *Cahiers du Sud* LI
       (April-May 1961), 276-89.
       Discusses the sources of ED's penetrating and contemplative
       poetry, especially her Puritan ancestry and her relationships
       with such people as Benjamin Newton, Leonard Humphrey, and
       Kate Anthon.
9.34   Tredant, Paul. "Lettre d'Amérique." *Les Nouvelles Littéraires*
       [Paris], No. 1043, Aug. 28, 1947, pp. 1-2.
       Brief mention of ED and Amherst in a literary tour of New
       England.
9.35   Winters, Yvor. *Aspects de la Littérature Américaine*, trans.
       Georges Belmont. Paris: Editions du Chêne, 1947.
       Includes a translation of Winters' "Emily Dickinson and the
       Limits of Judgment"; see 6.1200.

10.

German and Dutch

GERMAN: SEPARATE EDITIONS OF POEMS AND LETTERS

10.1   *Ten Poems by Emily Dickinson, 1830-1886.* Selected and trans. Rosey E. Pool. Calligraphy by Susanne Heynemann. Amsterdam: Widow J. Ahrend & Son, 1939. 22 pp.
> Reissued 1944. Unpaged [11 leaves].
An underground printing. Poems in English and German. The poems contained in this volume are listed by Galinsky (10.51), p. 241. Another underground volume was published in Amsterdam in 1940; see 10.79.

10.2   *Der Engel in Grau; aus dem Leben und Werk der amerikanischen Dichterin, Emily Dickinson.* Ed. and trans. Maria Mathi. Mannheim: Kessler, 1956. 221 pp.
Includes 49 letters in German and 50 poems in German and English. The poems and letters are listed by Galinsky (10.51), pp. 243-45.
<u>Reviewed:</u>
> Galinsky (10.51), p. 51
> Hohoff (10.54)

10.3   *Emily Dickinson, Gedichte.* Selected and trans. Lola Gruenthal. Berlin: Henssel, [1959]. 86 pp.
36 poems in German and English on facing pages, pp. 6-77, with an introduction to the poet and her work, pp. 79-86. The poems are listed by Galinsky (10.51), pp. 249-50.
<u>Reviewed:</u>

Galinsky (10.51), p. 51	Schmähling (10.71)
Meidinger-Geise (10.60)	Vordtriede (10.76)
Rüdiger (10.67)	

GERMAN: OTHER PUBLICATION OF
POEMS AND LETTERS

[10.47]   A. v.E., trans. "Emily Dickinson." *Der Westen* [Chicago], June
          19, 1898, Section 3, p. 1.
          Part II of this article (see 10.47) contains a German transla-
          tion of "If I can stop one Heart from breaking," "Much Mad-
          ness is divinest Sense," "The Heart asks Pleasure — first,"
          and "The Soul selects her own Society."

10.4   Ewald Flügel. "Die Nordamerikanische Literatur" in Richard
          Wülker, *Geschichte der englischen Literatur*. Leipzig and
          Vienna: Bibliographischen Instituts, 1907 (reissued 1911), pp.
          526-27.
          Two poems are translated into German: "I'm Nobody! Who
          are you," and "I shall know why — when Time is over."

10.5   Leonora Speyer. *American Poets: An Anthology of Contempo-
          rary Verse*. Munich: Kurt Wolff, 1923.
          Includes poems by ED in English.

[10.44]   A. Busse. "Amerikanischer Brief." *Die Literatur*, XXVII (Jan.
          1925), p. 239.
          Reprints the first four lines, in English, of "The Soul selects
          her own Society."

10.6   Toni Harten-Hoencke (Mrs. Schönemann), trans. *Amerikanische
          Lyrik*. Munich: Kastner & Callwez, 1925, pp. 45-46.
          Contains a German translation of "Heart! We will forget
          him!" and "If I can stop one Heart from breaking."

10.7   *Internationale Zeitschrift für Individualpsychologie*, VI (1928),
          386.
          Reprints, in English, the first verse of "Each Life Converges
          to some Centre."

10.8   Friedrich Bruns. *Die amerikanische Dichtung der Gegenwart*.
          Leipzig and Berlin: B. G. Teubner, 1930, pp. 73-74.
          Includes four poems in English: "To my quick ear the Leaves
          — conferred," "I felt a Funeral, in my Brain," "If I shouldn't
          be alive," and "My life closed twice before its close."

10.9   Otto F. Babler, trans. "Ich starbum Schönheit." *Dichtung und
          Welt*, II, No. 41 (Oct. 12, 1930), p. [1].
          A German translation of "I died for Beauty — but was scarce."

10.10   Louis Untermeyer, ed. *The Albatross Book of Living Verse:
          English and American Poetry from the Thirteenth Century to
          the Present Day*. European Edition. Hamburg: Albatross,
          1933, pp. 462-65.
          Includes eight poems by ED in English.

[10.53]   Hans Hennecke, trans. "Emily Dickinson (1830-1886); Gedichte
          eingeleitet und übertragen." *Europäische Revue*, XIII (April
          1937), 297-301.
          Three poems in German and English.

10.11   Julius Bab, trans. "'In alabasteren Räumen,' Gedichte." *Ameri-
          kanische Rundschau* [Purdue Univ.], IV (1948), No. 20, pp.
          65-68.

The ten Dickinson poems included here in English and in German translation are listed by Galinsky (10.51), p. 241.

10.12   Hans Hennecke, trans. *Lyrik des Abendlands*. Munich: Carl Hanser, 1948, pp. 429, 625; 2nd ed., 1953 (3rd ed., 1963), pp. 483-84, 690.
Reprints Hans Hennecke's translations of "Because I could not stop for Death" and "On the Bleakness of my Lot" which were first published in 1937 (see 10.53), and adds a brief biographical note on ED.

10.13   Paul Friedrich, trans. *Lyrik der Welt*, ed. Reinhard Jaspert. Berlin, 1948.
Two poems appear in German translation: "I never saw a Moor," and "My life closed twice before its close."

10.14   Josef Raith. *American Poetry*, Vol. I: *The Eighteenth and Nineteenth Centuries*. Munich: 1949, pp. 158-64.
A German school text with ED poems in English.

10.15   Julius Bab, trans. *Amerikas Dichter der Gegenwart*. Berlin and Hamburg: 1951, pp. 96-98.
Includes German translations of "If I shouldn't be alive," "I'm Nobody! Who are you?" "To my quick ear the Leaves — conferred," "I took one Draught of Life," and the last stanza of "I heard a Fly buzz — when I died" ("With Blue — uncertain stumbling Buzz").

10.16   Kurt Rüdiger and Julius Bab, trans. *Die Lyra des Orpheus: Lyrik der Völker in deutscher Nachdichtung*, ed. Felix Braun. Vienna and Hamburg: Jubiläumsausgabe, 1952, pp. 756-57.
Includes "The Gentian weaves her fringes," translated by Kurt Rüdiger, and a reprinting of Julius Bab's translation of "If I shouldn't be alive" (see 10.15).

10.17   Julius Bab, trans. *Amerikas neuere Lyrik*. Bad Nauheim: 1953, pp. 47-53.
Reprints, with some changes and the addition of two poems, the ten translations of ED's poems first published in 1948; see 10.11.

10.18   Georg von der Vring, trans. *Die Neue Zeitung*, No. 19, January 1953.
A German translation of "The Mountains — grow unnoticed."

10.19   Georg von der Vring, trans. *English Horn, Angelsächsische Lyrik von den Anfängen bis zur Gegenwart*. Cologne and Berlin: Phaidon, 1953, pp. 151-52.
Contains a German translation of "Go not too near a House of Rose" and a reprinting of an earlier translation of "The Mountains — grow unnoticed" (see 10.18).

10.20   Kurt Rüdiger, trans. *Amerikanisches Literaturbrevier*, ed. Norbert Krejcik and Emmy Sieberer. Vienna, 1954, p. 282.
Reprints Kurt Rüdiger's earlier translation of "The Gentian weaves her fringes" (see 10.16).

10.21   Hans Zehrer. *English and American Poetry*. English Authors Series, Vol. 50. Bielefeld: Velhagen & Klasing, n.d. (1954?), pp. 117-19.
A German school text with four poems in English: "I taste a

liquor never brewed," "These are the days when Birds come back," "The Brain — is wider than the Sky," and "Bring me the sunset in a cup." Brief biography and commentary on the poems appears in a supplementary volume, *Ergänzungsband*, pp. 40-41.

10.22   Kurt Rüdiger, trans. *Orpheus: Blätter für Dichtung*. Karlsruhe: 1955 (reissued 1957). Unpaged.
A German translation of "Heart, not so heavy as mine" is located on leaf 15.

10.23   Paul Friedrich, trans. *Psalter und Harfe: Lyrik der Christenheit*, ed. Heinz Coubier and Marianne Langewiesche. Munich, 1955, p. 224.
A German translation of "I never saw a Moor."

10.24   Karl Berisch and Hans Hennecke, trans. *Lyrik der Welt: Dichtungen des Auslandes*, ed. Reinhard Jaspert. Berlin, 1955 (reissued 1960), pp. 368-69.
Includes "The Crickets sang" and "To my quick ear the Leaves — conferred," translated by Karl Berisch, and a reprinting of Hans Hennecke's 1937 translation of "Because I could not stop for Death" (see 10.53).

10.25   Hans Hennecke, trans. *Gedichte von Shakespeare bis Ezra Pound*. Wiesbaden: Limes, 1955, pp. 254-61.
Six poems in German and English with an introduction (pp. 254-56). Three of the translations were originally published in 1937; see 10.53. The additional poems are: "Death is a Dialogue between," "Surgeons must be very careful," and "Look back on Time, with kindly eyes."

[10.63] Roswith von Freydorf, trans. John Crowe Ransom, "Emily Dickinson, Dichterin der puritanischen Sensibilitat," *Perspektiven*, No. 15 (Spring 1956), pp. 142-64.
This German translation of Ransom's essay includes ten poems quoted within the text. They are listed by Galinsky (10.51), p. 243.

10.26   Georg von der Vring, trans. *Unsterblich schone Schwestern. Frauenlyrik aus drei Jahrstausenden*. Munich, 1956, pp. 63-70.
Six poems by ED are translated into German.

10.27   Hans Hennecke and Lola Gruenthal, trans. *Irdene Schale, Frauenlyrik seit der Antike*, ed. Mechthild Barthel-Kranzbühler. Heidelberg, 1956, pp. 148-52.
Eight poems are translated into German, three by Hans Hennecke and five by Lola Gruenthal.

10.28   Kurt Erich Meurer, trans. *Religiöse Lyrik des Abendlands* (Lyrik aus aller Welt), ed. Johannes von Guenther. (Ullstein Buch 210). Berlin: 1958, pp. 129-30.
A German translation of "Bring me the sunset in a cup."

[10.77] Hans Schmidt, trans. Stanley T. Williams [Chap. 55, "Experiments in Poetry: Sidney Lanier and Emily Dickinson"], in *Literaturgeschichte der Vereinigten Staaten*, ed. Robert E. Spiller, *et. al.* Mainz: Matthias-Gruenwald, 1959, pp. 916-19, 921-25.

Twelve Dickinson poems and one letter quoted within the text
of Williams' chapter are translated into German.

[10.46]   Werner Peterich, trans. Marcus Cunliffe, *Amerikanische Litera-
turgeschichte. Munich, 1961, pp. 194-98, 390-91.
Twelve poems and parts of poems quoted within the text of
this volume are translated into German.

10.29   Paul Celan, trans. "Emily Dickinson: Acht Gedichte." *Die Neue
Rundschau* [Frankfort on Main], LXXII (1961), pp. 36-39.
A German translation of eight Dickinson poems. They are
listed by Galinsky (10.51), p. 246.

10.30   Robert E. Konrad, trans. *Dichtung und Bild. Gesammelte Werke
des Malerdichters*. Zurich: Die Arche, 1961, pp. 173-87.
Five poems in German translation, accompanied by the original texts in English: "I was the slightest in the House," "I
hide myself within my flower," "A Wife — at Daybreak I shall
be," "Bring me the sunset in a cup," and "Safe in their Alabaster Chambers." These five were selected from twelve
translations of Dickinson poems originally composed in 1948-
49.

10.31   *Three Centuries of American Verse*. Huebers Fremdsprachliche
Texte, No. 169. Munich: n.d. (1961?), pp. 30-31.
A German school text containing ED poems in English.

10.32   Georg von der Vring, trans. *Angelsächsische Lyrik aus sechs
Jahrhunderten*. Cologne and Berlin, 1962, pp. 241-47.
Includes three poems in both English and German: "Like Rain
it sounded till it curved," "The name — of it — is 'Autumn',"
and "If I shouldn't be alive."

10.33   Robert E. Konrad and Franz Peter Künzel, trans. *Documenta
poetica / englisch / amerikanisch in Original und deutscher
Übersetzung*, ed. Hans Rudolf Hilty. Munich: Kindler, 1962,
pp. 88-91.
English and German texts of two poems: "I started Early —
Took my Dog," translated by Franz Künzel, and "I was the
slightest in the House," translated by Robert Konrad (a reprinting; see 10.30).

10.34   *The Word Sublime. Poetry of the English-Speaking Communities*,
selected and ed. by Hans Combecher and Gustav Schad. Frankfort on Main; 1962, p. 94.
Includes six poems in English by ED.

10.35   Kurt Rüdiger, trans. & ed. *Wipfel des Menschen. Religiöse
Lyrik der Welt*. Karlsruhe: 1964, p. 28.
Three poems are translated into German: "At least — to pray
— is left — is left," "A Death blow is a Life blow to Some," and
"Our journey had advanced."

10.36   Kurt Rüdiger, trans. & ed. *Das Spinnjahr. Frauendichtung der
Welt*. Karlsruhe: 1965, pp. 43-44.
Four poems are translated into German: "Have you got a
Brook in your little heart," "If I shouldn't be alive," "I taste
a liquor never brewed," and "The Soul selects her own So-
ciety."

10.37   Hans Baumann, trans. & ed. *Ein Reigen um die Welt. 274 Gedichte aus 75 Sprachen*. Gütersloh: 1965, pp. 15, 166.

Includes a German translation of "Will there really be a 'Morning'?" and "The Moon was but a Chin of Gold."

10.38   *British and American Classical Poems.* Newly edited and annotated by Horst Meller and Rudolf Sühnel in cooperation with Arthur Brown and Richard Schade. Brunswick: 1966, pp. 104, 105, 237, 353. Includes three Dickinson poems in English with a biographical note.

10.39   *Learning English, Book of English Verse,* ed. Werner Hüllen and Wolfgang Schmidt-Hidding. Stuttgart: 1966, pp. 93-95.
A school anthology, this volume includes the English text of five Dickinson poems: "I like to see it lap the Miles," "The Brain — is wider than the Sky," "Because I could not stop for Death," "I never saw a Moor," and "The going from a world we know." Hans Hennecke's translation of "Because I could not stop for Death" (10.53) is reprinted on p. 122. See also the companion volume, *Interpretations* (10.72), by Wolfgang Schmidt-Hidding.

10.40   Hans Schmidt, trans. *Wege der amerikanischen Literatur: Eine geschichtliche Darstellung* by Martin Schulze. Frankfort on Main and Berlin: 1968, pp. 187, 188.
Reprints Hans Schmidt's 1959 translations of "Perception of an object costs" and "I measure every Grief I meet."

GERMAN: CRITICISM AND SCHOLARSHIP

10.41   Anon. "Emily Dickinson (1830-1886)" in *Die Amerikanische Dichtung der Gegenwart.* Leipzig: Teubner, 1930, pp. 73-74.

10.42   Berlet, Brigitte. "Die Bildersprache Emily Dickinsons." Ph.D. thesis. Frankfort on Main.

10.43   Brumm, Ursula. "Entwicklungszüge der amerikanischen Literatur" in *Amerikakunde* (Handbucher der Auslandskunde), ed. Paul Hartig. 4th ed. Frankfort on Main: 1966, pp. 671-72, 676.

10.44   Busse, A. "Amerikanischer Brief." *Die Literatur,* XXVII (Jan. 1925), 238-39.
Rev. of Bianchi, *Life and Letters* (4.36).

10.45   Combecher, Hans. *Muse in America. Vom eigenwilligen Weg amerikanischer Dichtung. Interpretationen. Die Neueren Sprachen,* Supplement I. Frankfort on Main: n.d., pp. 13-23.
Contains interpretations of "To make a prairie it takes a clover and one bee," "These are the days when Birds come back," "I never lost as much but twice," and "I never saw a Moor."

10.46   Cunliffe, Marcus. *Amerikanische Literaturgeschichte.* Werner Peterich, trans. Munich, 1961, pp. 194-98, 390-91.
A German translation of Prof. Cunliffe's volume, *The Literature of the United States* (see 6.242).

10.47   v.E., A. "Emily Dickinson." Part I: *Der Westen* [Chicago], June 12, 1898, Section 3, p. 1; Part II: June 19, 1898, Section 3, p. 1. This 3000-word essay appears to be the first foreign-language article on ED. Part I sketches her character and personality, quoting frequently from the letters and stressing the poet's

solitude. Part II argues briefly that ED's world view, for all
its penetration and even heresy, is not pessimistic, but rather
implies an acceptance of fate. Her love poems are among her
best and her poems on nature reflect their subject: sometimes rough and hard but never artificial.

10.48   Fischer, Walter. *Die englische Literatur der Vereinigten Staaten
         von Nordamerika.* Wildpark-Potsdam: Akademische Ver-
         lagsgesellschaft Athenaion M.B.H., 1929, p. 84.
         Brief introduction to ED in a literary history.

10.49   Frank, Josef. "Emily Dickinson (1830-1886)." *Prisma* [Munich],
         VI (April 1947), 21-23.
         ED's originality is explained in part as the result of a conflict
         between resignation and unsubdued passion (for Wadsworth):
         "Her only hour of being a female was paid for with a crown of
         thorns." She renounced maturity to adopt the pose of an eter-
         nal child and cosmic gnome. Her prankish humor resembles
         that of the German poet, Christian Morgenstern. In her isola-
         tion and loneliness, she took little snapshots of life and made
         them into allegories.

10.50   Galinsky, Hans. "Wege in die dichterische Welt Emily Dickin-
         sons" in *Spirit of a Free Society, Essays in Honor of Sen.
         James William Fulbright on the Occasion of the Tenth Anni-
         versary of the German Fulbright Program.* Heidelberg:
         Quille & Meyer, 1962, pp. 221-94. For a reprinting of this
         essay, see 10.51. Discusses literary and cultural sources
         which inform ED's poetic world and traces her creative de-
         velopment through close textual analysis of ten representa-
         tive poems.

10.51   ———. *Wegbereiter Moderner Amerikanischer Lyrik: Interpre-
         tations- und Rezeptionsstudien zu Emily Dickinson und Wil-
         liam Carlos Williams.* Heidelberg: Carl Winter, 1968.
         Two essays in this volume are concerned with ED. The first,
         pp. 9-44, discusses similarities in the recent critical recep-
         tion of Dickinson and Williams, especially in Europe. The
         second, pp. 47-113, is a reprinting, under the same title, of
         Prof. Galinsky's essay cited above (10.50). "Part I" of the
         latter essay is expanded to include a fuller account of German
         scholarly interest in ED. The appendix, pp. 240-50, contains
         a chart listing, by first line, German translations of Dickinson
         poems and letters, 1898-1968.

10.52   Granichstaedten-Czerva, Elizabeth. "Bildersprache bei Emily
         Dickinson." Thesis. Vienna, 1940. 123 pp.

10.53   Hennecke, Hans. "Emily Dickinson (1830-1886), Gedichte einge-
         leitet und übertragen." *Europäische Revue,* XIII (April 1937),
         297-301.
         A biographical and critical introduction with German and
         English texts of three poems: "Because I could not stop for
         Death," "I taste a liquor never brewed," and "On the Bleak-
         ness of my Lot" (a variant of "Soil of Flint, if steady tilled").

10.54   Hohoff, Curt. "Emily Dickinson, Zu einer Auswahl und Überset-
         zung von Gedichten und Briefen." *Das XX Jahrhundert*

[formerly *Die Tat*] (Jena), XXI, No. 233 (Aug. 25, 1956), p. 11.
Rev. of *Der Engel in Grau*, trans. Maria Mathi (10.2).

10.55   Ikle, Charlotte. "Emily Dickinson: 'Sag alles wahr, doch sag es schrag.'" *Du. Kulturelle Monatsschrift* [Zurich], XXI (1961), No. 9, pp. 63-64.

10.56   Lang, Hans-Joachim. *Studien zur Entstehung der neueren amerikanischen Literaturkritik*. Hamburg: Cram, de Gruyter, 1961, p. 51.
Notes that ED is treated only cursorily in literary histories published between 1896 and 1913. For a full discussion of ED's reputation among literary historians, see Lubbers, *Critical Revolution* (5.114), pp. 87-94, 184-95, 298-300, *passim*.

10.57   Leitel, Erich. *Die Aufnahme der amerikanischen Literatur in Deutschland: Übersetzungen der Jahre 1914-1944; Mit einer Bibliographie*. Thesis. Jena, 1958.

10.58   Link, Franz. "Vier Gedichte Emily Dickinsons." *Die Neueren Sprachen*, n.s. III (1954), No. 9, pp. 406-13.
Explications of "I like to see it lap the Miles," "My Life had stood — a Loaded Gun," "Although I put away his life," and "After great pain, a formal feeling comes." In German.

[5.114] Lubbers, Klaus. *Der literarische Ruhm Emily Dickinsons: Das erste Jahrhundert amerikanischer und britischer Kritik von Werk und Mensch*. Thesis. Mainz, 1967.

10.59   Lüdeke, Henry. *Geschichte der amerikanischen Literatur*. Bern: Francke, 1952, pp. 352-56, *passim*; rev. & enl. ed., 1963, pp. 281-84, *passim*.
Introduction to ED in a literary history. Discusses biographical, intellectual, and literary backgrounds to her poetry.

10.60   Meidinger-Geise, Inge. *Welt und Wort* [Munich], XIV (1959), 349.
Rev. of *Emily Dickinson, Gedichte*, trans. Lola Gruenthal (10.3).

10.61   Monnig, Richard. *Amerika und England im deutschen, österreichischen und schweizerischen Schrifttum der Jahre 1945-1949, Eine Bibliographie*. Stuttgart: Kohlhammer, 1951.

10.62   Oppens, Kurt. "Emily Dickinson: Überlieferung und Prophetie." *Merkur*, XIV (Jan. 1960), 17-40.
Discusses ED's cultural background and some of her themes, especially her belief in the creative imagination and in the imminence of this life. There is extensive comparison with Rilke. R. W. Franklin, *Editing* (5.28), pp. 125-26, comments on the editing of "It's like the Light" in this article.

10.63   Ransom, John Crowe. "Emily Dickinson: Dichterin der puritanischen Sensibilität," Roswith von Freydorf, trans. *Perspektiven* [Frankfort on Main], No. XV (Spring 1956), pp. 142-64.
A German translation of John Crowe Ransom's essay, "Emily Dickinson," in *Perspectives U.S.A.;* see 6.835.

10.64   Reitmayer, Sabine. "Emily Dickinson in deutscher Übertragung" in *Zulassungsarbeit zum Staatsexamen*. Mainz: 1966, pp. 96-98.

10.65   Riese, Teut Andreas. "Emily Dickinson und der Sprachgeist
          amerikanischer Lyrik." *Die Neueren Sprachen,* n.s. XII (April
          1963), 145-59.
          ED, like other major American poets, discards conventional
          poetic diction in favor of an indirect, almost formless language
          through which she can define and express a new sense of re-
          ality. Rev. by Robbins, *ALS, 1963* (6.851), p. 128.

10.66   ———. "Das Gestaltungsprinzip der Konkretion in der neueren
          amerikanischen Lyrik." *Jahrbuch für Amerikastudien,* No. 8
          (1963), pp. 136-47.
          In a discussion of realism in American poetry, the author ex-
          amines ED's characteristic attempt to find momentary signifi-
          cance in an otherwise enigmatic flow of concrete experience.

10.67   Rüdiger, Kurt. "Der geniale Dilettant: Emily Dickinson, Ge-
          dichte." *Der Karlsruher Bote,* Sept. 1960.
          Rev. of *Emily Dickinson, Gedichte,* trans. Lola Gruenthal
          (10.3).

10.68   Rus, Calvin. "Teaching American Poetry" in *Amerikanische
          Dichtung in der höheren Schule: Interpretationen amerikani-
          scher Erzählkunst und Lyrik,* by Hans Galinsky, Leo Marx,
          and Calvin Rus. *Die Neueren Sprachen,* Vol. III. Frankfort on
          Main: Diesterweg, 1961, pp. 64-66.

10.69   Schirmer, Walter F. *Kurz Geschichte der englischen Literatur
          von den Anfängen bis zur Gegenwart.* 1st ed., 1 vol. Halle/
          Salle: 1945, pp. 228, 277; reissued, Tübingen: Niemeyer,
          1949, pp. 231-32, 282. Later editions entitled, *Geschichte der
          englischen und amerikanischen Literatur von den Anfängen bis
          zur Gegenwart.* 2nd ed., 2 vols., Tübingen: Niemeyer, 1954,
          II, pp. 149, 229. 3rd ed., 2 vols., II (1960), pp. 153, 240, 247.
          4th ed., 2 vols., II (1967); reissued in 1 vol. (1968), pp. 619,
          683, 710.
          Brief mention of ED in a history of English and American lit-
          erature.

10.70   Schirmer-Imhoff, Ruth. *Anglia,* LXXI (1952-1953), 365, 366.
          Rev. of *Letters,* 1951 (4.80).

10.71   Schmähling, Walter. *Die Bücherkommentare,* VIII (1959), No. 4,
          p. 12.
          Rev. of *Emily Dickinson, Gedichte,* trans. Lola Gruenthal
          (10.3).

10.72   Schmidt-Hidding, Wolfgang. *Interpretations.* Stuttgart, 1966, pp.
          75-77, 94.
          A companion volume to *Learning English, Book of English
          Verse* (10.39).

10.73   Schulze, Martin. *Wege der amerikanischen Literatur.* Eine
          geschichtliche Darstellung. Frankfort on Main and Berlin:
          1968, pp. 187, 188.

10.74   Spitzer, Leo. "Baudelaire, Les Fleur du Mal: LXXVII —
          'Spleen,'" in *Interpretationen zur Geschichte der französis-
          chen Lyrik.* Heidelberg: Selbstverlag des Romanischen Sem-
          inars der Universität Heidelberg, 1961, pp. 170-179.
          Compares the idea of death in Baudelaire's poem and in ED's

"I felt a Funeral, in my Brain" and notes differences in the two poets' use of language.

10.75 ——. "Le Spleen" in *Romanische Literaturstudien*. Tübingen: 1959.

10.76 Vordtriede, Werner. "Die puritanische 'Droste.'" *Neue Deutsche Hefte*, VI (Dec. 1959), 857-59.
Rev. of *Emily Dickinson, Gedichte*, trans. Lola Gruenthal (10.3).

10.77 Williams, Stanley T. [Chap. 55, "Experiments in Poetry: Sidney Lanier and Emily Dickinson"] in *Literaturgeschichte der Vereinigten Staaten*, ed. Robert E. Spiller, *et. al.* Hans Schmidt, trans. Mainz: Matthias-Gruenwald, 1959, pp. 916-25.
A German translation of Stanley Williams' discussion of ED in the first edition of *Literary History of the United States* (6.1179).

10.78 Zuther, Gerhard H. W. *Eine Bibliographie der Aufnahme amerikanischer Literatur in deutschen Zeitschriften 1945-1960*. Munich: 1965, p. 37.
Notes translations, articles, and book reviews dealing with ED in German periodicals.

DUTCH: EDITIONS AND TRANSLATIONS

10.79 *Emily Dickinson, Selected Poems*. Selected by Simon Vestdijk. [Amsterdam]: A. A. Balkema, 1940. 70 pp.
An underground printing of 200 copies. The volume contains 59 poems in English only, selected from *Poems* [London], 1935 (3.173). Another underground volume was published in Amsterdam in 1939; see 10.1.

10.80 A. G. Van Kranendonk. *Geschiedenis van de Amerikaanse Literatuur*. Amsterdam: G. A. Van Oorschot, 1946, pp. 300-05.

[10.81] O. Postma and S. J. Van der Molen, trans. "Eat oer Emily Dickinson en har wurk." *Tsjerne*, VI (July 1951), 193-96.
15 poems are translated into Dutch.

DUTCH: CRITICISM AND SCHOLARSHIP

10.81 Molen, S. J. Van der. "Eat oer Emily Dickinson en har wurk." *Tsjerne* [Dokkum, Neterlands], VI (July 1951), 193-202.
Three poems are translated into Dutch by O. Postma, pp. 197-98. Another 12 poems are translated by S. J. Van der Molen, pp. 199-202. The latter provides an introduction to ED, pp. 193-96.

10.82 Vestdijk, Simon. "Over de Dickteres Emily Dickinson" in *Lier en Lancet*. Rotterdam: Nijgh & van Ditmar, 1939. Vol. I, pp. 9-51.

10.83 ——. "De Vlinder in de Kerk." *Critisch Bulletin* [Amsterdam], July-Aug. 1939, pp. 214-16.
Rev. of Whicher, *This Was a Poet* (5.104).

11.

Spanish and Portuguese

SPANISH: SEPARATE EDITIONS OF
POEMS AND LETTERS

11.1 *Emily Dickinson: Obra Escogida.* Introd. Juan José Domenchina;
trans. Ernestina de Champourcin and Juan José Domenchina.
S.A. México: Editorial Centauro, 1946. 131 pp.
67 poems appear in translation. Introduction, pp. 11-25. Back
matter includes biographical information, pp. 121-25 and a
bibliography, pp. 129-31.

11.2 *Emily Dickinson: Seis Poemas.* Trans. and notes by Ventura
Doreste. Colección El Arca. Las Palmas [Spain], 1954.
Reviewed:
C., J. L. (11.22)

11.3 *Emily Dickinson: Poemas.* Trans. Mariano Manent. Barcelona:
Editorial Juventud, 1957. 166 pp.
53 poems in Spanish and English with an introduction, pp. 5-15.
Reviewed:
Crusat (11.23)

SPANISH: OTHER PUBLICATION OF
POEMS AND LETTERS

11.4 Juan Ramón Jiménez. *Diario de un Poeta Recién Casado.* Ma-
drid: Casa editorial Calleja, Imprenta Fortanet, 1917.
Reprinted:
Juan Ramón Jiménez. *Diario de Poeta y Mar.* Madrid: Afro-
disio Aguado, 1955, pp. 239-40.
Translation of three poems from *Single Hound,* 1914 (3.114):
"The Soul that hath a Guest," "The gleam of an heroic Act,"
and "I send Two Sunsets."

11.5 *Antología de Escritores Contemporáneos de los Estados Unidos,*

ed. Allen Tate and John Peale Bishop. 2 vols. Santiago, Chile: Editorial Nascimento, 1944, I, 406-11.
Translation by "Santiago" [pseud.] of three ED poems from the anthology, *American Harvest*, ed. Allen Tate and John Peale Bishop. N.Y.: L. B. Fischer, 1942.

11.6 José Coronel Urtecho, trans. *Antología y Panorama de la Poesía Norteamericana*. Granada, Nicaragua: Envio del Autos, 1944.
Reprinted:
Reportorio Americano [San José, Costa Rica], XLI (Feb. 19, 1944), 37.
A translation of "There came a Wind like a Bugle."

11.7 Alberto Weis. *Poesía Estadounidense*. Buenos Aires: Continental, 1944.

11.8 Gastón Figueira, trans. "Life: XII." *Artigas* [Montevideo], Sept. 1946, pp. 102-03.
A translation of "I asked no other thing."

11.9 José Antonio Davila, trans. "Poemas Emily Dickinson." *Asomante* [San Juan, Puerto Rico], III, No. 1 (Jan.-Mar. 1947), pp. 18-23.
Six poems in Spanish and English.

11.10 Hildamar Escalante. *Breve Informe de Poesía Norteamericana*. Caracas: Tipografía La Nación, 1947, pp. 17-25.
Translation of four poems.

11.10a Agustí Bartra. *Una Antología de la Lírica Nord-americana*. México, D.F.: Edicions Lletres, 1951.
14 poems in Spanish, pp. 38-44, with an introduction, pp. 36-38.

11.11 Agustí Bartra. *Antología de la Poesía Norteamericana*. México: Colección Letras, 1952, pp. 88-100. Reissued: Libro-México, 1957.
29 ED poems are translated in the 1952 edition; 32 in the 1957 edition.

11.12 Guillermo Lücke, trans. "Cuatro Poemas de Emily Dickinson." *Centro*, No. 7 (1953), pp. 22-23.
Translation of "I'm 'wife' — I've finished that," "A word is dead," "Heart! We will forget him!," and "Our lives are Swiss." See also 11.36.

11.13 Manuel Mujica Lainez, trans. "Dos Poemas de Emily Dickinson." *Vistas* [Santo Domingo, Dominican Republic], No. 1 (Sept.-Oct. 1953), p. 4.

11.14 Sergio Fernández, trans. "Cuatro Poemas de Emily Dickinson." *Universidad de México*, XIV (Dec. 1959), 4.

11.15 Carlos López Narvaez, trans. "Dos poemas de Emily Dickinson: Estatura, Coloquio." *Nivel* [México, D.F.], No. 11 (Nov. 25, 1963), p. 8.
Translation of "I died for Beauty — but was scarce" and "I took my Power in my Hand."

[11.33] Rafael Pineda, trans. "Emily Dickinson." *Revista Nacional de Cultura* [Caracas], XXV (Jan.-April 1963), 139-45.
Translation of 25 ED poems.

SPANISH: CRITICISM AND SCHOLARSHIP

11.16   Arroyo, Anita. "La Poesía de Emily Dickinson." *Presencia*, No.
4 (Mar.-July 1958), pp. 3, 15.

11.17   Blackmur, Richard P. "Emily Dickinson: Notas Sobre Prejuicio
y Realidad" in *Antología de Escritores Contemporáneos de los
Estados Unidos*, ed. Allen Tate and John Peale Bishop. 2 vols.
Santiago, Chile: Editorial Nascimento, 1944, I, 443-78.
Translation of Blackmur's "Emily Dickinson: Notes on Preju-
dice and Fact" (6.107).

11.18   Bravo Villasante, Carmen. "Carta sobre los Epistolarios Feme-
ninos." *Asomante* [San Juan, Puerto Rico], XV (April-June,
1959), 7-19.
Very brief mention (p. 8) of ED's letters.

11.19   ———. "Las Escritoras Clásicas Norteamericanas." *Cuadernos
Hispanoamericanos* [Madrid], LXVI (May 1966), 205-22.
ED discussed, pp. 206-08.

11.20   ———. "Las Escritoras Norteamericanas." *Asomante* [San Juan,
Puerto Rico], XVIII (Oct.-Dec. 1962), 31-48.
A brief, appreciative introduction to ED, pp. 31-34.

11.21   Brooks, Van Wyck. "Emily Dickinson," trans. R. Lavandero.
Asomante [San Juan, Puerto Rico], III (Jan.-Mar. 1947), 24-35.
Translation of Chapter 15 of Brooks' *New England Indian Sum-
mer*, see 6.154.

11.22   C., J. L. *Insula* [Madrid], IX, No. 105 (Sept. 15, 1954), p. 7.
Rev. of *ED, Seis Poemas*, trans. Ventura Doreste (11.2).

11.23   Crusat, Paulina. "La Poesía de Emily Dickinson (Con Motivo de
Unas Versions de M. Manent)." *Insula* [Madrid], XII, No. 130
(Sept. 1957), p. 5.
Rev. of *Emily Dickinson, Poemas*, trans. M. Manent, 1957
(11.3).

11.24   Delgado-Arias, Eugene. "Emily Dickinson, Espiritu Esotérico."
Bitacora [Caracas], II (July 1943), 25-36.
Includes the translation of three poems.

11.25   Escalante, Hildamar. "Emily Dickinson, La Monja de Amherst."
El Nacional [Caracas], Feb. 6, 1949.

11.26   Figueira, Gastón. "Emily Dickinson y el Brasil." *Torre* [Rio
Piedras, Puerto Rico], X (Oct.-Dec. 1962), 121-25.
Discusses possible sources for ED's interest in Brazil.

11.27   ———. "21 Poetas Estadounidenses y un Estudio sobre Emily
Dickinson, por Conrad Aiken (Interpretación de Conie Lobell)."
Lírica Hispana [Caracas], XIV, No. 165 (Nov. 1956), pp. 3-64.
Includes a translation of Aiken's "Emily Dickinson" (6.20).

11.28   Frost, Lesley. "La Poesía Norteamericana Moderna." *Insula*
[Madrid], No. 19 (July 15, 1947), p. 2.
A brief allusion to ED's aesthetics.

11.29   Herrero Esteban, Jacinto. "Emily Dickinson y Pablo Antonio
Cuadra: Proximidad de dos Poemas." *Cuadernos Hispano-
americanos* [Madrid], LXI (Jan. 1965), 152-55.
Compares "I died for Beauty — but was scarce" with Cuadra's
"Interioridad de Dos Estrellas que Arden."

11.30   Manent, Mariano. "Un libro sobre Emily Dickinson." *Insula*
         [Madrid], X, No. 115 (July 15, 1955), p. 9.
         Rev. of Chase, *ED* (5.17).
11.31   Murciaux, Christian. "El Genio Puritano en el Siglo XIX." *Sur*
         [Buenos Aires], Nos. 215-216 (Sept.-Oct. 1952), pp. 84-108.
         Discusses elements of Puritanism in ED, Emerson, and Whit-
         man.
11.32   Onís, Harriet de. "Emily Dickinson." *Asomante* [San Juan,
         Puerto Rico], XII (April-June 1956), 23-38.
         An introduction to ED, especially in terms of her New England
         background. Several poems are translated in the notes. In
         Spanish.
11.33   Pineda, Rafael. "Emily Dickinson." *Revista Nacional de Cultura*
         [Caracas], XXV (Jan.-April 1963), 132-45.
         A general introduction, pp. 132-38, followed by translation of
         25 poems.
11.34   Ramón, José Antonio. *Panorama de la Literatura Norteameri-
         cana.* México: Ediciones Botas, 1935, pp. 104-05.
11.35   Ramón, Juan. *El Modernismo, Notas de un Curso (1953).* México:
         Aguilar, 1962, p. 140.
11.36   Ricardes, Fulton. "Emily Elizabeth Dickinson." *Centro,* No. 7,
         (1953), pp. 20-21.
         Introductory note to a translation of four poems: see 11.12.
11.37   Sánchez, Luis Alberto. *Nueva Historia de la Literatura Ameri-
         cana.* Buenos Aires: Editorial Americalee, 1944, pp. 304-05.
11.38   Stevens, Harriet S. "Emily Dickinson y Juan Ramón Jiménez,"
         Cuadernos Hispanoamericanos [Madrid], LVI (Oct. 1963), 29-
         49.
         Notes parallels between the two poets.
11.39   Tello, Jaime. "Emily Dickinson." *Bolívar* [Bogotá], No. 3 (Sept.
         1951), pp. 509-15.
         Brief biographical and critical introduction with translation of
         seven poems.
11.40   Vicuña, Magdalena. "Emily Dickinson." *Andean Quarterly* [San-
         tiago, Chile], Spring 1946, pp. 16-20.
11.41   Zardoya, Concha. "Emily Dickinson" in *Historia de la Literatura
         Norteamericana.* Barcelona: Editorial Labor, 1956, pp. 314-
         17.

PORTUGUESE: TRANSLATIONS

11.42   *Poetas Norte-americanos,* ed. Gastón Figueira. Rio de Janeiro:
         Bureau de Informações Pan-americano, 1943.
         Six ED poems are translated by Amparo Rodríguez Vidal, pp.
         101-03.
11.43   *Videntes e Sonâmbulos: Coletanea de Poemas Norte-americanos,*
         ed. Oswaldino Marques. Rio de Janeiro: Ministério da Edu-
         cação e Cultura, 1955.
         Five poems in Portuguese and English, trans. Manuel Bandeira,
         pp. 80-89. Includes a biographical note on ED, pp. 256-57.

11.44　　*Poesias Escolhidas de Emily Dickinson,* trans. Olívia Krahenbühl.
　　　　　São Paulo: Edição Sarama, 1956. 220 pp.
　　　　　Poems in Portuguese and English, with a prefatory note, pp.
　　　　　9-14.

PORTUGUESE: CRITICISM

11.45　　Nist, John. "Dois Poetas Norte-americanos e uma Aranha."
　　　　　Anhembi [São Paulo], XXXV (Aug. 1959), 480-84.
　　　　　For an English translation of this article, see 6.752.
11.46　　Silveira, Brenno. *Pequena História da Literatura Norte-*
　　　　　americana. São Paulo: Livraria Martins Editora, 1943, pp.
　　　　　184-85.

12.

Japanese

PUBLICATION OF POEMS AND LETTERS

12.1   Takeshi Saito, ed. and trans. *Choice Poems*. Tokyo: Kaibunsha, 1952, pp. 124-29.
Poems in English and Japanese with notes supplied by the editor.

12.2   *A History of American Literature: An Anthology*, ed. James E. Wood, Jr. Tokyo: Kenkyusha Ltd., 1952, pp. 251-54.
Introduction to ED and eight poems in English.

12.3   *American Poetry 1855-1955*, ed. William Moore. 4 vols. Tokyo: Kenkyusha Ltd., 1955, I, 37-63.
36 Dickinson poems in English.

12.4   Motoshi Karita, trans. *Gendai Sekai Shi-Sen [An Anthology of Modern World Poetry]*, ed. Rikutarō Fukuda. Tokyo: Mikasa Shōbō, 1959.

12.5   Ichirō Andō, trans. *Sekai Meishishu Taisei [A Definitive Collection of Famous World Poetry]*, Vol. 15 [North America]. Tokyo: Heibonsha, 1961.

12.6   Toshikazu Niikura, ed. and trans. *Emily Dickinson: Kenkyū to Shishō [Selected Poems]*. Tokyo: Shinozaki Shorin, 1962. 233 pp.
Published Sept. 15, 1962; second ed., Mar. 20, 1967.
The first book-length introduction to ED in Japan, this volume contains 77 poems in English and Japanese and a substantial critical essay. Poems follow the Todd-Higginson text with variants from the Johnson edition and are arranged under three headings: "Ecstatic Moments," "Immortality," and "Menagerie." In his introduction, pp. 1-83, the editor discusses the poet's life and cultural background and draws on his own recently published essays (see 12.20-21) for more extended treatment of the lyric and religious poems. Includes a translation of Allen Tate's essay (6.980), pp. 84-111. Mistakes are corrected and translations revised in the second edition.

195

12.7   *American Literature: Anthology,* ed. Keiichi Harada, *et. al.* To-
         kyo: Gakko Shuppan, 1964.
         An anthology for students. In English.

CRITICISM AND SCHOLARSHIP

12.8   Ando, Midori. "Emily Dickinson no Shuho — Sono 1" ["Emily
         Dickinson's Technique — Part I"]. *Gakuen,* April 1965.
12.9   ——. "On Death in the Poems of Emily Dickinson." *Gakuen,*
         No. 276 (Dec. 1962), pp. 56-66.
12.10   ——. "A View of Nature in Emily Dickinson's Poems." *Gakuen,*
         No. 280 (April 1963), pp. 63-76.
         ED grasped through nature the fragility and elusiveness of life.
[6.272] de Ford, Sara. *Lectures on Modern American Poetry.* Tokyo:
         Hokuseido Press, 1957.
12.11   Fukuda, Rikutarō. *English Teachers' Magazine,* XII (June 1963),
         32.
         A description of the ED Room, Jones Library, Amherst.
12.12   Funato, Hideo. "On Emily Dickinson." *Kamereon* [St. Paul's
         Univ., Tokyo], No. 5 (Autumn 1962), pp. 38-49.
         An evaluation.
12.13   Iwayama, Sataro. "Emily Dickinson no Shi no Variant Readings
         Kenkyu no Juyosei — Johnson ban ni taisuru Taido to shité"
         ["The Importance of Variant Readings in the Study of Emily
         Dickinson's Poetry — An Attitude Toward the Johnson Edi-
         tion"]. *Studies in English Literature,* XLII (March 1966),
         193-207.
12.14   ——. "Process of Transition of Emily Dickinson's Idea: From
         Death to Immortality." *Studies in Humanities* [Doshisha Univ.,
         Kyoto], No. 64 (March 1963), pp. 1-26.
12.15   Kato, Kikuo. "On the Death Poems of Emily Dickinson." *Bulletin
         of Tokyo Gakugei University,* XIV (March 1963), 7-10.
12.16   Miyanagi, Setsu. "Emily Dickinson — sono summer poem ni
         tsuite" ["Emily Dickinson — Her Summer Poem"]. *Hokusei
         Gakuen Women's Junior College Journal* (Sapporo, Hokkaido),
         No. 11.
12.17   Nakao, Kiyoaki. "Emily Dickinson's 'Irreverence.'" *American
         Literary Review* [Tokyo], XIX (April 1957), 5-8.
         In English.
12.18   ——. "Studies in American Poetry — The Individuality of Emily
         Dickinson." *Scientific Researches* [Waseda Univ., Tokyo], VI,
         pp. 1-12.
         Discusses biographical sources of ED's individuality and un-
         usual aspects of her poetry. In English.
12.19   Niikura, Toshikazu [Shunichi]. "Emily Dickinson's 'If you were
         coming in the Fall.'" *Meiji Gakuin Ronso* [Meiji Gakuin Univ.,
         Tokyo], No. 73 (Nov. 1962), pp. 139-50.
12.20   ——. "'Honest Doubt': Emily Dickinson's Religious Poetry."
         Meiji Gakuin Ronso [Meiji Gakuin Univ., Tokyo], Nos. 64-65
         (Oct. 1961), pp. 101-16. See also 12.6.

12.21   Niikura, Toshikazu [Shunichi]. "'Summer Poems' by Emily Dick-
        inson." *American Literary Review* [Tokyo], XXXIV (April
        1961), 11-12. See also 12.6.
12.22   Noda, Hisashi. "Emily Dickinson's Poetry: An Essay on the
        Symbols of 'Death.'" *Kyusha American Literature*, No. 6
        (April 1963), pp. 23-29.
        In English.
12.23   ———. "Notes on Emily Dickinson." *Kyusha American Litera-
        ture*, No. 5 (April 1962), pp. 63-70.
12.24   ———. "Notes on *This Was a Poet: A Critical Biography of Em-
        ily Dickinson* by G. F. Whicher (1938)." *Kyusha American
        Literature*, No. 9 (July 1966).
        In English.
12.25   Nogami, Akira. "Emily Dickinson." *America Bungaku* [Tokyo
        Univ. of Education], March 1949.
12.26   Omoto, Tsuyoshi. "Emily Dickinson's Poem 'No Rack can tor-
        ture me.'" *Hiroshima Studies in English Language and Liter-
        ature* [Hiroshima Univ.], IX (June 1963), 45-50.
12.27   Reyes, M. Philomene de los. "Emily Dickinson's 'White Elec-
        tion.'" *America Bungaku* [Tokyo Univ. of Education], No. 5.
12.28   Shikata, Noriko. "A Fairy-Tale-Like Aspect of Emily Dickin-
        son's Poems." *Yamazaki Gakuen Junior College Journal*,
        No. 3.
12.29   Takaku, Shinichi. "Paradoxical Quality in Emily Dickinson's
        Poems." *Hokusei Gakuen Women's Junior College Journal*
        (Sapporo, Hokkaido), No. 4 (1958), pp. 1-20.
12.30   ———. "Translation of Emily Dickinson's Poems." *Hokusei Ga-
        kuen Women's Junior College Journal* (Sapporo, Hokkaido),
        No. 3 (1957), pp. 31-51.
12.31   Yamamoto, Shuji. "Emily Dickinson and the Concept of Immor-
        tality." *Kyushu American Literature* [Fukuoka], No. 4 (Sept.
        1961), pp. 13-15.
12.32   ———. "Emily Dickinson: Person and Poetry." *Kyushu Ameri-
        can Literature* [Fukuoka], No. 3 (May 1960), pp. 15-20.

13.

Other Languages

NORWEGIAN

13.1 Brekke, Paal. *Amerikansk Lyrikk*. Et utualg i nor k gjendiktning ved Paal Brekke. Oslo: H. Aschehoug (W. Nygaard), 1957, pp. 26-32.
Contains twelve ED poems in Norwegian.

13.2 Smidt, Aagot Karner. "Emily Dickinson." *Vinduet,* XV (Summer 1961), 220-23.
Cites evidence of a Dickinson renaissance, criticizes ED's Freudian biographer-critics, and chides R. P. Blackmur for regarding her as a "great but minor poet." In Norwegian.

SWEDISH

13.3 Blomberg, Erik. *All Världens Lyrik*. Dikter från främmande språk i svensk tolkning. Urval av Anders Österling. Stockholm: Albert Bonniers, 1949, p. 367.
Swedish translation of "Success is counted sweetest" and "I never saw a Moor."

13.4 *Dikter av Emily Dickinson*. Trans. Erik Blomberg and Johannes Edfelt. Illus. Yngve Berg. Stockholm: Wahlström and Widstrand, 1949. 50 pp.
Poems in Swedish.

13.5 *Emily Dickinson*. En introduktion med lyriska tolkningar av Ellen Löfmarck. Stockholm: Natur och kultur, 1950. 130 pp.
Selected poems and letters in Swedish, with two critical essays.

13.6 Abenius, Margit. "Emily Dickinson." *Bonniers Litterara Magäsin,* III (Sept. 1934), 18-23. In Swedish.
Reprinted:
Margit Abenius. *Kontakter.* Stockholm: Albert Bonniers, 1944, pp. 93-104.

13.7   Edfelt, Johannes. "Detta Var en Poet." *Strövtåg* (1941), pp. 85-
            93.
            Rev. of Whicher, *This Was a Poet* (5.104).
[5.113]   Lindberg-Seyersted, Brita. *The Voice of the Poet: Aspects of
            Style in the Poetry of Emily Dickinson.* Uppsala, 1968.
13.8   Lindquist, Ebba. "Emily Dickinson efter många år." *Ord och
            Bild* [Stockholm], LV (1946), 581-85.

FINNISH

13.9   Tynni, Aale. *Tuhat Laulujen Vuotta Valikoima Lansimaista
            Lyriikkaa.* Toimittanut ja suomentanut Aale Tynni. Alkutek-
            stein varustettu laitos. Werner Söderström Osakeyhtio, 1957,
            pp. 508-09.
            Prints, in English and Finnish, "'Hope' is the thing with
            feathers" and "My life closed twice before its close."
13.10   Juvonen, Helvi. "Emily Dickinson." *Parnasso* [Helsinki], VII
            (Oct. 1958), 245-49.
            A general introductory essay, in Finnish. Defines some of the
            qualities and themes of ED's poetry, especially attitudes to-
            ward nature and death.

HUNGARIAN

13.11   Tabori, Paul. *Amerika uj Liraja; Antologia A Mai Amerikai
            Koltok Verseibol [New Lyrical Poetry in America; An Anthol-
            ogy of Modern American Poets].* Collected and trans. Paul
            Tabori. Ed. John Vajda Society. Budapest: A. Friedmann,
            1935, pp. 36-37.
            Contains four ED poems.

ROMANIAN

13.11a   Porumbacu, Veronica. "Emily Dickinson." *Gazeta Literară*
            [Bucharest], XI (Jan. 1968), 8.

POLISH

13.12   *Emily Dickinson: Poezje.* Przełożyła [I.] Kazimiera Iłłakowic-
            zówna. Wyd. 1. Warsaw: Państowowy Instytut Wydawniczy
            (Biblioteka poetów), 1965. 164 pp.
13.13   Dyboski, Roman. *Wielcy Pisarze Amerykanscy [Great American
            Writers].* Warsaw: 1958.
13.14   Marjańska, Ludmiła. "Emily Dickinson." *Wspołczesnośč Dwuty-
            godnik Literacki,* IX, No. 163 (April 27, 1964), p. 5.
            Five poems translated into Polish by the author accompany
            this brief introduction to ED's life and work.

13.15   Rakowska, Maria. "Emily Dickinson." *Wiadomości Literackie* [*Literary News*] [Warsaw], Nov. 24, 1929, p. 7.

[6.893a] Schlauch, Margaret. "Linguistic Aspects of Emily Dickinson's Style."

CZECH

13.16   Klášterský, Antonín. *Moderni Poesie Americka*. Prague, 1907. Contains translations of three ED poems; see 6.62.

13.17   Vočadlo, Otakar. *Současná Literatura Spojeníjch Státu* [*Modern Literature in the United States*]. Prague: Jan Laichter, 1934, pp. 45-46.

13.18   Vančura, Zdenek. "Objev Básní Emily Dickinsonové" [The Discovery of Emily Dickinson's Poems]. *Slovesná Veda* [Prague], I (1947-1948), 31-34.

13.19   *Emily Dickinsonová: Jediný Ohař* [*Single Hound*]. Trans. with an epilogue by Jiřina Hauková. In the arrangement of Jaroslav Sváb with a cover and frontispiece by Václav Bartovský. 1st. ed. Prague: Worker's Press, 1948. Illus. 64 pp.

13.20   *Emily Dickinsonová: Záblesky Melodie* [*Bolts of Melody*]. Selected and translated by Jiři Sledr. Illustrated by František Peterka. Series editor: Eva Masnerová. 1st. ed. Prague: Odeon, 1967. 136 pp.

CROATIAN

13.21   Slamnig, Ivan and Antun Soljan. *Americka Lirika*. Zagreb, Yugoslavia, 1952.

RUSSIAN

13.22   *Slýyshu, Poet Amerika*. [*I Hear America Singing*]. Edited by Ivan Kashkin. Moscow, Foreign Literature Publishing House, 1960. An anthology containing five poems by ED in Russian, pp. 40-41.

HEBREW

13.23   Avinoam, Reuben. *A Hebrew Anthology of American Verse*. Tel-Aviv: Om Oved, 1953, pp. 245-55. Ten poems translated into Hebrew.

13.24   Emily Dickinson: *Ošer Azev* [*Riches are Sad*]. Trans. Eliezra Eig. Illustrations by D. Rakia. Calligraphy by A. Yefenof. Tel-Aviv: Eked, 1965. [59] pp. Contains 28 poems in Hebrew only.

YIDDISH

13.25   Steinberg, Noah, ed. *Yiddish America*. N.Y.: Liben, 1929, pp. 199-200.
Four ED poems are translated into Yiddish by Dr. A. Asen.

VIETNAMESE

13.26   Nguyen-Khúc-Nha. "Emily Dickinson and the Renascence of Poetry in the United States." *Van-Hoa Nguyet-San [Culture Monthly Review]*, XIII (1964), 131-35, 294-306.
In Vietnamese.

THESES

14

Theses

This section is divided into two parts, "Doctoral Dissertations" (14.1-39) and "M.A. and B.A. Theses" (14.40-93). Arrangement within each part is chronological, with undated entries placed at the end. A number of doctoral dissertations are listed with annotations by Shelia T. Clendenning in her *ED: A Bibliography* (1.5), pp. 119-22. Summaries of theses appearing in *Dissertation Abstracts* are noted by the abbreviation *DA*, followed by volume and page number. Theses are unpublished except where publication is indicated.

DOCTORAL DISSERTATIONS

[10.52] Elizabeth Granichstaedten-Czerva. "Bildersprache bei Emily Dickinson." Vienna, 1940.

[2.2] Louise Kline Kelly. "A Concordance of Emily Dickinson's Poems." Pennsylvania State College, 1951.

14.1 R. P. Anis Samaan-Hanna. "Spiritual Values in the Poetry of Emily Dickinson." Univ. of Montreal, 1953.

14.2 Lee Biggerstaff Copple. "Three Related Themes of Hunger and Thirst, Homelessness, and Obscurity as Symbols of Privation, Renunciation, and Compensation in the Poems of Emily Dickinson." Univ. of Michigan, 1954. *DA*, XV, 821-22.

14.3 Norman Gregor. "The Luxury of Doubt: A Study of the Relationship Between Imagery and Theme in Emily Dickinson's Poetry." Univ. of New Mexico, 1955. *DA*, XVI, 956.

14.4 Martha Edelsberg Passe. "Criticism of Poetry in America During the Nineties." Ohio State Univ., 1957. *DA*, XVIII, 2147.

14.5 Sister Thomas C. Brennan. "Thomas W. Higginson: Reformer and Man of Letters." Michigan State Univ., 1958. *DA*, XX, 296.

14.6 Mordecai Marcus. "Nature Symbolism in the Poetry of Emily Dickinson." Univ. of Kansas, 1958.

14.7 Thomas W. Ford. "The Theme of Death in the Poetry of Emily

Dickinson." Univ. of Texas, 1959. *DA*, XX, 1786. (Published, see 5.27.)

14.8   Suzanne M. Wilson. "Structure and Imagery Patterns in the Poetry of Emily Dickinson." Univ. of Southern California, 1959. *DA*, XX, 3286-87. (Material from this thesis is incorporated in a published article, see 6.1191.)

14.9   Rowena Revis Jones. "Emily Dickinson's 'Flood Subject': Immortality." Northwestern Univ., 1960. *DA*, XXI, 1554-55.

14.10   Owen Paul Thomas, Jr. "The Very Press of Imagery: A Reading of Emily Dickinson." Univ. of California, Los Angeles, 1960.

14.11   John Stewart Wheatcroft. "Emily Dickinson and the Orthodox Tradition." Rutgers Univ., 1960. *DA*, XXI, 1186-87. (Material from this thesis is incorporated in two published articles, see 6.1112, 6.1113.)

14.12   David J. M. Higgins. "Portrait of Emily Dickinson: The Poet and Her Prose." Columbia Univ., 1961. *DA*, XXII, 246-47. (Published, see 5.34.)

14.13   Thomas Roscoe Arp. "Dramatic Poses in the Poetry of Emily Dickinson." Stanford Univ., 1962. *DA*, XXII, 2130.

14.14   Albert Joseph Gelpi. "The Business of Circumference: The Mind and Art of Emily Dickinson." Harvard Univ., 1962. (Published, see 5.29.)

14.15   Jack Lee Capps. "Emily Dickinson's Reading 1836-1886: A Study of the Sources of Her Poetry." Univ. of Pennsylvania, 1963. *DA*, XXIV, 1611-12. Noted by Robbins, *ALS, 1963* (6.851), p. 128. (Published, see 5.14.)

14.16   William F. Davis. "The Art of Peace: The Moral Vision of Emily Dickinson." Yale Univ., 1963. *DA*, XXIX, 896A.

14.17   Karl Keller. "The Metaphysical Strain in Nineteenth Century American Poetry: Emerson, Thoreau, Melville, and Emily Dickinson." Univ. of Minnesota, 1964.

14.18   David T. Porter. "The Art of Emily Dickinson's Early Poetry." Ph.D. Univ. of Rochester, 1964. *DA*, XXV, 1921. Noted by Robbins, *ALS, 1964* (6.851), pp. 135-36. (Published, see 5.69.)

14.19   William Robert Sherwood. "Circumference and Circumstance: Stages in the Mind and Art of Emily Dickinson." Columbia Univ., 1964. *DA*, XXVI, 2193. Noted by Robbins, *ALS, 1965* (6.851), p. 159. (Published, see 5.79.)

14.20   Sister Peter Marie Anselmo. "Renunciation in the Poems and Letters of Emily Dickinson." Univ. of Notre Dame, 1965. *DA*, XXVI, 2178. Noted by Robbins, *ALS, 1965* (6.851), p. 159.

14.21   Leta Perry Di Salvo. "The Arrested Syllable: A Study of the Death Poetry of Emily Dickinson." Univ. of Denver, 1965. *DA*, XXVII, 1816A. Noted by Robbins, *ALS, 1966* (6.851), p. 144.

14.22   Ralph William Franklin. "Editing Emily Dickinson." Northwestern Univ., 1965. *DA*, XXVI, 3335. Noted by Robbins, *ALS, 1965* (6.851), p. 159. (Published, see 5.28.)

14.23   Ruth Miller Kriesberg. "The Poetry of Emily Dickinson." New York Univ., 1965. *DA*, XXVII, 3872A. (Published, see 5.54.)

14.24 Francis Joseph Molson. "The 'Forms' of God: A Study of Emily
       Dickinson's Search For and Test of God." Univ. of Notre
       Dame, 1965. *DA*, XXVI, 5415-16. Noted by Robbins, *ALS,
       1966* (6.851), p. 144.
14.25 John Emerson Todd. "Emily Dickinson's Use of the Persona."
       Univ. of Wisconsin, 1965. *DA*, XXVI, 3309-10. Noted by Rob-
       bins, *ALS, 1966* (6.851), p. 144.
14.26 Bernhard Frank. "The Wiles of Words: Ambiguity in Emily
       Dickinson's Poetry." Univ. of Pittsburgh, 1966. *DA*, XXVII,
       1784A. Noted by Robbins, *ALS, 1966* (6.851), p. 144.
14.27 Robert Leland Lair. "Emily Dickinson's Fracture of Grammar."
       Ohio State Univ., 1966. *DA*, XXVII, 3052A-53A.
14.28 Margaret Vance Means McIntosh. "Emily Dickinson's Poems
       About Pain; A Study of Interrelated Moral, Theological and
       Linguistic Freedoms." Harvard Univ., 1966.
14.29 Cynthia Chaliff. "Emily Dickinson Against the World: An Inter-
       pretation of the Poet's Life and Work." New York Univ., 1967.
       DA, XXVIII, 1070A.
14.30 Robert Greene Flick. "Emily Dickinson: Mystic and Sceptic."
       Univ. of Florida, 1967. *DA*, XXIX, 227A-28A.
14.31 Ana María Fagundo Guerra. "The Influence of Emily Dickinson
       on Juan Ramón Jiménez' Poetry." Univ. of Washington, 1967.
       DA, XXIX, 258A-59A.
14.32 Emma J. Phillips. "The Mystical World View of Emily Dickin-
       son." Indiana Univ., 1967. *DA*, XXVIII, 2259A.
14.33 Edith Perry Stamm Wylder. "The Voice of the Poet: Selected
       Poems of Emily Dickinson with an Introduction to the Rhetor-
       ical Punctuation of the Manuscripts." Univ. of New Mexico,
       1967. *DA*, XXVIII, 4194A. (Material from this thesis is in-
       corporated in a published article, see 6.948.)
14.34 Mary Cynthia DeJong. "Structure in the Poetry of Ralph Waldo
       Emerson, Emily Dickinson, and Robert Frost." Univ. of
       Michigan, 1968. *DA*, XXIX, 867A.
14.35 Andrea Kay Goudie. "'The Earth Has Many Keys': A Study of
       Emily Dickinson's Response to Nature." Indiana Univ., 1968.
14.36 Robert Graham Lambert, Jr. "The Prose of a Poet: A Critical
       Study of Emily Dickinson's Letters." Univ. of Pittsburgh,
       1968. *DA*, XXIX, 1228A.
[10.42] Brigitte Berlet. "Die Bildersprache Emily Dickinsons." Frank-
       fort on Main, n.d.
14.37 Sister M. Jeremias Hall. "An Analysis of the Relationship of
       Love and Death in the Poetry of Emily Dickinson." Loyola
       Univ. [Chicago], in preparation, 1968.
14.38 James Hughes. "The Dialectic of Death: Transcendentalism and
       Death in Emerson, Poe, Dickinson, and Whitman." Univ. of
       Pennsylvania, in preparation, 1968.
14.39 Paula Putney. "Emily Dickinson's Theory of Poetry." Univ. of
       Missouri, n.d.

M.A. AND B.A. THESES

14.40   Helen Agnew Andrews. "The Poetry of Emily Dickinson." M.A.,
         Indiana Univ., 1911.
14.41   Paula Violet Cohn. "Emily Dickinson: A Study." M.A., Colum-
         bia Univ., 1918.
14.42   Isaranda F. Sanborn. "Emily Dickinson: An Interpretation of
         Her Mind." M.A., Columbia Univ., 1922.
14.43   Sara Saper Gauldin. "Emily Dickinson: A Study of the Common-
         place in Verse." M.A., Univ. of Missouri, 1925.
14.44   Josephine Pollitt. "New Light on Emily Dickinson." M.A., Co-
         lumbia Univ., 1925. (See also the author's *Emily Dickinson:
         The Human Background of Her Poetry,* 5.61.)
14.45   Anna Mary Wells. "Emily Dickinson." M.A., Southern Methodist
         Univ., 1927.
14.46   Julia Chaine. "The Poetry of Emily Dickinson." M.A., Columbia
         Univ., 1928.
[1.5]   Margaret Frances Parmalee. "Emily Dickinson: A Reading List
         of Books and Periodicals on Her Life and Poetry." M.A.,
         Univ. of Michigan, 1928.
14.47   Annie Laurie Robey. "Emily Dickinson: A Forerunner of Mod-
         ern American Poetry." M.A., Univ. of Oklahoma, 1928.
[24.7]   Palfrey Perkins. "Emily Dickinson, the Unique Poet." 1930.
14.48   Helen R. Adams. "The Prosody of Emily Dickinson." M.A.,
         Univ. of Pennsylvania, 1932.
[17.32] Elva E. Knight. "Bulletins from Immortality." Elmira College,
         1932.
14.49   Mary Baker. "Emily Dickinson's Knowledge of the Classical and
         European Philosophers and Their Influence on Her Prose and
         Poetry." M.S., Massachusetts State College [Amherst], 1933.
14.50   Jessie Estelle Canan. "The Religion of Emily Dickinson." M.A.,
         Univ. of Pittsburgh, 1933. Abstract: *University of Pittsburgh
         Bulletin,* XXX (Nov. 15, 1933), 496.
14.51   Sydney R. McLean. "Emily Dickinson's Year at Mount Holyoke."
         M.A., Mt. Holyoke College, 1933. (See also the author's arti-
         cle, "Emily Dickinson at Mt. Holyoke," 6.687.)
14.52   Harrison L. Reinke. "The Literary Criticism of Thomas Went-
         worth Higginson." M.A., Lincoln Univ., 1933. (Contains a
         chapter entitled "Emily Dickinson and T. W. Higginson," pp.
         55-60.)
14.53   Julia Frantz Shutts. "The Spirit of Childhood in the Poetry of
         Emily Dickinson." M.A., Univ. of Pittsburgh, 1933. Abstract:
         University of Pittsburgh Bulletin, XXX (Nov. 15, 1933), 501-02.
[24.8]   Nancy E. Russell. "The Domestic Life of Emily Dickinson."
         1934.
14.54   Elizabeth L. Reinke. "Puritan and Transcendental Influence on
         Emily Dickinson's Philosophy." M.A., Columbia Univ., 1935.
14.55   Sister Mary Irmina Shay. "Emily Dickinson's Prose: A Study of
         Her Letters." M.A., Boston College, 1935.
14.56   Margery McKay Cridland. "'Amazing Sense,' The Application of
         a New Method to the Poetry of Emily Dickinson." Honors

Thesis, Swarthmore College, 1936. (George Whicher comments on this thesis in *This Was a Poet* [5.104], pp. 211, 328.)

14.57   Iva Louise Handy. "Emily Dickinson: A Study of Her Kinship With Childhood, With Nature and With God." M.A., Cornell Univ., 1938.

14.58   Thomas Dillon Howells. "Images and Symbols in the Poetry of Emily Dickinson." M.A., Univ. of Chicago, 1938.

14.59   Katherine Kenyon Stewart. "French Criticism of Four American Poets: Poe, Whitman, Dickinson, Robinson." M.A., Univ. of Kansas, 1938.

14.60   Mary Ann Evans. "A History of Emily Dickinson Criticism (1890-1937)." M.A., Vanderbilt Univ., 1939.

14.61   Violet-Marie Krohn. "Emily Dickinson's Literary Background as Indicated in Her Letters: Emphasizing Her Relationship to Her Favorite Authors." M.A., Univ. of Chicago, 1940.

14.62   Addie Coffman. "Emily Dickinson's Verse Forms and Techniques." M.A., Univ. of Wyoming, 1942.

14.63   Ruth Harris. "Emily Dickinson, A Forerunner of Imagism." M.A., Boston Univ., 1944.

14.64   Anna Pederson. "The Romanticism of Emily Dickinson." M.A., Univ. of Minnesota, 1944.

14.65   Inez Elizabeth Crenshaw. "A Comparative Study of the Use of Imagery in the Works of Robert Frost and Emily Dickinson." M.A.(?), Univ. of Wisconsin, 1945.

[17.35]   Betty Lord. "A Study of the Life and Writings of Emily Dickinson in Preparation for a Dramatization of Her Life." M.A., Smith College, 1946.

14.66   Mary Charlotte Halpin. "The Metaphysics in Emily Dickinson's Poetry." M.A., Boston Univ., 1947.

14.67   Sister Rosaria Hogan. "An Evaluation of Emily Dickinson's Newly Discovered Poems." M.A., Boston College, 1948.

[1.15]   Russell St. Clair Smith. "A Dickinson Bibliography." M.A., Brown Univ., 1948.

14.68   Mary Rose Sweeney. "The Imagery of Emily Dickinson's Poetry." M.A., Univ. of Missouri, 1948.

14.69   Clare Louise McGowan. "The Question of Mysticism in the Poetry of Emily Dickinson." M.A., Boston College, 1950.

14.70   Vernon L. Ingraham. "Emily Dickinson — An Early Application of Modern Problems." M.A., Amherst College, 1951.

14.71   Thomas P. Roche, Jr. "Nature, Wit, and Emily Dickinson." Honors Thesis, Yale Univ., 1953.

14.72   Mary Louise Smith. "The Bible and Emily Dickinson: A Study in Indebtedness Conscious and Unconscious." M.A., Pennsylvania State Univ., 1954.

14.73   Charles Mitchell Watson. "Nature in the Poetry of Emily Dickinson." M.S., Indiana State Teacher's College [Terre Haute], 1955.

14.74   Sister Helen Miriam Cullen. "Color Imagery in the Poems of Emily Dickinson." M.A., Boston College, 1960.

14.75   Robert L. Gonsor. "Nature, Science and Emily Dickinson." M.A., Univ. of Massachusetts, 1961.

14.76   James Michos Hughes. "Death in the Poetry of Emily Dickinson." Honors Thesis, Harvard College, 1961. See also 14.38.

14.77   Jessie Alice Veach. "The Central Flint: A Consideration of Edward Dickinson as the Crucial Influence in the Development of the Poet, Emily Dickinson." M.A., Southern Illinois Univ., 1961.

14.78   Thomas E. Wood. "The Charms of Emily Dickinson." Honors Thesis, Amherst College, 1961.

14.79   Emily Louise Herring. "Domestic Imagery in the Poetry of Emily Dickinson." M.A., Wake Forest College, 1962. (Published on microcards, see 5.33.)

14.80   Sister Mary Michelle Reney. "Transcendentalism in Emily Dickinson's Poetry." M.A., Boston College, 1962.

14.81   Hilary Smith. "Emily Dickinson's Use of Precious Stone Imagery." M.A., Catholic Univ. of America, 1962.

14.82   Sister Alice Brennan. "The Influence of Sir Thomas Browne on Emily Dickinson." M.A., Boston College, 1963.

14.83   Louise B. Robeck. "The Poetry of Dickinson and Robinson." M.A., Pennsylvania State Univ., 1963.

14.84   Sister Helen Thomasina Sheehan. "Emily Dickinson, the Non-conventionalist, as Revealed in Her Legal Images." M.A., Boston College, 1964.

14.85   Lawrence A. Baldassaro. "Emily Dickinson and the Symbolist Tradition in Literature." Honors Thesis, Union College, 1965.

14.86   Philip L. Prim. "Animal Symbolism in Book One of the *Fairie Queen*, an Explication of Swinburne's 'Hertha,' and the Nature Poetry of Emily Dickinson." M.A., Pennsylvania State Univ., 1965.

14.87   Mahlon Conover Gaumer. "The Relevance of Dickinson Criticism." Honors Thesis, Arizona State Univ., 1965.

14.88   Cynthia Anne Craig. "Three Critical Studies in Poetry." M.A., Pennsylvania State Univ., 1966. (One study concerns death in the poetry of ED.)

14.89   Walter B. Kasell. "Emily Dickinson: Poetry in a Neutral Universe." Honors Thesis, Amherst College, 1966.

14.90   Hugh P. McGrath. "Convex and Concave Witness — The Confessional Stance of Emily Dickinson." Honors Thesis, Amherst College, 1966.

14.91   Frederick L. Morey. "The Tragic Implications of Emily Dickinson's Poetry." M.A., Univ. of Maryland, 1966.

14.92   Gerald Lane Dorgan. "Biblical Imagery in the Poetry of Emily Dickinson: The Revelation of St. John the Divine." M.A., Boston College, 1967.

14.93   Marian McConnell Wolk. "The Literary Background of Emily Dickinson As Seen Through Allusions and Comments in Her Letters and Poems." B.A., Westminster College, n.d.

JUVENILE LITERATURE

Books and Articles about
Emily Dickinson for Young People

15.1   Allen, Caroline C. "The Homestead in Amherst." *Horn Book,*
        XXXIII (Feb. 1957), 30-34.
        Recollections of the Dickinson family.
15.2   Auslander, Joseph, and Frank Ernest Hill. *The Winged Horse,*
        The Story of the Poets and Their Poetry. Garden City, N.Y.:
        Doubleday, Page, 1927. Reissued 1954.
        An introduction to ED, pp. 402-05.
15.3   Benét, Laura. "Emily Dickinson: A Poet Who Was Herself," in
        Famous American Poets. N.Y.: Dodd, 1950, pp. 75-80.
        A brief biography.
15.4   Classic Comics. "'The Railway Train' by Emily Dickinson."
        Classic Comics, No. 14. N.Y., [1946], 2 unnumbered pages.
        An illustrated reprinting of "I like to see it lap the miles."
15.5   Degnan, Marion Ruth. "Emily Dickinson." *Scholastic,* XVIII
        (May 2, 1931), 29.
        A prize grade school essay.
15.6   Emerson, Dorothy. "Emily Dickinson at Home." *Scholastic,*
        XXXIV (May 20, 1939), 25-E.
15.7   Fisher, Aileen, and Olive Rabe. *We Dickinsons, The Life of Em-*
        ily Dickinson as Seen Through the Eyes of Her Brother Austin.
        Decorations by Ellen Raskin. N.Y.: Atheneum; Toronto: Mc-
        Clelland & Stewart, 1965. 246 pp.
        A fictional biography for girls ages twelve to sixteen. Miss
        Fisher and Mrs. Rabe also wrote a four-page promotional
        leaflet for *We Dickinsons.* Entitled "A Poet Ahead of Her
        Time," it was published in 1965 by Atheneum.
        Reviewed:
15.8   Eaton, A. T. *Commonweal,* LXXXIII (Nov. 5, 1965), 160.
15.9   H., E. L. *Horn Book,* XLI (Dec. 1965), 642.
15.10   Jackson, Charlotte. *Atlantic Monthly,* CCXVI (Dec. 1965), 158.
15.11   Leavitt, H. D. *New York Herald Tribune Book Week,* Oct. 31,
        1965, p. 30.
15.12   Oppenheim, Shulamith. *New York Times Book Review,* Jan. 16,
        1966, p. 36.

15.13　　　Sheehan, Ethna. *America*, CXIII (Nov. 20, 1965), 646.
[3.216]　Godden, Rumer, ed. *Emily Dickinson: Letter to the World.*
15.14　　　Gould, Jean Rosalind. *Miss Emily.* Illustrated by Ursula Koering. Boston: Houghton, Mifflin, 1946. 220 pp. Published at $2.50.
　　　　　　A fictional biography.
　　　　　Reviewed:
15.15　　　Becker, M. L. *New York Herald Tribune Weekly Book Review,* May 12, 1946, p. 6.
15.16　　　Deutsch, Babette. *New York Times Book Review,* April 28, 1946, p. 32.
15.17　　　Griswold, Harriet Ford. *Christian Science Monitor,* April 13, 1946, p. 11.
15.18　　　H., R. F. *Springfield Republican,* April 27, 1946, p. 6.
15.19　　　Hill, Ruth A. *Saturday Review,* XXIX (Sept. 28, 1946), 42-43.
15.20　　　Jordan, Alice M. *Horn Book.* XXII (May-June 1946), 211-12.

[3.159]　Hampson, Alfred Leete, ed. *Poems For Youth.*
[6.532]　Hyde, Marietta, ed. *Modern Biography.*
15.20a　　Leipold, L. Edmond. "Emily Dickinson" in *Famous American Women.* Minneapolis: T. S. Denison, 1967, pp. 47-52.
15.21　　　Longsworth, Polly. *Emily Dickinson, Her Letter to the World.* N.Y.: Crowell; Toronto: Ambassador, 1965. 169 pp.
　　　　　　A biography for young people.
　　　　　Reviewed:
15.22　　　Anon. *New York Herald Tribune Book Week,* May 9, 1965, Spring Children's Issue, pp. 6, 29.
15.23　　　Balakian, Nona. *New York Times Book Review,* May 9, 1965, Children's Book Section, p. 8.
15.24　　　Bellows, Silence Buck. *Christian Science Monitor,* May 6, 1965, p. 4-B.
15.25　　　H., E. L. *Horn Book,* XLI (Aug. 1965), 397.
15.26　　　Maxwell, Emily. *New Yorker,* XLI (Dec. 4, 1965), p. 246.

15.27　　　Muir, Jane. *Famous Modern American Women Writers.* N.Y.: Dodd, Mead, 1959, pp. 17-26.
15.28　　　Perkinson, Grace E. "Emily Dickinson and Children." *Horn Book,* XXXIII (Feb. 1957), 19-27.
　　　　　　Discusses the appeal of ED's poetry to small children.
[3.210]　Plotz, Helen, ed. *Poems of Emily Dickinson.*
15.29　　　Scherman, David Edward, and Rosemarie Redlich. *America: The Land and Its Writers.* N.Y.: Dodd, Mead, 1956, pp. 53-54.
[6.917]　Shaw, John MacKay. *Childhood in Poetry.*
15.30　　　Simon, Charlie May. *Lays of the New Land.* N.Y.: Dutton, 1943.
　　　　　　A biographical sketch of ED, pp. 109-17.
15.31　　　Sweetser, Kate Dickinson. "Emily Dickinson, A Girl of Genius" in *Great American Girls.* N.Y.: Dodd, Mead, 1931, pp. 103-36.
　　　　　　A general introduction and appreciation. Contains the first printing of an 1874 letter to Mrs. Joseph A. Sweetser.
15.32　　　Untermeyer, Louis. "Emily Dickinson" in *Makers of the Modern World....* N.Y.: Simon & Schuster, 1955, pp. 132-38.
　　　　　　A brief biographical and critical introduction.
15.33　　　————. *Paths of Poetry: Twenty-Five Poets and Their Poems.* N.Y.: Delacorte Press, 1966, pp. 205-12.

CREATIVE TRIBUTES

16.

Fiction Based on
Emily Dickinson's Life

16.1   Benét, Laura. *Come Slowly Eden: A Novel About Emily Dickinson.* N.Y.: Dodd, Mead, 1942. 272 pp.
        Reviewed:

16.2   Feld, Rose. *New York Times Book Review,* Sept. 20, 1942, p. 6.
16.3   Jakeman, Adelbert M. *Springfield Republican,* Nov. 8, 1942, p. 7-E.
16.4   Oehser, Paul H. *Washington Post,* Oct. 11, 1942.
16.5   Ross, Mary. *New York Herald Tribune Books,* Sept. 13, 1942, p. 10.
16.6   Whicher, George F. *Atlantic Monthly,* CLXX (Nov. 1942), 138.

[15.7]   Fisher, Aileen, and Olive Rabe. *We Dickinsons....*
[6.309a] Higginson, Thomas Wentworth. That some of Higginson's fiction and one of his poems draw on the life of ED is suggested by Tilden G. Edelstein in *Strange Enthusiasm* (6.309a), pp. 308, 313, 345.

16.7   [Jackson, Helen Hunt]. "Esther Wynn's Love-Letters" by Saxe Holm [pseud.]. *Scribner's Monthly,* III (Dec. 1871), 164-76.
        Reprinted:
        Saxe Holm's Stories. First Series. N.Y.: Scribner, Armstrong, 1874.
        The situation between Esther Wynn and her lover and the discovery of hidden love letters suggest that this story was modeled after ED. See Whicher, *This Was a Poet* (5.104), pp. 124-27; Higgins, *Portrait* (5.34), pp. 171-75; Leyda, *Years and Hours* (5.49), II, 239, 295-96, 297, 472; Miller, *Poetry of ED* (5.54), pp. 18-19, and Lubbers, *Critical Revolution* (5.114), p. 223.

16.8   [———]. *Mercy Philbrick's Choice. No Name Series.* Boston: Roberts Brothers, 1876.
        ED may have provided the inspiration for Mercy Philbrick; see Whicher, *This Was a Poet* (5.104), pp. 127-133, Miller, *Poetry of ED* (5.54), pp. 18-19, and Lubbers, *Revolution* (5.114), p. 223.

16.9   Jenkins, MacGregor. *Emily*. Indianapolis: Bobbs-Merrill, 1930.
          296 pp.
          Reviewed:
16.10   Anon. *Boston Transcript*, Aug. 13, 1930, p. 2.
16.11   Anon. *Nation*, CXXXI (Oct. 22, 1930), 450.
16.12   Anon. *New York Times Book Review*, Sept. 28, 1930, p. 24.
16.13   Ellis, [Harold] Milton. *Portland* [Maine] *Evening News*, Nov. 22,
          1930, p. 5.
16.14   F., F. S. *Springfield Sunday Union and Republican*, Oct. 5, 1930,
          p. 7-E.
16.15   Gilman, Dorothy Foster. *New York Herald Tribune Books*, Sept.
          21, 1930, p. 18.
16.16   S., J. F. *Boston Evening Transcript*, Oct. 4, 1930, Book Section,
          p. 1.
16.17   Untermeyer, Louis B. *Saturday Review*, VII (Dec. 6, 1930), 424.

17.

Drama Based on
Emily Dickinson's Life

17.1   Anon. "Noel Coward Considering a Musical Based on the Life of Emily Dickinson." *New York Times*, July 20, 1958, Section 2, p. 11.

17.2   Beals, Julia. "Past Midnight, Past the Morning Star." ED poems, letters, and memorabilia adapted for the stage and performed by Julia Beals.
Reviewed:

17.3   Anon. *New York Times*, Nov. 30, 1966, p. 58.

17.4   Broner, Esther. "Colonel Thomas Wentworth Higginson." Music by Morton Zieve. A musical based on the life of Higginson in which ED is one of the important characters. Presented at a meeting of the Michigan Academy of Science, Arts, and Letters, Wayne State Univ., Detroit, April 10, 1968. Unpublished. See also 6.1159a.

17.5   Gardner, Dorothy. *Eastward in Eden: The Love Story of Emily Dickinson.* N.Y. and Toronto: Longmans, 1949.
Reprinted:
The Burns Mantle Best Plays of 1947-1948, ed. John Chapman. N.Y.: Dodd, Mead, 1948, pp. 237-63.
Produced in Boston and New York, 1947-48. Beatrice Straight played the part of ED. Also performed as an opera; see 17.12.
Reviewed:

17.6   Anon. *Christian Science Monitor*, Nov. 5, 1947, p. 5.

17.7   Brooks Atkinson. *New York Times*, Nov. 20, 1947, p. 39.

17.8   Otis L. Guernsey, Jr. *New York Herald Tribune*, Nov. 20, 1947, p. 23.

17.9   Joseph Wood Krutch. *Nation*, CLXV (Dec. 6, 1947), 628-29.

17.10   George F. Whicher. *Amherst Journal*, Dec. 12, 1947, p. 4.

17.11   Walter Pritchard Eaton. *New York Herald Tribune Weekly Book Review*, Aug. 14, 1949, p. 12.

17.12   Dorothy Gardner. *New York Times*, May 23, 1954, Section 2, p. 7.

Dorothy Gardner writes of the circumstances behind her adaptation of "Eastward in Eden" for opera with music by Jan Meyerowitz. Performed at Hunter College and reviewed by Olin Downes, *New York Times*, May 27, 1954, p. 35.

17.13 Arthur Gelb. "Eastward in Eden is Revived in Village," *New York Times*, April 18, 1956, p. 24.

17.14 Glaspell, Susan. *Alison's House*. N.Y.: Samuel French, 1930.
Reprinted:
Six Plays. London: Gollancz, 1930, pp. 579-672.
Produced in New York and Boston, 1930 and 1931. Received the Pulitzer Prize in 1931.
Reviewed:

17.15 Anon. *New York Herald Tribune*, Nov. 30, 1930, Section 8, p. 1.
17.16 John Mason Brown. *New York Evening Post*, Dec. 2, 1930, p. 12.
17.17 Brooks Atkinson. *New York Times*, Dec. 3, 1930, p. 29.
17.18 Robert Littell. *New York World*, Dec. 3, 1930, p. 11.
17.19 Arthur Ruhl. *New York Herald Tribune*, Dec. 3, 1930, p. 18.
17.20 Robert Garland. *New York Telegram*, Dec. 4, 1930, p. 18.
17.21 E. C. S. *Christian Science Monitor*, Dec. 6, 1930, p. 10.
17.22 Anon. "An Impression of 'Alison's House.'" (Drawing.) *New York Times*, Dec. 7, 1930, Section 9, p. 1.
17.23 Anon. *Time*, XVI (Dec. 15, 1930), 22.
17.24 Harry Hansen. *New York World*, Dec. 23, 1930, p. 9.
17.25 Otis Chatfield-Taylor. *Outlook and Independent*, CLVI (Dec. 31, 1930), 711.
17.26 Harry Hansen. "Among the New Books." *Harper's Magazine*, CLXII (Feb. 1931), among front advertising pages.
17.27 Brooks Atkinson. "Pulitzer Laurels." *New York Times*, May 10, 1931, Section 8, p. 1.
17.28 Katharine Lyons. "Prize Play to Open Here Monday." *Boston Traveller*, Oct. 24, 1931.
17.29 James G. Peede. *Boston Herald*, Oct. 25, 1931, p. 2-D.
17 30 T. H. P. *Boston Evening Transcript*, Oct. 27, 1931.
[6.85] May Lamberton Becker. "The Reader's Guide." *New York Herald Tribune Book Week*, X, No. 8 (Oct. 29, 1933), p. 25.

17.31 Johnson, Lockrem. "A Letter to Emily." A Chamber Opera in One Act and Two Scenes. Music by Lockrem Johnson, Op. 37. Libretto adapted by the composer from the play, *Consider the Lilies*, by Robert Hupton. Typescript. 16 leaves. Performed in 1955.
Concerns T. W. Higginson's first visit to ED. Copy in Jones Library, Amherst. Unpublished.

17.32 Knight, Elva E. "Bulletins from Immortality." Based on the Life and Legends of Emily Dickinson. Three brief acts and an epilogue. Produced as an Elmira College Workshop play, Mar. 19, 1932. Unpublished.
Copy of a typed manuscript in Jones Library, Amherst, and Amherst College Library.
Reviewed:

17.33 Anon. *Springfield Sunday Union and Republican*. April 17, 1932, pp. 2-E, 3-E.

17.34   Leaf, Margaret. "Adventures in Reading." Dramatized epi-
         sodes from the life of Emily Dickinson. Script by Margaret
         Leaf in collaboration with Helen Walpole. June Walker in
         the leading role. Recorded in 1940 by Audio-Scriptions, Inc.,
         1619 Broadway, New York, N.Y. Four records, 78 r.p.m.
         Broadcast over Radio Station WJZ on the Blue Network be-
         tween 2:00 and 2:30 p.m., Aug. 12, 1940.

17.35   Lord, Betty. "A Study of the Life and Writings of Emily Dick-
         inson in Preparation for a Dramatization of Her Life." Un-
         published M.A. Thesis, Smith College. Northampton, Mass.,
         1946. Copy in Jones Library, Amherst.

17.36   MacLeish, Archibald, and Ezra Laderman. "Magic Prison." A
         dialogue for music with two narrators and orchestra. Mate-
         rials for the text gathered from the poems and letters of
         Emily Dickinson and the recollections of T. W. Higginson by
         Archibald MacLeish. Music written by Ezra Laderman. ED
         played by Anne Draper; T. W. Higginson by E. G. Marshall.
         Performed at Lincoln Center, New York City, June 12, 1967.
         André Kostelanetz commissioned the work and directed the
         New York Philharmonic Orchestra for this performance.
         Text printed in *Saturday Review*, L (Oct. 28, 1967), 21-23.
         Introduction to the text by Mr. MacLeish, p. 21.
         Reviewed:

17.37   *New York Times*, June 13, 1967, p. 56.
17.38   Rosten, Norman. "Come Slowly, Eden; A Portrait of Emily
         Dickinson." *Nassau Review*, I (Spring 1966), 1-87.
         Reprinted:
         N.Y.: Dramatists Play Service, 1967. 61 pp.
         A play in two parts. "Two performances as parts of ANTA's
         Matinee Theatre Series presented at Theatre De Lys, New
         York City, Dec. 6, 1966. The play was first produced by the
         Theatre Workshop of Nassau College, May 3-15, 1966; see
         22.26.
         Reviewed:

17.39   Dan Sullivan. *New York Times*, Dec. 7, 1966, p. 56.
17.40   Tracy, Lorna. "Noon and Paradise." A dramatic reading by
         Lorna Tracy. Presented at the Theatre of the Riverside
         Church, New York City, May 9, 1965.
         A copy of the program is in the Jones Library, Amherst.

[6.1159a] White, William. "Emily on the Stage."
17.41   York, Vincent, and Frederick Pohl. *Brittle Heaven.* A Drama
         in Three Acts. N.Y.: Samuel French, 1935. 149 pp. Copy-
         right 1932, under the title *Stardust and Thistledown.* Pro-
         duced in New York City in 1934 with Dorothy Gish as ED.
         The play is based on Josephine Pollitt's *Human Background*
         (5.61).
         Reviewed:

17.42   Anon. *New York Times*, Aug. 20, 1933, Section 9, p. 1.
17.43   Anon. *Boston Herald*, Sept. 10, 1933, p. 32.
17.44   Anon. *Boston Globe*, Sept. 12, 1933, p. 22.

17.45   Frank Prentice Rand. *Amherst Record*, Sept. 20, 1933, p. 4.
17.46   Robert Garland. *New York World-Telegram*, Nov. 8, 1934, p. 30;
          Nov. 14, 1934, p. 26; Nov. 19, 1934, p. 14.
17.47   Anon. *New York Times*, Nov. 11, 1934, Section 10, p. 1.
17.48   John Mason Brown. *New York Post*, Nov. 14, 1934, p. 13.
17.49   John Whitney. *Newark* [N.J.] *Evening News*, Nov. 14, 1934.
17.50   Anon. *News-Week* [Dayton, Ohio], IV (Nov. 17, 1934), 26-27.
17.51   Anon. *Literary Digest*, CXVIII (Nov. 24, 1934), 20.
17.52   Anon. *New Mexico Lobo*, XLI (May 6, 1939), 1.

Poetry about Emily Dickinson

(An anthology of 45 contemporary poems in tribute to Emily Dickinson, entitled *Emily Dickinson: Letters from the World,* collected by Marguerite Harris, is scheduled for distribution by Corinth Books [N.Y.] in 1970.)

18.1   Adelman, Joseph. "Emily Dickinson" in *Poetic Portraits.* Los Angeles: Welzel Pub. Co., 1934, p. 65.

18.2   Adler, Frederick Herbert. "Thoughts While Reading Emily Dickinson." *The Rectangle* [Sigma Tau Delta, Univ. of Minn.], II (May 1926), 14.

18.3   Aldis, Dorothy. "Emily Dickinson." *Poetry,* XXXVI (Aug. 1930), 238.
This poem was expanded and revised for inclusion in the author's volume, *Any Spring* (N.Y.: Minton, Balch & Co., 1933), p. 6.

18.4   Allen, Fred Raphael. "Emily Dickinson — Her Poems" in *In Sonnet Wise.* Boston: Gorham Press, 1911, p. 35.

18.5   Angoff, Charles. "Emily Dickinson Advises Her Biographers." *American Mercury,* LXI (Sept. 1945), 352.

18.6   Anon. "Pen-Drift (Opus 943 — by tf)." *Brattleboro Reformer,* Dec. 11, 1930.

18.7   ———. "Zeno," "Ivory Tower." [Poems on a clipping in the Jones Library, Amherst.]

18.8   Asquith, Doris. "Emily Dickinson's Grave." *Amherst Record,* Nov. 10, 1937.

18.9   Auslander, Joseph. "Letter to Emily Dickinson." *Palms* [Guadalajara, Mex.], VI (Feb.-Mar. 1929), i-viii.
Reprinted:
Joseph Auslander. *Letters to Women.* N.Y.: Harper, 1929, pp. 37-48.
Prize Poems, 1913-1929, ed. Charles A. Wagner. N.Y.: Boni, 1930, pp. 226-35.
For comment on this poem, see 6.91.

18.10   Austin, Ethel. "Emily Dickinson." *Hartford Courant*, April 28,
        1935, Part 2, p. 2-A.
18.11   Baker, Phyllis. "Emily Dickinson." *Yankee*, XXIV (Feb. 1960),
        96.
18.12   Barr, Isabel Harriss. "Wreath for Emily Dickinson." *New York
        Tribune*, Aug. 20, 1933, Section 2, p. 6.
        Reprinted as part "I" of a two-poem tribute entitled "Wreath
        for Emily Dickinson" in Isabel Harriss Barr, *Sword Against
        the Breast* (N.Y.: Putnam's, 1935), p. 27. Although the second
        poem, subtitled "II" in *Sword Against the Breast*, p. 28, is
        cited by Charles R. Green (see 1.17) under the title "For Em-
        ily Dickinson" as published in the *New York Herald Tribune*
        for Mar. 16, 1935, I was unable to locate it in the newspaper
        for that date.
18.13   Benét, William Rose. "Firefly Serenade." *New York Herald
        Tribune*, Nov. 20, 1933, p. 13.
        Reprinted:
        William Rose Benét. *Starry Harness*. N.Y.: Duffield & Green,
        1933, pp. 90-91.
        This poem is addressed to Christina Rossetti, ED, and Elinor
        Wylie.
18.14   Bergquist, Catharine. "To Emily Dickinson." *Poetry World and
        Contemporary Vision*, III (Mar. 1932), 6.
18.15   Bianchi, Martha Dickinson. "Beneath the Hills" in *Within the
        Hedge*. N.Y.: Doubleday & McClure, 1899, pp. 119-27.
18.16   Bidgood, Mary Emmeline. "For Emily Dickinson." *Wings* [Lit-
        erary Guild of America], IV (Summer 1927), 10.
        I was unable to locate this poem in the first four volumes of
        Wings, dated 1927-1930. The citation is from Smith, "A Dick-
        inson Bibliography" (1.15).
18.17   Blair, Edward Williams. "To Emily Dickinson" in *The Second
        Angle*. New Haven, Conn., 1953, p. 12.
18.18   Blanchard, Edith Richmond. "Love Poems of Emily Dickinson."
        Providence Journal, Oct. 30, 1929, p. 13.
18.19   Bowen, Margaret Barber. "Emily Dickinson ('When She Took Up
        Her Simple Wardrobe and Started for the Sun')" in *Singing
        Places*. Boston: Cornhill, 1919, p. 19.
18.20   [Bowen], M[ary]. "To Emily Dickinson." *The Unit* [Grinnell Col-
        lege, Iowa], V (Oct. 29, 1892), 53.
        Reprinted:
        *Under the Scarlet and Black: Poems Selected from the Under-
        graduate Publications of Iowa College*, ed. Hervey S. Mc-
        Cowan and Frank F. Everest. Grinnell, Iowa: Herald Pub-
        lishing Co., 1893, p. 27.
        Dial, XV (July 16, 1893), 43.
18.21   Brady, Eunice. "Emily Dickinson." *Forum* [N.Y.], XCIV (Aug.
        1935), 125.
18.22   Brinnin, John Malcolm. "A Visiting Card for Emily" in *New
        Michigan Verse*, ed. Carl Edwin Burkland. Ann Arbor: Univ.
        of Michigan Press, 1940, p. 98. The poem is dated "Amherst,
        1938."

Reprinted:
Accent, I (Winter 1941), 96-97.
John Malcolm Brinnin. *The Garden Is Political.* N.Y.: Macmillan, 1942, pp. 70-71.

18.23   Buchman, Marion. "Epitaph for Emily Dickinson" in *A Voice in Ramah.* N.Y.: Bookman Associates, 1959, p. 67.

18.24   Burch, Claire. "Poem by Emily Dickinson." *Providence Sunday Journal,* July 24, 1949, Section 6, p. 8.
Reprinted:
Poetry, LXXIV (July 1949), 205.

18.25   Cane, Melville. "Dickinsons and Todds." *Saturday Review,* XXVIII (June 9, 1945), 48.
Reprinted:
Melville Cane. *A Wider Arc.* N.Y.: Harcourt, Brace, 1947, p. 132.
Melville Cane. *So That It Flower.* N.Y.: Harcourt, Brace, 1966, p. 150.
A poem occasioned by the publication of *Ancestors' Brocades* (5.5). For a reply in verse, see 18.105.

18.26   ———. "Emily Dickinson." *Literary Digest,* CVIII (Jan 3, 1931), 18.
Reprinted:
Melville Cane. *Poems New and Selected.* N.Y.: Harcourt, 1938, p. 10.
Poems for Modern Youth, ed. Adolph Gillis and William Rose Benét. Boston: Houghton, Mifflin, 1938.
Melville Cane. *A Wider Arc.* N.Y.: Harcourt, Brace, 1947, p. 131.
Melville Cane. *So That It Flower.* N.Y.: Harcourt, Brace, 1966, p. 149.

18.27   Capetanakis, Demetrios. "Emily Dickinson." *Portfolio: An Intercontinental Quarterly* [Washington, D.C.], The Black Sun Press, I (Summer 1945), p. [12].
Reprinted:
Demetrios Capetanakis. *The Shores of Darkness; Poems and Essays.* N.Y.: Devin-Adair, 1949, p. 25.

18.28   [Chalmers, Roberta Swartz]. "Emily Dickinson. One Hundred Years Old." *Mt. Holyoke Alumnae Quarterly,* XIV (Jan. 1931), 244-45.

18.29   Christman, W[illiam] W[eaver]. "The Hidden Heart." *Bozart and Contemporary Verse* [Oglethorpe Univ.], V (Sept.-Oct. 1931), 16.

18.30   Coffin, Robert P[eter] Tristram. "A Summer Christmas Tree (Emily Dickinson's Garden, Amherst, Mass.)." *Book Collector's Packet,* III (Mar. 1939), 12.
Another printing of this poem in the *New York Herald Tribune* for Jan. 29, 1939 is noted by Charles R. Green in the *Bulletin of Bibliography* (see 1.17). I was unable to locate the poem in the newspaper for that date.

18.31   Coglan, Leo. "Emily Dickinson." *The Spectator* [Portland, Ore.], LXV (Aug. 1940), 28.

18.32   Conant, Isabel Fiske. "Directions for Saddling Pegasus for Em-
         ily Dickinson." *Saturday Review,* VII (Jan. 10, 1931), 528.
18.33   ———. "Emily Dickinson." *Saturday Review,* VII (Mar. 14, 1931),
         670.
18.34   ———. "Emily Dickinson in the Kitchen." *New York Herald
         Tribune,* Dec. 19, 1937, Sections 2-4, p. 10.
         Reprinted:
         Isabel Fiske Conant. *Orange Feather.* Boston: Bruce Hum-
         phries, 1939, p. 39.
18.35   ———. "For Emily Dickinson." *Scrapped Silver.* Portland,
         Maine: Mosher Press, 1928, unpaged.
18.36   ———. "New-Englanders." *Remembered Journey.* Dallas: Ka-
         leidograph Press, 1938, p. 67.
18.37   ———. "On the Air." Typewritten copy from the author in the
         Jones Library, Amherst.
18.38   ———. "Ordeal of Genius." *Saturday Review,* VII (Mar. 14,
         1931), 670.
18.39   ———. "Philadelphia Sunday." *New York Herald Tribune Books,*
         Dec. 21, 1930, p. 13.
18.40   ———. "Quatrains for Emily." *Remembered Journey.* Dallas:
         Kaleidograph Press, 1938, pp. 48-49.
18.41   ———. "Ruby-Crowned Kinglet." Typewritten copy from the au-
         thor in the Jones Library, Amherst.
18.42   ———. "Two New England Girls." *Window-Shopping.* Dallas:
         Kaleidograph Press, 1940, p. 36.
18.43   ———. "Two New Englanders." *Orange Feather.* Boston: Bruce
         Humphries, 1939, p. 26.
18.44   Cooke, Le Baron. "Emily Dickinson." *Rutland* [Vt.] *Herald,*
         Mar. 2, 1933.
18.45   Corso, Gregory. "Emily Dickinson, The Trouble With You Is —"
         Big Table, I (Spring 1960), 87.
18.46   Crane, Hart. "To Emily Dickinson." *Nation,* CXXIV (June 29,
         1927), 718.
         Reprinted in collected editions of Hart Crane's poetry and in
         Blake and Wells, *Recognition* (5.13), p. 130. See also Crane's
         reference to ED in *The Bridge* (*Collected Poems* [N.Y.: Live-
         right, 1930], pp. 47-48).
18.47   Crowell, Annie L. "Emily Dickinson's Garden." *The Triad An-
         thology of New England Verse,* ed. Louise Hall Littlefield.
         Portland, Maine: Falmouth Book House, 1938, p. 48.
18.48   Crowell, Grace Noll. "Emily Dickinson." *New York Herald
         Tribune,* Sept. 20, 1936, Section 2, p. 14.
18.49   Cutler, Mary G. "Fulfillment." *Unity* [Chicago], XXVI (Jan. 22,
         1891), 171.
18.50   De Vito, Ethel Barnett. "Emily Dickinson." *Catholic World,*
         CLXXXVI (Mar. 1958), 462.
18.51   Doyle, Joseph. "Emily Dickinson." *The CEA Critic,* XXXI (Nov.
         1968), 15.
18.52   Engle, Paul. "Emily Dickinson." *Poetry,* LVIII (Sept. 1941),
         298-99.
         Reprinted:

Paul Engle. *West of Midnight.* N.Y.: Random House, [1941],
 p. 66.
Anthology of Magazine Verse for 1938-1942 and Yearbook of
 American Poetry, ed. Alan F. Pater. N.Y.: Paebar Co.,
 1942, p. 145.
Poet to Poet: A Treasury of Golden Criticism, ed. Houston
 Peterson and William S. Lynch. N.Y.: Prentice-Hall, 1945,
 p. 309.

18.53 Evans, Nellie Seelye. "Emily Dickinson." *Poems.* Englewood,
 N.J.: Press Printing Establishment, 1906, p. 71.

18.54 Ford, Emily E. F[owler]. "Eheu! Emily Dickinson." *Springfield*
 Republican, Jan. 11, 1891, p. 2. Dated "Brooklyn, Jan. 3,
 1891."
 Reprinted:
 Springfield Weekly Republican, Jan. 16, 1891, p. 10.

18.55 Foster, Charles H[owell]. "To Emily Dickinson." *The American*
 Spectator, I (Dec. 1932), 11.

18.56 Gilbert, Anne Kelledy. "Postscript to Emily Dickinson." *Con-*
 temporary Verse, XXV (Sept. 1929), 4.
 Reprinted:
 New York Times Book Review, June 8, 1930, p. 31.

18.57 Giltinan, Caroline. "Emily Dickinson." *Catholic World,* CXXXII
 (Nov. 1930), 150.

18.58 Ginsburg, Louis. "Emily Dickinson." *New York Herald Tribune,*
 Aug. 30, 1931, Section 2, p. 8.

18.59 ———. "Emily Dickinson." *English Journal,* XXXIV (Nov. 1945),
 502.

18.60 ———. "Emily Dickinson." *New York Herald Tribune,* Mar. 6,
 1946, p. 22.
 Reprinted:
 Guests In Eden (5.59), p. 44.

18.61 ———. "Emily Dickinson." *English Journal,* XLII (Jan. 1953), 15.

18.62 Goodman, Mae Winkler. "Emily Dickinson." *Washington* [D.C.]
 Star, May 4, 1945, p. A-8.
 Reprinted:
 The Poetry Society of America Anthology, ed. Amy Bonner,
  et. al. N.Y.: Fine Editions Press, 1946, pp. 72-73.

18.63 Gould, Wallace. "To Emily." *The New American Caravan,* ed.
 Alfred Kreymborg, *et. al.* N.Y.: Macaulay, 1929, pp. 323-27.

18.64 Green, Robert Alan. "To Emily Dickinson on Viewing Her Home."
 Springfield Union, April 6, 1933.

18.65 Griffith, William. "Emily Dickinson." *Commonweal,* IX (Feb. 6,
 1929), 396.
 Reprinted, with changes:
 Literary Digest, C (Mar. 2, 1929), 36.
 The Garden Book of Verse, ed. William Griffith and Mrs. John
  Paris. N.Y.: William Morrow, 1932, Book I, pp. 15-16.

18.66 Heider, Werner. "Emily Dickinson. *Griffin Seed.* Francestown,
 N.H.: Golden Quill Press, 1955.
 Reprinted:
 New York Times Book Review, Dec. 30, 1956, p. 2.

18.67 Hickey, Agnes MacCarthy. "Emily Dickinson's Grave, West
       Cemetery, Amherst." *Out of Every Day; Book III.* Cedar
       Rapids, Iowa: Torch Press, 1953, p. 29.
18.68 ——. "The Home of Emily Dickinson, Amherst." *Out of Every
       Day, Book III.* Cedar Rapids, Iowa: Torch Press, 1953, p. 28.
18.69 Holahan, Martha Eileen. "The Poet's Epitaph" in Bingham, *An-
       cestors' Brocades* (5.5), pp. 180-81. Dated May 1, 1892.
18.70 Huff, Robert. "Emily Dickinson and Patanjali Examine a New
       Soul." *Saturday Review,* XL (May 4, 1957), 28.
18.71 Hunting, Constance. "Miss Dickinson." *Massachusetts Review,*
       III (Autumn 1961), 40.
18.72 Jacoby, Grover I., Jr. "To Emily Dickinson. *The Human Patina
       and Other Poems.* Hollywood, Calif.: The Press of Holly-
       crofters, Inc., 1938, p. 60.
18.73 Jenkins, W[ill] F. "To Emily Dickinson." *Nature Magazine,*
       XXXVII (Oct. 1944), 394.
18.74 Jonas, Ann. "Post Mortem: Emily Dickinson." *Colorado Quar-
       terly,* XV (Winter 1966), 274.
18.75 Kennedy, Leo. "With a Volume of Emily Dickinson." *Canadian
       Forum,* XIII (Dec. 1932), 96.
18.76 Lakin, R. D. "I Never Saw a Moor, Either." *Midwest Quarterly,*
       VIII (Spring 1967), 354.
18.77 Landauer, Hortense Pandres. "For Emily Dickinson." *Saturday
       Review,* X (May 5, 1934), 674.
       Reprinted:
       Louis Untermeyer and Carter Davidson. *Poetry: Its Appre-
           ciation and Enjoyment.* N.Y.: Harcourt, Brace, 1934, pp.
           140-41.
18.78 Landrum, Grace Warren. "To Emily Dickinson." *Sewanee Re-
       view,* XXXVI (Jan. 1928), 20.
18.79 Leader, Pauline. "Poem to Emily Dickinson." *Poetry,* XXXVI
       (May 1930), 85.
18.80 Lennen, Elinor. "Emily Dickinson." *Ave Maria* [Notre Dame,
       Ind.], LIV (Aug. 30, 1941), 266.
       Reprinted:
       Ave Maria, LV (Jan. 3, 1942), 8.
18.81 Leyda, Jay. *A House to Be Born In.* Wood Engravings by George
       Lockwood. Northampton, Mass.: The Gehenna Press, 1958.
       A poem on ED's home. Separately bound in paper covers.
18.82 Lloyd, J. William. "Emily Dickinson." *Wind-Harp Songs.* Buf-
       falo: Peter Paul Book Co., 1895, p. 31.
18.83 Losh, J. Horace. "To Emily Dickinson." *Driftwind* [North Mont-
       pelier, Vt.], VIII (Feb. 1934), 252.
18.84 Loveman, Robert. "Proclamation." *A Book of Verses.* Phila-
       delphia: Lippincott, 1900, p. 32.
18.85 Lowell, Amy. *A Critical Fable.* Boston: Houghton, 1922 (reis-
       sued 1924), pp. 7, 44, 73.
       The protagonist in this poem defends her admiration for ED
       against James Russell Lowell who is cast as a disapproving
       philistine.

18.86   Lowell, Amy. "The Sisters" in *What's O'Clock*. Boston: Hough-
         ton, Mifflin, 1925, pp. 127-37.
         Reprinted:
         Amy Lowell. *Selected Poems*, ed. John Livingston Lowes.
           Boston: Houghton, Mifflin, 1927, pp. 50-56.
         The author pays homage to ED as one of her poet-sisters, pp.
         133-37. See also 6.261a.
18.87   McC[ausland], E[lizabeth]. "For a New England Nun: Emily
         Dickinson, Poet." *Springfield Sunday Union and Republican*,
         Dec. 7, 1930, p. 4-E.
         Reprinted:
         Elizabeth McCausland. *Hot Nights and Other Poems*. Spring-
           field, Mass.: privately printed, 1934, unpaged.
18.88   Marcellino, Ralph. "Letter to Emily Dickinson." *New York Sun*,
         Dec. 21, 1937, p. 24.
18.89   McLean, Sydney R. "Emily Dickinson: Partial Portrait." *Mas-
         sachusetts Review*, VII (Autumn 1967), 650-51.
         Four separately titled sonnets: "Cousin," "Niece," "Editor,"
         "Poet."
18.90   Meredith, G. E. "The Poems of Emily Dickinson." *Literary
         World*, XXII (April 11, 1891), 128.
18.91   Miner, Virginia Scott. "Amherst Town." *Saturday Review*, XXII
         (July 6, 1940), 24.
18.92   Moffit, J. "To Emily Dickinson." *Atlantic Monthly*, CXCIX (Mar.
         1957), 72.
18.92a   Moreland, John Richard. "To Emily Dickinson." *The Moon
         Mender*. Dallas: Kaleidograph Press, 1933, p. 68.
18.93   Morse, Samuel French. "Emily Dickinson." *New Republic*,
         LXXXVI (April 15, 1936), 282.
18.94   Osgood, E. L. "The Range, Along a Road Well Known to Emily
         Dickinson." *New York Herald Tribune*, Nov. 20, 1933, p. 13.
18.95   Padgett, Ron. "Most Sensual of Recluses, Faint." *C: A Journal
         of Poetry* [N.Y.], May 1963, p. [9].
         This mimeographed publication lacks a volume or issue num-
         ber. A copy of the untitled poem (here cited by its first line)
         is at the Jones Library, Amherst.
18.96   Page, Myriam. "Emily Dickinson." *Springfield Sunday Union and
         Republican*, April 3, 1932, p. 4-E.
18.97   Parks, Ruth M. "Emily Dickinson." *Hartford Courant*, June 14,
         1931, p. 2-A.
18.98   Peale, Edward. "Four Poems Not Yet Released (or Even
         Dreamed of) by Any Branch of the Family of Emily Dickin-
         son." *Bookman* [N.Y.], LXXIII (Aug. 1931), 584-85.
         The first lines of these parodies of ED are: "Eternity's as
         long as time," "If you have found an inward lake," "Leap up
         my soul and caper," and "The first part is the hardest."
18.99   Phillips, Le Roy. "The Poems of Emily Dickinson." *Amherst
         Literary Monthly*, VI (June 1891), 90-91.
         Reprinted:
         New England Magazine, n.s. V (Nov. 1891), 311.

18.100   Phillips, Paul C. "Emily Dickinson." *Springfield Sunday Union and Republican,* Feb. 25, 1934, p. 4-E.

18.101   Porter, Katherine I. H. "The Poet's Gown." *Springfield Sunday Republican,* July 30, 1916, p. 14. Dated "Natal, Brazil, Aug. 17, 1911."

18.102   Pyun, Y[ung] T[ai]. "To Emily Dickinson." "To the Same." *Songs from Korea.* Seoul: International Cultural Association of Korea, 1948, pp. 83, 84.
          Both poems are in English.

18.103   Rand, Frank Prentice. "From Letters by Emily Dickinson." *Heart O'Town.* Amherst, Mass.: privately published (printed by E. L. Hildreth & Co.), 1945, pp. 69-81.
          ED appears as one of the speakers in this poem.

18.104   Renon, Erika. "To Emily Dickinson." *American Scholar,* XXX (Winter 1960-1961), 66.

18.105   Reynolds, Virginia Dickinson. "Round Emily's Name." *Saturday Review,* XXVIII (July 28, 1954), 21.
          This poem replies to Melville Cane's satire, "Dickinsons and Todds"; see 18.25.

18.106   Rich, Adrienne. "E." in Gelpi, *Mind of the Poet* (5.29), p. xiii.
          Reprinted:
          Adrienne Rich. *Necessities of Life, Poems 1962-1965.* N.Y.: W. W. Norton, 1966, p. 33. Entitled "'I am in Danger — Sir.'"

18.107   Roseliep, Raymond. "With Red Plums and Her Poems." *Poetry,* CXI (Feb. 1968), 300.

18.108   Russell, Sydney King. "Emily Dickinson." *New York Sun,* Oct. 9, 1937, p. 22.

18.109   Sandburg, Carl. "Accomplished Facts." *Poetry,* XV (Feb. 1920), 243.
          Reprinted:
          Carl Sandburg. *Smoke and Steel.* N.Y.: Harcourt, Brace, 1922, p. 169.
          Carl Sandburg. *Collected Poems.* N.Y.: Harcourt, Brace, 1950, p. 226.

18.110   ———. "Letters to Dead Imagists." *Chicago Poems.* N.Y.: Holt, 1916, p. 176.
          Reprinted:
          Carl Sandburg. *Collected Poems.* N.Y.: Harcourt, Brace, 1950, p. 73.

18.111   ———. "Public Letter to Emily Dickinson." *Atlantic Monthly,* CLXXIX (Mar. 1947), 44.
          Reprinted:
          Carl Sandburg. *Collected Poems.* N.Y.: Harcourt, Brace, 1950, p. 670.

18.112   Saner, Reginald A. "To Emily D." *Midwest Quarterly,* VIII (Spring 1967), 330.

18.113   Schacht, Marshall. "Not to Forget Miss Dickinson." *A Little Treasury of Modern Poetry, English and American,* ed. Oscar Williams. Rev. ed. N.Y.: Scribner's, 1952, p. 582.

18.114   Schneider, Flora. *Collected Poems.* Canton, Ohio: privately printed, 1959.

This volume contains four poems about ED: "Camphor-Wood
Chest (Containing Poems of Emily Dickinson)," p. 37; "Emily
Dickinson," p. 38; "I'm Nobody!" p. 22; "Lavinia Dickinson,"
p. 39.

18.115   Scott, Winfield Townley. "Emily Dickinson." *Atlantic Monthly*,
CLXXV (June 1945), 61.
Reprinted as "'After Great Pain a Formal Feeling Comes'":
Winfield Townley Scott. *Mr. Whittier and Other Poems*. N.Y.:
Macmillan, 1948, pp. 6-7.
Winfield Townley Scott. *Collected Poems: 1937-1962*. N.Y.:
Macmillan, 1962, pp. 127-28.

18.116   Shapiro, Karl. "Emily Dickinson and Katherine Anne Porter."
Poetry, XCVIII (April 1961), 2-3.
Reprinted:
Karl Shapiro. *Selected Poems*. N.Y.: Random House, 1968,
p. 324.

18.117   Slote, Bernice. "To Emily" in McNaughton, *Imagery of ED* (5.53),
p. iii.

18.118   Smith, John I. "To Emily Dickinson." *Scholastic*, XV (Jan. 4,
1930), 8.

18.119   [Smith, Russell St. Clair.] Paul Revere, pseud. "To Emily Dick-
inson." *Tampa* [Fla.] *Morning Tribune*, Jan. 12, 1932.
Reprinted:
Tampa [Fla.] *Morning Tribune*, May 6, 1932.

18.120   Speyer, Leonora [von Stosch]. "Emily Dickinson." *Bookman*
[N.Y.], LXV (April 1927), 149.

18.121   Storrs, Mary Elwell. "Emily Dickinson, 1830-1886." *Springfield
Republican*, May 22, 1891.
I was unable to locate the poem in either the daily or weekly
edition of the *Republican* for that date. The citation is from
Lubbers, *Critical Revolution* (5.114), p. 277.

18.122   T., R. "The Grave of E.D., Amherst." *New York Herald Tribune*,
May 15, 1934, p. 19.

18.123   Taggard, Genevieve. "Dedication" to *Life and Mind* (5.81), pp.
vii-viii.
Reprinted:
Genevieve Taggard. *Collected Poems, 1918-1938*. N.Y.:
Harper, 1938, pp. 89-90. The poem is dated "Amherst, 1930."

18.124   ———. "Two Poems to Emily Dickinson (In her own language)"
in *Collected Poems, 1918-1938*. N.Y.: Harper, pp. 87-88.
The poems are dated "New York, 1934."

18.125   Taylor, G. A. "Emily Dickinson's Garden." *Hampshire Daily
Gazette*, April 1, 1933.
Reprinted:
Cincinnati Fine Arts Journal, V (June 1933), 10.
Amherst Record, Jan. 2, 1935.

18.126   Thompson, Dorothy Bowen. "Emily Dickinson Among Her Biographers." *Saturday Review*, XXVIII (Mar. 31, 1945), 16.

18.127   Thompson, Peggy. "For E.B.B. and E.D." *American Scholar*,
XVIII (Winter 1948), 67.

18.128   Troubetzkoy, Dorothy Ulrich. "From Emily Dickinson's Hill."
          New York Herald Tribune, April 22, 1946, p. 20.
          Reprinted:
          Guests In Eden (5.59), p. 38.
18.129   Tuttle, Helen Barton. "Emily Dickinson." *American Voice*.
          N.Y.: Harbinger House, 1942, pp. 34-35.
18.130   Untermeyer, Jean Starr. "Hidden Meteors." *New York Herald
          Tribune Books*, Aug. 11, 1929, p. 6.
          Reprinted:
          Voices, No. 86 (Summer 1936), p. 49.
          Jean Starr Untermeyer. *Winged Child*. N.Y.: Viking Press,
             1936, p. 55.
          Jean Starr Untermeyer. *Job's Daughter*. N.Y.: W.W. Norton,
             1967, p. 82.
18.131   Van Doren, Mark. "Emily Dickinson." *Kenyon Review*, IX (Win-
          ter 1947), 71.
          Reprinted:
          Mark Van Doren. *New Poems*. N.Y.: William Sloane, 1948,
             p. 50.
          Mark Van Doren. *Collected and New Poems, 1924-1963*.
             N.Y.: Hill and Wang, 1963, p. 339.
18.132   Vauclain, Margaret. "Emily Dickinson Dies." *The Griffin* [N.Y.],
          XIII (April 1934), 21.
18.133   Vernon, Frances E. "Emily Dickinson" in *Guests In Eden* (5.59),
          p. 42.
18.134   Wattles, Willard. "The Bench. (In Memory of Emily Dickin-
          son.)" *Amherst Graduates' Quarterly*, VI (May 1917), 185.
18.135   Wesenberg, Alice Bidwell. "Emily." *Mt. Holyoke Alumnae
          Quarterly*, XIII (Jan. 1930), 192.
18.136   Wilbur, Richard. "Altitudes." *Things of This World*. N.Y.:
          Harcourt, Brace, 1956, pp. 3-4.
          Reprinted in succeeding collections of Richard Wilbur's poetry,
          e.g., *The Poems of Richard Wilbur*, N.Y.: Harcourt, Brace,
          [1963], pp. 63-64. Also reprinted in *In Other Words*, ed. Hor-
          ace Hewlett (6.459), pp. 145-46.
18.137   Winters, Yvor. "To Emily Dickinson." *Boston Herald*, Dec. 6,
          1930, p. 15.
          Reprinted:
          Yvor Winters. *The Proof*. N.Y.: Coward-McCann, 1930, p.
             47.
          Yvor Winters. *Collected Poems*. Denver, Colo.: Alan Swal-
             low 1952 (rev. ed. 1960), p. 49.
18.138   Wise, M. J., Jr. "To Emily Dickinson." *Amherst Graduate
          Verse 1931*, ed. David Morton. Amherst, Mass.: Poetry So-
          ciety of Amherst College, 1931, p. 71.
18.139   Witt, Harold. "Bees, Suns, and Blueberry Muffins at the Dickin-
          sons." *Approach*, No. 61 (Fall, 1966), pp. 20-22.

19.

Tributes by Other Artists

Additional musical settings are listed in earlier bibliographies; see
Blanck, 1.4; Jones Library, 1.8; Lubbers, 5.114; White and Green, 1.17.

19.1   Bacon, Ernst. "Five Poems by Emily Dickinson." Boston:
        George Schirmer, 1944.
            Musical settings to five poems: "It's all I have to bring today,"
        "So bashful when I spied her," "Poor little Heart," "And this of
        all my Hopes," and "To make a prairie it takes a clover and
        one bee."
19.2   ————. "The Grass So Little Has To Do." N.Y.: Associated Mu-
        sic Publishers, 1944.
            Musical setting.
19.3   ————. "Is There Such a Thing As Day?" N.Y.: Associated Mu-
        sic Publishers, 1944.
            Musical setting for "Will there really be a 'Morning'?"
19.4   ————. "No Dew Upon the Grass." Bryn Mawr, Pa.: Merion Mu-
        sic, Inc. (New Music Edition), 1942.
            Musical setting for "The Sun kept setting — setting — still."
19.5   ————. "Velvet People." N.Y.: Carl Fischer, 1948.
            Musical setting for "Pigmy seraphs — gone astray."
19.6   Bain, Murray. "Safe in Their Alabaster Chambers." N.p., 1964.
        9 pp.
            Musical setting for chorus, cello, and English horn.
19.7   Barber, Samuel. "Let Down the Bars, O Death." Opus 8, No. 2.
        N.Y.: Carl Schirmer, n.d. (Composed in 1936.)
            Musical setting for chorus.
19.8   Blanchard, Robert. A drawing of Emily Dickinson in Monroe
        Heath, *Great Americans at a Glance* (6.457), p. 19.
19.9   Copland, Aaron. "Twelve Poems of Emily Dickinson Set to Mu-
        sic." N.Y. and London: Boosey and Hawkes, 1951.
            Musical setting for voice and piano. Discussed, see 6.568.
19.10   Franchetti, Arnold. "Aria Variata" for contralto and orchestra on

poetry of Emily Dickinson. Signed by the composer at Lyme,
Conn., Aug. 9, 1957. 46 pp. A microfilm of the manuscript is
owned by the Newberry Library, Chicago.

The lyrics are drawn from several poems, among them "Good
Morning — Midnight," "He found my Being — set it up," "Let me
not mar that perfect Dream," "I have no Life but this," and "As
subtle as tomorrow."

19.11   Graham, Martha. "Letter to the World."
Modern dance for five characters based on the life of ED.
Reviewed:

19.12   Anon. *Harper's Bazaar*, LXXV (April 1941), 80-81.
19.13   Anon. *Smith College Monthly*, II (Nov. 1941), 13-16.
19.14   Anon. *Life* [Chicago], XXII (Mar. 17, 1947), 102-03.
19.15   Margaret Lloyd. "Jubilee Fortnight of a Dance: Premieres and
Revivals Presented on Broadway." *Christian Science Monitor*,
April 18, 1953, p. 4.
19.16   Seymour Peck. "Graham: Explorer of Dance Frontiers." *New York
Times Magazine*, Mar. 30, 1958, pp. 22-23.

19.17   Hays, Hobart V. A drawing of Emily Dickinson in Martha W. England and John Sparrow, *Hymns Unbidden* . . . (6.316), p. 115.
19.18   Johnston, David A. "Meditations, 1958." N.p., 1964. Musical settings of Dickinson poems for voice and piano.
19.19   Lee, Doris. "Emily Dickinson: The Rose is Out of Town." *Vogue*,
CXXIII (April 15, 1954), 92-93.
A painting inspired by "The morns are meeker than they were."
19.20   Pinkham, Daniel. "An Emily Dickinson Mosaic." N.Y.: C.F.
Peters, 1963. 22 pp.
Musical settings of six poems for a chorus of women's voices
and piano or small orchestra. Performed at Nassau College,
May 1966; see 22.26.
19.21   Reeves, Ruth. "Exhibition of Tapestry Entitled 'Homage to Emily
Dickinson.'" *Art Digest*, V (Dec. 15, 1930), 21.
Reprinted:
Atelier, I (April 1931), 258.
Craft Horizons, V (Feb. 1946), 4.
Guests in Eden (5.59), p. 32. Alma G. Watson comments on
the tapestry, p. 33.
A design in textile depicting events in ED's life. Owned by the
Jones Library, Amherst.
19.22   Rorem, Ned. "Musical Settings by Ned Rorem of American Po-
etry," a program performed at the Town Hall, New York City,
Dec. 12, 1968. The program included two musical settings of
ED's "Love's stricken 'why'" sung by Beverly Wolff. For a
note on this performance, see the *New York Times*, Dec. 8,
1968, p. D-23.
19.23   Swan, Barbara. "Emily Dickinson."
A lithograph portrait, signed: "Swan." Plate, 76.5 x 56.5 cm.
Fifteen copies were made, one of which is owned by Harvard
Univ.
19.24   Thurber, James. A cartoon. *New Yorker*, X, No. 19 (June 23,
1934), p. 12.

RECORDINGS, BROADCASTS, FILMS

20.

Recordings

Only records wholly devoted to ED are listed.

20.1   *Emily Dickinson. Fourteen Poems.* Austin Warren, reader. Recorded forewords by E. G. Burrows. International Literature Series, ed. Emily S. Teachout. Recorded Dec. 1951 by Idiom Recording Co., 809 Amherst, Ann Arbor., No. E1-LQC-12958. One 12-in. record, 33 1/3 r.p.m.

20.2   *Poems of Emily Dickinson.* Nancy Wickwire, reader. Original music composed and played by Don Feldman. Released *ca.* 1959 by Spoken Arts, Inc., 95 Valley Road, New Rochelle, N.Y., No. 76. One 12-in. record, 33 1/3 r.p.m.

20.3   *Poems and Letters of Emily Dickinson.* Julie Harris, reader. Directed by Howard Sackler. Released in 1960 by Caedmon Records, Inc., 505 Eighth Ave., New York, N.Y., No. TC 119. One 12-in. record, 33 1/3 r.p.m.

20.4   *The Letters of Emily Dickinson* [and] *A Reminiscence by T. W. Higginson from* The Atlantic Monthly, *Oct. 1891.* Samuel Barclay Charters, reader. Includes the printed text of the recording with a biographical note and critical introduction by Samuel Charters. Released in 1963 by Folkways Records, 165 W. 46th St., New York, N.Y., No. FL 9753. One 12-in. record, 33 1/3 r.p.m.

20.5   *Lucyle Hook Reads Poems of Emily Dickinson.* Sixty-seven poems are read. Brief comment on the poems by Henry Wells. Released *ca.* 1961 by The National Council of Teachers of English, 508 South Sixth St., Champaign, Ill., No. RL20-5. One 12-in. record, 33 1/3 r.p.m. For text and study questions to accompany this recording, see 6.1219.
    <u>Reviewed:</u>
      Muri (6.738a)
      Roach (6.848)

20.6   *Emily Dickinson: A Self Portrait.* Julie Harris, reader. Twenty poems and twenty-seven letters are interspersed. Released

in 1968 by Caedmon Records, Inc., 505 Eighth Ave., New York,
N.Y., No. S-2026. Two 12-in. records, 33 1/3 r.p.m.
Reviewed:
    Searles (6.901a)

Radio and Television
Broadcasts and Films

21.1 Percival Hunt. Radio talk broadcast Feb. 18, 1928. Text published; see 6.524.

21.2 Ted Malone. "Ted Malone from Home of Emily Dickinson." "Pilgrimage of Poetry" series, N.B.C. Broadcast over Radio Station WJZ, May 19, 1940. Transcribed by Audio-Scriptions, Inc., 1619 Broadway, New York, N.Y. Two records, four sides, 78 r.p.m. (Mr. Malone spoke from ED's brother's home, The Evergreens.)

Press notices:

21.3 *Amherst Record*, May 15, 1940, p. 1.

21.4 *Amherst Record*, May 22, 1940, p. 1.

21.5 *Springfield Sunday Union and Republican*, May 19, 1940, p. 6-A.

[17.34] Margaret Leaf. "Adventures in Reading." Radio broadcast of dramatized episodes from the life of Emily Dickinson, Aug. 12, 1940.

21.6 John Dando. "Behind the Pages with John Dando: Emily Dickinson." Broadcast over Radio Station WTIC, Nov. 21, 1951. Text in Jones Library, Amherst.

21.7 Lyman Bryson, John Ciardi, and T. H. Johnson. "Invitation to Learning" series, C.B.S. Broadcast April 24, 1955.

21.8 Stuart Gerry Brown, Edwin H. Cady, and Albert J. George. "Books and Ideas" series, a 30 min. telecast of an informal conversation on Emily Dickinson between three Syracuse Univ. professors, produced in 1956 by Arthur Weld for the Educational Television and Radio Center, Syracuse Univ. A film of this telecast was distributed by National Educational Television in 1958.

21.9 F. D. Claudfield. A radio talk on Emily Dickinson by F. D. Claudfield, Dept of English, Univ. of Alberta, Oct.-Nov. 1964. Text in Jones Library, Amherst.

21.10 Denis Donoghue. "Emily Dickinson: Connoisseur of Chaos," a recorded lecture in the series, "Against the Sky: A Short View of American Poetry, 1850-1950." 1 hour. Delivered at the Univ. of Cincinnati. Distributed in 1965 by the Univ. of Cincinnati under the auspices of the National Association of Educational Broadcasters. See Mr. Donoghue's essay, "Emily Dickinson" (6.293).

21.11   Joseph Morgenstern. "Movies That Teach." *Newsweek*, LXXI (Mar. 25, 1968), 86, 89-90.
Notes preparation of an educational film on ED.

21.12   A. E. Claessyens and Mari Lyn Henry. "One to One" series, a 30 min. telecast of a lecture on Emily Dickinson by Mr. Claessyens with readings of poems by Miss Henry. Produced in 1968 by WETA-TV, Washington, D.C., under the auspices of the American Home Library Program.

COMMEMORATIONS AND EXHIBITIONS

Commemorations and Exhibitions

BOSTON PUBLIC LIBRARY EXHIBIT, DEC. 1923

[6.443]   Zoltan Haraszti. "An Emily Dickinson Collection." *Boston Evening Transcript*, Book Section, Dec. 8, 1923, p. 6.

1930 CENTENARY CELEBRATIONS

Mt. Holyoke Alumnae Conference, Mt. Holyoke College, Nov. 8-9, 1929

22.1   "Notices." *Mt. Holyoke Alumnae Quarterly*, XIII (July 1929), 112. Notice of "Founder's Day . . . a homecoming occasion in honor of Emily Dickinson for alumnae who are interested in poetry."

22.2   "Notices." *Mt. Holyoke Alumnae Quarterly*, XIII (Oct. 1929), 173 and facing page.

22.3   "'Play and Poetry Talk Shop' Opens at Mt. Holyoke Friday." *Springfield Sunday Union and Republican*, Nov. 3, 1929, p. 2-E.

22.4   "Program." Alumnae Association of Mt. Holyoke College. Emily Dickinson Weekend, Nov. 8-9, 1929. Copy of the program in Jones Library, Amherst.

22.5   "Founder's Day is Observed at Mt. Holyoke." *Springfield Daily Republican*, Nov. 9, 1929, pp. 1, 2.

22.6   "Mt. Holyoke Honors Founder and Emily Dickinson. Principals in Clash Over Christmas Fast." *New York Herald Tribune*, Nov. 10, 1929, Section III, p. 7.

22.6a   "Emily Dickinson Under Discussion at Mt. Holyoke." *Springfield Sunday Union and Republican*, Nov. 10, 1929, pp. 1A, 2A.

22.7   "Alumnae Conference Impressions," *Mount Holyoke Alumnae Quarterly*, XIII (Jan. 1930), 188-92. Articles are contributed by the following: Rowena Keyes (6.569), pp. 188-90; Sydney McLean (6.684), p. 190; Jane Mesick (6.699), p. 190; Esther Skeel (6.927), pp. 191-92.

[6.972]   Genevieve Taggard. "The Little 'Scholar' of 1848." *Journal of Adult Education*, II (Jan. 1930), 75-76.

Hampshire Bookshop Observance of the Emily Dickinson Centenary, Northampton and Amherst, May 1930

[6.681]   Elizabeth McCausland. "They Will Gather at Amherst in Homage to Emily Dickinson." *Springfield Sunday Union and Republican*, May 4, 1930, p. 3-E.

[6.85a]   May Lamberton Becker. "The Reader's Guide." *Saturday Review*, VI (May 10, 1930), 1030.

22.8   "The Emily Dickinson Centenary." (An editorial.) *Springfield Republican*, May 10, 1930, p. 10.

22.9   "Emily Dickinson, Poet, Is Honored at Northampton." *Springfield Sunday Union and Republican*, May 11, 1930, pp. 1-A, 2-A.

22.10   "Homage to Memory of Emily Dickinson." *Boston Globe*, May 12, 1930, p. 15.

22.11   "Homage Paid Memory of Emily Dickinson." *Hampshire Daily Gazette* [Northampton, Mass.], May 12, 1930, pp. 1, 4, 8.

22.12   "Pilgrimage." *Hampshire Daily Gazette* [Northampton, Mass.], May 12, 1930.

22.13   "Bibliographic Notes on Emily Dickinson (May 1930)." *Book Scorpion Miscellany* [Hampshire Bookshop, Northampton, Mass.] [Oct. 1930.]
          Unpaged. See also the Hampshire Bookshop bibliography of ED (1.6) and M.E.D., "The Bookshop and Emily Dickinson" (6.254).

Centenary Celebration, Amherst, Dec. 10, 1930

[6.822]   James Powers. "World Acclaims Emily Dickinson, But She's Still 'The Queer Poet' to Amherst." *Boston Sunday Globe*, Nov. 23, 1930, pp. 6, 7.

22.14   "Emily Dickinson's Home Town Observes Centenary of Her Birth." *Hartford Courant*, Dec. 7, 1930, p. 6-E.

22.15   "Emily Dickinson Centenary at Amherst." *Springfield Sunday Union and Republican*, Dec. 7, 1930, p. 4-A.
          Also discusses the Jones Library bibliography (1.8).

22.16   "Centenary of Emily Dickinson Observed." *Springfield Daily News*, Dec. 8, 1930.

22.17   "Dickinson Centenary Observed at [Jones] Library." *Springfield Republican*, Dec. 10, 1930, p. 2.

22.18   "Today is Centennial Anniversary of Birth of Poet, Emily Dickinson." *Springfield Union*, Dec. 10, 1930, p. 7.

22.19   "The Emily Dickinson Centenary." *Current Literature* [London], No. 266 (Feb. 1931), pp. 42-43.

[6.1031] Louis Untermeyer. "Thoughts After a Centenary." *Saturday Review*, VII (June 20, 1931), 905-06.

Yale University Library Exhibition, Dec. 10, 1930

22.20   "Yale University 'Birthday Party' for Emily Dickinson." *New York Herald Tribune Books*, Dec. 21, 1930, p. 13. A bibliography was issued in conjunction with this celebration; see 1.1.

Miscellaneous Centenary Material

22.21   *Springfield Sunday Union and Republican*, June 7, 1931, p. 7-E.

LATER COMMEMORATIONS

22.22   "50th Anniversary of Death of Emily Dickinson." *Hampshire Daily Gazette* [Northampton, Mass.], May 15, 1936.

22.23   "The Emily Dickinson Exhibition." *Gazette of the Grolier Club* [N.Y.], II (April 1946), 169-73.
         Description of the ED exhibition at the Grolier Club, 47 E. 60th St., New York City, Oct. 18-Nov. 7, 1945.

22.24   Emily Dickinson Day, Amherst, Mass., Aug. 28, 1954. "A Day of Commemoration to the Amherst Poetess by the Dickinson Association of America." Copy of the program in the Robert Frost Library, Amherst College.

22.25   "Emily Dickinson Born 125 Years Ago." *Amherst Journal Record*, Dec. 8, 1955, pp. 1, 4, 7, 10.

22.26   "This Was a Poet," An Emily Dickinson Festival, Nassau Community College [Garden City, N.Y.], May 6-8, 1966. Dedicated to Millicent Todd Bingham. The program included special performances of Norman Rosten's "Come Slowly Eden" (17.38), of music by Ernst Bacon (19.1-5), and of "An Emily Dickinson Mosaic" by Daniel Pinkham (19.20). A summary of the events of the festival is printed as the final page of an 8-page program for the play, "Come Slowly Eden."

22.27   *Nassau Community College Library Newsletter*, Vol. I, Nov. 3, part 1 (May 1966), pp. 1-4.
         Issued in connection with the Nassau College ED Festival (22.26), this number of the *Newsletter* contains a brief tribute, "Homage to Emily Dickinson" by Paul A. Doyle, pp. 1-2, and an annotated listing of some volumes by and about ED on display in the College Library, pp. 2-4.

MISCELLANEA

Miscellanea

EMILY DICKINSON'S DICTIONARY

23.1   *An American Dictionary of the English Language,* Exhibiting the
Origin, Orthography, Pronunciation, and Definitions of Words.
By Noah Webster ... Revised Edition. .... N.Y.: Harper, 1846.

NEWSPAPER NOTICES OF EMILY DICKINSON'S
LAST ILLNESS AND DEATH

23.2   *Springfield Daily Republican,* May 17, 1886, p. 6.
      Reprinted:
      Leyda, *Years and Hours* (5.49), II, 472.
23.3   *Northampton Daily Herald,* May 17, 1886.
      Reprinted:
      Leyda, *Years and Hours* (5.49), II, 472.
23.4   *Springfield Daily Republican,* May 18, 1886, p. 7.
      Reprinted:
      Leyda, *Years and Hours* (5.49), II, 472.
[6.285]   *Springfield Daily Republican,* May 18, 1886, p. 4.
      An obituary by Susan Dickinson.

DICKINSON FAMILY MATERIALS

23.5   Edward Dickinson. [A toast to Hadley] in *Celebration of the Two
Hundredth Anniversary of the Settlement of Hadley, Mass. at
Hadley, June 8, 1859.* [booklet]. Northampton: Bridgman and
Childs, 1859, pp. 77-79.
Hadley's bicentennial celebration occasioned a brief, formal
statement of good wishes by Edward Dickinson on behalf of
Hadley's "daughter city," Amherst.

23.6   Reunion of the Dickinson Family at Amherst, Mass., Aug. 8th and
           9th, 1883. Binghampton Publishing Co., 1884.
           The printed program of the reunion. See Leyda, *Years and
           Hours* (5.49), II, 402-03.

23.7   Frederick Dickinson, comp. *"To the Descendants of Thomas
           Dickinson, Son of Nathaniel and Anna Gull Dickinson, of Weth-
           ersfield, Conn. and Hadley, Mass."* Chicago: W. D. Grant,
           1897. A genealogy of the Dickinson family. See also Judd,
           6.559; Lee, 6.604; and Whicher, 5.104, pp. 315-17.

POEMS ERRONEOUSLY ASCRIBED TO EMILY DICKINSON

23.8   "I Saw the Sun To-day and Laughed." *The Mahogany Tree*, I
           (Mar. 26, 1892), p. 198.
           An eight-line poem signed "E---y D--k----n." For two other
           poems ascribed to ED, see 6.1162.

OTHER MISCELLANEA

23.9   *Eleventh Annual Catalogue of the Mount Holyoke Female Semi-
           nary in South Hadley, Mass., 1847-8,* Amherst [Mass.]:
           Press of J.S. & C. Adams, 1848.
           ED is listed among the pupils of the "Middle Class," p. 6.
           An appendix describes the course of study and requirements
           for admission. Lists the names of 235 students in 3 classes.

23.10   Paper leaflet published in memory of Leonard Humphrey, Jan.
           14, 1851 by Alpha Delta Phi, Amherst College.

23.11   "Emily Dickinson Contest Number." *Circle, A Journal of Verse,*
           IX (1932), No. 2, pp. 29-45.
           This issue includes the printing of an "Emily Dickinson $50.00
           Prize Poem." The previous issue (No. 1, p. 28) reprints two
           ED poems.

23.12   "The Emily Dickinson House." Amherst, Mass.: Amherst Col-
           lege, 1966. Unpaged.
           A twelve-page pamphlet prepared by Amherst College for vis-
           itors to the Dickinson home. Contains full-page photos and
           four pages of text devoted to the history, furnishings, and
           landscaping of the house. See also 6.494 and 7.56-57.

23.13   Elizabeth Kingsley. "Double Crostics No. 8." *Saturday Review,*
           X (May 19, 1934), 706. "Solution" (May 26, 1934), 717.
           A puzzle featuring ED.

UNPUBLISHED MATERIALS

24

Papers Delivered at Scholarly Meetings
and Other Unpublished Essays

This section collects various papers and addresses which in 1968 were still unpublished. Papers read before professional societies which have been published are located in other sections. Only those unpublished materials which could not be conveniently placed elsewhere are listed here; for unpublished theses, for example, see section 14. The following list does not claim to be exhaustive. The arrangement is alphabetical.

24.1 Bowen, Clayton R. "Do You Know Emily Dickinson?" [Subheading:] "Unpublished article for Prof. of New Testament Interpretation and Libraries at Meadville Theological School, Dec. 1931." Copy in Jones Library, Amherst.

24.2 Haskell, Juliana. "Perils of Posthumous Publication."
An address to the Zeta Chapter, Phi Delta Gamma, Dec. 1945.

24.3 Hsu, Kai-yu. "Tension and Conflict in the Poems of Emily Dickinson and Li Ch'ing-chao." Noted, *PMLA*, LXXXIII, No. 4, Part 1 (Sept. 1968), p. 1008.
Paper delivered at the Annual Meeting of the Philological Association of the Pacific Coast, Nov. 1967.

24.4 Lauber, John F. "Independent Ecstasy: The Aesthetic of Emily Dickinson." Noted, *PMLA*, LXXX, No. 4, Part 2 (Sept. 1965), p. 51.
Paper delivered at the Annual Meeting of the Philological Association of the Pacific Coast, Nov. 28, 1964.

24.5 Miller, F. De Wolfe. "Emily Dickinson's Assumption of Aristocratic Values." Noted, *PMLA*, LXXVII, No. 2 (May 1962), p. 51.
Paper delivered at the Annual Meeting of the Modern Language Association, Dec. 28, 1961.

24.6 Oppens, Karl. "Der Literarische Ruhm Emily Dickinsons." Ruth Miller in *Poetry of ED* (5.54), p. 432, notes that the author of this unpublished manuscript documents the critical reception of *Poems, First Series,* by collecting "a multitude of ephemeral reviews" published in England and America. This citation is

apparently the result of a confusion between Klaus Lubbers'
study of ED's reputation (5.114) and Kurt Oppens, another German scholar (see 10.62).

24.7   Perkins, Palfrey. "Emily Dickinson, the Unique Poet." 1930.
Copy in Jones Library.

24.8   Russell, Nancy E. "The Domestic Life of Emily Dickinson." May
25, 1934. Copy in Jones Library, Amherst.

24.9   Thomas, Owen. "Syntactic Deletions in the Poetry of Emily Dick-
inson: An Experiment in Transformational Analysis."
Paper delivered at the Annual Meeting of the Modern Language
Association, Dec. 1965.

24.10   Turner, Clara Newman. "My Personal Acquaintance With Emily
Dickinson," ed. Clara Newman Pearl.
Excerpts printed:
Leyda, *Years and Hours* (5.49), I, 136; II, 67-68, 141-42, 226,
383-84, 481.
Copy in Jones Library, Amherst. Noted by Whicher, *This Was
a Poet* (5.104), p. 319.

24.11   Wylder, Edith (Perry Stamm). "The Speaker of Emily Dickinson's
'My Life Had Stood a Loaded Gun.'" Noted, *PMLA*, LXXXIII,
No. 4, Part 1 (Sept. 1968), p. 1003.
Paper delivered at the Annual Meeting of the Rocky Mountain
Modern Language Association, Oct. 1967.

Explication Index

Poems are listed alphabetically by first line. Numbers in parentheses following the first lines are the numbers assigned to the poems in the 1955 Johnson edition (3.197). Explications are arranged chronologically; the author's name is followed by entry and page numbers. Short titles follow the author's name when page numbers refer to a reprinting. The index is comprehensive in the sense that it includes textual as well as critical comment on individual poems, but it cannot claim to be complete. On its limitations and for help in locating additional explications, see the Preface, page xi.

A first mute coming (702)
  Capps, 5.14, 38, 149

A fuzzy fellow without feet (173)
  Porter, 5.69, 95-96

A house upon the height (399)
  Lindberg, 6.617, 345-46

A lady red amid the hill (74)
  Miles, 6.703, 148
  Herring, 5.33, 53-54
  Porter, 5.69, 29, 94-95, 111

A light exists in spring (812)
  Winters, *In Defense of Reason,* 6.1200,
    296-97
  Griffith, 5.31, 85-86, 88-89, 92, 97-100,
    161
  Pickard, 5.60, 66-67

A little bread, a crust, a crumb (159)
  Capps, 5.14, 31
  Porter, 5.69, 144

A little east of Jordan (59)
  Ward, 5.97, 43
  Duncan, 5.24, 51
  Capps, 5.14, 33, 38, 70, 149, 213
  Porter, 5.69, 46

A little madness in the spring (1333)
  Anderson, 5.2, 81
  Sherwood, 5.79, 197-98

A loss of something ever I felt (959)
  Chase, 5.17, 155
  Ward, 5.97, 14
  Gelpi, 5.29, 70, 85

A mien to move a queen (283)
  Porter, 5.69, 41-43, 53

A narrow fellow in the grass (986)
  Whicher, 5.104, 118, 239
  Blair and Chandler, 6.111, 258-60
  Spicer, 6.942, 135-43
  Adams, 6.11, 143-45
  Ciardi, 6.210, 801-02
  C. R. Anderson, 5.2, 120, 121
  Lindberg, 6.617, 348-49
  P. W. Anderson, 6.43, 79-80
  Pickard, 5.60, 63-64

A nearness to tremendousness (963)
  Thackrey, 5.95, 9-10
  Porter, 5.69, 127-28

A pang is more conspicuous in spring
    (1530)
  Capps, 5.14, 157

A pit but heaven over it (1712)
  Franklin, 5.28, 40, 44-46

A poor torn heart, a tattered heart (78)
  Capps, 5.14, 97, 172

A precious mouldering pleasure 'tis (371)
  Whicher, 5.104, 206-07
  Capps, 5.14, 25-26

A prison gets to be a friend (652)
  Capps, 5.14, 80
  Porter, 5.69, xi

A prompt executive bird is the jay (1177)
  P. W. Anderson, 6.43, 81

A route of evanescence (1463)
  Higginson, 6.477a, 402
  Whicher, 5.104, 262
  Davidson, 6.266, 407-08
  Smith, 6.929
  Johnson, 5.44, 202; 6.544, 269-70
  Patterson, 6.780, 12-19
  Adams, 6.11, 139-42
  Anderson, 5.2, 114
  Pearce, *Continuity,* 6.784, 178
  Galinsky, 10.50, 237-43, *passim*
  Fish, 6.351, 109
  Waggoner, *Am. Poets,* 6.1058, 197-98,
    672
  Capps, 5.14, 65, 185
  Lynen, 6.631, 131-32
  Porter, 5.69, 76-77, 113, 149
  Pickard, 5.60, 60
  Sandeen, 6.877, 498-99

A secret told (381)
  Ward, 5.97, 78

A sepal, petal, and a thorn (19)
  Gelpi, 5.29, 138
  Franklin, 5.28, 104-05, 125

A single clover plank (1343)
  P. W. Anderson, 6.43, 82-83
  Donaldson, 6.292a, 579-80

A single screw of flesh (263)
  Porter, 5.69, 162

A slash of blue (204)
  Porter, 5.69, 111

A sloop of amber slips away (1622)
  Reeves, 6.841, 108

A solemn thing it was I said (271)
  Chase, 5.17, 243
  Wheatcroft, 6.1113, 143
  England, *BNYPL,* 6.316, 103
  Gelpi, 5.29, 118
  Miller, 5.54, 14-15

A something in a summer's day (122)
  Porter, 5.69, 30

A spider sewed at night (1138)
  Nist, 11.45, 480-84
  Anderson, 5.2, 125-26
  Gelpi, 5.29, 151-52
  Laverty, 6.599, 13

"Go tell it" — What a message (1554)
    Marcellino, 6.653, 140
    Capps, 5.14, 108, 188
    Trilling, 6.1007, 917-19

Go thy great way (1638)
    England, *BNYPL*, 6.316, 114

God is a distant, stately lover (357)
    Whicher, 5.104, 183
    Gelpi, 5.29, 50
    Capps, 5.14, 120, 179

God is indeed a jealous God (1719)
    Gelpi, 5.29, 93
    Capps, 5.14, 150

God made a little gentian (442)
    Chase, 5.17, 186
    Frye, *Fables of Identity*, 6.375, 213-14

God made no act without a cause (1163)
    Wheatcroft, 6.1112, 105

God permits industrious angels (231)
    Ward, 5.97, 8

Going to heaven (79)
    Whicher, 5.104, 111-12
    C. R. Anderson, 5.2, 255
    Porter, 5.69, 64-68, 71

Good night, because we must (114)
    Porter, 5.69, 158

Good to hide and hear 'em hunt (842)
    Capps, 5.14, 144

Great Caesar! Condescend (102)
    Capps, 5.14, 64, 184

Great streets of silence led away (1159)
    Winters, *In Defense of Reason*, 6.1200,
        287-88
    Chase, 5.17, 184
    Baldi, *Sewanee Review*, 8.36, 439
    Reeves, 6.841, xxxv
    Pickard, 5.60, 117-18

Growth of man like growth of nature (750)
    Gelpi, 5.29, 95
    Sherwood, 5.79, 173-74

Had I known that the first was the last
        (1720)
    Capps, 5.14, 47

He ate and drank the precious words
        (1587)
    C. R. Anderson, 5.2, 44
    Capps, 5.14, 21, 210

He forgot and I remembered (203)
    Capps, 5.14, 54, 189, 161

He fumbles at your soul (315)
    Chase, 5.17, 204-05

C. R. Anderson, 6.35, 157
    Griffith, 5.31, 171-73; 6.427, 99
    Sherwood, 5.79, 108-09

He is alive this morning (1160)
    Ward, 5.97, 171

He lived the life of ambush (1525)
    Wells, 5.101, 280

He outstripped time with but a bout (865)
    Gelpi, 5.29, 43

He preached on "breadth" till it arguéd
        him narrow (1207)
    C. R. Anderson, 6.35, 158

He put the belt around my life (273)
    Glenn, 6.404, 580-82
    Griffith, 5.31, 177
    Gelpi, 5.29, 116
    Porter, 5.69, 112
    Franklin, 5.28, 28-29
    Miller, 5.54, 13-15, 240, 442

He strained my faith (497)
    Lindberg-Seyersted, 5.113, 176, 203-04

He was weak, and I was strong, then (190)
    Gelpi, 5.29, 118

Heaven is so far of the mind (370)
    Pickard, 5.60, 52

"Heaven" is what I cannot reach (239)
    Porter, 5.69, 33-34, 109, 117-18

"Heavenly Father" take to thee (1461)
    Chase, 5.17, 178
    Welland, 6.1085, 76
    Gelpi, 5.29, 44
    Capps, 5.14, 152

Her grace is all she has (810)
    Marcellino, 6.647, 22

Her "last Poems" (312)
    Patterson, 6.778, 47
    Capps, 5.14, 87, 168
    Ford, 5.27, 128-29

Her little parasol to lift (1038)
    Wheatcroft, 6.1113, 140-41

Her sweet turn to leave the homestead
        (649)
    Ford, 5.27, 137-38

His mind of man, a secret makes (1663)
    Donaldson, 6.292a, 580-81

Hope is a strange invention (1392)
    C. R. Anderson, 6.33, 301-02

"Hope" is the thing with feathers (254)
    Porter, 5.69, 147, 171

I'm ceded, I've stopped being theirs (508)
    Chase, 5.17, 156-57
    Ward, 5.97, 57; 6.1070, 24
    C. R. Anderson, 5.2, 178
    Frohock, 6.373, 100-04
    Griffith, 5.31, 174-75
    Porter, 5.69, 75
    Sherwood, 5.79, 146-48

I'm nobody! Who are you (288)
    Taggard, 5.81, 178-79
    Whicher, 5.104, 223
    Moseley, 6.731, 12
    Capps, 5.14, 65, 139
    Porter, 5.69, 162
    Backus, 6.62a, 1-7
    Franklin, 5.28, 135

I'm "wife" — I've finished that (199)
    Johnson, 5.44, 91
    Griffith, 5.31, 174-75
    Gelpi, 5.29, 116
    Porter, 5.69, 52, 68-70, 93-94, 164

Image of light, adieu (1556)
    Gelpi, 5.29, 75

Immured in heaven (1594)
    Johnson, 5.44, 229-30; 6.543
    Cambon, 6.172, 35-36

In ebon box, when years have flown (169)
    Porter, 5.69, 162

In falling timbers buried (614)
    Gelpi, 5.29, 36

In rags mysterious as these (177)
    Miller, 5.54, 102

In snow thou comest (1669)
    Waggoner, *Amer. Poets*, 6.1058, 674-76

In thy long paradise of light (1145)
    Gelpi, 5.29, 93

In winter in my room (1670)
    Whicher, 5.104, 186
    Griffith, 5.31, 177-83, 284-88
    Pickard, 5.60, 84-85

Is bliss then such abyss (340)
    Merideth, 6.694, 441-42

Is heaven a physician (1270)
    Gelpi, 5.29, 47
    Ford, 5.27, 144-45

It always felt to me a wrong (597)
    Gelpi, 5.29, 38
    Capps, 5.14, 36, 55, 161, 212

It can't be "summer" (221)
    Warren, 6.1072, 585

It ceased to hurt me, though so slow (584)
    Stevens, 11.38, 48-49

It did not surprise me (39)
    Porter, 5.69, 154

It don't sound so terrible, quite, as it did
    (426)
    England, *BNYPL*, 6.316, 106-07
    Ford, 5.27, 132-34; 6.362, 202

It dropped so low in my regard (747)
    Reeves, 6.841, xlv-xlvi
    Main and Seng, 6.641, 87-88

It feels a shame to be alive (444)
    Ford, 5.27, 134-35; 6.362, 202
    Capps, 5.14, 109, 188

It is an honorable thought (946)
    Marcellino, 6.651, 126

It is dead — find it (417)
    Ford, 5.27, 101-02

It is easy to work when the soul is at play
    (244)
    Porter, 5.69, 50, 161
    J. Q. Anderson, 6.41, 46-47

It rises, passes on our south (1023)
    C. R. Anderson, 6.40, 407

It sifts from leaden sieves (311)
    Chase, 5.17, 214-15
    Johnson, 5.44, 193
    C. R. Anderson, 5.2, 159-60; 6.40, 410-12

It sounded as if the streets were running
    (1397)
    C. R. Anderson, 5.2, 140-41; 6.40, 408-09
    Herring, 5.33, 50

It tossed and tossed (723)
    Van der Vat, 6.1032, 250

It troubled me as once I was (600)
    Capps, 5.14, 105, 216

It was not death, for I stood up (510)
    C. R. Anderson, 5.2, 212
    Ward, 5.97, 59
    Griffith, 5.31, 187-92
    Pickard, 5.60, 96-97

It was too late for man (623)
    Van der Vat, 6.1032, 250

It will be summer eventually (342)
    C. R. Anderson, 5.2, 144
    Franklin, 5.28, 92, 109-10

It would have starved a gnat (612)
    Chase, 5.17, 155
    Ward, 5.97, 11

It's coming, the postponeless creature
    (390)
    McNaughton, 5.53, 49

Much madness is divinest sense (435)
C. R. Anderson, 6.35, 149
Capps, 5.14, 64

Musicians wrestle everywhere (157)
Porter, 5.69, 149-50

Must be a woe (571)
Johnson, 5.44, 144
Gelpi, 5.29, 108

My cocoon tightens, colors tease (1099)
C. R. Anderson, 5.2, 269
Waggoner, *Am. Poets,* 6.1058, 201-02
J. Q. Anderson, 6.41, 44

My eye is fuller than my vase (202)
Porter, 5.69, 64

My faith is larger than the hills (766)
England, *BNYPL,* 6.316, 103

My first well day since many ill (574)
Sandeed, 6.877, 491-92

My life closed twice before its close
(1732)
Whicher, 5.104, 107-08
Perrine, 6.797, 126-27
Franklin, 5.28, 88-90

My life had stood a loaded gun (754)
Taggard, 5.81, 306-07
Whicher, 5.104, 279
Link, 10.58, 408-09
Johnson, 5.44, 138-40
Poetry Workshop, 6.805
C. R. Anderson, 5.2, 172-73
Perrine, 6.791
Avery, 6.58, 49
Goffin, 6.405, 185-86
Patterson, 6.779, 343
Pickard, 5.60, 85-86
Cody, 6.220b, 161-80

My reward for being was this (343)
Franklin, 5.28, 39

My river runs to thee (162)
Porter, 5.69, 101

My wheel is in the dark (10)
Miles, 6.703, 150
Van Doorn, 6.1035, 132-33
Whicher, 5.104, 232
Howard, 6.508
Porter, 5.69, 48

My worthiness is all my doubt (751)
Chase, 5.17, 140, 160

Myself was formed a carpenter (488)
Thackrey, 5.95, 2

Nature affects to be sedate (1170)
C. R. Anderson, 5.2, 122

Nature and God – I neither knew (835)
Chase, 5.17, 164-65
Griffith, 5.31, 264
Capps, 5.14, 106

Nature assigns the sun (1336)
Gelpi, 5.29, 141

"Nature" is what we see (668)
Johnson, 5.44, 183
C. R. Anderson, 5.2, 82
Gelpi, 5.29, 82
Capps, 5.14, 116-17

Nature the gentlest mother is (790)
McNaughton, 5.53, 34-36
Johnson, 5.44, 184

No crowd that has occurred (515)
Pickard, 5.60, 113

No ladder needs the bird but skies (1547)
Capps, 5.14, 45, 156

No man saw awe nor to his house (1733)
Capps, 5.14, 36, 149, 211
Waggoner, *Am. Poets,* 6.1058, 674-76

No other can reduce (982)
Sherwood, 5.79, 170-71

No rack can torture me (384)
Glenn, 6.404, 577-78
Omoto, 12.26, 45-50

No romance sold unto (669)
Barbot, 6.67, 694

Not any higher stands the grave (1256)
Wells, 5.101, 126
Ford, 5.27, 161
Franklin, 5.28, 87-88

Not probable – the barest chance (346)
Johnson, 5.44, 252-53

Not with a club the heart is broken (1304)
Chase, 5.17, 175
C. R. Anderson, 5.2, 193
Marcus, 6.654
Griffith, 5.31, 177
Franklin, 5.28, 111

Obtaining but our own extent (1543)
Gelpi, 5.29, 100
Ford, 5.27, 169

Of all the souls that stand create (664)
Whicher, 5.104, 284-85
Chase, 5.17, 159
Childs, 6.204, 458-59
Johnson, 5.44, 101
C. R. Anderson, 5.2, 171-72
Wilbur, 6.1174, 44

Of all the sounds despatched abroad (321)
Johnson, 5.44, 115-16

C. R. Anderson, 5.2, 249-50
Griffith, 5.31, 139-40, 143

Our little kinsmen after rain (885)
England, *BNYPL*, 6.316, 112

Our lives are Swiss (80)
Pohl, 6.806, 522
Parsons, 6.770, 19-20
Capps, 5.14, 107-08
Porter, 5.69, 92-93, 148-49, 170

Our share of night to bear (113)
P. W. Anderson, 6.43, 75-76

Ourselves we do inter with sweet deri-
sion (1144)
Ward, 5.97, 173
Waggoner, *Criticism*, 6.1058, 315

Ourselves were wed one summer, dear
(631)
Johnson, 5.44, 40-41
Patterson, 6.778, 47-48
Stefanini, 8.96a, 48-51

Out of sight! What of that (703)
Adams, 6.11, 135

Pain has an element of blank (650)
Griffith, 5.31, 293, 294

Papa above (61)
Welland, 6.1085, 68-70
Gelpi, 5.29, 37
P. W. Anderson, 6.43, 73-74
Capps, 5.14, 45, 54, 160
Porter, 5.69, 91

Paradise is of the option (1069)
Wheatcroft, 6.1112, 118-19
Capps, 5.14, 31

Paradise is that old mansion (1119)
Gelpi, 5.29, 91
Capps, 5.14, 33, 148, 211

Pass to thy rendezvous of light (1564)
C. R. Anderson, 5.2, 226
Pearce, *Continuity*, 6.784, 185
Ford, 5.27, 170-71

Peace is a fiction of our faith (912)
Capps, 5.14, 118

Perception of an object costs (1071)
Anon., 4.48, 674
Miles, 6.703, 156
Whicher, 5.104, 296
C. R. Anderson, 5.2, 90
Bolin, 6.125, 29
Gelpi, 5.29, 135

Peril as a possession (1678)
Whicher, 5.104, 184

Pigmy seraphs gone astray (138)
Pohl, 6.806, 522
C. R. Anderson, 6.35, 150-52

Pink, small, and punctual (1332)
C. R. Anderson, 5.2, 98
Pickard, 5.60, 59

Poor little heart (192)
Wheatcroft, 6.1113, 137
Capps, 5.14, 75-76, 169
Laverty, 6.599, 14
Franklin, 5.28, 7, 9

Portraits are to daily faces (170)
Johnson, 5.44, 22
Tugwell, 6.1012, 342

Prayer is the little implement (437)
Whicher, 5.104, 273
Griffith, 5.31, 60-61

Presentiment is that long shadow on the
lawn (764)
Blackmur, *Language as Gesture*, 6.107,
48
Chase, 5.17, 140-41
Hirsch, 6.492, 36-37
Griffith, 5.31, 84, 86, 92
Duncan, 5.24, 63
Perrine, 6.793, 119

Publication is the auction (709)
C. R. Anderson, 5.2, 59-60
Ward, 5.97, 194
Wheatcroft, 6.1113, 140

Quite empty, quite at rest (1606)
Johnson, 5.44, 230

"Remember me" implored the thief
(1180)
McNaughton, 5.53, 14-15

Remembrance has a rear and front (1182)
Frye, *Fables of Identity*, 6.375, 215-16

Remorse is memory awake (744)
Griffith, 5.31, 201-04, 205

Renunciation is a piercing virtue (745)
Blackmur, *Expense of Greatness*, 6.107,
119-23
Ward, 5.97, 69; 6.1070, 33
Wheatcroft, 6.1112, 115-18
Porter, 5.69, 127
Pickard, 5.60, 98-99

Reportless subjects to the quick (1048)
Marcus, 6.656, 498

Reverse cannot befall (395)
C. R. Anderson, 6.34

Revolution is the pod (1082)
Whicher, 5.104, 239

Some rainbow coming from the fair (64)
  Porter, 5.69, 152, 160

Some things that fly there be (89)
  Porter, 5.69, 31-32, 80, 83-84, 164

Some too fragile for winter winds (141)
  Ford, 5.27, 83

Some work for immortality (406)
  Merideth, 6.694, 449-51
  Pickard, 5.60, 50-51

Somewhere upon the general earth (1231)
  Ward, 5.97, 153

Soul, take thy risk (1151)
  Gelpi, 5.29, 34

Soul, wilt thou toss again (139)
  Ward, 5.97, 44
  Porter, 5.69, 158

South winds jostle them (86)
  Johnson, 5.44, 114
  Porter, 5.69, 160

Speech is a prank of parliament (688)
  Higgins, 3.211, 12-13

Split the lark and you'll find the music
    (861)
  Reeves, 3.202, 106
  C. R. Anderson, 5.2, 89
  P. W. Anderson, 6.43, 79

Spring comes on the world (1042)
  Gelpi, 5.29, 137-38

Still own thee, still thou art (1633)
  Ford, 5.27, 159

Strong draughts of their refreshing minds
    (711)
  Childs, 6.204, 458
  Johnson, 5.44, 145
  C. R. Anderson, 5.2, 45

Struck was I, not yet by lightning (925)
  Frye, *Fables of Identity*, 6.375, 215
  Gelpi, 5.29, 117-18

Success is counted sweetest (67)
  Winterich, 6.1197, 2311-13
  Whicher, 5.104, 202-03
  Wilbur, 6.1174, 40-41
  Welland, 6.1085, 62-63
  Cambon, 6.172, 36
  Merideth, 6.694, 446-47
  Porter, 5.69, 170
  Sherwood, 5.79, 60-61

Superfluous were the sun (999)
  Tugwell, 6.1012, 342-43
  Lindberg, 6.617a, 179-80

Surgeons must be very careful (108)
  Avery, 6.58, 50

Suspense is hostiler than death (705)
  Lindberg-Seyersted, 5.113, 132, 153-54

Sweet hours have perished here (1767)
  Franklin, 5.28, 95-97

Sweet is the swamp with its secrets
    (1740)
  Adams, 6.11, 142-43
  Franklin, 5.28, 99, 101

Sweet, safe houses (457)
  C. R. Anderson, 6.35, 161-63
  J. Q. Anderson, 6.42, 9-10
  Lindberg-Seyersted, 5.113, 67, 68, 87-
    88

Take all away from me (1640)
  Ward, 5.97, 112; 6.1069, 106
  Higgins, 3.211, 5

Take your heaven further on (388)
  Wheatcroft, 6.1113, 135

Taken from men this morning (53)
  Ford, 5.27, 94-95

Talk with prudence to a beggar (119)
  Chase, 5.17, 222
  Parsons, 6.770, 20
  Miller, 5.54, 102-103, 113-14, 444

Tell all the truth but tell it slant (1129)
  Porter, 5.69, 122

That after horror, that 'twas us (286)
  Porter, 5.69, 166-67
  Pickard, 5.60, 97-98

That I did always love (549)
  Martz, 6.660, 564

That is solemn we have ended (934)
  Miles, 6.703, 157

That it will never come again (1741)
  Marcellino, 6.650, 231-32

The admirations and contempts of time
    (906)
  Gelpi, 5.29, 74
  Ford, 5.27, 106-07
  Sandeen, 6.877, 492
  Sherwood, 5.79, 187-88

The auctioneer of parting (1612)
  C. R. Anderson, 5.2, 197
  Galinsky, 10.50, 253-257, *passim*

The bat is dun with wrinkled wings (1575)
  C. R. Anderson, 5.2, 108-10
  Pickard, 5.60, 64-65

The Bible is an antique volume (1545)
  Whicher, 5.104, 155
  Warren, 6.1072, 574
  C. R. Anderson, 5.2, 19
  Duncan, 5.24, 54

Index of Persons,
Periodicals, and Subjects

MLN, see *Modern Language Notes*
Modern Drama, 6.813a
Modern Language Journal, 6.997
Modern Language Notes, 6.36-38, 6.327,
    6.336, 6.645, 6.721, 6.880, 6.945, 6.1180,
    6.1207
Modern Language Quarterly, 6.667,
    6.910a, 6.911
Modern Language Review, 6.131-132
modern poetry, ED as a forerunner of,
    Cestre, 9.20; Gelpi, 5.29, pp. 153-75;
    Griffith, 5.31, pp. 223-72; Lombardo,
    8.67; Perosa, 8.9; Reeves, 6.840; Reid,
    6.844; Robey, 14.47; Untermeyer,
    6.1023; Vigorelli, 8.102; Wells, 6.1102;
    Wilson, 6.1190; Wood, 6.1202; see also
    French Symbolist poets, Imagist verse,
    Italian poets, poetic tradition, and in-
    dividual poets listed by name
Moderna Språk, 6.147
Moffit, J., 18.92
Moldenhauer, Joseph J., 6.716
Molen, S. J. Van der, 10.81
Molson, Francis Joseph, 14.24
Monatshefte für Deutschen Unterricht,
    6.577
Mondo, Il, 8.17, 8.37, 8.43, 8.89
Mondo Occidentale, 8.58
Monnig, Richard, 10.61
Monro, Harold, 6.717
Monroe, Harriet, 6.718
Montague, G. H., 7.41, 7.43, 7.46
Montale, Eugenio, 8.17, 8.76-77; ED
    compared to, Vigorelli, 8.102
Monteiro, George, 3.212, 6.719-721
Month at Goodspeeds, 4.71
Montreal, University of, thesis, 14.1
Moore, Geoffrey, 6.722
Moore, Marianne, 6.723
Moore, Virginia, 6.724-726
Moore, William, 12.3
moral experience in ED's poetry (see
    also social attitudes), Winters, 6.1200;
    ED's "moral vision," Davis, 14.16
Moran, Helen, 6.727
*More Books, Bulletin of the Boston Public
    Library* (see also *Boston Public Library
    Quarterly*), 5.107
Morehouse, Charles F., 6.182
Moreland, John Richard, 18.92a
Morey, Frederick L., 1.21, 1.29, 14.91
Morgenstern, Christian, ED compared
    to, Frank, 10.49
Morgenstern, Joseph, 21.11
Morgrage, Louise, 6.728
Morison, Samuel Eliot, 6.729
Morley, Christopher, 6.730
Morse, Samuel French, 18.93
Morton, David, 18.138
Moseley, Edwin, 6.731

motion in ED's poetry (see also change),
    Adams, 6.10; C. R. Anderson, 5.2, pp.
    131-62; De Witt, 6.282; Johnson, 5.44,
    pp. 200-02; McNally, 6.688; McNaughton,
    5.53, pp. 19-20; Patterson, 6.780; Por-
    ter, 5.69, pp. 75-105; Sherwood, 5.67,
    pp. 112-15
Mottram, E. N. W., 6.732
Moulton, Louise Chandler, 6.733-734;
    compared to ED, Higginson, 6.477b
Mount Holyoke Alumnae Quarterly, 4.49,
    6.227, 6.237-238, 6.569, 6.684, 6.686,
    6.699, 6.927, 6.1091-1092, 6.1124, 18.28,
    18.135, 22.1-2, 22.7
Mount Holyoke College, 7.48, 22.1-7;
    thesis, 14.51
Mount Holyoke Female Seminary, ED at
    (see also Lyon, Mary), Anon., 7.22,
    7.32; Bass, 6.73; Chase, 5.17, pp. 50-
    65; Gelpi, 5.29, pp. 15-16, 31-32; Hig-
    gins, 5.34, pp. 43-48; Johnson, 5.44, pp.
    12-15; McLean, 6.687, 14.51; Pollitt,
    5.61, pp. 41-50; Taggard, 5.81, pp. 51-
    59; Wheatcroft, 14.11; Whicher, 5.104,
    pp. 58-76, 319-20; Ed's textbooks at,
    Capps, 5.14, pp. 105-11, 189-91; *Elev-
    enth Annual Catalogue of*, 23.9
Mount Holyoke News, 4.34
Mudge, Jean McClure, 6.734a
Muir, Jane, 15.27
Muirhead, James Fullarton, 6.735
Mullican, James S., 6.735a
Mumford, Lewis, 6.736
Munn, L. S., 6.737
Murciaux, Christian, 9.33, 11.31
Murdock, Kenneth B., 6.738
Muri, John T., 6.738a
Murphy, Esther, 6.739
Murray, Marian, 6.740
music and musical settings, Bacon, 19.1-
    5; Bain, 19.6; Barber, 19.7; Copland,
    19.9; Feldman, 20.2; Franchetti, 19.10;
    Johnson, 17.31; Johnston, 19.18; Lader-
    man, 17.36; Meyerowitz, 17.12; Pink-
    ham, 19.20; Rorem, 19.22; Zieve, 17.4;
    musical settings discussed, Archibald,
    6.46; Frump, 6.374; Kerman, 6.568;
    musical settings listed, Blanck, 1.4;
    Jones Library, 1.8; Lubbers, 5.114, pp.
    275-77; White, 1.17
musical terminology in ED's letters,
    Giuliani, 5.58a, pp. 115-16
Musser, Grace S., 6.741
Mutiny, 3.209
mutability, theme of, see change
mystical experience in ED's poetry,
    Blackmur, 6.107; Blunden, 6.118; Bogan,
    6.119; Chase, 5.17, p. 184; Drew, 6.300a;
    Flick, 14.30; Jacoby, 9.23; Johnson,
    5.44, pp. 141-42; Keleher, 6.563; Mary

Poulet, Georges, 6.819
Pound, Ezra, ED compared to, Wilson, 6.1190
Powell, Desmond, S., 6.820
Power, Sister Mary James, 5.72, 6.821
Powers, James H., 6.822
Prace Filologiczne, 6.893a
Prairie Schooner, 6.655, 6.689, 6.1164
Prampolini, Giocomo, 8.12, 8.81-82
Praz, Mario, 8.13, 8.83-84
Prescott, Frederick Clarke, 6.823
Presencia, 11.16
"presentiment," Hirsch, 6.492; Perrine, 6.793; Reeves, 6.843
Price, James, 6.824
Price, Lawrence Marsden, 6.824a
Price, Warwick James, 6.825-826
Prim, Philip L., 14.86
Princeton University Library Chronicle, 6.221
Prisma, 10.49
prison imagery, Schreiber, 6.895; poems employing, listed, Miller, 5.54, pp. 381-82
privation, theme of, see renunciation, suffering
process, theme of, see change, nature as process
Progresso Italo-americano, 8.56
prose, ED's (see also letters), Higgins, 5.34, 6.469, 14.12; Lambert, 14.36, C. C. R., 6.827; Schappes, 6.890; development of, Todd, 6.999; vocabulary of, Guiliani, 8.58a; poems buried in, Fain, 6.327; Williams, 3.209
prosody, ED's (see also form), Adams, 14.48; Allen, 6.26; Brinnin, 3.206; Coffman, 14.62; England, 6.316; Fussell, 6.377; Herbert, 6.458; Johnson, 5.44, pp. 84-87, 6.550; Lindberg-Seyersted, 5.113, pp. 118-96; Porter, 5.69, pp. 106-24; Wells, 5.101, pp. 255-75, 6.1120; Whicher, 5.104, pp. 227-75
Providence [R.I.] *Journal*, 3.38-39, 6.900, 18.18, 18.24
Provincia, La, 8.57
psychological study of ED, problems in, Wells, 6.1093; West, 6.1108
Public Ledger, see *Philadelphia Public Ledger*
Public Opinion, 3.107, 6.1205
publication, ED's attitude toward, Johnson, 5.44, pp. 56, 96, 103-14; Patterson, 5.55, pp. 212-16; Ward, 5.97, 6.1068; Welland, 6.1085; Whicher, 5.104, pp. 113-15; pressures on ED to publish, Johnson, 5.44, pp. 110-16, 164-69, 175; Miller, 5.54; ED's publication history, see reputation, history of

Publications of the Modern Language Association, see *PMLA*
Publishers' Weekly, 1.7, 1.11, 2.5, 3.170, 3.198, 6.1197, 6.1199, 7.23, 7.44
Pulitzer Prize, 1931, awarded to *Alison's House*, 17.14; see also Atkinson, 17.27
punctuation, ED's (see also dash, handwriting), C. R. Anderson, 5.2, pp. 306-07; Blackmur, 6.108; Franklin, 5.28, pp. 117-28; Lindberg-Seyersted, 5.113, pp. 180-96, 6.617; Stamm, 6.948, 14.33; Ward, 6.1071
Puritan tradition, ED and (see also Calvinism), Berti, 8.39; Block, 6.115; Donoghue, 6.293; England, 6.316; Feuillerat, 9.21; Ford, 5.27, pp. 35-46; Gelpi, 5.29, pp. 89-93; Jacoby, 9.23; Larrabee, 6.597; Miller, 6.712; Murciaux, 11.31; Reinke, 14.54; Rosati, 8.89; Sherwood, 5.79, pp. 137-79; Tate, 6.980; Van der Vat, 6.1032; Ward, 6.1067; Welland, 6.1085; Wheatcroft, 6.1112-1113, 14.11; Whicher, 5.104, pp. 156-64; Zolla, 8.104
Putney, Paula, 14.39
Pyun, Yung Tai, 18.102

Quarles, C. Francis, ED's possible reading of, Miller, 5.54, pp. 421-23, 438-39, 447
Quarterly Journal of Speech, 6.991
Quarterly Review of Literature, 6.971
Queen's Quarterly, 6.574-574a, 6.862
Quest, 6.1079
quest, theme of (see also aspiration), Porter, 5.69, pp. 16-54; Sherwood, 5.79, pp. 23-67; poems on, listed, Miller, 5.54, pp. 374-76
Quinn, Arthur Hobson, 6.406
Quotidiano, 8.53

R., C.C., 6.827
R., J.J., 6.845
Rabe, Olive H., 6.828, 15.7
Rackliffe, John, 6.670
Radcliffe Quarterly, 6.101
radio talks and programs on ED, 17.34, 21.1-7, 21.9-10
Rahv, Philip, 6.980
Raine, Kathleen, 6.829
Raith, Josef, 10.14
Rakia, D., 13.24
Rakowska, Maria, 13.15
Ramón, José Antonio, 11.34
Ramón, Juan, 11.35
Rand, Frank Prentice, 6.830-831, 17.45, 18.103
Rand, Jerry, 6.832-833
Rand, W. J., 6.834
Ransom, John Crowe, 6.835, 10.63

Walton, Eda Lou, 6.1065-1065a
Want, M. S., 6.1065b
Ward, Alfred Charles, 6.1066
Ward, Samuel G., 6.1067
Ward, Theodora, 1.31, 3.197, 4.76, 4.90,
  5.97, 6.1068-1071
Warner, Mary, 6.237-238
Warren, Austin, 6.1072-1073, 6.1085a,
  20.1
Warren, Richard, 3.201
Warren, Robert Penn, 6.151; emotional
  paralysis in *All the King's Men* and an
  ED poem compared, Satterwhite, 6.880
Washington, University of, thesis, 14.31
Washington [D.C.] *Post*, 6.634, 6.804, 16.4
Washington [D.C.] *Star*, 6.308, 18.62
Wasson, Mildred, 6.1074
Waterman, Nixon, 6.1075
Watson, Alma G., 5.59, 19.21
Watson, Charles Mitchell, 14.73
Wattles, Willard, 18.134
Watts, Isaac, ED's use of (see also hymn
  meter, prosody), Davidson, 6.268; En-
  gland, 6.316; Porter, 5.69; Stephenson,
  6.953; Wheatcroft, 14.11
Waugh, Dorothy, 6.1076-1079
Wayne State University, paper delivered
  at, White, 6.1159a
Weber, Carl J., 4.72
Week End Review, 6.48, 6.1082
Wegelin, Christof, 6.1080
Wehmeyer, W. A., 6.1080a
Weirick, Bruce, 6.1081
Weis, Alberto, 11.7
Welby, T. Earle, 6.1082-1083
Weld, Arthur, 21.8
Welland, Dennis S. R., 6.1084-1085
Wellek, René, 6.1085a
Wellesley [Mass.] *Townsman*, 7.39
Wells, Anna Mary, 6.1086-1093, 14.45
Wells, Carlton F., 5.13
Wells, Carolyn, 6.1094
Wells, Henry Willis, 5.101, 6.1095-1104,
  20.5
Welshimer, Helen, 6.1105
Welt und Wort, 10.60
Wesenberg, Alice Bidwell, 18.135
West, Edward Sackville, 6.1106
West, H. F., 6.1107
West, Ray B., Jr., 6.1108
Westbrook, Perry D., 6.1109
Westen, Der, 10.47
Western Humanities Review, 6.94, 6.205,
  6.706
Westminister College, thesis, 14.93
Wetcho, W. F., 6.1110
Wetherell, J. E., 6.1111
Wharton, Araminta, Joseph Lyman's (q.v.)
  friendship with, Sewall, 5.76, pp. 761-64

Wheatcroft, John Stewart, 6.1112-1113,
  14.11
Wheeler, Charles B., 6.1114
Whicher, George Frisbie, 1.8, 3.194,
  5.104, 6.437, 6.1115-1144, 16.6, 17.10
Whicher, George M., 6.1145
Whicher, Harriet Fox, 6.1123, 6.1141
Whicher, "J.M.," 6.1145
Whicher, Stephen, 6.1146
Whitbread, Thomas, 6.1147
white, see color
White, Gertrude, 6.1148
White, James E., 6.1149
White, William, 1.17, 6.56, 6.1150-1164
Whitesell, Edwin, 6.1060
Whiteside, Mary Brent, 6.1165
Whiting, Lilian, 3.56, 4.22, 6.1166-1171
Whitman, Walt, ED's relation to, Bates,
  6.75; Blackmur, 6.107; Cambon, 8.46;
  Catel, 9.16; Chase, 5.17; D'Agostino,
  8.50; Dailey, 6.257; Deutsch, 6.278;
  Griffith, 5.31, pp. 267-69; Lombardo,
  8.67; Marcus, 6.656; Martz, 6.661; Mil-
  ler, 5.54, pp. 65-67; Murciaux, 11.31;
  Nist, 6.752, 11.45; Parks, 6.769; Simon,
  6.925a; Waterman, 6.1075; Whicher,
  6.1123; White, 6.1148
Whitman, William, 6.1172
Whitney, John, 17.49
Wiadomości Literackie, 13.15
Wicks, Frank S. C., 6.1173
Wickwire, Nancy, 20.2
Wilbur, Richard, 6.1174, 18.136; ED com-
  pared to, Lombardo, 8.68
Wilder, Thornton, 6.1175-1176
Wilkinson, Mrs. William H., see Hum-
  phrey, Jane
Williams, Oscar, 3.209, 18.113
Williams, Paul O., 6.1177
Williams, Sidney, 6.1178
Williams, Stanley T., 6.1179-1180, 10.77
Williams, Talcott, 6.1181
Williams, William Carlos, 6.580a; ED's
  and WCW's critical reception in Ger-
  many compared, Galinsky, 10.51
Williams-Ellis, A., 6.1181a
Willy, Margaret, 6.1182-1184
Wilson, Edmund, 6.1184a
Wilson, James R., 6.1185
Wilson, James Southall, 6.1186-1188
Wilson, Rufus Rockwell, 6.1189
Wilson, Suzanne Marie, 6.1190-1191, 14.8
Wineberg, Michael, 1.31
Wingate, Charles E. L., 6.1192-1195
Wings, 6.166, 6.1037, 18.16
Winterich, John Tracy, 6.1196-1199
Winters, Yvor, 6.1200, 9.35, 18.137
Wisconsin, University of, theses, 14.25,
  14.65